REFORMING THAI POLITICS

The **Nordic Institute of Asian Studies** (NIAS) is funded by the governments of Denmark, Finland, Iceland, Norway and Sweden via the Nordic Council of Ministers, and works to encourage and support Asian studies in the Nordic countries. In so doing, NIAS has been publishing books since 1969, with more than one hundred titles produced in the last decade.

REFORMING THAI POLITICS

Edited by
Duncan McCargo

NIAS

First published in 2002 by NIAS Publishing
Nordic Institute of Asian Studies
Leifsgade 33, DK–2300 Copenhagen S, Denmark
tel: (+45) 3254 8844 • fax: (+45) 3296 2530
E–mail: books@nias.ku.dk • Website: http://eurasia.nias.ku.dk/publications/

© Nordic Institute of Asian Studies (NIAS) 2002

All rights reserved. While copyright in this volume as a whole is vested in NIAS, copyright in the individual papers belongs to the authors. No paper may be reproduced in whole or in part without the express permission of author and publisher. The responsibility for facts and opinions in this publication rests exclusively with the editor and contributors, and their interpretations do not necessarily reflect the views of the publishers.

British Library Cataloguing in Publication Data
Reforming Thai politics
  1.Thailand - Politics and government
  I.McCargo, Duncan
  320.9'593

ISBN 87-87062-94-1 (cloth)
ISBN 87-87062-93-3 (paper)

CONTENTS

NOTES ON CONTRIBUTORS ... vii

PREFACE AND ACKNOWLEDGEMENTS ... xi

1   INTRODUCTION: UNDERSTANDING POLITICAL REFORM
    IN THAILAND by *Duncan McCargo*... 1

PART I: THE MEANINGS OF POLITICAL REFORM

2   AN OVERVIEW OF POLITICAL REFORM ISSUES
    by *Prawase Wasi* ... 21

3   GOOD GOVERNANCE: A STRATEGY TO RESTORE THAILAND
    by *Thirayuth Boonmi* ... 29

4   FRAMING THE 'PEOPLE'S CONSTITUTION'
    by *Michael Connors* ... 37

5   THE MONARCHY AND CONSTITUTIONAL CHANGE SINCE 1972
    by *Kobkua Suwannathat-Pian* ... 57

6   HUMAN RIGHTS AND POLITICAL REFORM IN THAILAND
    by *David Streckfuss and Mark Templeton* ... 73

7   DEMOCRATIZATION AND SOCIAL WELFARE IN THAILAND
    by *Johannes Dragsbæk Schmidt* ... 91

PART II: THE POPULAR SECTOR

8   CIVIL SOCIETY AND STREET POLITICS: LESSONS
    FROM THE 1950s by *James Ockey* ... 107

9   CIVIL SOCIETY AND DEMOCRATIZATION IN THAILAND:
    A CRITIQUE OF ELITE DEMOCRACY
    by *Somchai Phatharathananunth* ... 125

10 RESPONDING TO ECONOMIC CRISIS: THAILAND'S LOCALISM
    by Kevin Hewison ... 143

11 POLITICAL REFORM THROUGH THE PUBLIC SPHERE:
    WOMEN'S GROUPS AND THE FABRIC OF GOVERNANCE
    by Philippe Doneys ... 163

12 NGOS AND GRASSROOTS PARTICIPATION IN THE POLITICAL
    REFORM PROCESS *by Naruemon Thabchumpon* ... 183

PART III: ELECTORAL REFORM

13 THE 1997 CONSTITUTION AND THE POLITICS
    OF ELECTORAL REFORM *by Sombat Chantornvong* ... 203

14 POLITICAL REFORM AND CIVIL SOCIETY AT THE LOCAL LEVEL:
    THAILAND'S LOCAL GOVERNMENT REFORMS
    by Daniel Arghiros ... 223

15 THAILAND'S JANUARY 2001 GENERAL ELECTIONS:
    VINDICATING REFORM? *by Duncan McCargo* ... 247

16 CONCLUSION: ECONOMICS, POLITICS AND CIVIL SOCIETY
    by John Girling ... 261

BIBLIOGRAPHY ... 267

INDEX ... 283

NOTES ON CONTRIBUTORS

Daniel Arghiros has conducted research on Thai provincial politics and rural enterprise and is the author of *Democracy, Development and Decentralisation in Provincial Thailand* (Richmond: Curzon 2001). He is currently working as a development advisor in Cambodia on secondment from the University of Hull, UK, where he is a lecturer. Contact e-mail: D.Arghiros@bigfoot.com

Michael Connors is currently revising his 2000 University of Melbourne PhD thesis – which examines how statist and liberal actors have attempted to construct 'ideal' Thai citizens – for publication by Routledge. He previously taught at Thammasat and La Trobe Universities, and is presently a lecturer in politics at the University of Leeds. Contact e-mail: mkconnors @hotmail.com

Philippe Doneys is completing a PhD at the Institut d'Études Politique de Paris. His research focuses on ways non-state actors shape state policies and public decision-making structures, and he is currently researching non-state actors' contribution to HIV/AIDS planning in Thailand. Contact e-mail: phdoneys@aol.com

John Girling is a political scientist who lives in France. Although now retired from the ANU, he continues to publish widely. His best-known contributions to Thai studies are the books *Thailand: Society and Politics* (Ithaca: Cornell, 1981) and *Interpreting Development: Capitalism, Democracy and the Middle Class in Thailand* (Ithaca: Cornell Southeast Asia Program, 1996).

Kevin Hewison is a professor in the Department of Applied Social Studies, The City University of Hong Kong. His most recent book was the edited collection *Political Change in Thailand: Democracy and Participation* (London: Routledge, 1997). Contact e-mail: SSKEVIN@cityu.edu.hk

Kobkua Suwannathat-Pian is dean of the School of Liberal Studies, Universiti Tenaga Nasional, Malaysia. A historian by training, she has lectured on Thai and Southeast Asian history at Chiang Mai University, Thailand, and at the National University of Malaysia. Her books include *Thai–Malay Relations: Traditional Intra-Regional Relations from the Seventeenth to Early Twentieth Centuries*

(OUP, 1988) and *Thailand's Durable Premier: Phibun through Three Decades 1932–1957* (OUP, 1995). Contact e-mail: kobkua@uniten.edu.my

Duncan McCargo is a senior lecturer in the Institute for Politics and International Studies, University of Leeds, UK. His other books include *Chamlong Srimuang and the New Thai Politics* (London: Hurst, 1997) and *Politics and the Press in Thailand: Media Machinations* (London: Routledge, 2000). He is the editor of the Routledge book series 'Rethinking Southeast Asia'. Contact e-mail: d.j.mccargo@leeds.ac.uk
    For more information, see the Leeds Thai Politics Website at http://www.leeds.ac.uk/thaipol

Naruemon Thabchumpon is a lecturer in the Department of Government, Faculty of Political Science, Chulalongkorn University. She has published several articles on the politics of popular participation in Thailand, and is currently working at the University of Leeds on a PhD thesis dealing with grassroots politics and the Forum of the Poor. Contact e-mail: junaruemon@hotmail.com

James Ockey is a senior lecturer in political science at Canterbury University in Christchurch, New Zealand. He has written extensively on Thai politics and is currently working on a monograph on the 'Hyde Park' era in Thailand. Contact e-mail: j.ockey@pols.canterbury.ac.nz

Prawase Wasi is professor of medicine emeritus at Mahidol University. A distinguished physician, medical researcher, and Magsaysay Award winner, he is one of Thailand's leading social critics and 'senior citizens'. Dr Prawase chaired the Democracy Development Committee in 1994–1995, and has published numerous books and articles in Thai on political reform, civil society and social change.

Savitri Gadavanij is a lecturer at the National Institute of Development Administration (NIDA) in Bangkok. She is currently working on her PhD – which examines the political discourse of Thai parliamentary debates – at the University of Leeds. Contact e-mail: ipisg@leeds.ac.uk

Johannes Dragsbæk Schmidt is associate professor at the Research Center on Development and International Relations (DIR), Aalborg University, Denmark. He is currently conducting a comparative study of the economic policy-making process in Southeast Asia. Among his latest publications are the co-edited volumes *Social Change in Southeast Asia* (Harlow: Longman, 1998), and *Globalization and Social Change* (London: Routledge, 2000). Contacts and info: www.i4.auc.dk/development and jds@i4.auc.dk

NOTES ON CONTRIBUTORS

Sombat Chantornvong is an associate professor at the Faculty of Political Science, Thammasat University. A political philosopher by training, he has published numerous books on subjects ranging from political theory and Thai literature, to elections and party politics. Contact e-mail: tim6373@tu.ac.th

Somchai Phatharathananunth is a lecturer in politics at Mahasarakham University, Thailand. He gained his PhD from the University of Leeds in 2001, with a thesis entitled 'Civil Society in Northeast Thailand: The Struggle of the Small Scale Farmers' Assembly of Isan'. Contact e-mail: schph @hotmail.com

David Streckfuss finished his PhD in Southeast Asian History and recently won the John Smail Prize for the best dissertation in Southeast Asian Studies at the University of Wisconsin. He now works with the Council on International Educational Exchange, based in New York City. Contact e-mail: dstreckfuss@yahoo.com

Mark Templeton graduated with a J.D. at Yale Law School in 1999 and was a Robert L. Bernstein Fellow in International Human Rights at the Yale Law School 1999–2000. He has been working on human rights issues in South and Southeast Asia and is a member of the California bar. Contact e-mail: mark_n_templeton@hotmail.com

Thirayuth Boonmi is a former student leader from the 1970s, and a graduate of the Institute of Social Studies in The Hague. Now a lecturer in sociology at Thammasat University, he is a prominent public intellectual and the author of many publications in Thai commenting on current social and political issues.

PREFACE AND ACKNOWLEDGEMENTS

The Seventh International Conference on Thai Studies, held in Amsterdam in July 1999, was a Thai Studies conference like no other. Over several glorious summer days, in the liberal atmosphere of a great European city, hundreds of scholars came together in a spirit of open debate about the serious issues challenging their understandings of Thai society. Away from Thailand, far from the hierarchical mores that so often limit the parameters of domestic discourse, Thai scholars and their non-Thai counterparts engaged in vigorous discussion of salient questions. The conference theme of 'Thailand: A Civil Society?' set the tone: this was a conference focused on critical questions about the nature of Thai society, broadly defined. There were many highlights, but among the strongest contenders were: the intense and sometimes emotional debate over Wat Thammakai in the Buddhism panel; moving accounts of hill-tribe oppression in a late evening session (which reached the ears of the prime minister via the BBC Thai Service, and subsequently provoked uproar in Thailand); and a brilliantly provocative keynote lecture on memory and the two Octobers by Thongchai Winichakul.

This book arises out of an Amsterdam panel entitled 'Reforming Thai Politics? The Politics of Thailand's Reforms'. With two exceptions (Streckfuss/Templeton and Connors) all the chapters in this book are by Amsterdam participants; and all Amsterdam paper-presenters are contributors to the book (with the exception of Hewison's co-presenter Malcolm Falkus, and Pei-Hsiu Chen, who was unfortunately unable to give his paper due to illness). The aim of the Amsterdam panel was to generate debate: participants who held radically different views of the political reform process were deliberately invited to take part. We were very fortunate in being joined by Dr Prawase Wasi, one of the main public figures behind the reform movement. A distinctive feature of the panel was the opportunity it created for more mainstream reformists such as Dr Prawase and Thirayuth Boonmi, to debate with prominent and outspoken scholars of different persuasions, including Sombat Chantornvong and Kobkua Suwannathat-Pian. A second dimension was the way in which up-and-coming local academics Naruemon Thabchumpon and Somchai Phatharathananunth were given space to present new perspectives – while international scholars such as Daniel Arghiros, Philippe Doneys, John Girling, Kevin Hewison, James Ockey and

Johannes Schmidt brought their own very different vantage points to the debate.

I am extremely grateful to everyone who helped make this book possible, and to the various funding bodies that enabled participants to travel to Amsterdam. Viggo Brun and Søren Ivarsson inadvertently set me off on this project, by inviting me to Copenhagen to give some lectures on Thai political reform at the end of 1997. Special thanks must go to Han ten Brummelheis and Leontine Visser, the Amsterdam conference organizers, and to conference coordinator Arno Ooms. Several of the contributors did far more than write their own chapters: Dr Prawase Wasi was my original inspiration when he first shared his ideas on political reform with me back in mid-1995; Naruemon Thabchumpon liaised with other Thai panellists on my behalf; Sombat Chantornvong discussed political reform issues with me over countless buffet lunches around Bangkok, as well as supplying me with materials for my own chapters; Savitri Gadavanij helped out with transliterations; and Michael Connors, who arrived in Leeds at the tail end of the project, has been a constant source of information and second opinions. I am also very grateful for input from Shawn Crispin, Krisadawan Hongladarom, Michael Nelson and Walailak Piriyuvasak. Gerald Jackson, Leena Höskuldsson and the editorial team at NIAS bravely took on that publisher's nightmare, the 'academic conference volume', and helped transform mounds of paper into the present book.

It is hoped that the resulting volume will convey something of the rich flavour of the Amsterdam panel on Thai political reform, bolstered by some additional chapters, and updated to take account of the Senate and parliamentary elections that took place in 2000 and 2001.

Duncan McCargo
Leeds, December 2001

1

INTRODUCTION: UNDERSTANDING POLITICAL REFORM IN THAILAND

Duncan McCargo

BACKGROUND

Thailand had a truly amazing year in 1997: the economy collapsed, and the political order was reconstituted. A series of elections in 2000–01 offered a chance to assess the degree of Thailand's economic recovery, and more especially to evaluate the extent to which structural political problems had been surmounted. This book seeks to analyse the debates and processes surrounding political developments in Thailand around the turn of the millennium.

Since the end of the absolute monarchy in 1932, Thai politics has undergone numerous political 'reforms', often accompanied by constitutional revisions, and shifts in the location of power. The student-led popular uprising against military authoritarianism in October 1973 was a major breakthrough in Thai politics, clearly demonstrating the potential for political change to arise from grassroots agitation. Yet the bloody restoration of authoritarianism in October 1976 illustrated the residual strength of conservative forces. From 1977 onwards, under premiers Kriangsak Chomanan and Prem Tinsulanond, Thailand saw a gradual process of liberalization: parliamentary politics appeared to be progressively institutionalized. Yet the rise of money politics fuelled by the country's remarkable economic growth undermined the credibility and legitimacy of the elected Chatichai Choonavan government. The military capitalized on public disquiet, staging an opportunistic and ultimately anachronistic coup d'état in February 1991. Following the events of May 1992 – when troops shot dead scores of unarmed protesters in the streets of Bangkok – there were strong pressures from various groups in Thai society for a fundamental overhaul of the political order.

The 1991 coup had briefly raised unsatisfied expectations that corruption could be curtailed and the quality of politics improved. These pressures for change were acknowledged by the first Chuan Leekpai government in 1994, when it established the Democratic Development Committee (DDC) under Dr Prawase Wasi, to devise proposals for political reform. The momentum generated by the DDC culminated in the drafting and promulgation of a new constitution in 1997.

Yet this process of constitutional change was only one element in a broad package of reforms under discussion, including electoral reform, educational reform, reform of the bureaucracy, health sector and welfare reform, media reform, reform of universities and academic research, and, most ambitious of all, civil society reform. To these might be added, more controversially, the need for a serious overhaul of the military, a review of the workings of the Buddhist sangha, and a more open debate about the role of the monarchy. At the same time, not everyone genuinely favoured reform. Conservative forces remained extremely powerful, and institutions such as the Ministry of Interior remained dedicated to preserving their power by resisting substantive reforms. Like the larger processes of political change in Thailand after 1932, the reform process of the 1990s was not a smooth or a seamless one, but a site of bitter contestation and struggle between competing interest groups.

Since the end of the absolute monarchy in 1932, Thailand has had 16 different constitutions, with an average duration of just over four years. While in many countries constitutions serve almost as national monuments – enduring political and historical markers – in Thailand constitutions are regularly torn up and rewritten, reflecting small or large shifts in the political order. A new constitution can legitimate a military coup, or signal a period of greater liberalization; yet each new charter becomes the basis for a fresh round of political contestation. In the Thai context, constitutionalism means the use of constitutions as an instrument of day-to-day politics. There have been several main phases of Thai constitutionalism in the post-1932 period. For the 26-year period from December 1932 onwards, constitutions subordinated the power of parliament to that of the executive. From 1959 to 1968, the Sarit and Thanom regimes used an interim constitution to suspend parliamentary politics. But the promulgation of the 1968 constitution signalled the first signs of an opening; Thanom's attempts to backpedal by suspending the fledgling parliament and reverting to the more authoritarian 1972 constitution led directly to the anti-authoritarian popular movement of 1973. Apart from a brief but significant setback in 1976, constitutional politics since 1973 have been an important area in which liberal and progressive forces have sought to promote their political agendas in the face of resistance from conservative elements.

While many of the constitutional debates in Thailand over the past three decades have been important ones, a kind of constitution drafting industry has emerged. The relationship between this industry and the wider political process is not always a wholesome one. There are numerous well-known figures, including former politicians, bureaucrats, public lawyers and academics, who hanker after the chance to serve on committees or other bodies associated with constitutional change. One of the functions of the constitution-drafting process is simply to provide 'jobs for the boys': titles, meeting allowances and media attention for those seeking to relaunch a career or ensure a place in the history books. While many of these people were undoubtedly well-intentioned and sincere, some of the figures concerned could be described as 'professional constitution drafters', eager to be associated with what they hoped would be the definitive Thai constitution. Riggs famously described Thailand as a 'bureaucratic polity' (Riggs 1966); an alternative description of Thailand in the 1990s might be the 'constitutional polity', in which the great and the good pursued aggrandizement through extended processes of constitutional revision. It has even been argued that consitutionalism is 'a political "disease" that paralyses and distorts Thai public life' (McCargo 1998: 7).

Not all constitutional change in Thailand has been concerned with reforming or overhauling the political order. Just as often, revising the constitution has been a matter of consolidating elite power, diverting dissenting voices into committee-room corridors. On one level, the preoccupation with revising the constitution manifested in Thailand reflects deep insecurities about the direction and purpose of the political order. Yet whenever a process of constitutional revision begins, a kind of political space is opened up, a Pandora's box of competing interests and associated demands. As Thai politics has become more pluralistic in the post-1973 period, so the claims of the different interest groups for a share of the constitution-drafting cake have become louder. As the capacity of state elites to monopolize the political agenda has been increasingly eroded by a growth in pluralism and by the undermining of state capacity which is linked to globalization of the economy, so the potential for reformist opportunities to emerge during the constitution-drafting process becomes greater.

ALTERNATIVE MEANINGS OF POLITICAL REFORM

Crucial in advancing the reform cause in the run-up to the passage of the 1997 constitution was a tactical alliance between liberal, progressive and conservative forces to check the power of elected politicians. As chairman of the Democracy Development Committee (a body established by parliament to examine questions of political reform in 1994),

Dr Prawase Wasi argued that Thailand was experiencing 'parliamentary dictatorship' – exactly the same phrase used to justify the military coup of February 1991. His well-chosen words had a powerful appeal to conservatives and bureaucrats who felt uneasy about the rise of elected politicians over the previous two decades. Prawase rightly judged that it was essential to bring on board conservative elites, and to seek their support for the reform process. As Connors has observed (Connors 1999: 210), Prawase was a syncretist, an unusual figure who could bring together both conservatives and progressives. Yet, as Prawase notes in his contribution to this volume, the participation of conservative forces in the reform process was a double-edged sword. Some groups sought to undermine the constitution-drafting process, arguing that the 1997 draft charter posed a threat to the monarchy, or did not go far enough in recognizing the special status of Buddhism. Building an alliance for change was a complex process, since the catch-all catch-phrase 'political reform' plainly meant different things to different people. It is worth briefly reviewing some of the alternative meanings of political reform (for more detail, see McCargo 1998: 13–22).

While conservatives saw reform as essentially about checking the power of elected politicians, another meaning of political reform – that favoured by Prawase himself – placed little emphasis on legalistic solutions. Rather, the focus was on a broad package of changes aimed at transforming the way society was organized. A new constitution could prove helpful insofar as it provided some momentum for change, a springboard for further reforms. Because Thailand is a highly legalistic society, this approach sought to tap into the legalism of the elite in order to build up pressures for more fundamental changes.

Another possible meaning of political reform was an attempt to head off social disorder, the violence that might be generated through intense conflicts over resources and opportunities in a society rife with injustice and inequality. In other words, by introducing reforms prior to the outbreak of a major social crisis, disorder could be pre-empted. While the possible basis of a crisis was never specified, one source of anxiety about the future concerned the succession question. While the king had performed an important refereeing role in national crises (especially in May 1992), it was necessary to ensure the stability of political institutions in any future eventuality. By promulgating a more inclusionary constitution which would check abuses of power, popular faith in the political order could be strengthened, and a potential crisis of state legitimacy averted.

On another level, one meaning of political reform was checking the 'dark influences' associated with provincial business elites that had achieved such a powerful grip on the political process. These influences were neatly symbolized for many by Sanoh Thienthong, the interior minister at the time the 1997 constitution was promulgated. Sanoh was the provincial power-broker behind the short-lived premierships of Banharn Silpa-archa (1995–96) and Chavalit Yongchaiyudh. The rise of such figures dismayed both conservatives and progressives alike: public order was being enforced by people whose own commitment to the rule of law was widely questioned. Ninety per cent of Thai voters lived in rural areas, and frequently elected 'rural machine politicians' of limited competence and integrity to parliament. Bangkokians, accustomed to ruling over the provinces, found themselves governed by less than respectable provincial businesspeople. In large part, the concerns of the reformers were justified. At the same time, substantive reforms would have empowered rural people to select politicians who really reflected their interests, a change that would have had adverse consequences for cosseted and resource-rich Bangkok.

Another meaning of political reform was a desire for technocracy. The Anand 1 and Anand 2 administrations – which were wholly unelected – have often been praised as Thailand's best ever governments. It was widely felt that the existing Thai political order made it impossible for 'good people' (of whom Anand was the chief representative) to gain major political office. Reforms should create the conditions for such people to enter politics. This idea underlay a consistent preoccupation with separating the executive from the legislature, culminating in the 1997 constitutional provisions which made it impossible for a constituency MP to serve as a minister. The popularity of Anand and the widespread hankering for competent as opposed to electorally legitimate government demonstrated that the political reform process that culminated in the 1997 constitution was only shallowly rooted in democratic principles.

Democratic ideas, however, did animate some sections of the pro-reform coalition, especially non-governmental organizations and people's organizations. Their essential aim was to see more power devolved to the grassroots and more emphasis on addressing the concerns of ordinary people. In this, they were supported by some progressive academics and public intellectuals. At the same time, the non-governmental sector (as Naruemon explains in this volume) was by no means unified: there was significant debate within the NGO movement about the most appropriate form of popular participation, and something of a divide emerged between urban-based NGOs and rural people's organizations. Overall, however, the groups in this sector stood to gain from almost any reform process that weakened the powers of the state, and introduced greater checks and balances concerning the activities of politicians. Accordingly, grassroots organizations were willing to go along with quite minor reforms in the hope of building upon these small gains in future: they saw reform as a long-term process of popular empowerment.

THE CONTEXT OF THE CRISIS

The economic crisis that engulfed Thailand in 1997 led to a widespread questioning of the country's social and political structures. As redundant urban factory workers and labourers returned to their villages, scepticism about the prevailing mode of development became quite widespread, and there was a new interest in principles of self-sufficiency and decentralization. To a large extent, this interest was a revisiting of earlier ideas associated with the community culture school of thought (see Chatthip 1991). Broadly speaking, this school had criticized mainstream economic development, arguing that Thais should emphasize their cultural roots as villagers who had been self-reliant and mutually supportive in a pre-monetary order. By reducing engagement with the global economy and making do with a modest standard of living, people could lead fuller lives without such a high degree of vulnerability to the forces of international capitalism. These themes were highlighted in successive birthday speeches by the King from 1997 onwards. With the sudden end of rapid economic growth, the urgency of reform and adaptation to Thailand's changing circumstances became vastly more acute: the scaling down of economic desires and demands was one rather Buddhistic solution, placing the responsibility for adaptation firmly upon individual citizens.

At the same time, there is considerable evidence that large-scale political failure – seen in a lack of political leadership, lack of effective representative structures, electoral and structural corruption, the decline of bureaucratic competence, and above all colossal over-centralization – was one of the major causes of the Thai economic crisis. Thai politics could only be reformed by addressing structural problems as well as making individual moral choices.

Thailand has suffered from serious failures of political leadership; with a handful of exceptions, Thailand's leading politicians during the final two decades of the twentieth century were unimpressive and parochial individuals with negligible international standing. Capable and upstanding figures were rarely attracted to the murky world of Thai politics, which was rife with electoral fraud and corruption (see Surin and McCargo 1997). It was virtually impossible to be elected to parliament outside Bangkok without engaging in vote-buying and other abuses. Staggering sums were spent in manipulating the results of elections at all levels. It was similarly difficult to serve as a minister without participating in corrupt practices, or at least without colluding in – or passively condoning – the corruption practised both by fellow politicians and by bureaucrats. Ministers routinely received commissions or kickbacks on major contracts under their supervision; provincial governors took a cut in the profits from illegal lotteries; military commanders, police chiefs and local politicians shared in the spoils from smuggling, drug-dealing and other criminal activities. Under such conditions, mediocre leaders thrived, and capable individuals either succumbed to temptation or quickly abandoned politics.

Despite the fact that general elections took place with remarkable regularity (three in the 1980s and four in the 1990s), parliament was not an effective forum for representing popular interests. Politicians owed their loyalties to the faction bosses and the business interests that had financed their very expensive election campaigns, rather than to the voters themselves. MPs had no offices at parliament, and often paid little attention to the concerns of their constituents, other than by providing a very crude form of social welfare (supplying ice and drinks for ordinations, funerals, weddings and other celebrations, for example). While a small number of MPs sought to develop expertise in areas of public policy, the great majority had no such interests. Serving as an MP was a kind of racket, with fact-finding junkets arranged by the various parliamentary committees, perks and trips paid for by business interests angling for contracts, and even spells of overseas 'training' funded by well-intentioned but usually misguided international bodies.

Vote-buying, a longstanding Thai practice, was actually exacerbated by new legislation passed at the end of the 1970s, intended to clean up elections and restructure political parties. By the 1995 and 1996 elections it had reached epidemic proportions: to stand a serious chance of winning a typical upcountry seat, a basic investment equivalent to nearly 1 million US dollars was required. While the Bangkok intelligentsia and business community ritually denounced such practices, it was an open secret that the very largest and most respected Thai companies were directly funding vote-buying on a massive scale, hoping to reap material rewards from each new government. Since the outcome of the elections was usually unclear, and all Thai governments were coalition administrations with five or more partners, putting all your eggs into a single party basket was unwise. Accordingly, most major companies funded all the major parties. And although self-righteous-sounding government officials ritually denounced abuses of the electoral system, it was well known that winning a parliamentary seat often depended on the cooperation of provincial governors and police chiefs. The electoral system had become a massive exercise in benefit-sharing, the slicing up of a cake which grew larger and more sumptuous with each election. Most of the eating, however, was done by elites: the process was an essentially exclusionary one.

While earlier views of Thailand as a 'bureaucratic polity' have recently been strongly disputed (see Hewison 1996), there is little doubt that civil servants and military officers have long exerted an important influence in the Thai political order. During the 1980s, however, the private sector grew in importance. Whereas the best and the brightest young Thais had traditionally aspired to public sector careers in organizations such as the army, the police, the Interior Ministry, the Finance Ministry and the Bank of Thailand, by the late 1990s local and international companies and private sector organizations were offering greater remuneration, more rapid promotion prospects, and more inviting opportunities. The private sector gained the upper hand in the labour market, not only attracting the majority of able young graduates, but also luring away the most able mid-career civil servants. Ammar Siamwalla (1997) argued that those charged with running the economy and regulating the financial system (notably officials in the Bank of Thailand and the Ministry of Finance) failed to keep abreast of the complex changes taking place in the international financial system, and thus made crucial mistakes that contributed to the economic crisis. In other words, the technocratic competence that underpinned a strong Thai economy from the 1960s onwards had been seriously eroded by the end of the century. This hollowing-out of public sector competence, though most evident in the central state financial institutions, significantly undermined the performance of the Thai state as a whole. During a period of staggeringly rapid change on the domestic, regional and global levels, Thai civil servants did not manage to keep pace, failing sufficiently to adapt and to innovate.

At the core of structural impediments to reform in Thailand lay the extraordinary degree of centralization. With the honourable exception of the Bangkok Metropolitan Authority, Thailand had no local government truly worthy of the name in 1997. While liberalism and pluralism were flourishing at the national level, out in the countryside provincial governors and other state officials continued to exercise an exceptional degree of political control. There were elected municipal and provincial councils, but these were weak bodies whose powers were tightly delimited by Bangkok ministries. The great majority of councils had been captured by construction contractors and other business interests. Crucially, moves to make the office of provincial governor an elected position were firmly resisted throughout the constitution-drafting process. As career bureaucrats in the Interior Ministry, sent out from the capital to administer the provinces in a quasi-colonial fashion, provincial governors were one of the largest obstacles to progressive change. Indeed, while Thailand's political order was undergoing extensive reform during the second half of the 1990s, the officials in numerous provinces were building themselves immense new *salakan jangwat* (provincial halls) at vast expense. These monumental structures symbolized their determination to resist the forces of decentralization at literally any cost. Unless the progressive rhetoric which informed the constitution-drafting debate was backed by a real shift in power away from Bangkok and towards ordinary people in towns and villages across the country, reform would remain procedural rather than substantive.

The present book seeks to address questions such as the following:

- What reforms were needed?
- Why was reform necessary, or not necessary?
- How could reform be implemented?
- How effective had previous attempts at reform proved?
- Who were the key actors and groups pursuing or obstructing reform agendas?
- What were the competing reform agendas in circulation?
- And how realistic were the goals advanced by reformers?

THE 1997 CONSTITUTION

The Constitution of 1997 has been heralded as a 'people's constitution' (for a discussion, see Connors, this volume). The constitution was 'popular' in two main senses. The first sense involved the composition of the Constitution Drafting Assembly, 73 of whose 99 members were provincial representatives who had been chosen by a complicated nomination process. In reality, however, politicians had the final say concerning the selection of these people's representatives (see Ockey 1997: 313–315). The second popular dimension was the emphasis on public consultation and debate, including a series of 'public hearings' across the country. Yet Prawase himself lamented the fact that genuine popular participation was very limited (*Bangkok Post* 'Constitution special', 27 March 1997). To a great extent, the drafting process was an elite led affair. A third potentially popular dimension of the process was never pursued: if parliament had rejected the draft constitution, a nation-wide referendum would have been held in order to reach a final verdict. This hybrid procedure (the people would only get to decide if the elite were arguing amongst themselves) contrasted with, for example, that used to approve the Philippine constitution of 1987: in the Philippine case, the decision was made by citizens as a whole, with no veto privileges for parliamentarians. In the event, the Chavalit Yongchaiyudh government – already facing economic collapse and desperately hoping to remain in office – reluctantly allowed the passage of the new charter, and no popular referendum was held.

The 1997 Thai Constitution is a long document, comprising 336 Articles. Because it represents the confluence of numerous competing interests, the constitution is not especially consistent: rather, it includes a mixture of liberal, progressive and conservative clauses. Three broad areas are of particular importance: those Articles dealing with reform of the electoral system; those Articles that establish new bodies charged with checking and balancing abuses of the political process; and those Articles dealing with popular rights.

The following Articles dealt with important electoral reforms:

- Voting was made compulsory (Article 68).
- An appointed Senate was replaced by an elected Senate of 'non-partisan' figures (Articles 126, 127).
- The old multi-member constituency system was replaced by a mixture of single-seat constituencies and proportional representation (using a 'party-list' system) (Article 98).
- Constituency MPs would no longer be allowed to serve as ministers (to do so, they would have to step down as MPs) (Article 118).
- MPs would need at least a bachelor's degree (Article 107, 3).
- Ministers could come from the party list (Article 119).
- MPs would not be allowed to switch parties during the 90 days preceding an election (Article 107, 4).

The clear thrust of these changes was an attempt to separate the executive and legislature: parties were expected to place senior, reputable figures on the party list so that they could be ready to assume ministerial posts, while local hoodlums, if elected to parliament at all, were to be confined to representing their districts. It was hoped that compulsory voting would make vote-buying more expensive and difficult, while smaller parliamentary constituencies would create a more genuine bond between citizens and their elected representatives (Borwornsak and Burns 1998). Senators were supposed to be wise men and women, standing above the fray of day-to-day politics, and bringing their wisdom to bear on important legislative matters.

The most distinctive feature of the 1997 constitution was the range of new bodies it established, in order to monitor and referee the political order. These were as follows:

- the Election Commission, an independent body with sweeping powers to oversee the electoral process, including the rights to investigate questionable elections, and if necessary to order new elections (Articles 136 to 148);
- the National Counter-Corruption Commission (NCC), with extensive powers to scrutinize the financial affairs of politicians and

their families, including the right to propose that the Senate remove politicians from office (Articles 291 to 307);
- the Constitutional Court to adjudicate on any matters concerning the interpretation of the constitution (Articles 255 to 270);
- up to three ombudsmen to investigate complaints concerning the performance of state officials (Articles 196 to 198);
- Administrative Courts to adjudicate in disputes arising from administrative acts of state officials (Articles 276 to 280);
- the National Human Rights Commission to investigate and report acts that violate human rights (Articles 199 and 200)
- the State Audit Commission (Article 312).

It was hoped that these new bodies would curtail abuses of power by both elected politicians and government officials, thus creating a new climate of transparency and critical scrutiny. In practice, however, much depended on how the new bodies would be able to function in practice. Some bodies with similar functions had existed in previous guises (such as the old Office of State Audit, and the old Counter-Corruption Commission), but these had experienced serious difficulties preserving their independence and credibility. While the constitution set out basic guidelines for the workings of these new bodies, their detailed operations were to be governed by a series of organic laws, covering: the election of parliamentarians, the Election Commission, the ombudsmen, political parties, counter-corruption, criminal procedures for those holding political positions, state audit, and referendums. In other words, the constitution contained within it a large body of unfinished business, the detailed pursuance of which would rely upon further legislation.

A third key area of the 1997 Constitution was the inclusion of provisions that enhanced the rights of citizens to challenge the power of politicians and the state. These included:
- provision for individuals to sue the state for pursuing projects harmful to the environment (Article 56);
- the right to gain access to public information from state agencies (Article 59);
- a requirement that where proposed legislation is deemed to concern children, women, the elderly or the disabled, representatives of these groups should take part in ad hoc committee discussions at the House of Representatives (Article 190);
- The right of 50,000 voters to petition the National Counter Corruption Commission to have a politician or high-ranking official accused of corruption removed from office (Article 304).

Although these Articles were somewhat woolly and ambiguous, they did offer considerable scope for individuals and non-governmental organizations to challenge the entrenched power possessed by both the state and particular politicians.

STRUCTURE OF THIS BOOK

This volume seeks to explore the politics behind the promulgation of Thailand's sixteenth constitution in October 1997, and how the reforms embodied in the new constitution have unfolded in the period that culminated in the January 2001 general election. Yet the essays here are not narrowly focused on institutional and legalistic concerns. Appropriately for a book gestated at a conference organized around the theme of 'Thailand: a Civil Society?' (the Seventh International Conference on Thai Studies, held in Amsterdam, 4–8 July 1999), this volume seeks to explore and reflect the debate engendered by the political reform movement in Thai society. The constitution-drafting and wider reform processes are seen as inherently contested, illustrating conflicts and differences – to take one example, disputes between elites who have sought to change Thailand's political and social order from above, and those at the grassroots who have challenged prevailing orthodoxies. The aim of this volume is not so much to give a narrative account of the reform process, but to provide some insight into competing issues and interests that have contributed to that process. It also seeks to reveal the ways in which the discourses and realities of reform have impacted on Thai society more generally.

The first few chapters examine important questions behind the reform movement. They begin with a first-hand view of the reform process from Prawase Wasi, one of the architects of Thailand's political reforms. Prawase explains how he first advocated constitutional reform immediately after the events of May 1992, when he wrote a personal letter to then interim Prime Minister Anand Panyarachun. He was concerned that unless shortcomings in the political order could be rectified, there was a potential for social disorder culminating in violence. Prawase subsequently hit upon the term 'political reform' as 'a marketable catch-phrase' with which to popularize these concerns. His appointment as chairman of the Democracy Development Committee (DDC) by the president of parliament in June 1994 gave Prawase the opportunity to push his political reform agenda. At the same time, he makes it clear that he never harboured any illusions that the government of the day would act on the Committee's recommendations. His strategy was one of 'social empowerment', creating a broad pro-reform coalition. The discourse of reform promoted by the DDC had an important impact on the 1995 election campaign. Prawase used a clever strategy of

INTRODUCTION

appealing to the new prime minister Banharn Silpa-archa's humanism and sense of family, effectively flattering him into thinking that support for reform could bolster his shaky political reputation. Banharn established the Political Reform Committee (PRC) to pursue the reform agenda, and during Banharn's premiership, parliament approved the establishment of the Constitution Drafting Assembly (CDA). Once the CDA had been created, the shape of the new constitution became a matter of fierce contestation. Prawase frankly acknowledges that some conservatives and political parties sought to disrupt the drafting process and to sabotage attempts to introduce significant reforms. Yet he insists that it was not simply the economic crisis of 1997 that ensured the passage of the new charter. Rather, the success of the process reflected the strength of public participation that helped to forge a social movement for political reform. The reform movement could then proceed to build upon the new constitution to seek the reform of other areas of society. He ends with a call for academics to contribute to an informed debate leading to public empowerment.

Thirayuth Boonmi similarly calls for the transformation of Thai society, seeing the economic crisis of 1997 as a wake-up call. His preferred solution is what he terms 'good governance', a strategy that embraces political and public sector reform as well as social, community and individual transformation. At the heart of the good governance project is a quest for substantive political legitimacy, based on popular sovereignty and broad democratic participation. Thirayuth also stresses the need for Thai people to achieve greater awareness of their rights. His concept of good governance has been an influential one in post-crisis Thailand; however, he has been at pains to stress that the concept is not identical with the technical notions of good governance advanced by the World Bank and other bodies, but includes a more holistic, communitarian vision.

In his chapter, Michael Connors provides a general analysis of the process by which the 1997 constitution was framed. He acknowledges that the process was highly contested and deeply flawed, yet also argues that the new constitution could only have emerged on the basis of a broad liberal consensus among key sections of the elite. Accordingly, he argues that the political reform process does hold out real hope for substantive and even radical change in Thailand. An alliance has emerged between liberal elements of the elite and progressive elements in the NGO and activists communities, placing traditional state power and the dark forces of money politics on the defensive. While essentially critical of the elite, Connors arrives – by a very different route – at a surprisingly optimistic conclusion, not so different from the prognoses of Prawase and Thirayuth.

In a rare analysis of the political role of the monarchy, Kobkua Suwannathat-Pian traces the evolution of King Bhumibol's changing constitutional position since 1972. She chronicles significant developments in the powers of the monarch which appeared in the 1991 and 1997 constitutions. In practice, she argues, the King has been able to exert an extra-constitutional role that commands wide popular support (as for example, when he appointed Anand Panyarachun interim prime minister in June 1992, instead of elected MP Somboon Rahong). Kobkua sees this informal royal authority as a function of Thailand's defective democratic institutions and processes. She therefore ends with a rhetorical and still hypothetical question: would successful political reform that genuinely strengthened the legitimacy of parliamentary politics transform the role of the monarchy into a more ceremonial one?

David Streckfuss and Mark Templeton bring their combined historical and legal expertise to bear in assessing the extent to which the 1997 Constitution marks a genuine breakthrough for human rights in Thailand. While noting certain positive developments, their main focus is on the shortcomings of the charter when judged by the standards of the International Covenant on Civil and Political Rights. They argue, for example, that the recent Wat Thammakai case highlighted the hollowness of religious freedom in Thailand; that the banning of the film *Anna and the King* demonstrated a disturbing lack of freedom of expression; and that constitutional provisions under which only degree-holders may run for parliament limit the access of the underprivileged to effective political representation. They are sceptical about the likely effectiveness of new bodies such as the National Human Rights Commission and the Constitutional Court. In conclusion, they argue that Thailand's citizens continue to lack a clear human rights consciousness, without which it will prove difficult to sustain the momentum of reform.

The chapter by Johannes Schmidt links the institutional themes of the early part of the book with the discussions of civil society and grassroots participation which follow in the later chapters. Examining the origins of the 1997 economic crisis and the subsequent responses of the Thai state, Schmidt argues that the crisis served to highlight the extent to which Thailand's remarkable economic growth had failed substantially to benefit large sections of the population. He insists that only systematic state intervention could ameliorate the structural inequalities in the Thai economic and social order that were laid bare by the crisis. Thus constitutional reform needed to be followed up by the introduction of proper mechanisms of social welfare. Schmidt is highly critical of the recent vogue for 'civil society' in Thailand, arguing that non-governmental organizations cannot replace the state, and are no substitute for substantive government measures to counter major socio-economic problems of poverty and inequality.

INTRODUCTION

James Ockey's discussion of the 'Hyde Park' street politics of the 1950s begins a group of chapters on the popular dimensions of reform. Ockey argues that demands for more grassroots participation in political debate are nothing new in Thailand. When Prime Minister Plaek Phibunsongkhram returned from his world tour in 1955, he set up a Thai version of the 'Speakers' Corner' that he had seen in London's Hyde Park. The Thai Speakers' Corner – a regular forum at the Sanam Luang – attracted considerable interest and became a focal point for mass rallies with many thousands of participants. Phibun was obliged to ban the forum after only six months, though to this day 'Hyde Park' remains a Thai appellation for a protest meeting. Ockey draws several important lessons from these historical developments, cautioning that it is inadequate to define civil society simply as organizations outside the state's control, since control is always a matter of degree. He stresses the importance of noting who is organizing movements and interest groups; and argues that the street politics of the 1950s closely prefigure the role of people's organizations such as Forum of the Poor in the 1990s. A common strand of both forms of protest was their lack of middle-class orientation.

In his critique of what he calls 'elite democracy' in Thailand, Somchai Phatharathananunth also raises critical questions about the meaning of civil society. He is concerned that metropolitan elite liberals such as fellow contributors Prawase Wasi and Thirayuth Boonmi have placed too much emphasis on the capacity of the state to initiate reform, and even to reshape civil society itself. For Somchai – who teaches in his native Northeast – allowing the Thai state to intervene in civil society is fundamentally misguided, offering meddlesome politicians and bureaucrats the right to interfere in the concerns and livelihoods of ordinary people, especially in rural areas. He dismisses the idea of a 'partnership' between the state and grassroots organizations, on the grounds that the fundamental inequalities of power between the two sides make a genuine partnership unworkable: the state will simply attempt to coopt and control local groups and organizations. Somchai argues that all substantive democratic change in Thailand has come from below; and there is no reason to believe that the state has sincerely embraced principles of democratic participation. The key to real political reform is thus the emergence of a vibrant and oppositionist popular sector.

Kevin Hewison examines Thai responses to the economic crisis of 1997, arguing that one important response was the emergence of a discourse of localism. Drawing upon earlier notions of cultural nationalism such as the community culture school, the new localism attracted attention from many different sectors of Thai society. One of its chief proponents was King Bhumibol himself, who articulated a 'new theory' of subsistence agriculture in his 1997 and 1998 birthday speeches. This discourse of localism implied a rejection of consumerism and the global capitalist order, and an emphasis on the primacy of the rural sector. Yet Hewison notes that – as with Somchai's elite-penetrated civil society – localist rhetoric has sometimes simply licensed state officials to interfere in rural problems, to the detriment of genuinely bottom-up initiatives. For Hewison, this new localism is highly nationalistic, not to mention 'reactionary, romantic, anti-urban and chauvinist'. Though himself highly critical of capitalist neo-liberalism, Hewison rejects Thai localism for failing to offer a coherent alternative to the prevailing order.

The chapter by Philippe Doneys takes as its main focus the role of women's organizations in the drafting of the 1997 Constitution. He insists that successful political reform requires institutional linkages between state and non-state actors. Using a Habermasian analysis, he argues that the Thai constitution-drafting process exemplified the construction of a public sphere in which non-state actors shared space with the state. He traces the emergence of women's civic groups in Thailand, examining the way in which they have moved from mere philanthropy to vigorous policy advocacy. Doneys questions the hard-and-fast distinction between state and civil society employed by critics such as Somchai. In effect, he develops a theoretical rationale for the kind of partnership between state and non-state actors advocated by social activists and commentators like Prawase and Thirayuth. Doneys argues that the role of women's organizations in the constitutional debate illustrates the extent to which the 'fabric of governance' in Thailand is increasingly influenced by non-state actors.

In her discussion of the role of NGOs in the political reform process, Naruemon Thabchumpon argues that the creation of 'substantive' reforms (as distinct from merely 'procedural' ones) requires greater popular empowerment and deeper participation. She is careful, however, not to lump all NGOs into a single, catch-all category. Rather, she differentiates between 'elite-urban' and 'rural-popular' components of Thai civil society. While elite-urban elements are largely Bangkok-based organizations – often with a middle-class orientation and a limited understanding of the real struggles and conflicts facing the poor – rural-popular groups are closer to the grassroots. For Naruemon, the real challenge for NGOs is to broker alliances and collaborations between these two dimensions of Thai civil society: in short, to bring together progressive Bangkokians and poor farmers. Like James Ockey, Naruemon argues for a more nuanced understanding of Thai civil society. Her sympathies clearly lie with the creation of 'a broad alliance for change', which would see a range of civil society groups form strong strategic linkages. Yet unlike Doneys, she is rather sceptical that such alliances are already emerging.

Sombat Chantornvong's is the first of three chapters that address the electoral dimensions of the reform process. Sombat evaluates the changes implemented in the electoral system with a sceptical eye, arguing that many of the reforms are superficial or technical, and will do little to undermine the longstanding abuses that plague Thai elections at all levels. Specifically, he discusses the problematic (and repeatedly re-run) Senate elections of 2000, and the ensuing controversy about the proper powers and duties of the Election Commission. He notes the persistence of practices such as vote-buying and the poaching of MPs from one party to another. He also examines the nature of factions and political clans, and discusses the way in which leading families have sought electoral office at various levels in many provinces. Sombat's overall analysis is deeply critical of the post-1997 reforms.

The chapter by Daniel Arghiros deals with local government reforms in Thailand and asks whether a genuine process of democratic decentralization is taking place in the provinces. Reviewing the workings of elected provincial and subdistrict councils, Arghiros (who has done extensive fieldwork on Thai rural politics) raises serious questions about their accountability and effectiveness. Rather than functioning as representative bodies, these elected organizations have developed authoritarian institutional cultures. Worse still, elections for these bodies are dominated by vote-buying and other corrupt practices. Both provincial and sub-district councils therefore have a very low level of accountability to the electorate. As Arghiros himself observes, his chapter makes for 'dismal reading'. Nevertheless, he is adamant that even Thailand's flawed experiments in democratic decentralization are worth making, and expresses the hope that socio-economic changes will gradually enhance the prospects for genuinely representative politics.

Reviewing the general election of 2001, Duncan McCargo attempts to unpack the significance of the landslide victory by Thaksin Shinawatra's Thai Rak Thai Party. Could the triumph of such a well-funded political machine really mean the decline of money politics? For some commentators, the election saw a shift towards party voting and the growing importance of policy platforms. Widespread challenges to electoral outcomes testified to a new spirit of civic consciousness. Yet vote-buying and electoral manipulation were more rampant than ever, and the credibility of monitoring agencies such as the Election Commission was greatly undermined in the ensuing furore. The jury was still out on the long-term impacts of changing electoral procedures.

The book concludes with a thoughtful essay by John Girling, who examines the inter-relationship between economics, politics and civil society in the Thai context. Girling emphasizes the central role that non-state actors and social forces will play in any effective process of substantive reform, arguing that the emergence of a strong civil society will be crucial if Thailand's political reforms are to succeed.

This volume does not set out to offer a definitive account or explanation of Thailand's political reforms. Rather, it seeks to celebrate the 'spirit of Amsterdam' – the vigorous and open debate that characterized the Seventh International Conference on Thai Studies in 1999 – by offering a range of perspectives and interpretations about these important and fiercely contested developments. It is hoped that the arguments here will stimulate further analysis, discussion and even controversy.

PART I

THE MEANINGS OF POLITICAL REFORM

2

AN OVERVIEW OF POLITICAL REFORM

Prawase Wasi

INTRODUCTION: FROM ABSOLUTE MONARCHY TO CIVIL SOCIETY

Political events from 1932 to the present day may be briefly summarized as follows. On 24 June 1932 there was a revolution to change the absolute monarchy to a constitutional one. The main ideology of the revolution was one of political and socio-economic reform. Power moved down vertically, shifting from the king into the hands of a small group of revolutionaries known as the 'Khanasaradorn', or people's group. In 1947 the military seized absolute power which remained in its hands for 26 years until the student uprising of 14 October 1973. In 1976 the military returned to suppress the students by violent means. However, the 20 years that followed the October student revolution saw a gradual decline in the power of the military, accompanied by the growth of the middle class, and increased public participation in a wide range of societal spheres. The coup d'état staged by the military in 1991 did not accord with the prevailing political context, and was met by popular resistance which led to the bloody events of May 1992 – events which put an end to the military role in politics forever. Since then, politics has been in the hands of civilian politicians who are engaged in playing money politics. Vote-buying, abuses of power, corruption and inefficiency are rampant. A movement for constitutional political reform began in 1994. With unprecedentedly wide public participation, a new constitution based on principles of political reform was promulgated in 1997. The 1997 constitution is an important milestone in Thai politics, aimed at checking abuses of power by politicians while opening the way for a civil society movement. The constitution thus plays an important function at a historic turning point between the vertical descent of political power to the emergence of a horizontally based civil society. It is widely recognized that civil society is a necessary condition for true democracy which brings about socio-economic development.

The process of rewriting a constitution and having the new version promulgated by peaceful means is extremely difficult – in fact, next to impossible. George Washington was responsible for initiating the American constitution of 1787; Charles de Gaulle was given a free hand to write the 1958 French constitution; and it took defeat in World War II to produce constitutional political reform in Japan and Germany. Yet the Thai constitution of 1997 was written by people who were not in power, and in the face of disagreement on the part of politicians. How this was done – the politics of political reform – should be the subject of careful research. What is described below is based on personal experience and knowledge, since I was the chairman of the Democracy Development Committee (DDC) which recommended that Thailand should produce a new constitution to advance the cause of political reform.

ORIGINS OF THE DEMOCRACY DEVELOPMENT COMMITTEE

The DDC was appointed on 9 June 1994, with myself as chairman. How this came about will be briefly described. In 1992, following the bloody May incident and the appointment of Anand Panyarachun as prime minister for the second time,[1] he was poised to dissolve parliament. I wrote him a personal letter suggesting that parliament not be dissolved yet, but that it should first be urged to amend the constitution in order to create a better political system. This was my first rudimentary proposal for political reform.

Some time in 1993 Borvornsak Uwanno, the legal expert, and his assistant Jaroen Compeerapap, came to see me at Siriraj Hospital, saying that the constitution then in force would lead to further bloody conflict. Throughout that year Amorn Chandara-Somboon[2] published in instalments a long paper on 'constitutionalism', which he proposed as a solution to Thailand's national problems (Amorn 1994). This paper was the result of a constitutional research project initiated by Chai-Anan Samudavanija.[3]

Hidden in the 'constitutionalism' paper was the key phrase 'political reform', which I seized upon as a marketable catch-phrase to win public support for the movement to change the constitution.

In May 1994, during the first Chuan government, Chalard Vorachad[4] staged a hunger strike in front of parliament, demanding that all administrative office-holders should be elected. Various groups of people who felt frustrated with the political situation expressed their support for Chalard, but later the situation polarized into a tense confrontation between two opposing camps. Chalard vowed that he would fast unto death. This provided an optimal moment for me to declare, on 1 June

1994, that 'the death of Chalard should lead to political reform'. There was then a sudden uproar demanding 'political reform'. Marut Bunnag, the Democrat Party-appointed President of Parliament, established the Democracy Development Committee (DDC) on 9 June 1994, hoping to persuade Chalard to end his hunger strike. I was appointed chairman of the DDC.

THE WORK OF THE DDC

The DDC was in existence from 9 June 1994 to 28 April 1995. The DDC recommended the rewriting of the constitution to implement political reform. However, the DDC knew from the beginning that politicians would not support political reforms that would curb their power. Thus the main strategy of the DDC was social empowerment. To do this, it was necessary to engage in information dissemination and public participation with the involvement of the media. It was essential that the information disseminated was clear, firm, easy to understand, and presented in such a way as to capture popular sentiment. The public already felt a mixture of loathing and exasperation concerning the behaviour of politicians, but did not know how to address the problem. 'Rewrite the constitution to curb the power of bad politicians' they were told. The way to do this was to 'amend Article 211 of the present constitution to create a new constitution-drafting mechanism'. Amending Article 211 was a message simple enough for everybody to grasp. We were engaged in a strategic campaign, rather than an academic debate. Detailed academic debate usually fails to arouse public interest. Public participation and media involvement were carefully designed so that demands for political reform became a social movement.

The DDC ceased to exist on 28 April 1995, when it presented its token recommendations to the President of Parliament (see Democratic Development Committee 1995a, 1995b). This self-dissolution was done at the behest of the chairman, to prevent the DDC from becoming a political organization entangled in the messy and dirty business of day-to-day politics. I felt that the DDC ought to give a very clear and strong message, and then immediately dissolve itself; any further activities would tarnish its image.

The DDC did not expect the President of Parliament or the government to do anything with its recommendations – and indeed they took no action based on the Committee's findings. Importantly, however, public consciousness of the political reform issue had already been raised.

MAKING POLITICAL REFORM A POLITICAL ISSUE

The first Chuan government could not continue to function, and parliament was dissolved in May 1995. During the general election campaign that followed, Banharn Silpa-archa, leader of the Chart Thai Party, announced that his party endorsed 'political reform as advocated by Prawase', running big advertisements in newspapers, and promising the public that Chart Thai would implement political reform if elected. This declaration was apparently the work of Surakiart Sathianthai,[5] former dean of the Faculty of Law, Chulalongkorn University, member of the DDC, and a close friend of Bovornsak and adviser to Banharn Silpa-archa. When a major political party made political reform part of its election campaign platform, political reform automatically became a continuing political issue, since the media began questioning other political parties about their stance on the policy, and the public demanded clear pledges from other politicians. It should be pointed out that opposition political parties are more likely to embrace innovative or reforming recommendations than government parties, which typically prefer to maintain the status quo and avoid risk. Thus in the politics of reform, this should be kept in mind.

As expected, when the Chart Thai Party won the election and formed the new government, the media and the public demanded that the party's election promises of political reform be carried out. Banharn Silpa-archa, the prime minister, had to honour his promises by asking parliament to set up the Political Reform Committee (PRC), chaired by his brother, Chumpol Silpa-archa. The task of the PRC was to recommend the amendment of Article 211 of the constitution, so as to set up a constitution-writing mechanism. There was extensive public debate and discussion concerning the best structures for the rewriting of the constitution to support political reform. Finally, the parliamentary scrutiny committee chaired by Chai-Anan Samudavanija recommended the formation of the Constitution Drafting Assembly (CDA). At this point, parliamentary approval of the recommended amendment to the constitution was vital. The role of the prime minister in pushing it through was crucial. I never hesitated to use a 'family or wife strategy' at such critical moments. I wrote an article in a newspaper entitled 'The Silpa-archa Family, Humanism and Political Reform', saying that Banharn's family was his greatest asset, and they should push together for political reform. His daughter Kanchana[6] wrote me a letter saying that her father was sincere and would push wholeheartedly for political reform. The subsequent approval of the amendment of Article 211 by parliament paved the way for the work of the CDA.

THE CONSTITUTION DRAFTING ASSEMBLY

The CDA established by the amendment of Article 211 was composed of 76 provincial representatives and 33 experts in law, political science, or government. The process of its formation attracted a lot of public interest and participation. The CDA elected Uthai Pimjaichon, former President of Parliament, as its chairman, Anand Panyarachun, former prime minister, as chairman of the Constitution Drafting Committee (CDC) and Bovornsak Uwanno, a key person from the DDC, as the CDC secretary. The CDA also included many other prominent academics and public figures.

The CDC and CDA functioned very painfully and experienced numerous difficulties amidst a lack of understanding, conflicts of interest, disagreements, and hostile accusations. Conservatives in both the lower and upper houses and outside parliament repeatedly attacked the CDA, accusing it of wanting to change the system so as to affect the monarchy. Some groups even threatened to mobilize the Village Scouts in order to protest against the CDA. Some Buddhist groups demanded that Buddhism be specified as the national religion, and threatened to boycott the promulgation of the new constitution. Some members of the CDA who were elected from the provinces were regarded as stooges of political parties, coming in to disrupt the constitution-drafting process; these suspicions were not entirely unfounded.

However, as a result of good academic input, good leadership in the CDC and CDA, and broad public participation, the process gradually gained ground and improved in quality. The social movement for political reform was a strong force which curtailed opportunities for disruption. The CDA was able to finish the constitution drafting by the legal deadline. The government seemed to be reluctant to endorse the draft, and some personalities in the ruling group voiced strong objections to it. However, on the basis of broad public pressure, MPs and senators overwhelming approved the draft, and thus the new constitution was promulgated in October 1997 – another step forward for political reform.

Some have claimed that only the economic crisis of 1997 pushed the new constitution through. This may be the case, but as chairman of the DDC, I predicted in 1994 that Thailand would have a new reformist constitution in 3–4 years. I did so on the basis that problems and conflicts resulting from bad politics would ultimately lead to a crisis, with no other way out except political reform. The promulgation of the 1997 constitution was a historic event which has set Thailand on a path towards social reform.

SOCIAL REFORM: A NATIONAL AGENDA

In our modern, interconnected, multidimensional and rapidly changing complex society, social crises are bound to occur. Social crises are extremely difficult or impossible to solve because existing social institutions are not powerful enough to cope with new problems –

whether they be bureaucratic, academic or religious institutions. There is a need for social reform in at least the following major areas, in order to create

1. new social values and consciousness,
2. sufficient economy and civil society;
3. good governance in the financial system;
4. political and bureaucratic reform;
5. education reform;
6. media reform;
7. legal reform.

These components of reform are interlinked and need to be carried out simultaneously. Courage and lessons should be drawn from the process of the movement which led to the 1997 constitution. There must be further social movements supported by relevant research. Key people in different areas will be necessary for the success of these reforms. The whole spectrum of social reform may be viewed as a process of promoting good governance, or building civil society.

CONCLUSION

Modernizing reforms in Siam during the period 1850–1932 were led by the monarchy. The modernization process bred a European-educated elite group which was the main actor in the 24 June 1932 revolution. Although the military ruled from 1947, the democratic spirit and expanded education resulting from the 1932 revolution contributed to the student-led uprising against the military in 1973. While the military resumed its rule after the suppression of students in 1976, the military's grip on power and legitimacy gradually waned with the rise of the middle class. In the meantime, because of the spread of materialism and consumerism coupled with a curriculum that emphasized rote learning, the students' role in the reform movement faded. Thus in the final resistance to military rule in 1992, it was not the students – as in 1973 – but the middle class who led the fighting. In the constitutional reform movement of 1997 there was wide public participation. The roles of NGOs, community leaders, academics and the media have increased and contributed greatly to the reform movement – a transformation in civil society.

The wide-ranging social reforms mentioned in the previous section will be very difficult to implement, but are extremely necessary. Intersectoral collaboration and public participation are elements of the new politics, not simply the narrow activities of traditional politicians. Poverty and environmental problems will destabilize society and may lead to violent conflicts. The money-oriented economy makes the country crisis-bound. The complexity of the interlinked economy is too difficult for the public to understand, and it is too difficult for the public to develop the necessary coping skills. The empowerment of the public to enable them to understand modern complexity is crucial for the reform movement. For this purpose, traditional academics who confine themselves to their own disciplines and place all their emphasis on purely academic analysis do not lead to the generation of adequate social energy. The politics of reform at present needs to develop a cadre of academics of high integrity, who understand the complexity of modern society, who have a vision for the future, can synthesize things, can develop strategies, and can communicate with the public. Only through public empowerment based on relevant knowledge can the social reform process advance through the forest of obstacles. Legitimate organizations of the poor are crucial to promote a more balanced direction of development policies. And finally, the politics of reform should understand the significance of spiritual development. External reform alone cannot lead to peace and sustainability. Internal reform is also necessary to create new development paradigms.

NOTES*

1 Anand served two terms as an appointed prime minister in 1991 and 1992.
2 Professor of Law at Thammasat University.
3 Prominent political scientist and former professor at Chulalongkorn University.
4 Chalard staged a number of politically-inspired hunger strikes – most famously in April and May 1992, when his protest provided the catalyst for mass demonstrations which culminated in the resignation of Prime Minister Suchinda Kraprayoon.
5 Dr Surakiart later became finance minister in Banharn's first cabinet.
6 Also a Chart Thai MP for the family's home province

* The editor is responsible for the notes in this chapter.

3

GOOD GOVERNANCE: A STRATEGY TO RESTORE THAILAND

Thirayuth Boonmi

Edited and translated by Savitri Gadavanij

I warned in an article entitled 'The Second Rattanakosin Crisis' (*Matichon Weekly*, 26 August 1997) that 'if we cannot get through the crisis, we might become a nation with a bankrupt economy, an enfeebled society, a people dispirited and hopeless, and a country that is a regional basketcase'.

That warning has come true: social problems are more severe, unemployment is up, and the misery and poverty of the people are increasing. It will take eight years to clear our foreign debt of 5 million million baht (according to the current currency exchange rate), if we commit 800,000 million baht from the national budget annually. To do this the government would not be able to repair even one road, pay even one civil servant, or supply even one hospital. Moreover, if we had pre-crisis levels of productivity but strictly economized by allocating 10 per cent of our GDP, it would take us 10–15 years to pay off this amount of debt.

Aside from loans, the government has created debt from its bail-out of different financial institutions, from the BBC to the 58 finance companies, commercial banks and other financial institutions, amounting to approximately 1.2 million million baht. It is hard to see where the government will find the finances apart from increasing taxes and massively cutting the budget for public utilities. There seems to be no other option than not to repair, not to build, and to let the nation degenerate for ten years until the debt can be repaid.

However, we cannot let society deteriorate, leave people with no hope and in a constant state of stress. I have proposed the concept of *thammarat* (good governance) as a solution to this problem. It refers to a collaboration between the public, social and private sectors to create governance and administration that are transparent, legitimate, accountable and effective. I have suggested this solution because our problem stems from the festering depravity in our political system, bureaucracy, technocracy and the business sector, while the popular sector is weak, lacking in knowledge to monitor policy and the work of the other sectors. The result is a disastrous loss to the economy, finances and treasury of the nation. The ultimate solution must be the reform of various systems in society. However, instead of having any one side demanding that another side reform, the call is for society to reform itself.

There are two reasons behind this demand. One is because we have to confront the foreign economic intrusion together. Another is because a large part of society is responsible for the crisis. *Thammarat haengchat,** or good governance, is the right strategy to tackle the economic crisis, because it is a strategy to increase political, social and cultural capital in order to increase economic capital. We must accept that we have lost all our economic capital and have become deeply indebted. What we have left is political capital, which is the system of democracy and the reform of the constitution derived from the 14 October 1976 and May 1992 incidents, and political reform. This political capital is invaluable and should be maintained as the basis for solving the crisis. However, we also need to promote an increase in social and behavioural-normative capital, that is, to ensure reform in many different systems, including having the Thai people conduct business, work and their lives in society and communities more efficiently, so that they are more professional and have higher standards.

Thai society has been fighting for democracy for a long time. We have witnessed the end of absolute monarchy in 1932, the 14 October 1973 incident and the Black May events of 1992. It can be said that in terms of political reform we have had a measure of success. People now have enough faith in the political system to solve the crisis, without calling on the military, as would have occurred previously. It can be said that for 25 years after the 14 October 1973 incident, we struggled until we won political rights. Yet what we lack, and what should be our objective, are detailed rights and freedoms which are the micro-structures of power, such as consumer rights, and the rights to protect oneself, the community, the environment, and to develop one's own morality.

Good governance entails cooperation between people, institutions, political organizations and society. This cooperation need not be formal as long as the parties involved actively work together. It will cultivate good morale, knowledge, morality and will be a symbol of hope for people living in extreme tension and misery.

Good governance is a product of collaboration. It is not a construct of power but of morality and wisdom for the purpose of creating a correct body of knowledge for people; that is, knowledge about how to solve problems without blaming others, for example the USA, the IMF, without seeking a debt moratorium, or asking for help from outsiders. The right solution is to choose the middle way, which is one of self-reliance, and to reinforce a Thai spirit which is internationally minded. Good governance is a powerful movement of local institutions and communities to understand their own problems, so that they can rely on themselves and reform themselves. By helping themselves, they can be more independent and also be strong enough to truly monitor what is not good in their community. Good governance is the only way to boost the country's immune system, making it strong and healthy in the future.

DEFINING GOOD GOVERNANCE

Good governance means a form of public administration that is good and efficient in every aspect, and at every level. This ethical administration can be realized only when we believe that people, bureaucrats and the government are partners in determining the fate of the country. However, partnership is no guarantee of good governance. Good governance also refers to the rules and regulations that make the country's administration transparent, accountable, efficient and just. Good governance is an interactive relationship between the state, the society, the private sector and the general public. The aim of the collaboration is to monitor the country's administration to be efficient, transparent, just and accountable.

In the past, we viewed governance as a matter of the government being the centre of power for issuing 'administrative' policy. There was a distinct borderline between the powerful and the powerless; those who dictated fate, and those whose fate was dictated; the governors and the governed.

However, a new concept has recently emerged and has become widely accepted by the UN and World Bank, as well as the IMF. According to this new thinking, good governance should be an interactive collaboration between democratic government and society, which includes the private sector and NGOs. It emphasizes participation, transparency and accountability. There should be a share in policy making and increased self-management within the social sector. These changes will lead to a more sustainable and equal development.

GOOD GOVERNANCE AS A NEW SOURCE OF LEGITIMACY

Thai people have always believed that the state is the most important thing, that we need as many politicians and civil servants as possible. In today's world, thinking about democracy has changed for the better, so that it is no longer deemed that democracy is sufficient: good governance is also necessary.

Good governance is an idea that has evolved beyond Western political science and practices, with its rigid division of power into the legislature, the judiciary, the executive and popular sovereignty. Good governance is a new way of looking at political power as something flexible, interacting with the people's sector and increasingly divided. New ideas about power and legitimacy should be as follows:

1. The people are sovereign. They are partners in the governing of the country. The state should reduce its size and power so that the social and people's sector can have more power.
2. Nowadays the economic sector is bigger and more complex than the governmental and bureaucratic sector. The interaction between the economic sector and the people is highly complicated and diverse. It is difficult for the governmental and bureaucratic sector to supervise it effectively. Therefore, people must have more direct participation (participatory democracy) in order for the economic sector to be more just and efficient.
3. To have good governance at every level means establishing legitimacy at every level of society, or distributing legitimacy through micro-legitimation processes at many levels. All these levels are interrelated:

- *Individual good governance* – each individual is aware of his/her power and is able to exercise it responsibly and justly;
- *Community good governance* – the coordination between community rights and power, and local administration;
- *Business and private sector good governance* – the management of private sector and public enterprises so that they are accountable, transparent and efficient and take on social responsibility;
- *Political and bureaucratic good governance* – decentralization of good administration and management. There should be a system to check their administration both internally and between offices so that they become more efficient and develop a heightened sense of responsibility for the public.

CONDITIONS TO ESTABLISH GOOD GOVERNANCE

Good governance can be established when Thai society has reached an appropriate level of maturity, such that

- it can perceive that the society has complexity and diversity, and that it cannot be divided into clear-cut compartments;
- each part of the society develops positively, for example political parties accept the new conventions of political reform, even though many drawbacks may persist, such as vote-buying and corruption in politics;

- Thai people are more enthusiastic and the politicians and bureaucrats do not look down upon them as foolish or uneducated;
- each part of society embarks on its own internal reform.

However, the public and media are still the major forces in setting the good governance movement in motion.

GOOD GOVERNANCE: A REFORM OF THE SOCIAL SYSTEM

The economic crisis that happened indicates that the problem we have is a structural one. Therefore a reform of the system is the solution to that problem. The reforms should be executed in four areas.

The first area concerns the private sector and the Bank of Thailand. There should be a more effective mechanism to monitor the country's financial system. There should be a system capable of signalling in advance an impending economic crisis. Legal means must be able to prevent any kind of unlawful monopoly of land and concessions. They should be able to promote proper business ethics, an account audit system and the assessment of tax and assets. The tax system also needs reform so that it can yield more social justice.

The second area in need of reform is the public sector. The governmental sector needs three main reforms. The size of public services needs to be reduced while increasing their efficiency. Services such as the police department and the forestry department should be decentralized. The role of the social sector should be increased by turning over government activities such as education and management of natural resources to local communities. Universities and hospitals should be transformed into autonomous bodies, for example, partly funded by the government. The role of the media in the public sphere should be strengthened, so that it is able to monitor and evaluate the administration's performance.

The third area is that of people's social and economic rights. Contemporary Thailand is characterized by socio-economic complexity. The Thai people are not aware of their new status and rights. As a result, they do not realize that their rights are being seriously violated. For example, the media — radio and television broadcasts and newspapers — pay insufficient attention to the consumer's right to know the truth, and hospitals take advantage of their patients. Thai people are subject to unfair terms and conditions when they buy cars and properties, and have to deal with bureaucratic and private services that take advantage of consumers.

Another indispensable reform is the reform of law and the legal process, so encouraging people to exercise their rights. For example, there should be a class action law. Also, we should consider lowering the cost of lawsuits so that consumers can afford to go to court whenever necessary.

THE FORM OF GOOD GOVERNANCE

Good governance refers to the promotion of social collaboration of different parties, namely: the public sector, social sector and private sector; the nation's major institutions; and various levels of the country (community, regional and national). This collaboration should be concrete and strong. It could take the form of a National Convention for the Good Governance of Thailand or the establishment of an Economic and Social Council according to the new constitution. Yet, since good governance is an ideal, we must be careful that no organization bears a name such as 'Good Governance Committee' or 'Good Governance Forum'. It must be named 'Committee *for* Good Governance' or 'Forum *for* Good Governance' because those who participate are not representatives of the ideal, but are simply advancing its cause.

By being conscious about the abstract nature of good governance, we can prevent arguments about who has the legitimate right to speak for 'good governance'. As people voluntarily participate, they will have different sources of legitimacy: for example, a politician's legitimacy comes from election, an official will be legitimized by their respective institution, and any person can legitimately speak according to their social role.

In sum, good governance is a form of unity and genuine cooperation of the government, private sector, scholars, leaders of major institutions and community networks in a time of national crisis. The cooperation is in the form of think-tanks rather than power-holding. Good governance is not a formal office but it is capable of bringing into being formal organizations as allowed by the constitution and law, such as the National Economic and Social Development Board (NESDB). It can also promote a social movement at many levels in order to solve problems.

DUTIES AND RESPONSIBILITIES OF GOOD GOVERNANCE

The collaboration of many institutions at various levels can be a symbol of hope for Thai people in a time of crisis. It also shows the world community the strong will of the Thais to solve their own problems. Thais need to analyse their previous failures and mistakes thoroughly. This is better than letting the government – which had a hand in the problem – diagnose the problem by itself. We can also establish an office to monitor governmental policy and to send out warnings prior to economic crises, should they occur again. Administrative reform must be encouraged. The administration should be transparent, just, accountable and effective, which is the meaning of good governance.

It is also important to develop a public understanding that solving the country's economic woes is a problem of structural nature concerning economics, society and culture. It will, therefore, take a long time, and demand patience and dedication. It is impossible for a few people to solve this problem in a short period of time. We also need to establish a body of knowledge to set up a strategy to restore the nation in every dimension. As it is a long-term project, those behind good governance will not be directly responsible for short-term economic problems such as the value of the baht or interest rates, because these are the government's responsibility. Yet, they may give government advice.

Participating institutions should demonstrate a constructive role by expressing their public commitment and suggesting how they can help solve the problem. It is important to employ the correct perspective to solve problems, that is through self-reliance and self-reform both in terms of values and institutional arrangements. Together, we should define national goals such as adopting the concept of 'moderate existence' according to the King's proposals, or sustainable development. Together we must define concrete goals to address immediate grievances such as resolving unemployment, introducing saving schemes, supporting Thai products and helping the poor in urban and rural areas.

We need to empower people and communities by ensuring that the organic laws flowing from the new constitution are faithful to its intention. This includes encouraging NGOs to cultivate people's awareness about their rights, such as their right to have access to information, their right to be protected as consumers, and their right to look after their community. NGOs should create platforms for people to speak up about their problems and their solution to those problems, in order to relieve social tensions. Finally, we should encourage members of the community or society to be considerate and help one another as much as possible.

EDITOR'S ACKNOWLEDGEMENT

This article is based on an article that appeared in *Matichon Weekly*, 27 January 1998, supplemented by some unpublished material supplied by the author. Thanks to Somchai Phatharathananunth and Michael Connors for their comments and suggestions on the translation, and Naruemon Thabchumpon for liaising with the author.

---

* TRANSLATOR'S COMMENT: In the original article, the author uses the term *thammarat haengchat* (national *thammarat*) for his Thai version of good governance. However, there are some differences between Thirayuth's concept of *thammarat*, and 'good governance' as defined by international organizations such as the World Bank. While *thammarat* emphasizes the voluntary collaboration of institutions at various levels of society, good governance simply refers to governance that is transparent, legitimate and accountable.

4

FRAMING THE 'PEOPLE'S CONSTITUTION'

Michael Kelly Connors

In the 1990s, a loose coalition of Thai reformers emerged to push through a liberal political agenda against authoritarian and corrupt elements in both the state apparatuses and political organizations. The main outcome of this movement was the promulgation in 1997 of Thailand's sixteenth constitution, the so-called 'People's Constitution'. The reformers aimed to break the impasse of a system of money politics that they characterized as having 'malfunctioning' political parties (non-representative and failing to aggregate interests), an electoral system oiled by vote-buying, and a corrupt and unaccountable political and bureaucratic elite. Reformers pitted themselves against all manifestations of money politics, hoping that through a new system of checks and balances, and the establishment of a series of independent bodies such as a Counter Corruption Commission and an Electoral Commission, the political system would be made more responsive, representative and stable.

FRAMING THE CHANGE: ELITES OR 'THE PEOPLE'?

In this chapter I shall demonstrate that the 'People's Constitution' was the outcome of a coherent and deliberate elite project for liberal reform in the difficult context of a spatially bifurcated political system. Aiming to establish public institutions and processes that could check the arbitrary use of power by both politicians and bureaucrats, and secure stable executive government, reformers also had to address the rural–urban electoral divide which was seen as pivotal to the existence of money politics. The dominance of clique-based political parties in parliament was seen by reformers as a consequence of an unsophisticated rural electorate, itself a product of underdevelopment, returning undesirable politicians, either because of client-based loyalty or because of vote-buying and -selling (see Anek 1996; Nelson 1998). Opposed to this account of political reform, two general positions may be discerned.

First, McCargo suggests that the passing of the constitution was partly an outcome of the 'disorderly pluralism of Thailand's multiple elites' (1998: 26), and reflected the diseased Thai preoccupation with 'constitutionalism', which saw competing elites tailoring constitutions to their own advantage (ibid.: 5–9). This diseased constitutionalism stood in implicit contrast with a 'Western' constitutionalism, which embraces the liberal end of restraining arbitrary power (Vile 1967). McCargo rightly points out the multiple 'meanings' attached to reform by different groupings (1998: 13–22). However, I shall argue that such contestations occurred within a shared framework of political liberalism. By this I mean that while reformers' ideological orientation may be plotted across a communitarian-liberal continuum, they each pragmatically subscribed to the construction of institutions that would facilitate checks on the exercise of power. Against the resulting pessimism that flows from McCargo's analysis, I remain cautiously optimistic that the constitution, coupled with socio-economic changes, has laid a firm basis for the long-term emergence of Thai liberalism.

The rise of provincial capitalist and 'godfather' (*jao pho*) influence over the party and parliamentary system in the 1980s (Pasuk and Baker 1997: 29–32), which became institutionally consolidated by the 1990s, meant that reformists chose to bypass the parliamentary arena. To them parliament was an untrustworthy forum; substantive debate over political reform therefore shifted to a wider public arena. The reform movement consequently appeared to be a popular affair, giving credence to the idea of an invigorated public sphere and mass engagement in political debate. This encouraged an interpretation of the new constitution as reflecting the views of the 'people', particularly because much was made of the people's participation in the drafting process. Supporters could point to numerous public hearings, and the mobilization of the press, NGOs and other organizations in support of political reform (Naruemon 1998: 46–47; Prudhisan 1998: 272–273).

However, what is important here is not the spectacle of popular involvement, as though there existed a channel for some fictitious collective will, but the strategies pursued by non-elite actors. In strategic terms, progressive organizations broadly supported the elite reform project, and fought for some concessions within that ambit. This scenario reflects the strategy of some NGOs to support the establishment of 'progressive capitalism', while simultaneously pursuing a deepening of the democratic process at the local level, once described as 'the minimum programme' (Chatthip 1991: 138). Also, supporting this linkage between NGOs and the liberal project was a shared critique of the state as overbearing and in need of limitation. This produced some degree of convergence between liberals and progressive activists around a shared project of creating civic-mindedness among the Thai people (Connors 2000: 336–372).

This chapter will elaborate these two basic arguments; first, that the constitution reflects a coherent liberal project, and second that NGOs and the varied organizational 'grassroots' alliances were not instrumental agents in setting the reform agenda, but provided support for the reformist project. First, however, let me trace a bare outline of the history of political reform.

A STALLED REFORM MOVEMENT

In the 1980s, despite a penchant for sanctimonious national hypocrisy and authoritarianism, the military, bureaucratic and business elites were able to effect a relatively smooth transition to political democracy (see Ockey 1992). This transition did not entail a deepening of democratic processes; rather it was limited to procedural aspects such as competitive elections and the expansion of provincial capitalists' power through the medium of political parties. All this occurred at the expense of the bureaucratic and military establishment. The transition also occurred in the context of a relatively free press that sought to elicit middle-class engagement in politics (McCargo 2000: 1–12).

The transition was apparently halted in 1991 when the self-proclaimed National Peace Keeping Council (NPKC) led a coup against the elected Chatichai government. The NPKC's motivations were multi-layered, mixing academy-class rivalry and opposition to unprecedented political interference in military affairs. General Suchinda Kraprayoon, a key coup leader, speaking of military appointments by the deposed government, had told a reporter: 'My stars are being rubbed off my shoulders' (*The Nation*, 24 February 1991). Beyond these sectional interests there was also a concern about the erosion of bureaucratic power (Hewison 1993b: 164–166).

The NPKC's criticisms of 'parliamentary dictatorship', vote buying and the malaise of politics under capitalist politicians apparently won cautious support among the Bangkok middle classes, particularly after the junta installed a credible technocratic cabinet, and selected a leading representative of globally engaged Thai capitalism, Anand Panyarachun, as prime minister. The reluctance of the NPKC to assume direct political power, and yet exercise it behind closed doors, suggested cognisance of the social and economic changes of the preceding decade that had made direct military rule untenable. The coup ostensibly aimed to revamp the system by creating strong executive control and undermine the influence of provincial capitalists. Yet this agenda was derailed, and the 'clean' coup degenerated inexorably into a 'dirty' coup.

The derailment derived from the NPKC's ambitions, which entailed formalization of the group's power even after the restoration of constitutional democracy. This intention expressed itself in constitutional chicanery throughout 1991, when liberal and conservative projects for a stable executive form of government were scuttled by the appointment of a Constitutional Scrutiny Committee (CSC) closely connected with the coup group. The CSC built into the draft constitution a provision allowing the NPKC to select the Senate and a clause allowing an outsider to take the premiership – seen by critics as a pathway for Suchinda to take power. Supporters of the coup group also created Sammakhi Tham, a catch-all political party. After an election in March 1992 held under the new constitution, this party formed a coalition government and invited Suchinda to take the premiership. He accepted.

A mass movement arose in opposition to this military aggrandizement, involving the intelligentsia and activists, labour groups and a mobilized population from a cross-section of classes. The progressive intelligentsia and students consistently attacked the actions of the military, with support from sections of the urban middle classes (Connors 1997: 137–138). Those workers and union leaders who were not entangled in military patronage also mobilized (Ji 1997: 108–112; Brown 1997: 175–177). Finally, thousands of people, mobilized by various forces, especially parties and prominent individuals such as the Bangkok governor, Chamlong Srimuang (see McCargo 1997: 247–263), swelled the protests. In May 1992 these strands coalesced as hundreds of thousands of protestors took to the streets to oppose Suchinda's constitutional path to power. Cornered, the military tried to shoot its way out, resulting in scores of protestors dying. With dissension in the ranks of the military making armed clashes possible (see *The Nation*, 20 May 1992), King Bhumibol intervened, ending the crisis, yet leaving the substantive issues unresolved. The King's intervention effectively demobilized both sides, a testament to his pivotal crisis management role on the side of conservatism and gradual change (Hewison 1997a: 68–73).

Without effective leadership, and demobilized by palace intervention, the movement stopped short of developing beyond its anti-Suchinda demands. In place of a radically reconstructed political system, the events of 1992 resulted in the continuation of parliamentary ascendancy. Constitutional amendments passed within days of the King's intervention, principally required that the prime minister be an elected MP. After elections in September 1992 the quasi-liberal Democrat Party, led by Chuan Leekpai, assumed the reins of government.

Importantly, the May protests established the conditions for future political change. Firstly, by sending the disgraced military back to the barracks, the movement defused military capacity to sidetrack future reform programmes. The mass movement also laid the basis for broader participation in politics so that when the question of political reform emerged again, it would not be confined to the shadowy gatherings of constitutional engineers.

RESURGENT REFORM AFTER 1992

Post-May politics returned to something resembling the pre-coup days: rampant corruption, coalition party infighting, and inaction on crucial issues such as decentralization. The experience of the Chuan administration's sluggish legislative output (1992–95), broken promises, corruption and apparent coldness towards NGOs, were important in shaping a post-May demoralization among many people.

While no major changes in the system were yet in sight, business groups reverted to their money-patterned way of relating to political parties and parliament. However, in late 1993 and 1994 a parliamentary committee on constitutional amendments, led by liberal elements within parliament, made far-reaching recommendations supporting greater governmental transparency, decentralization and wider political participation (see *Raignan khanakammathikan wisaman* 1993). Much hope was placed in the committee's recommendations, particularly hotly contested measures for decentralization, but conservatives in the opposition and the Senate allied so that only minor amendments were passed in late 1994 (Quigley 1996).

Parliamentary prevarication increased non-parliamentary pressure for reform and in 1994 the liberal democrat Marut Bunnag, President of Parliament, established the Democracy Development Committee (DDC) and charged it with diagnosing the problems of the political system and prescribing solutions. The DDC drew on longstanding conservative concerns about 'parliamentary dictatorship' (the seemingly arbitrary power of majority coalition governments). Former secretary-general of the Council of State Amorn Chandara-Somboon had, for several years, been articulating a strategy of 'parliamentary rationalization' to enhance the power of the executive and diminish the capacity of the legislature to 'interfere' (Amorn 1994). The DDC explicitly adopted much of his analysis (DDC 1995a: 6–7). It also tapped into populist notions of participatory democracy and human rights. The DDC was fronted by the ubiquitous Prawase Wasi, widely seen as a wise and virtuous figure, and so acceptable to a broad cross-section of groups (Connors 1999: 207–211). Its intellectual leadership was provided by law professor Bowornsak Uwano, a former advisor to the Chatichai government, and an active exponent of constitutional change. By 1995 the DDC was able to turn the reform agenda into a political project that sought to put an end to money politics and remoralize the public sphere by promoting civic virtue (DDC 1995a). The DDC's proposed process indicated that political reform was conceived as a technical exercise with people's involvement minimized. An unelected special committee composed of former prime ministers, experts from the fields of law and political science and others appropriately experienced would draft the constitution, submit it to parliament for scrutiny, and then finalize the draft. This would then be put to a referendum. When the July 1995 general election was called just months after publication of the proposals, activists and journalists pressured political parties to take a stance on political reform. Banharn's Chart Thai Party emerged as the main victor in the election, having pledged to take up the DDC's proposals. It did so, however, by reasonably establishing the Political Reform Committee (PRC), to consider alternative means of instituting reform.

By 1996 it would be fair to say that the demands for political reform were becoming louder and more widespread, attracting a broad range of support from business groups, technocrats, NGOs and the press. Interestingly, the central public clash was not between reformers and non-reformers, but around the issue of how far MPs would be involved in the reform process. The sitting government and political parties sought parliamentary involvement in drafting the constitution, while the reform movement was firm on locking politicians out of the process. This battle was fought inside and outside the PRC. By late 1996 a compromise was struck that kept politicians out of the drafting process, but allowed Parliament to select 76 provincial representatives from a collegiate of 760, and to select 23 experts from extensive lists presented by universities and other bodies (see Ockey 1997: 313–315).

From this process the Constitutional Drafting Assembly (CDA) was born. Uthai Phimchaichon, a one-time political prisoner in the 1970s, and Anand Panyarachun provided the CDA's public leadership. Though divided on a number of issues, liberals within the CDA largely subscribed to the broad demands of the reform movement. These demands had been codified by the DDC, which had commissioned a series of reports that effectively mapped out the reform programme. Furthermore, the Thailand Research Fund had supported various studies to be used in drafting the constitution. Outcries from critics that this constituted interference in the workings of the CDA meant that these documents were utilized discreetly in the drafting of the CDA's constitution (*Bangkok Post*, 5 and 7 December 1996; *Matichon*, 11 December 1996). According to Bowornsak, the careful drafting of publications indicated concern that public involvement had to be guided into the right channels, otherwise people would talk about their local problems, such as landlessness, which were not directly related to the constitution (Interview with the author, 15 January 1998 in Bangkok).

The intentions of the CDA were set out in its pamphlet 'Preliminary Framework for Drafting the Constitution', which formed the basis for discussion at public forums in early 1997 (CDA 1997a). What the above suggests is that behind the rhetoric of a 'People's Constitution' lay a carefully engineered reform programme which would be legitimized through public hearings and involvement.

The liberalism of the movement becomes clear if one considers how 'Preliminary Framework' addressed three key problems: rights, accountability and the political structure. Firstly, in extending rights and freedoms, it was argued that limiting the arbitrary power of the state was crucial. Implicitly, too, the authors of the document suggested that constitutional rights should take precedence over laws that sought illegitimately to limit such rights. Any limitation of rights, it was suggested, must find justification within the constitution. Furthermore, it was argued that the right of political participation had previously been curtailed because of the limited decentralization of power (CDA 1997a: 13–16). Also proposed was the establishment of a Constitutional Court to deliberate on contentious matters relating to rights violations and unconstitutional behaviour. This court would give unprecedented rights to citizens to seek redress if their individual rights were violated, but it would also have the power to determine whether any behaviour was contrary to the 'nation, religion and monarchy', thus ensuring rights stayed within the elite-defined normative civic culture of 'Thainess' (CDA 1997a: 14–17; Reynolds 1991). Secondly, a series of liberal checks and balances was proposed to make bureaucrats and politicians more accountable. Such proposals included the establishment of constitutional and administrative courts, an independent counter-corruption agency, a parliamentary ombudsman, and the requirement of asset declarations by cabinet members and senior bureaucrats (CDA 1997a: 28–39). Third, the document proposed a review of the political structure with the aim of eliminating money politics and restoring legitimacy to the political process. Regarding political parties, it was suggested that party structures be reformed in a democratic direction so as to limit the influence of rogue capitalists. Central to the reform programme was the attempt to sever the links between cabinet and the legislature. It was proposed that MPs who became cabinet members would lose their parliamentary status. Direct or indirect elections for the Senate were also suggested (CDA 1997a: 40–50).

The CDA held numerous public hearings throughout Thailand in the first half of 1997, soliciting ideas, dispensing advice and seeking the support of the rural population. It had to contend with significant opposition from a number of senators, bureaucrats and politicians. In August 1997 the CDA presented its draft constitution to parliament. It was essentially faithful to the reform programme. Facing economic crisis after the currency collapse of July 1997, and potential political crisis should it oppose the reform project, the incumbent government of Chavalit Yongchaiyudh, which had earlier publicly opposed the draft, reluctantly allowed it to become law.

In the remaining part of this chapter I shall analyse the key social forces behind the reform movement, and I address the question of why the 1997 constitution became law, despite the strong opposition it faced.

ELITES: GLOBAL IMPERATIVES AND LOCAL INITIATIVES

If the passing of the constitution represented a tentative victory for liberalism, it would be wrong to imagine this is a new force in Thailand, since such currents are scattered throughout Thailand's history (Connors 2000: 303–310). The relevant question is why liberalism became an emergent force challenging the anarchic and hierarchical pluralism of money politics. The answer, surely, lies in the changing nature of the Thai economy and its articulation with the global economy. Clearly, the events leading to the new constitution of 1997 were underwritten by structural factors which forced sections of the capitalist and state elite towards reform. Crucially, political order and stability were seen as prerequisites for Thailand to survive in a reforming global economy increasingly hostile to 'crony capitalism'.

Under the conditions of the Cold War, the US had countenanced various non-liberal forms of capitalism, and enlisted to the cause of the 'free world' countless despots and thugs. With the Cold War gone, and with the strategic advantage afforded by the Asian currency crisis, it was apparent that the US – as world hegemon – was eager to revive its historic liberal agenda, and promote forms of governance it believed could enhance stability and facilitate market-friendly policy processes (Catley 1999).

During the 1990s, a nascent international neo-liberalism emerged which promoted the ideal of a technocratically enabled state able to establish a legal and normative order, free from the constraints and muddying influence of partisan politics (Jayasuriya 1999: 321–325). The ideal character of this state is embodied in the World Bank's promotion of good governance, encompassing transparent public administration and policy-making that is efficient and accountable. This transparency is primarily designed to bolster the confidence of investors, to ensure optimal use of capital resources, and to secure a responsive system to guard against the myriad risks of political instability. In Thailand the project of establishing good governance partly took shape in the public and political institutions fought for by the reform movement.

The coincidence of the institutional needs of global capitalism and a domestic coalition for political reform is surely what most clearly defines the events under discussion in this chapter. Admittedly, it is hard to locate the centre of the elite-driven reform movement. Certain key players are identifiable in framing and popularizing ideas, among them Prawase Wasi and the liberal royalist Bowornsak Uwanno, but without support from powerful elite circles, these ideas would have been the mere outpourings of public intellectuals. Whatever the precise motivations of individual reformers and framers may have been, they took a backseat to the impatient and thwarted liberalism of some sections of the Thai elite.

It would be reasonable to suggest, following Surin (1993), that there has been a generational change among the Thai elite, marked by a new liberal orientation to political order. Representatives of this change may be found in many government agencies, political parties and public organizations. Organizationally the change is best expressed in the work of the Thai Development Research Institute (TDRI), which brings together some of Thailand's most powerful technocrats and academics. Since the mid-1980s, TDRI has functioned as an 'independent think-tank', dispensing advice on all and sundry matters to government. In the various research and policy works of the TDRI, one can sense the distaste for the machinations of Thai politics felt by leading governmental advisers and researchers.

Reflecting this feeling was an important paper 'Beyond Patronage: Tasks for the Thai State', by Scott Christensen and Ammar Siamwalla (1993), which echoed much of the World Bank's thinking on good governance. The authors' basic argument was that the increasing complexity of Thai society required a remaking of state–society relations. They reaffirmed the state's role as the indispensable administrator of a complex society, and as the neutral arbiter of societal conflict. To operationalize this ideal, society–state relations needed to be mediated by a remade political process that would allow the state to tap into societal knowledge on complex problems. This was especially true for issues of sectional interest, where knowledge and interest could aid the state in policy formation (this sentiment partly explains the rise of public hearings in Thailand). In this paper, democracy was seen as a means to rational policy outcomes in a complex society. Interestingly, democracy was said to be manifest in the concept of 'accountability' – a word absent, the authors claimed, in the Thai language. They went on to note that:

> Accountability – the very word is itself bourgeois – comes about at a particular time in a country's economic history, and is part and parcel

of the differentiation and specialization of society made possible by the development of markets. (Christensen and Ammar 1993: 8–9)

In highlighting the word 'accountability', the TDRI authors were betraying the influence of the World Bank's idea of good governance as the key to stable growth. 'Beyond patronage' was a programmatic statement of political reform in the interests of collective capital: the patronage state must be dismantled because it serves the sectional interests of those who access the state. A highly prescient paper, its prescription for a regulatory state was partly echoed in the programme of the political reform movement.

Business groupings, particularly those from the provinces, took a different stance on reform. It was largely because of the experience of 'money politics', associated with provincial capitalists, that Bangkok-based big-business groupings proved willing to work with the military and bureaucracy in 1991. The events of May 1992 led to a rethink by some: they could not countenance a return to military authoritarianism, yet they remained sceptical about the parliamentary system. They feared both the provincial capitalist politicians who had made the parliamentary system their plaything, and the intrusion of national politicians into the economic policy sphere (see Pasuk and Baker 1997: 29). Yet the elections of 1995 and 1996 witnessed the highest levels of vote-buying ever. Many watched in horror and distaste as money politics reached inflationary heights under the Banharn (1995–96) and Chavalit (1996–97) administrations (see Callahan and McCargo 1996; Surin and McCargo 1997). Despite an increasingly demanding global environment, the Thai political system seemed incapable of adaptation and reform.

Nevertheless, increasing pressure was exerted by managers of international capital and its technocratic mediators in Thailand. Thailand's capital markets had been liberalized under the first Anand administration, and Thailand had attracted significant volumes of capital. Increasingly, foreign chambers of commerce were critical of corrupt practices, as were domestic commentators. In September 1996, a Bank of Thailand official warned the administration: '[T]he government should run a tight ship from now on. Projects initiated with the political agenda should be left out. It takes ages to restore credibility' (*Bangkok Post*, 13 September 1996). Pressures for a clean-up were growing, particularly as Bangkok's export and property boom began to slide, and those who had speculated, invested or entrusted billions after the opening of Thailand's financial sector began to rein in their investments. This uncertain atmosphere provided fertile ground for recruitment to the cause of political reform.

However, despite the apparent interest in politics and reform among some in the capitalist class, large sections of that class had become implicated in the vast networks of corruption. Demobilized as a collective political force by its various sectionalized practices of corruption or by political nepotism, business awaited strategic leadership. It was in this context of political immobilism by business as a whole, that the reform movement became increasingly important in providing programmatic leadership for business and reforming technocrats. Early in the drafting process the CDA successfully sought support from business associations. Significantly, great support for measures of state accountability and transparency from business groupings was recorded and publicized (CDA 1997b).

At public hearings of the CDA, peak business organizations such as the Thai Chamber of Commerce and Thai Bankers' Association more or less repeated ideas of reform that had been circulating for several years. While there was a broad recognition of the need for political change, organized business groups did not consider themselves as leaders in the process. Perhaps the general position of business reformists is summed up in the words of one provincial business leader: 'The Thai economy has been hundreds of miles ahead of society and politics. We need reforms so that all sectors of the country can move ahead together' (*The Nation*, 9 December 1996). While business had been behind the economic surge, there was no suggestion that it should also lead the political initiative. On the influence of organized business in the drafting of the new constitution, Bowornsak has commented that '[t]he business sector [was] not interested in the constitution, they know nothing, they just pay politicians ... they proposed what had already been proposed' (interview with the author, 15 January 1998, Bangkok).

Even towards the end of the drafting process, when efforts had been made to enlist business actively behind the reform process, the CDA was lamenting the lack of business understanding of the draft (*Phujatkan Daily*, 21 August 1997). The business sector did, however, seek to include pro-capitalist statements in the constitution, including measures to support free competition and self-regulation. It also sought a greater say in legislative programmes, including laws relating to unfair trading practices and decentralization. Business-people expressed support for decentralization, and for the exclusion of MPs from the cabinet. Business concerns found their way into the preliminary and final CDA drafts, exemplified by an article committing the state to support free trade.

ACTIVISTS AND NGOS

I now wish to consider the more problematic engagement of NGOs in the reform movement. Certainly, NGO involvement was significant and productive, yet it was subsidiary to the real politics of elite conflict over political reform. While acting as a popular counterweight to conservative and vested resistance to reform, as well as providing an organizational medium for more radical proposals, the prime function of NGOs was effectively to legitimize the rhetoric of the 'People's Constitution', by mobilizing their constituencies to attend meetings, and drumming up support for the CDA. Publicly, NGOs aired support for the broad aims of the CDA, while arguing over details. This subordinate role needs to be seen in historical context.

With the political left in disarray after the crushing of the popular movement in the 1970s, a modest 'movement' based on local developmental problems gradually took hold. As Srisuwan explains, between 1979 and 1980 a number of progressive intellectuals consciously shifted towards small-scale NGO-type activity, seeing this as localized and unthreatening to those in power (1996: 156–157). Their local focus provided a breeding ground for new strategies that eventually merged into a loose national network, aiming to promote sustainable development and participatory democracy.

There were many ideological tendencies in the NGO movement; hence on one level Thai NGOs defy collective ideological characterization. However, by the mid-1980s most progressive developmental NGOs presented a broadly united front, critical of mainstream development (with its macro-economic focus, support for industrialization and emphasis on GDP) and authoritarianism. They also rejected strategies of mass mobilization and class struggle (Thai Volunteer Service 1987: 10).

Another factor influencing NGOs was the overwhelmingly foreign nature of funding. International NGOs and foreign governments, via international agencies, were funding NGOs according to their own agendas. Some of these funding mechanisms might be seen as promoting the expansion of either international social democracy or liberalism, depending on the funding body (Petras 1999). To the extent that NGOs were dependent on funding, they were required to plan, justify and develop programmes in line with the international developmental ethos with the endpoint of 'just' or 'human' capitalism. Equally, the funding relationship meant developing professionalism and accountability (Prawase 1991: 9–10), as well as integration with international agendas of 'just' development. Inevitably there was a degree of bureaucratization and career-mindedness among some activists.

Suthy Prasartset (1995) suggests that despite the diversity of NGOs, it is possible to characterize the movement as a whole by what he calls the 'four corner' strategy. Tracing the development of NGOs through the 1980s to the 1990s, Suthy argues that initially NGOs embarked on a 'search for alternative livelihood', characterized by promoting small cooperatives and various commodity banks (Suthy 1995: 104). Developing from this first stage was the second cornerstone of NGO strategy:

networking amongst NGOs and People's Organizations (POs). This resulted in the formation of national networks based on information exchange and solidarity (Suthy 1995: 107–108). Third, as Thailand entered its accelerated boom in the mid-1980s, placing pressure on natural resources, a generalized conflict emerged, 'pitting the state and corporate sector against the popular sector' (ibid.: 108). This situation led NGOs to articulate policy alternatives and raise public awareness – the third cornerstone. Finally, Suthy notes that NGOs began consciously to devise a strategy of alliance building – the fourth cornerstone – with state officials and others, so as to coordinate their projects and win greater legitimacy (Suthy 1995: 118). Furthermore, they aimed at galvanizing broad support from the urban middle class and academics (ibid.: 119).

The NGOs' role in supporting the CDA must be seen as partly conditioned by this engagement with governing institutions, particularly planning agencies, and a desire to be seen as legitimate actors. Despite their meagre size and resources, many NGOs have sought involvement in big-picture policy formation, trying, for instance, to influence the National Economic and Social Development Board (NESDB). This reflected their attempts to connect local concerns to broad political questions, given the failure of parliament to do so. The CDA drafting process provided another opportunity to do this. For their part, some officials in different agencies welcomed such involvement, for it both legitimized decisions as consultative, and served to discipline NGOs as 'responsible' political actors. This pattern of responsible engagement was evident throughout the proceedings of the CDA.

During the drafting process many coordinating groups formed to aggregate and lobby on behalf of the NGOs and People's Organization. One such group was the Women's Constitution Network (WCN), a grouping of women's organizations seeking gender equality. The Network exemplified the general NGO approach to the CDA. Rather than challenging the fundamental structure of the evolving liberal and rationalized parliamentary regime, the aim was to ensure a position in the constitution for its constituency. The Network comprised dozens of different women's organizations, ranging from women's labour groups to provincial women's craft organizations (WCN newsletter 1997a: 30). The group's primary effort was focused on ensuring gender equality in the constitution. It also sought proportional representation in political parties and parliament. Supportive of the general measures outlined by the CDA, the Network additionally sought a guaranteed female presence in the proposed Constitution Court and other reform institutions (WCN 1997). In many ways, it was an extension of the broad liberal current of Thai feminism represented by organizations such as Friends of Women (*Friends of Women Newsletter* 1990). The Network succeeded in overturning some sections of the draft where sexist language was present, or where there was no mention of women when specific reference was warranted. The Network did not succeed in establishing a constitutional requirement for women to be represented in cabinet, or in other political and statutory agencies of the state. However, one significant success was the winning of a constitutional requirement for women's involvement in legislation related to women and children.

The Network's approach to CDA largely reflects the position of most NGOs, namely one of critical support. This is best illustrated by briefly looking at the role of the Campaign for Popular Democracy (CPD), an organization made up of members from NGOs, student groups and professional associations. After May 1992, the CPD, which had played a crucial and brave role in organizing resistance to the 1991 coup, went into severe decline. This decline reflects the nature of an organization that was dependent on NGO support. With the military-backed regime gone after May 1992, NGO activists were less interested in pursuing directly political questions, and returned to their particular issues of concern. Critical reports from the CPD's meetings confirm this organizational decline (see Khanakammakan ronarong prachatippatai 1995). The organization was aware of its failure to lead: 'To summarize the work of CPD in developing democracy, it is clear that its activities have been mostly responsive to the situations that arise from the political games of the politicians (*Jotmai Khao Kho Ro Po*, May–April 1995: 8).

The organizational crisis was somewhat alleviated when the CDA formed, and the core group in the CPD became the coordinating body for a number of democracy and NGO groups regarding issues arising from the drafting process. With the prospect of a political battle ahead, the remnants of the CPD were able to gather together a loose body of democracy organizations and map out a basic strategy. By January they were offered financial support from a government committee for political reform, to assist in coordinating public hearings on the constitution. This role summarizes a major contribution of the NGOs – assistance in facilitating the expression of marginalized voices and linking these with the reform project.

The CDA generated a great deal of interest among NGOs. Submissions were received from hundreds of organizations. In 'Proposals for the Thai Constitution' submitted by a loose coalition of NGO, labour, women's and democracy groups, an attempt was made to provide a united response to the CDA framework (Ongkan chaoban 1997). The preface of 'Proposals' outlined the political philosophy of the groups:

> Humans and society have development and equality but also have respect for difference and diversity ... they have integrity and concern and are able to live peacefully and harmoniously with nature.

The state, communities and the private sector are able to progressively develop the economy by helping benefit the whole nation...

The political system, administration and judicial process are transparent, honest and just. They are responsible to the people by allowing the people to have a broad participatory role within them. (Ongkan chaoban 1997: 4)

This brief preamble to the broad 'people sector' philosophy provides a clear insight into the ideals of this sector, essentially aspiring to a unity between state, communities and the private sector. While NGOs were ideologically to the left of liberalism, they did not use the drafting process to push for an outcome that would have fundamentally altered the political structure beyond that afforded by liberal democracy. Rather, they attempted to stretch what was on offer, while embracing the broad goals of a 'rationalized' parliament.

Regarding the first frame, 'Proposals' envisaged extending rights discourse well beyond the abstract rights proposed by the CDA, and sought protection for labour, women, tribal peoples, the environment and extensive community rights (ibid.: 6–28). Many of these proposals, especially relating to labour rights to organize and tribal rights to citizenship, were not carried into the final CDA draft, hinting at the limits CDA liberals were willing to go. In terms of the second frame, 'Proposals' endorsed the CDA's suggestions, only pushing for more people's involvement in various scrutiny measures (ibid.: 34). In terms of the third frame, on political institutions, a split was recorded between the democracy organizations and the broader NGO currents. While the democracy groups argued for the abolition of the Senate, the broader NGO groupings sought its retention with provision for a direct election. However, on the central issue of separation of power (the exclusion of MPs from cabinet), all groups offered an overwhelming endorsement.

'Proposals' was, like many other submissions to the CDA, a log of claims by non-state organizations. Yet, in practice, such organizations found themselves fighting more for the CDA proposals than for their own ideas. Given the opposition from the political parties to the overall reform process, many progressive actors were willing in practice to have their own agendas sidelined, in order to support the CDA draft. To be fair, there was a certain pragmatism among activists in their support for the CDA draft. Many were conscious of its elitist nature, particularly the stipulation for parliamentary candidates to hold an undergraduate degree. But many appeared indifferent about the evolving technocratic state embodied in the draft, seeing this as an issue of inter-elite conflict: what mattered most was the provision for enforceable rights. In reality, critical support for the general approach of the CDA existed very early on, despite the 'log of claims' submitted. The generally supportive and subordinate stance taken by the NGOs reflects their lack of capacity to mobilize a genuinely mass movement for social change, however this was conceived. Instead, they aligned themselves with what they saw as reformist elites. The hope was that the new framework of politics would ultimately facilitate their own reform agendas.

WHY DID THE CONSTITUTION PASS?

To answer this question it is useful to consider the basis of opposition the CDA faced. There were three principal sources of opposition. The first came from actors within the political system. Many MPs opposed the CDA's exclusion of MPs from the drafting process, and especially the proposals that would prevent them from taking cabinet seats (*Bangkok Post*, 6 March 1997 and 23 May 1997). Their principal argument was that they knew the system best, and could devise the most realistic constitutional measures. To the existing unelected senators, the CDA's endorsement of direct Senate elections came as a shock. A senate vote against the draft was therefore widely expected. For many senators and MPs, the CDA project was too hasty, too ambitious and too technical, and they were very sceptical that constitutional provisions could really clean up politics.

The principal opposition, however, came from hard-core practitioners of money politics, and sections in the bureaucracy who stood to lose from change. These two groupings formed something of an alliance to thwart the draft, mobilizing their rural constituencies through party connections and local units of government (Connors 2000: 290–298). Such measures had worked in 1994, when they defeated efforts at decentralization.

The year of 1997 was a different time. There was a total exasperation with the non-responsive system of money politics, best symbolized by rural grievances and business scandals. The largest physical manifestation of this weariness was the yearly march to Bangkok by thousands of peasants and farmers, bringing with them numerous grievances (Praphat 1998). Each year governmental committees were convened to address their needs. Yet there existed no infrastructure, political necessity or political will to tackle the host of problems plaguing rural Thailand. This was symptomatic of a failure to govern. On the business side there was the criminal conduct by officials of the Bangkok Bank of Commerce (BBC), aided and abetted by prominent politicians (MacIntyre 1999: 149). As the scandalous story of unsecured loans, favours and fraud unfolded from 1994 onwards, the BBC became emblematic of the business–political nexus as a whole – and a reason to clean up. Weariness, however, does not push through a new constitution.

It is difficult not to conclude that the compelling factor that forced the opposition to the CDA draft to surrender was the political circumstances resulting from the economic crash of 1997. Summing up the impact of the crisis on his thinking, the influential Senate President Meechai Ruchapan explained why he chose to drop opposition to the draft and push for the Senate to support it:

> At the time I changed my position because when the constitution was finished the economic crisis broke out. If we looked around we could see the people had placed their hope in the constitution ... if we rejected the constitution, the people's hope would be exhausted and it would create a severe crisis...If it didn't pass ... problems would break out ... and the country would not survive. (Interview, Bangkok, 8 January 1998)

While Meechai responded quickly to the changed circumstances, the governing party did not. Prevaricating his way through various possibilities, Prime Minister Chavalit finally succumbed after pressure had been exerted by the military, business, reformist politicians, the press, and persons close to the palace, to accept the draft (*Siam Post*, 6 September 1997). The crisis clearly strengthened the reformist hand, making it impossible for the oppositionists to play various cards they held in reserve, such as amending the article governing the CDA so that parliament could amend the draft constitution or stirring up rural opposition during a referendum.

SLIDING DOORS: A CONCLUSION IN RESERVE

This chapter has not dwelt on the opposition to the CDA. That opposition took shape most clearly in the powerful Interior Ministry, supported by the minister of the interior. It was involved in mobilizing public protests against the CDA draft on the grounds that it opposed 'the unitary state' and also threatened the monarchy. This opposition is on the public record. Less discernible is the way in which oppositionists used figures within the CDA itself to advance their cause. While it is not possible to be definitive about this, something needs to be said.

It may be possible that CDA representatives who were close to the governing party promoted many of the apparently progressive elements in the constitution. Their aim in radicalizing the draft (including direct senate elections, for example) was to ensure that the senate would vote against it. Had such a vote occurred, a referendum on the constitution would have been called. Given their networks of political and bureaucratic influence throughout the provinces, the oppositionists could have been confident of winning a 'no' vote against the draft.

Although we await a proper history of the drafting process, this line of argument does have some plausibility. When the CDA was convened, many noted that its composition closely resembled the favoured list circulated by the governing party (*The Nation*, 27 December 1996;

Matichon, 27 December 1996). Furthermore, throughout the drafting process the press was constantly awash with stories of manipulation of CDA delegates by forces close to the governing party. In June and July a battle waged in the CDA over two separate issues: senate elections and the wording of Article 3. When the CDA endorsed direct elections for the senate, the press cried foul, arguing that dark forces were manipulating the provincial delegates into forcing the senate to oppose the draft. (*Krungthep Thurakit*, 17 July 1997; *Bangkok Post*, 23 July 1997). Similar charges were made when the CDA changed Article 3 of the draft from 'sovereignty comes from the people' to 'sovereignty belongs to the people'. Conservative elements saw this change as attacking the 'traditional' right of the monarch to exercise sovereignty through the executive, legislature and courts. Interestingly, opponents hoped that the amendment to Article 3 would lead to the CDA draft being ruled unconstitutional, since it altered the position of the monarchy (*Bangkok Post*, 6 June 1997).

If we accept this line of argument, we are then left with a rather comical scenario. In the first place this argument would suggest that it was oppositionists who were partly responsible for a number of the progressive articles in the constitution. Secondly, the oppositionists, surely among the best practitioners of money politics, were compelled by the intervening economic crisis into accepting a draft they had engineered to fail. If this is the case, the money politicians of Thailand have left a strange and perhaps welcome legacy. It was Banharn Silpa-archa's administration, a model of money politics, that allowed through constitutional amendments that made the CDA possible, and it was Chavalit Yongchaiyudh's administration – no stranger to the world of money politics – which not only passed the constitution, but may have had a hand in its radical articles.

This is an uncomfortable conclusion because liberals, in their battles against money politics, draw sustenance from their claim that they are following the 'voice of the people', as expressed in the constitution. In 1997 claims and counter-claims of interference were rife. Now that the Constitution has become 'sacred', it seems no one wants to look at the grubby machinations that may lie behind its final form.

SLIDING DOORS: THE REAL CONCLUSION

No matter how messy the reform process was, no matter how contradictory the stance of some players, the CDA produced a constitution that retains the potential to move Thai politics towards a rule-based system. Each significant measure in the constitution has become a battleground between the forces for change and those against. It is clear that the coupling of reformist elites and activists around a joint programme of reform has provided the basis for the emergent liberal Thai state gradually to build over the morass of money politics and the old state. The basis for this shift is also reinforced by the transformation of the economy and the impact of global forces, an impact greatly accelerated after the 1997 crash. However, given the wily and ingenious ways in which vested interests have already subverted aspects of the reform programme – political influence in the senate and whittling down aspects of enabling legislation – setbacks will be suffered. In the Senate elections of 2000 and the House of Representative elections of 2001 it is apparent that the new Election Commission of Thailand has provided unprecedented succour to the cause of reform. In punishing scores of recalcitrant and corrupt politicians by ordering new elections, the ECT is striking a blow against old-style electioneering. This is but one example.

The new struggles waged around political reform are unlikely to be a clear zero-sum contest between two sides. Compromises will be struck, accidents may advance the cause, the new institutions may be corrupted from within, their scope curtailed, and erstwhile reformers may decide that ends are not obliged to means. But no matter what transpires, it is now clear that political reform's impact is in implanting a new rule-based dynamic which will, however unevenly, generate new patterns of political behaviour. Despite setbacks, it is hard to imagine another time when Thai liberalism has been so well placed to shape the political system.

ACKNOWLEDGEMENT

The author would like to thank Duncan McCargo and Michael Nelson for their challenging criticisms and helpful suggestions in response to an earlier draft.

5

THE MONARCHY AND CONSTITUTIONAL CHANGE SINCE 1972

Kobkua Suwannathat-Pian

The decade of the 1970s has certainly gone down in Thai history as a time of great socio-political instability, a time of serious threats and significant changes, reflected in a series of uprisings, coups and constitutions promulgated.[1] Compared with the subsequent decades which only brought into existence two constitutions – the 1991 and 1997 Constitutions – the 1970s appear particularly unstable, even by the standards of Thailand's roller-coaster politics. It was during the past three decades, however, that two significant socio-political 'novelties' were achieved. These were the development of the socio-political power of the throne, and the reform of Thai politics. The focus of this paper is on the former, namely the development of the real socio-political power of the constitutional monarchy in Thailand.

CONSTITUTIONAL POWER OF THE MONARCH

The history of the present constitutional monarchy harks back to the year 1957. In fact, 1957 was, as one Thai scholar puts it, 'the beginning of a new phase in Thai political history' (Thak 1979: 121). Between the years 1957 and 1972, King Bhumibol Adulyadej, gradually but steadily, assumed the position of the sole power legitimizer. Basically, this meant that His Majesty took over the role of popular sovereignty in bestowing a legitimate right to rule upon otherwise democratically illegitimate regimes. Since 1957, the principal political function of the throne was to legitimize (or not to legitimize) the regime in power. The fall of the Thanom-Praphat regime in October 1973 following a student-led uprising, as well as the students' success in toppling that regime, clearly revealed the monarchy's role as an independent legitimizer of power. Not only the military but also politicians, progressive elements and the

Thai masses had by 1973 come to regard the King as the ultimate socio-political power with immeasurable wisdom to tackle the political ups and downs of the country when all other means had failed. Thus emerged the principle of a royal power legitimization on which Thailand's present-day constitutional monarchy is constructed. It is a home-grown principle born out of the failure of the Western version of democracy, and of a time-honoured Thai tradition that saw the monarchy as the centre of Thai socio-political life. This tradition was nurtured back to active life, after a lengthy period of a political hibernation, by Field Marshal Sarit Thanarat (1957–63) who made it possible for the throne to work hand in hand with the military regime he set up for the benefit of all parties concerned.

To this foundation, a significant 'novelty' was added to enhance the powers of the throne by the 1974 constitution – commonly known as the King–People Joint Effort Constitution, or *ratthathammanoon chabab ratcha-pracha samasai*.[2] It required the President of the Privy Council to countersign the royal appointments of members of the Senate (Article 107). Article 107 was objected to by both the King and Pridi Phanomyong, by then the grand old man of Thai democracy. In his comment before signing the draft, King Bhumibol clearly stated that His Majesty 'strongly disagrees' with Article 107 as 'it violates the principle that the King is above politics'. In his royal opinion, the said article turned the President of the Privy Council into a political agent 'which is in conflict with Article 17'.[3] This royal disagreement led to the amendment of the constitution on 19 January 1975. The prime minister replaced the President of the Privy Council as the official who was to countersign the royal appointment of the appointed members of Parliament. Besides this controversial 'novelty', the 1974 Constitution also widened the Law of Succession whereby all the King's children, regardless of their sex, were, with parliamentary approval, eligible to succeed His Majesty. The King however retained the right to name his heir if he so desired.[4]

A comparison between the two most recent constitutions promulgated in 1991 and 1997 clearly reveals the unassailable position of the monarchy in Thai socio-political life.[5] The chapter on 'The King' in most of the constitutions passed since 1972 remained essentially unchanged. In both 1991 and 1997 Constitutions, the rights and privileges of the King in that chapter are almost identical. The King is the head of state, upholder of religion, the ultimate commander of the Thai forces. His person is sacred and inviolable, he confers and recalls decorations, creates and removes titles, appoints and dismisses privy councillors and palace officials (Constitution 1991, Articles 2, 6–11; Constitution 1997, Articles 2, 8–17). The King's absolute authority over the appointments and dismissals of the Privy Council is a novelty since in the past his choice of the President of the Privy Council had to be approved by Parliament. He likewise has a final say in the matter concerning the appointment of the regent. Only when the King is unable or does not wish to appoint a regent is Parliament empowered to exercise its right to approve the candidate(s) for the regency submitted to it by the Privy Council. (Constitution 1991, Articles 16–18; Constitution 1997, Articles 18–20). On the question of succession, the King is given the power to amend or alter the 1924 Law of Succession as His Majesty deems necessary. Parliament is to be informed of any changes, and it is the duty of the President of Parliament to have the changes gazetted. The King reserves the right to appoint his successor in accordance with the Palatine Law of Succession 1924. In the case of the throne becoming vacant and the immediate reigning monarch having failed to name his successor, the Privy Council will submit the names of candidates (which may include those of royal princesses) for the approval of Parliament (Constitution 1991, Articles 20–21; Constitution 1997, Articles 22–23.)

The King's veto power over legislation remains a suspending one. It may be overridden by the vote of a two-thirds majority of the total number of members in both Houses after 90 days. Another 30-day waiting period after the second submission to the King is required before the bill automatically becomes law, regardless of whether the King has signed it or not (Constitutions 1991 and 1997, Article 94). The dignity of the throne is conspicuously emphasized in both constitutions. Before taking office, cabinet members, judges and jurors are required by the constitution to swear an oath of allegiance to the King in which they pledge their personal loyalty to His Majesty (Constitution 1991, Articles 164 and 192; Constitution 1997, Articles 204 and 252). The practice evidently implies that each minister and judiciary official is first of all a loyal subject and official of the King. They perform their duty on behalf of His Majesty. Each owes his monarch personal loyalty which implicitly overrides loyalty to others. For instance, the practice implies that cabinet ministers are not simply the subordinate colleagues of the prime minister; their relationship with and collective loyalty to the premier comes second to their duty to the King. By implication, therefore, no prime minister can now act as either an equal of the King (as in the case of Sarit), or as a higher leader than the King (as in the case of the pre-war period). Prime minister, cabinet ministers and judicial officials are all loyal subjects of the throne.

Both the 1991 and 1997 Constitutions are to a high degree the outcomes of the great shift of political power most evident since the 1973 'revolution' against a military regime. Both charters affirm the incomparable public and personal powers and prestige exercised by King

Bhumibol since that date. Fundamentally, the two charters stress King Bhumibol's socio-political achievements rather than assign to the throne the powers and prestige the throne obviously commanded in reality even before these august documents came into existence. For example, the two constitutions state that 'Thailand is a constitutional democracy with the King as Head of State' (Article 2). It is almost impossible to think that there could be a change in the political system of Thailand in the foreseeable future that does not accord the King the highest position in the country. It can be correctly said that Article 2 is superfluous. Whether it is written into the Constitution or not, the monarchy is definitely an inherently indivisible part of Thailand, at least as long as King Bhumibol is on the throne. The 1991 Constitution introduced a new article which declared that 'The State is required to protect the monarchy, sovereignty, and unity of the nation', if necessary even by the use of force (Articles 59, 60). These articles actually aim to provide the armed forces and their leaders with a legitimate role in the affairs of the nation. But it is unfortunate that the military should have made the monarchy the focus of their protection. The 1997 Constitution possesses no such articles. Based on national experience since 1973, such articles go against the trend of modern Thai politics. It is the King who proffers his 'protection' to the nation, not the nation that protects the King. But for the gracious interventions of His Majesty, Thailand would have faced national calamities of the greatest kind at least twice, in 1973 and in 1992.

Most interesting perhaps are the efforts by the 1997 Constitution to strike a positive balance between Thailand's unique monarchy and the universal concept of the role of a constitutional monarch. A constitutional monarch, according to a general understanding, is neutral and above politics. His main functions as far as state affairs are concerned are to be consulted, to warn and to give advice (which may or may not be taken by the administration). Constitutionally, the King is accorded such rights. As the Senate is now an elected body, the King's constitutional right to be consulted is in the areas concerning the appointments of: the prime minister (on the advice of the President of Parliament, Article 201), the Electoral Commission (Article 136), the Constitutional Court presdient and 14 judges (Article 255) the State Audit Commission (Article 312), the National Human Rights Commission (on the advice of the president of the Senate, Article 199), and the National Counter-Corruption Commission (Article 297).

As the monarch is above politics, every official document signed by the King – law, royal correspondence, decree or speech – must be countersigned by a cabinet minister or by officials specified in the Constitution. However, the King's rights to give advice and to be consulted are not simply a formality. It is common knowledge that His

Majesty takes his constitutional rights seriously, and has demonstrated his willingness to test their meanings to the limit. When a situation requires a royal intervention, the rights to be consulted and give advice assume a most tangible form. For example, King Bhumibol openly rejected the parliamentary choice of a designated prime minister in 1992 and instead appointed a candidate of his own choice who was not even member of parliament. The fact that the royal choice received wide public endorsement tells much about both the King's political astuteness and the royal political muscle vis-à-vis Parliament. It also reveals the peculiar aspect of the Thai constitutional monarchy which, though it principally resembles those of other countries, yet in practice differs so widely from them. The constitutional monarchy in Thailand represents paradoxes in which the King is above politics but also in politics; in which his powers are prescribed by the constitution yet he may choose with impunity to exercise powers beyond limits set by that august charter; in which he is a constitutional monarch, yet may act like a traditional absolute ruler. King Bhumibol is without question a constitutional monarch in his own class.

The recent version of constitutional monarchy as portrayed in the 1997 Constitution appears to represent the desire of the elected Constituent Assembly to accommodate both the real powers and prestige of the King and the formal concept of the monarchical system within legal boundaries.[6] It also appears that the boundaries so set represent only a guarantee against the possibility of power abuse in the case the occupant of the throne turned out to be inexperienced, less self-disciplined, and perhaps not so dedicated to royal responsibilities and to the well-being of his people. The Assembly certainly had no intention whatsoever of applying such limitations to the incumbent monarch: not that had the Assembly wished to limit the powers of the incumbent, such a desire could have been implemented in any effective manner. King Bhumibol has, through sheer perseverance, patience, a high personal sense of morality and dedication, established his own version of constitutional monarchy which has clearly received the endorsement of his people.

THE ROYAL VERSION OF CONSTITUTIONAL MONARCHY

King Bhumibol came to the throne at a most tragic and trying time. His elder brother, King Ananda Mahidol who was 21, suddenly and mysteriously died of a gunshot wound in the early hours of 9 June 1946. For most of the following six years – before the King returned to take up permanent residence in his kingdom – he was an absentee ruler, living and studying in Lausanne, Switzerland. On his return in early December 1951, Bhumibol was the first mature King to take up permanent residence in Thailand since the abdication of his uncle,

King Prajadhipok, in March 1935. Greeting the King as his ship entered Thai waters was the 'silent coup', carried out by the 1947 coup group. This 1951 coup abrogated the royalist constitution of 1949, and thus pre-empted any possible constitutional moves by the monarch that could weaken or restrain the power of the then ruling military elite. In fact, King Bhumibol's early experiences as Thailand's reigning constitutional monarch left a profound impression on the young ruler. Between 1951 and 1957, the King had to accept the constitutional role prescribed by the amended 1932 Constitution of 1952, which basically defined the monarch as a ruler placed above politics, whose main duty was to do whatever the government told him – a ceremonial ruler or, put less kindly, a figurehead or a 'rubber-stamp', to be used whenever necessary by the ruling elite. During these years, the King exercised neither political power nor traditional prestige of any significant kind. The 1947 coup leaders and the government also saw to it that the King had no opportunity to develop his dynamic potential or re-establish traditional links with his subjects.

Prior to the 1957 coup, the only means left for King Bhumibol to express his unhappiness or displeasure with those in power was to withhold his royal approval of or support for those government policies or programmes to which he strongly objected. It was evident that the King found his position during these years unpalatable and almost unbearable. Yet, throughout this trying period, King Bhumibol was a tower of patience and a perfect master of the art of waiting. He must have realized that time was on his side. Most contemporary documents available confirm that when an opportunity presented itself for him to move against his political opponents, King Bhumibol did not hesitate to seize it. For example, he supported Sarit and the 1957 coup, even though at the time His Majesty was not really certain of Sarit's intentions. Nevertheless, the King supported the Sarit coup in 1957 which successfully toppled the Phibun government, and the 1947 coup leaders who had played the role of royal jailers for the past six years.[7]

Soon it became clear that a strong partnership had been formed between the young and inexperienced King and the hard-drinking, hard-working and action-oriented coup leader and prime minister, Field Marshal Sarit Thanarat, a partnership which afforded the King the opportunity that he had so patiently awaited. Sarit provided his monarch with the freedom actively to participate in and positively contribute to the affairs of the nation (Thak 1979). The King was again ready to take a clearly independent step against an unpopular military regime in 1973 in support of the new liberal political forces led by students.

Between 1973 and the 1990s, the King successfully established what he strongly believes to be the most suitable form of constitutional monarchy for Thailand, one that acknowledges the positive and proactive role of the monarch, and, at the same time, gives to the people and their representatives political power in accordance with the basic principles of democracy.[8] His success has led to worldwide admiration and praise. In a 1985 article on the King, a foreign magazine stated that King Bhumibol 'is not an ordinary King, and he rules as head of state by unusual standards'. It further commented that Bhumibol was 'more than a constitutional monarch' because he possessed the power of love.[9] In an exclusive interview granted to the same magazine, the King expounded upon his understanding of his role as constitutional monarch. It is significant to realize the differentiation that the King then made between the legal role of the constitutional king which clearly stands on the constitutional principle that 'the [constitutional] king can do no wrong' – because specified officials and/or the government have to accept the responsibility for the King's official actions – and the traditional role that His Majesty has inherited from his Chakri forefathers (ibid.).

As a constitutional monarch, the King is head of state but not the political figurehead often associated with this role. In the King's understanding, as head of state the monarch must, on the one hand, change with the country and, on the other hand, preserve 'the spirit of the country' as he is 'the soul of the nation'. As a Chakri King, Bhumibol understands his royal duty to be protector and guardian of his people and their well-being. In other words, King Bhumibol understands his role within the constitutional monarchical context to be of a dual nature: a personified symbol of both the traditions and the modern characteristics of the nation; a proactive ruler who tirelessly strives for the betterment of his people. The dual facets of kingship – traditional and modern – should not be in conflict, but should be and blend together.

For instance, legally, under the constitutional monarchy, 'the king can do no wrong'. King Bhumibol adds his own interpretation to this modern principle. The King 'can do no wrong', he says because 'he has love, especially in a country that upholds many traditions'. This implies that with the traditional love and reverence that he commands, whatever he does can only be for the good of the country, and thus can never be wrong. It follows that the public powers of the King emanate not from a written constitution, but from the affection, devotion and trust that the Thai people have for him. These sentiments, as implied by the royal stand, form the very foundations of the King's legitimate right to intervene or to be proactive in the affairs of the nation. This right overrides all other written legal authorities, be they the constitution or other man-made laws. This is not surprising. What the King puts forward by way of an explanation for the modern understanding of constitutional kingship entirely reflects what His Majesty has performed as a symbolic gesture of the supreme authority traditionally invested in the person of the anointed monarch during the coronation. Since ancient times, Thai monarchs have placed the royal crown on their own august heads during the coronation ceremony, as it has always been considered that no other person in the realm, no matter how pure or how powerful, could ever claim a higher authority than the King himself. No one deserves such a distinctive honour but the King.

Bhumibol nonetheless admits that as a constitutional monarch, the King is both above and under the law. The King is, by Bhumibol's inference, above all man-made laws in the land, but is under the law prescribed by the teachings of the Lord Buddha. The King is bound by the 'Tenfold Practice of Duties of Kingship' in accordance with the political ideology of Theravada Buddhism. This requires the King, among other things, to be 'truthful, diligent and do things with care'. Consequently, the King can never be an autocrat as he has to live by a higher and different kind of code of ethics and responsibilities. (Dhani 1954: 91–104; Kobkua 1988: 30–33, 44–48). The royal explanation very much follows the line of argument put forward by the traditionalists and royalists concerning the nature of Thai kingship (Dhani 1954). The differences only appear in the choice of terminology and principles behind such explanations. For instance, in the traditionalist-royalist exegesis, Thai kingship is a limited one based on both law and popular consent: *Phra Thammasat, dasabidha-rajadharm* (the laws), and *anekchonnikon samononsommuttithep* (the consent of the people). The laws by which a Thai king of old had to abide were those of the universal law and the teachings of Theravada Buddhism; while his virtue earned him the love and respect of his people who, by inference, unanimously selected individual kings as their rulers (Batson 1984: 285–286).[10] Both the King and the royalists agree that in practice the King's supreme position is above man-made laws, and the consent of the people makes Thai monarchs democratic ones. It is apparently upon these principles of 'divine' laws and popular 'election' that King Bhumibol fundamentally stakes his supreme rights and powers above all other institutions in the affairs of the nation.

Since 1963, King Bhumibol has revealed his adroitness in performing the function of a constitutional monarch 'by unusual standards'. For example, on the monarch's constitutional power to appoint the prime minister on the advice of the President of Parliament, the King's stand is that he 'may have more power [than what is stated by the Constitution] because the people have faith in their King'. Thus in certain situations the King will exercise this unwritten power for the good of the nation. King Bhumibol has in fact demonstrated his readiness to employ his power as 'king-maker' in both a positive and a negative manner. For instance, in 1963 the King came out quickly in support of Thanom as Sarit's successor, and effectively forestalled brewing power struggles among the military elite after the death of Field Marshal Sarit. Again in 1973, he personally appointed an interim prime minister in a quick move to restore order and confidence after the overthrow of the Thanom-Praphat regime. In fact Prime Minister Sanya Thammasak has gone down in the Thai political history of the post-1932 period as the only prime minister who was personally selected and appointed by the King.

Perhaps most conspicuous of all King Bhumibol's exercises of his 'king-maker' power was the negative royal response to the selection of a designated prime minister in 1992. The King not only declined to appoint the parliamentary candidate whose credentials were most questioned by well-informed sectors of the country, but also approved a candidate of his own choice who became an interim prime minister. The royal appointment of Anand Panyarachun as interim prime minister in 1992 had no constitutional basis whatsoever (Prasan *et al.* 1998: 194–198). In fact, it contravened the letter and spirit of the constitution. It was blatantly obvious, however, that this bold move by King Bhumibol was widely supported by his subjects all over the kingdom. The President of Parliament willingly countersigned the royal appointment.[11] Such royal initiatives simply confirm his people's acceptance of King Bhumibol's extra-constitutional role which, when exercised, takes precedence over all other legal authority.

It is more than evident that King Bhumibol may technically be a constitutional monarch. But he is definitely not a constitutional monarch of an ordinary kind. Since 1973, the King has come to wield immense powers, both public and personal, over his people and the nation. His is the highest authority in the land, towering over the military, constitution and parliament. It is a great personal achievement of a once young, shy and inexperienced monarch who was very much the passive charge of the all-powerful military elite of the pre-1957 era. In the eyes of the world, the source of Bhumibol's unique power is the respect, esteem, love and trust of his people. Bhumibol has made his own version of constitutional monarchy a reality. To cite his own words in reply to a question on the power and influence the King obviously wields over the affairs of the nation,

> [If] the Chief of State is no good they will make him into a rubber-stamp. But if the Chief of State is better, they will perhaps ask for his opinion because the opinion is respected – that is the difference. But how can I have the respect of the people? It is because I don't use the

power as you describe – I don't use it. If there is a rule I go by the rule. But if there is no rule then my opinion would be heard. (National Archives, File S.B. 15/5)

It is clear that as King Bhumibol's stature increases in the reckoning of his people, so also do his public powers to intervene and to dictate Thailand's socio-political course as His Majesty deems necessary. Two incidents in the 1980s demonstrated the King's enhanced role in politics. The failed April 1981 and September 1985 coups to topple Prime Minister Prem Tinsulanond confirmed that any attempt to overthrow the government which did not receive royal sanction would fail. In the aborted 1981 coup in particular, the King's response to the attempt to overthrow his favourite prime minister was unexpected. First, His Majesty declined to grant the coup leaders who had successfully seized control of all strategic buildings in Bangkok an audience, and thus sanction the coup as he had previous coups. Moreover, the King and the royal family left the capital in an apparent desire to offer moral support to the beleaguered Prem, who had set up a command headquarters to fight against the rebels at Korat, a town about 300 kilometres northeast of Bangkok. Queen Sirikit made a broadcast from the Korat base, urging a peaceful solution and expressing support for the government. These shows of royal displeasure against the coup were too much for the Revolutionary Council. Within three days, the coup collapsed.

It was then observed that the moment the King had joined Prem on the helicopter out of Bangkok, the chances for the coup to emerge victorious 'became almost nil'. This was because 'the people ... revere and love their King. Where the King extends his hand, the people of Thailand extend theirs' (Wedel 1988: 94–95). It is evident that Bhumibol had sharpened his role from a passive to an active, or more accurate, to a proactive participant. As His Majesty stated in a 1980 interview: 'If you don't defuse the bomb, it will blow up.' Since that statement was made, the King has defused many political bombs and saved his kingdom from a national calamity. As if to answer some critics that active royal involvement in politics could well backfire, the King warned that any attempts to use the throne in the wrong way, that is, not in the best interest of the country or the people, would fail 'to [the] detriment' of those who tried (Lockhart 1990: 576). General Sant Chitpatima and his Revolutionary Council painfully learned this lesson in April 1981. From that time onwards, the King has implicitly reserved for himself the right to intervene in, and actively guide, the affairs of the nation whenever royal guidance and intervention are required. The royal constitutional monarchy has reached its ultimate goal.

The King sees behind his command of the near absolute respect and love of his subjects, his own love, concern for, and willingness to give in order to improve the well-being of his people, as reasons why such a close bond between the monarchy and the people remains alive and dynamic at all times. It is King Bhumibol's ardent belief that a monarch, or any world leader for that matter, cannot and should not take for granted the affection and devotion of the people. He must, if he aspires always to retain high public esteem and trust, work to maintain these attributes; he should 'give more and take less'. It is to King Bhumibol's credit that His Majesty always acts on what he preaches. If ever there were doubts as to the King's political authority, the 17–20 May 1992 bloody clash between the military junta and the pro-democracy demonstrators proved beyond question that King Bhumibol has successfully created a constitutionally supreme monarchy, in accordance with his own political and dynastic principles. In the 1990s, this royal version of constitutional monarchy has almost unconsciously become an accepted socio-political norm and is often referred to as 'the Thai way of constitutional monarchy'. Thai people have come to expect that their King will always be a knight clad in the shining armour of love, rushing in to resolve not just intermittent political crises but whatever insurmountable difficulties and sufferings his subjects encounter in their lives.

In practice, the King now receives support from both the ruling elite and the Thai masses. This royal popularity affords His Majesty an unprecedented latitude in public affairs, one never even dreamt possible by the Chakri royal family when it faced the political challenges that followed the events of 1932. Former Prime Minister Anand Panyarachun very much approved of the way the King exercises royal informal authority which, according to Anand, the King 'has put to good use, whenever circumstances require' (Vatikiotis and Fairclough 1996: 22). Yet in solving and reaching for acceptable solutions to the difficulties facing his country and the throne, King Bhumibol has yet to exercise the legislative veto power accorded him by the Constitution. It would be interesting to find out whether, in the event of a direct clash between the King and a popular parliament over a particular item of legislation, the parliamentary collective will would prevail over the royal veto. So far Bhumibol has chosen to employ informal approaches, such as royal comments or audiences granted to ministers and bureaucrats as a means of effecting changes and correcting what he sees as inaccurate or unsuitable policies.

However, the King is also capable of displaying his will or wishes which are apparently contrary to the prevailing public sentiments in a most conspicuous manner. For instance, during the heightened political tension in 1976 created by the unexpected return from the political exile of former prime minister Thanom Kittikachorn, the King and Queen paid a visit to Thanom, a monk in the royal temple of Bowornives

Viharn, and offered alms. The royal gesture unmistakably indicated the palace's blessing of Thanom's return amidst clamouring demands that he be forced to resume his exile abroad. The cabinet was then informed that the return of the former prime minister had received palace approval (Morell and Chai-Anan 1981: 270–272). In that particular incident, the King won his point against the demands of the ever-increasingly vocal student body and the liberals who protested against the government's lenient treatment of the ex-military dictator. Thanom was allowed to stay and the demands for his expulsion subsided.

In sum, the royal version of constitutional monarchy which Bhumibol himself has partly resurrected from the traditional concept of Thai kingship, and mainly recreated and readjusted to suit the requirements of his time, derives its authority not from the written constitution but from His Majesty's personal close bond with his subjects. This bond, though it has its origins in the traditional devotion of the Thai masses to the monarchy throughout its long history, is consciously and consistently cultivated and nourished by the service, devotion and affection with which the King has showered his people through his apparently 'selfless giving'. His devotion to the people is legendary. A story is often told of the time of the King's departure to complete his studies in Switzerland. The crowds lining the street to see him off urged the King not to desert his people. Bhumibol was supposed to have replied: 'I will not desert my people so long as the people do not desert me.' Throughout his long reign of over 50 years, King Bhumibol has kept his promise. He continuously and tirelessly works for the betterment of his subjects. The Thais have reciprocated with a degree of affection, reverence and absolute trust rarely seen in the world today. They clearly take great pride in their working monarch, not simply because he has their best interests at heart, but also because the King achieves an unbelievably high standard of personal moral attainment (Grey 1988: 166–174). For an ordinary Thai, King Bhumibol deserves to be loved and revered on two main counts: he is a good King and he is an extraordinary good man. In a Thai Buddhist context, King Bhumibol's power derives from his subjects' appreciation of his personal vast reservoir of merit, his *bun-barami*, which is beyond compare with those in public or private life. Most of his subjects regard it as their great fortune to live under his benevolent and enlightened reign.

One question often arises up concerning the strength of this 'Thai way of constitutional monarchy' since it is tied up so closely with the personal merit of the King. Would it be better to have at least some of the public powers exercised by King Bhumibol written into the constitution? Most royalists think not (Anuraj 1992: 27–28). They tend to prefer the status quo of 'flexibility in kingship', namely, that individual monarchs should be given room to exercise their own discretion. This royalist stand is not surprising. It would be more harmful to the monarchy if the constitution were to prescribe all the powers now enjoyed by King Bhumibol as constitutional powers of the monarch. Harmful because in the hands of – to borrow the King's own term – a 'no good' monarch, such powers would certainly lead to untold damage to the monarchy. As things stand, the constitution has no negative effect on the power and prestige of the King, but if necessary it can be an instrument preventing abuses of power by a head of state who is 'no good' and who thus deserves to be treated as 'a rubber-stamp'. In such a situation, the dignity and prestige of the throne can effectively be safeguarded. Perhaps the royal version of the constitutional monarchy is not so much a royal as a King Bhumibol-tailored version of the constitutional system with the King as head of state.

POSTSCRIPT

In more ways than one, the passage of the 1997 Constitution was unquestionably a watershed in the progress of the Thai constitutional monarchical system. For the first time a Thai constitution conscientiously provides for genuine popular participation in politics and in the running of the country. If this socio-political reform so engineered proves effective, it would mean there would be a parliament representing the interests of the people, and thus the true representative of popular sovereignty. During the period of guided democracy, the throne has rightly claimed that it had a political responsibility to the people. Many Thais regard the supreme authority of the throne over the affairs of the nation as partly stemming from the political retardation of democracy in the country and therefore a temporary feature required during the socio-political transition period. Would the principle of constitutional monarchy as practised by the King be fundamentally affected by an emergence of a people's parliament? Would there be a clash of sovereign will: the throne's and parliament's? Would the monarchy retreat behind an official façade of pomp and ceremony? The answers to all these queries are unclear. What is clear is that, more likely than not, the monarchy represented by the most revered King Bhumibol Adulyadej will be as Thailand's greatly beloved monarch desires it to be. The future will have to take care of itself.

NOTES

1 Five constitutions were promulgated during the 1970s: the 1972 (interim), 1974, 1976, 1977 and 1978 constitutions.
2 The *ratcha-pracha samasai* constitution was considered a joint effort between the King and the people because it was the King who appointed

2,436 Thai citizens from all walks of life as delegates to the national convention set up after the October 1973 'revolution'. Its sole duty was to select 299 members for a new National Assembly, replacing the one appointed in 1971 by the ousted Premier Thanom. The new 299-member assembly was to pass a new constitution drafted by its subcommittee. The result was the 1974 Constitution, which at the time was regarded as the first positive step towards establishing true democracy in Thailand.

3   King Bhumibol's comment, quoted in Pridi 1992: 155–156. During the drafting, it was proposed that the Privy Council should put forward 300 names of those qualified for parliament. These 300 would then select 100 from their number to be members of the Senate. It was finally agreed that the 100 senators – all well-qualified persons of 35 years and above – should be appointed by the King, with the President of the Privy Council countersigning the royal appointment. As Pridi rightly pointed out, this was first proposed by the Boworadet Rebellion, and was put into practice by the 1947 interim constitution.

4   King Bhumibol in fact invested his only son, Prince Vajiralongkorn, with the title of *Sayam-mongkut-ratcha-kuman*, or the Crown Prince of Thailand in a traditional and religious ceremony in December 1972. It was a time of great rejoicing. The celebration lasted two days, climaxing in a glittering garden party attended by both Thai and foreign dignitaries. By investing his son with the heir-apparent title of crown prince, the King looked to guarantee a smooth succession to the throne.

5   The 1991 Constitution was drafted by the Legislative Assembly set up after the February 1991 coup. As such, it was another version of previous military constitutions. It reflected the political designs of the new military ruling elite, which aimed to safeguard its political power under the guise of democracy: crucially, the prime minister was not required to be an MP. On the 1997 Constitution, see the Introduction to the present volume.

6   The official translation of the 1997 constitution uses the term 'Constituent Assembly'. However most authors writing in English (including other authors in this volume) prefer the unofficial translation 'Constitution Drafting Assembly'.

7   Actually it was more the coup leaders, especially Phao, rather than Premier Phibun, who were concerned about the King's potential power and influence – to the point that they ignored Premier Phibun's advice against staging a coup at the time King Bhumibol and his consort, Queen Sirikit, were on their way back to take up residence in Thailand. See Kobkua (1995: 75–79).

8   The following analysis of King Bhumibol's political principles is based on His Majesty's own expressions as given in the form of press interviews and such like. See National Archives, File S.B. 15/5 'Give more, take less, His Majesty King Bhumibol Adulyadej'. See also an overall analysis of the monarchy in Hewison (1997a).

9 National Archives, File S.B. 15/5 'Miracles happen, gentlemen, but they don't come cheap', *Leader Magazine,* 1985.

10 In his *Problem of Siam,* King Prajadhipok confirmed that the tradition of the 'election' of Thai kings continued to the time of King Chulalongkorn. The latter replaced it with the creation of the title of crown prince 'who succeeded to the throne without question' (Prajadhipok 1974: 13–14).

11 The events leading to royal intervention were both comic and tragic. The five political parties that supported the candidacy of Somboon Rahong, a retired air marshal, were so certain of his appointment that they had arranged for a party to celebrate his appointment during the hours the premier-designate was waiting for the expected royal command. But in a quick succession of events at the palace on the eve of 10 June 1992, House Speaker and President of Parliament Arthit Urairat had countersigned the royal appointment of ex-Premier Anand Panyarachun as the new interim prime minister. It had appeared that Somboon's appointment would send the country into another round of dangerous political tension. The King's decision not to accept Somboon's nomination was apparently made in a desire to break this impasse. The King's move fully displayed his position as 'the country's supreme authority' and was in line with His Majesty's understanding of his role as constitutional monarch.

6

HUMAN RIGHTS AND POLITICAL REFORM IN THAILAND

David Streckfuss and Mark Templeton

Most major human rights assessments seem to agree that Thailand has entered a new threshold in protecting the rights of its citizens. Recent US State Department annual reports on human rights in Thailand say that the 'Government generally respected the human rights of its citizens', despite the occurrence of a few extra-judicial killings, some incidents of torture, 'an ingrained culture of corruption', a pattern of poor treatment of immigrants, and abuses against minority mountain peoples.[1] Human Rights Watch reports that for 'Thai citizens ... the scope for human rights protection increased'.[2] Like Amnesty International, Human Rights Watch focuses almost exclusively on the maltreatment of refugees.[3]

It is true that Thailand has made great strides since the army brutally suppressed pro-democracy protesters in 1992. The country adopted a new Constitution in 1997 with promises of better protection for civil liberties. By ratifying the International Covenant on Civil and Political Rights (ICCPR) in 1999, the government agreed to respect the human rights of all persons in its territory, to adopt legislation to give effect to those rights, and to afford remedies for rights violations. And Thailand certainly has had a better rights record than some of its Southeast Asian neighbours.

But Thailand has a long way to go before it deserves the high marks that the international community has given it. In this chapter, we shall argue that recent controversies regarding the freedom of religion, the freedom of expression (and to receive new ideas), and the electoral process show that old laws, attitudes and mores have trumped the spirit of reform. While the 1997 Constitution is generally an improvement over its predecessors, it neither meets nor exceeds the international standards in these three areas. Institutions designed to promote and protect these rights either have not yet begun to function or have disappointed many with what they have done. Unless a general awareness of human rights develops among the Thai people, it will be difficult to maintain and extend the freedoms for which many have struggled and some died.

FREEDOM OF RELIGION

Freedom of religion is a core human right, and the 1997 Constitution protects a slightly wider range of religious activity than its recent predecessors. The new charter states:

> [A] person shall enjoy full liberty to profess a religion, a religious sect or creed, and observe religious precepts or exercise a form of worship in accordance with his or her belief; provided that it is not contrary to his or her civic duties, public order or good morals. In exercising the liberty referred to in paragraph one, a person is protected from any act of the State, which is derogatory to his or her rights or detrimental to his or her due benefits on the grounds of professing a religion, a religious sect or creed or observing religious precepts or exercising a form of worship in accordance with his or her different belief from others. (Constitution 1997: Article 38)

The 1991 and 1978 Constitutions employ almost exactly the same language; however, they do not state that a person has the full liberty to 'observe religious precepts' (cf. Constitution 1991, Article 27; Constitution 1978, Article 25). This additional phrase protects actions that a person undertakes related to his or her religious belief, but that may not occur during formal worship practices.

International human rights agreements such as the ICCPR shield religious beliefs and practices to a greater extent than the 1997 Constitution or its predecessors in at least six ways.

- First, the ICCPR states that a person has the freedom 'to have or to adopt a religion or belief of his choice' (ICCPR, Article 18.1). The Constitution states only that a person has the freedom to profess a religion; one who wants to constrain religious freedom could argue that the Constitution does not protect the freedom to adopt a religion or to change faiths.
- Second, the ICCPR states that a person can exercise his religious freedom 'either individually or in community with others and in public or private' (ICCPR, Article 18.1). Because the Constitution does not contain a similar clause, it is possible that a court would hold that the Constitution protects personal expression of beliefs, but not collective demonstrations of faith.
- Third, the ICCPR lists 'teaching' as a protected activity; since the Constitution does not, one could argue that instruction is not covered.[4]

- Fourth, the ICCPR states that 'no one shall be subject to coercion which would impair his freedom' (ICCPR, Article 18.2). Because the Constitution does not have a like clause, one opposed to religious liberty could argue that the state, a group or a person could strongly encourage a person to change his or her beliefs without violating the specific terms of the Constitution.[5]
- Fifth, the ICCPR stipulates that states may constrain religious freedom, but requires governments to follow strict standards and procedures: 'Freedom to manifest one's religion or beliefs may be subject only to such limitation as are prescribed by law and are necessary to protect public safety, order, health or morals or the fundamental rights and freedoms of others' (ICCPR, Article 18.3). According to the ICCPR, religious freedom can be constrained only by law; an executive or judicial official cannot restrict religious observance sua sponte (in this context, 'on its own motion'). Since the Thai Constitution does not have similar provisions, judicial officials could uphold restraints placed on an individual by finding that the person violated his or her 'civic duties, public order or good morals', but without reference to a specific law.
- Sixth, the ICCPR protects the rights of parents and legal guardians to educate their children in conformity with their own convictions (ICCPR, Article 18.4). The Thai Constitution does not have these specific guidelines.

Even if one focuses on the fact that the new Constitution is a modest improvement over its predecessors with regard to the freedom of religion, there is still a dismaying gap between the letter of Constitution and the way that authorities have applied existing laws regarding religion. The passage of the new charter seems to have had little effect on how these officials think about matters of religion and the appropriate extent of their powers.

THE CASE OF THAMMAKAI

The clearest failure of the government to uphold the freedom of religion despite the new Constitution is the case of the Thammakai (Dhammakaiya) Buddhist group. The group and its leader, Dhammachayo, were well known for conducting aggressive donation drives, undertaking ambitious building projects, and claiming that followers would experience miracles. The abbot's meditation method declared 'the existence of Nirvana' and implied that 'Nirvana was atta (self), which meant it had a form'.

Although in early 1999 mundane charges of illegal land purchases and embezzlement of temple funds were made against the abbot, most critics condemned primarily his teaching on Nirvana. Dhammachayo's opponents claimed that Nirvana 'can only be achieved, not experienced', and that Theravada Buddhism teaches that 'Nirvana is anatta [no-self] and has no form'. The Buddhist hierarchy described the abbot's philosophy as 'heresy', and the Supreme Sangha Council ordered the abbot to renounce his teachings in March of 1999 (*The Nation*, 12 January, 19 May, 6 August 1999).

But the matter did not end with the Supreme Sangha Council's proclamation. Emerging in full force was a national security apparatus, which has been largely undisturbed by all the commotion over political reform and which has been dedicated for well over half a century to defining and then intimidating and silencing enemies of the state.

In early January, top national security officials met to see if the abbot had violated any security laws and admitted that 'intelligence and security apparatus were closely monitoring Dhammachayo'. They feared that the abbot might turn his 'popularity into an unsanctioned personality cult' which then could mobilize his followers (*The Nation* 14 January, 19 January 1999).

In February, the House Committee on Religious Affairs, worried about the controversy's 'long-term, adverse impacts on the nation and monarchy', came out with a report that called for the removal of the abbot 'on grounds of religious violations, national security and undermining of the monarchy'. The National Security Council voiced concern that Thammakai 'could erode the foundation of Buddhism, causing divisiveness in the country', and that the temple's frequent use of the monarchy in soliciting donations 'could also tarnish the country's most revered institution'. The report concluded that the government should set up a permanent body 'to monitor religious activities, aimed at ensuring the security of Buddhism' (*The Nation*, 25 February 1999).

In May, the Ministry of Education's Religious Affairs Department (RAD) charged Dhammachayo with having 'propagated false teachings on Nirvana, causing divisiveness among monks and spreading heretic doctrines'. The department also said that it 'had formed three panels to be responsible for the dissemination of information relating to the controversy, and to pre-empt any adverse impact on Buddhism' (*The Nation*, 22 May and 28 May 1999). Various laws such as the Religious Organizations Act of 1969 give great powers to the RAD to make determinations about religious matters, including the recognition of new religions.[6]

Throughout this entire affair, religious and state officials intimated that the abbot had violated a criminal law concerning the profession of a religion. At various times there were calls for, or threats by, the authorities to arrest the abbot for 'distorting religion', 'damaging' or 'destroying Buddhism', 'heresy', 'propagating false teachings', and so on. In fact, these types of acts do not violate the law. Simply said, heresy is not a crime, even in Thailand.

What is disturbing is that few have spoken out against the treatment of the Thammakai group as a human rights abuse.[7] A distressingly large number of those generally associated with the defence of human rights have supported the state's suppression of Dhammachayo.[8] Leading progressive human rights activists and NGOs have expressed in private the need for Dhammachayo to be defrocked.[9] Rather than coming to the defence of the accused, the head of the Law Society of Thailand has suggested ways to 'cut out all the red tape' so that heretical monks could be more efficiently and quickly defrocked. Such measures, he said, were needed 'for the sake of the religion' (*The Nation*, 20 June 1999).

Others have suggested that the state should permit Thammakai followers to believe what they will, but that it should deny them the right to call themselves Theravada Buddhists.[10] However, this 'solution' is probably unacceptable in terms of human rights. It is not for the government to determine whether Thammakai adherents are actually practising Buddhism or whether they can call themselves 'Buddhists'.

Even if Thammakai followers did 'stop' being Buddhists and attempted to set up their own sect, it is uncertain whether the state would permit them to follow their beliefs. With the phrase from the Constitution, 'religion, religious sect or creed' unclear, with the legal proviso that religious practice may not be contrary to 'civic duties, public order or good morals', and with intolerance of religious diversity among the public, groups like Thammakai would always risk being denied rights. A lurking danger is that the Constitutional Court relies on the RAD's definition of religion in order to determine whether an organization is a legitimate 'religious sect', and a belief an acceptable 'creed'. And that would bring us back to the RAD, the state organ that has already found fault with the Thammakai religious doctrine.

Charles Keyes has argued that the appearance and continued popularity of Buddhist religious groups such as Thammakai or Santi Asoke indicate not the 'triumph of politicized Buddhism' but rather the creation of a 'civil religion' in Thailand that 'accommodates a diversity of Buddhisms'. No longer, writes Keyes, can the meaning of Buddhism 'be determined by the state'. Events in the past 30 years have 'fundamentally undermined the dominance of an establishment Buddhism' and although fragmented, 'allowed diverse and competing religious and social elements to emerge' (Keyes 1999).[11]

The dominance of the Buddhist hierarchy may certainly be in question. But the core of Keyes's observations, in light of the reactions of the state and a good deal of the population, seems too benign. If a 'diversity of Buddhisms' has emerged, it has featured both conflict and calls of condemnation. Many of the other controversies surrounding Buddhism in Thailand in the past few years have involved monks accused of breaking key Theravada Buddhist monastic rules – having sexual relations with women – and were not debates over orthodoxy. But the Dhammachayo case has been a doctrinal debate, as was the conflict over Santi Asoke, the latter ending with excommunication.

Robb Stewart comes closer to the mark when he states baldly that 'freedom of religion does not exist in Thailand' (Stewart 1999: 2). He argues persuasively that the state has adopted Theravada Buddhism as the de facto state religion and has helped to define and defend a particularly conservative interpretation of it. As a result, the state can hardly be a protector of religious freedom. In effect, the state neither guarantees fully the right to profess a religion other than Buddhism, nor permits persons to follow non-sanctioned forms of Buddhism.

While the Constitution's provisions on religious freedom furnish a modest improvement over previous charters, in practice the same authoritarian attitudes and forces remain, as does a fundamental intolerance of diversity by elite civil society leaders. As the Dhammachayo controversy demonstrates, improved protection for the freedom of religion on paper does not evince real substantive political reform.

FREEDOM OF SPEECH

Freedom of speech is another core human right, and the 1997 Constitution protects expressive activity to a somewhat greater degree than did the 1991 Constitution. The new charter states:

> A person shall enjoy the liberty to express his or her opinion, make speeches, write, print, publicize, and make expression by other means. The restriction on liberty under paragraph 1 shall not be imposed except by virtue of the provisions of the law specifically enacted for the purpose of maintaining the security of the State, safeguarding the rights, liberties, dignity, reputation, family or privacy rights of other person, maintaining public order or good morals or preventing the deterioration of the mind or health of the public. (Constitution 1997, Article 39: 1–2)

The 1991 Constitution contains similar language. However, the two documents differ with regard to whether and when the government can prevent dissemination of particular publications and information.

The 1997 Constitution states that 'the closure of a publishing house or a radio or television station in deprivation of the liberty under this section shall not be made' (Constitution 1997, Article 39: 3), whereas the 1991 Constitution permits shutting publications if the government secures a 'judgment or order of court' (Constitution 1991, Article 39: 3). The 1997 Constitution states:

The censorship by a competent official of news or articles before their publication in a newspaper, printed matter or radio or television broadcasting shall not be made except during the time when the country is in a state of war or armed conflict; provided that it must be made by virtue of the law enacted under the provisions of paragraph two. (Constitution 1997, Article 39: 4)

The 1991 Constitution also permitted censorship during 'a state of emergency or martial law' (Constitution 1991, Article 39: 4). By forbidding the government from closing publishers and electronic broadcasters, and by reducing the number of circumstances that permit censorship, the 1997 Constitution is a step forward in protecting freedom of speech.

International human rights agreements, such as the ICCPR, shield freedom of speech to a greater extent than did the 1997 Constitution or its predecessors in at least three significant ways.

- First, and perhaps most important, the ICCPR contains a broader definition of protected activity. The ICCPR states that the freedom of speech includes the 'freedom to seek, receive and impart information and ideas of all kinds' (ICCPR, Article 19.2). None of the previous Thai Constitutions protected the freedoms to seek or to receive information – listeners' or viewers' rights – in this way.[12]

- Second, the ICCPR requires the restrictions to be 'necessary' (ICCPR, Article 19.2.); the Thai Constitutions do not. The Thai Constitutions permit limitations that advance certain social objectives but which could be achieved through other, less restrictive means, such as warnings, education or presentation of alternative information or ideas.

- Third, the ICCPR states that 'everyone shall have the right to hold opinions without interference' (ICCPR, Article 19.1). Because the Constitution does not have a like clause, a person opposed to expressive freedom could argue that the state, a group, or a person could strongly encourage a person to change his or her opinion without violating the specific terms of the Constitution.[13]

THE CASE OF *ANNA AND THE KING*

As was the case with regard to religious freedom, officials' attitudes towards and actions against free speech are at odds with the new Constitutional guarantees for the freedom of expression. The clearest case is the banning of the screening of *Anna and the King* in Thailand by the Film Censorship Board in late 1999.

When the board acted, its head, an officer in the Special Forces or essentially political police, claimed that the movie 'intentionally tries to undermine the monarchy and seriously distorts Thai history', which 'could create unrest in our society'. Ominously, he went on to say: 'The screening would be against the peace and security of our society as it would incite riots among those who are loyal to the monarchy. It would be out of our control' (*The Nation*, 29 December 1999).

The exact items deemed offensive need not delay us long. According to the Board, insults ranged from the film making the king look like a 'cowboy' to the impossibility of his kissing his daughter on the lips or his smoking cigars, to making Thai women look stupid and moody (*The Nation*, 29 December 1999; see also ibid. 29 November 1998).

There are two basic human rights issues at work here: the right to expression and the right to receive new ideas. Both are central to the intellectual and artistic life of individuals and to the national community. How did the Constitution fail to prevail, and in what way did other laws impinge on the case?

Provision 112 of the Thai Code punishes persons who indulge in lèse-majesté, or insults to the royalty. The lèse-majesté provisions quite explicitly provide protection for only four persons – the king, queen, heir-apparent and regent – and not for the institution of the monarchy as such. In legal exegeses, Thai scholars argue that the law presumably would not cover previous kings. However, in practice, calls have been made occasionally for the arrest of those who have supposedly insulted past kings.[14] Strangely, despite democratic reforms and a general opening of society, the penalty for this crime has ever increased throughout the twentieth century, for example expanding in 1976 from a prison term of not more than 3 years to a sentence of 3–15 years (for more details, see Streckfuss 1995).

Opponents of *Anna and the King* claim that the film violates the law of lèse-majesté. Does it? The king portrayed in the film, King Rama IV (1851–68), is the great-grandfather of the present monarch. Would insulting the great-grandfather be equal to insulting the great-grandson? How could such an important law be so loosely applied? The accusation of lèse-majesté is often made in Thai society and with the heavy penalty there is no wonder that the law provides a weighty damper on the free expression of art, history and politics.

The legal restrictions controlling what may be shown in films have also increased steadily over time. The Cinema Act of 1930 simply forbade anything that might be against public order and morals. In 1972, a coup proclamation forbade the showing of any film that 'might cause contempt for government or nation' and banned any 'political' content in movies that may 'adversely affect governance or incite the creation of disquietude in the country'. In 1991, areas of violation included also films that insulted the 'noble morality, culture and traditions of the nation' or disturbed the 'peace and order and security of the nation'.

Specifically, the new provisions forbade any movie that would 'ridicule, mock, scorn or insult the institution of the Thai monarchy' or that was a 'clear expression in the nature of insult to the state or nation or government, or inciting to cause disquietude in the land' (Interior Ministry 1991).

The Film Censorship Board has also consistently rejected any film scripts deemed critical of past dictators, on the grounds of defamation. The result is that there are virtually no critical historical documentaries or movies covering any modern historical period. In this area, there are only dreary and pedantic faux-documentaries celebrating royalty.

In the *Anna and the King* case, the government has clearly violated the rights of citizens to receive new ideas by suppressing any versions of history not in accordance with its own. Human rights standards permit the state to press its social agenda, but not at the exclusion of other views. Quite freely, the head of the Board maintained that the problem with *Anna and the King* was that 'the story still doesn't glorify the monarchy as an institution' (*The Nation*, 26 December 1998). Another member of the Board pointed out that there were 'some factual errors [that] may create historical confusion' (ibid., 23 December 1998).

The rationale in banning the film has all the trappings of a human rights violation – a paternalistic attitude towards free access, a defence of suppression based on abstract notions of national institutions, and even an assumption that there is something seriously criminal in propagating 'false interpretations'. As in the case of Thammakai where the state was eager to forward its views of religion, the state here advances its own view of the monarchy. But in this case the state is not just violating the rights of a given group, as with Thammakai, but those of everyone in society. Even with the heavy punishment as an incentive for silence, it is still remarkable how acquiescent the public has been in regard to its own rights. Rarely did the public debate over the film focus on the question of rights.[15]

The question here is not so much whether Fox has the right to show its film in Thailand. Rather, it is whether Thai society has the right to make free and informed decisions on which books, art, films, newspapers and so on it receives. It is disappointing that many pro-democracy forces in society were either uninterested in this case or were silent because they believed it to be solely a matter of American cultural imperialism. Unfortunately, both instances show how limited human rights consciousness is in Thailand.

ELECTORAL FREEDOMS

A third fundamental human right is that of the citizens to participate in the political affairs of their country. Surprisingly, the 1997 Constitution does not protect the rights of Thai citizens to vote, to choose their representatives freely, or to hold elected office as well as did the 1991 charter. First, the new charter disenfranchises any person 'detained by a warrant of the Court or by a lawful order' (Constitution 1997, Article 106: 3), whereas the 1991 Constitution prohibited voting by persons 'detained by a warrant of the Court' (Constitution 1991, Article 110: 3). Therefore, the new Constitution additionally disenfranchises people restrained by administrative or military officials.

Second, the new charter protects the right to vote for those who are listed in the house register for 'not less than 90 days up to the date of the election' (Constitution 1997, Article 105: 3), whereas the 1991 Constitution did not impose a minimum residency requirement. While the purpose of such a provision may be to prevent chicanery in the voting process, it also potentially limits the rights of citizens who recently moved to select their representatives.[16]

Third, and perhaps most important, the new Constitution requires those who seek positions in the National Assembly or Senate to have college degrees.[17] Its predecessors had no such preconditions. While the purpose of such a provision may be to improve the quality of the legislative body by requiring its members to have more formal education, it also curtails the rights of citizens who have less schooling or fewer educational opportunities to represent the Thai people (Constitution 1997, Article 105: 2). The few, tiny improvements in electoral access under the 1997 charter[18] do not change the fact that the net result of the 1997 Constitution is a reduction in the voting rights of and electoral options for Thai citizens.

The new Thai Constitution continues to restrict voting rights and opportunities to seek political office more than international human rights agreements permit. The ICCPR states that

> every citizen shall have the right and the opportunity ... without unreasonable restrictions, (a) To take part in the conduct of public affairs, directly or through freely chosen representatives; (b) To vote and to be elected at genuine periodic elections which shall be by universal and equal suffrage and shall be held by secret ballot, guaranteeing the free expression of the will of the electors; (c) To have access, on general terms of equality, to public service in his country.[19]

The United Nations Human Rights Committee, which has the responsibility for evaluating how well signatory states have complied with ICCPR provisions, has stated that governments should make the political process as inclusive as possible. It has stated that 'exercising the right to vote... should be available to every adult citizen'.[20] But the Thai Constitution automatically disenfranchises Buddhist priests, novices, monks and clergy (Constitution 1997, Article 106: 2) in blatant disregard of the ICCPR provision prohibiting discrimination on the basis of religion and religious status.[21] It prevents voting by all persons detained by warrants of the Court or a lawful order (Constitution 1997, Article 106: 3), regardless of whether those persons have been convicted of a crime. It unreasonably prohibits naturalized citizens from voting in elections for the first five years after naturalization, in essence discriminating against them on the basis of residence and descent (Constitution 1997, Article 105: 1). The Human Rights Committee has also stated that '[p]ersons who are otherwise eligible to stand for election should not be excluded by unreasonable or discriminatory requirements such as education, residence or descent or by reason of political affiliation' (Committee on Civil and Political Rights 1996, Article 15). As discussed above, the 1997 charter imposes significant educational requirements on those who want to serve as representatives without clear, direct benefits for those burdens (see Constitution 1997, Articles 107: 3, 125: 3). The 1997 Constitution simply does not meet the international standards for protection.

EXCLUSION OF PERSONS FROM LESS PRIVILEGED BACKGROUNDS

The new educational requirements have already affected elections and politicians, and not necessarily for the better. In the first senate contest under the new Constitution, there were no female candidates in 28 provinces, despite the conventional wisdom that women at the local level are more involved politically than urban women. Many said that they could not seek seats because they lacked the necessary formal degrees, even though they had first-hand experience working in their communities and fighting corruption (*The Nation*, 8 March 2000).

It is ironic that Ramkhamhaeng University started a programme in late 1999 to help politicians comply with the letter, if not the spirit, of the Constitution's new educational requirements. The Ramkhamhaeng course reduces the time that it takes elected officials to earn a Bachelor of Arts degree by granting credits for their practical experience. The dean of the Faculty of Political Science, Associate Professor Pornchai Theppanya, defended the programme, stating that the National Education Act 1999 stresses that 'students can obtain education through informal or unconventional methods such as self-study, social experiences, media and other sources of knowledge (*The Nation*, 1 February 2000). But a former member of the Constitutional Drafting Assembly, a lecturer at Chulalongkorn University's Faculty of Education and a current politician have said that they fear that the programme will result in lower educational standards (*The Nation*, 31 January 2000, 28 October 1999).

On the one hand, it is laudable that a university is willing to recognize practical experience. On the other hand, it is inappropriate for existing national politicians to receive credits and opportunities to participate in these programmes when community leaders do not.[22] Furthermore, it flouts the spirit of the Constitution if the purpose of the programmes is merely to help elected officials comply with the new formal requirements. Thus, the new educational requirements keep competent people from serving, while those in power can manipulate the system to maintain their positions. They have fortified the notion that the privileged are the most capable to lead by not recognizing or rewarding sufficiently the experience of those who are not formally educated but who have hands-on knowledge about the interests of the people.

NEW MECHANISMS: THE NATIONAL HUMAN RIGHTS COMMISSION AND THE CONSTITUTIONAL COURT

The effective promotion and protection of human rights require institutional mechanisms for monitoring and addressing violations of civil, political, economic, social and cultural rights. The 1997 Constitution mandated the establishment of the National Human Rights Commission and the Constitutional Court, among other institutions, for these purposes.

The subsequent National Human Rights Commission (NHRC) Act of 1999 created what could be a powerful, relatively independent organization for promoting civil, political, economic, social and cultural liberties. The Commission may investigate alleged abuses, propose remedial measures when appropriate, recommend changes to laws, rules and regulations, promote human rights education, and report annually to the National Assembly and the public on the situation of human rights in Thailand (NHRC Act, 1999 Article 15). The Commission may receive petitions from persons who allege human rights violations or from non-governmental organizations that represent the interests of those persons (Articles 23, 24). The Commission or a subcommittee may undertake independent investigations. They may

- require persons or organizations to respond to charges (Article 25)
- issue summons to government officials and private persons (Article 32)
- seek warrants for entering into dwellings or other places (Article 32)
- propose remedial measures (Article 28)
- mediate between violators and victims (Article 27).

The Commission may also undertake an investigation of its own accord. No one can serve on the commission and work as a government official, an employee of a state agency or enterprise, a local government administrator, a businessperson, or 'an employee of any person' at the same time (Article 7). The Commission's president has charge and control of execution of the Act creating the organization, rather than the legislature, the prime minister, or another governmental agency or official as had been proposed (Article 4). Thus, the commission has a broad mandate and wide-ranging powers to fulfil it. However, at present, it is impossible to determine how effective the Commission will be. Only time will tell how effectively the Commission and its office will investigate human rights abuses and promote civil, political, economic, social and cultural liberties.

The other major constitutional body charged with protecting civil liberties, the Constitutional Court, is at best a modestly upgraded version of the previous Constitutional Tribunal. Like its predecessor, it has the power to review legislation after passage by the National Assembly but before presentation to the King.[23] It can rule on the constitutionality of 'any law' in 'any case' if a court or a party before it questions the legality of the provision.[24] And its rulings apply to all undecided cases. The 1997 Constitution spells out slightly greater powers and requirements for the new court:

- The Constitutional Court's decisions are explicitly binding on the 'National Assembly, Council of Ministers, Courts and other State organs' (Article 268).
- The Court has the enumerated 'power to demand documents or relevant evidence from any person or summon any person to give statements of fact' (Article 265).
- The Court has an 'independent secretariat' (Article 270)
- The Court must follow procedure which takes account of 'fundamental guarantees with regard to the openness of hearing, the opportunity to the parties to express their opinions before the decision of the case, the right of the parties to inspect documents relating to them, the opportunity to challenge the judge of the Constitutional Court and the reasoning of the decision or order of the Constitutional Court' (Article 269).

Many critics argue that Constitutional Court judges are neither using their new prerogatives wisely nor are adhering the spirit of the 'People's Constitution'. For example, the new charter states that persons sentenced to imprisonment may not serve as ministers (Article 216: 4). But the Constitutional Court held that Newin Chidchob could continue to serve as deputy agriculture and cooperatives minister – even though he was convicted of a crime that requires detention – because the lower court suspended his sentence of six months' imprisonment. The critics, including 42 of 44 members of the Constitutional Drafting Assembly, believed that the decision was 'wrong and incompatible with the charter's spirit' because the purpose of the provision was to clean up cabinet-level politics and make government more responsive to the people, according to Professor Amorn Raksasat (*The Nation*, 26 June 1999). In another case, the Constitutional Court ruled that the Election Commission could not ban senate candidates who had violated election rules on multiple occasions. Yuwarat Kamolvej of the Commission said that progress made on the road to political reform could be limited. 'Don't talk to me about the spirit of the constitution', he said. 'This shows that we, in Thailand, interpret the law to the letter. The spirit of the law has no meaning' (*Bangkok Post*, 17 June 2000). Leaders of some non-governmental organizations have stated that they will pursue impeachment of Constitution Court judges who have engaged in behaviour indicating a bias towards a plaintiff accused of corruption (*The Nation*, 19 and 22 June 1999).

Defenders of the Court contest these claims. They argue that the job of the Court is to interpret the text of the Constitution as it was given to the Court, not to engage in a guessing game about what the 'people' wanted when their representatives drafted the document. They also note that the Court sent a clear message about corruption and made a significant impact on Thailand's political culture when it upheld the National Counter-Corruption Commission's decision to ban then-interior minister Sanan Kachornprasart from politics for five years for fabricating a loan in his ministerial declaration of assets and liabilities (see *Bangkok Post*, 11 August 2000). However, fresh controversy over the workings of the Court broke out when Prime Minister Thaksin Shinawatra was acquitted of failing properly to declare his assets in August 2001 (see the discussion by McCargo, Chapter 15). As with the National Human Rights Commission, it will be possible to judge the Court's willingness and ability to clean up Thailand's political system and to protect fundamental rights only over time. What is clear right now is that many believe that the Court has not yet earned the trust of the people.

CONCLUSION

In modern constitutional democracies, the constitution serves as the backdrop, the document containing the principles and definitions by which the legal system is understood. In Thailand, however, the constitution can only be understood by looking at the laws on the books and the play of various political and social forces on the ground. There have been almost 20 constitutions in the past 70 years and it seems rash to believe that this latest Constitution will suddenly effect an oceanic change in the Thai attitude toward constitutions. It is, after all, merely a document. It cannot be expected to reverse the effects of more than 100 years of authoritarian regimes, the worst of which took the bulk of the past century. Laws were enacted only to be suspended by coup decrees, only then to be papered over by yet others.

Support of diversity and strengthening of civil society are the only effective counters to the authoritarian impulse. Rather than seeing suppression as key to strengthening

Thai society, it needs to be recognized that Thailand benefits most in the long run when civil liberties are supported in general, even for those with whom one does not agree. It has been the mistake of indigenous and international human rights groups to dismiss the importance of the suppression of Thammakai, the banning of *Anna and the King*, or election requirements that disenfranchise the vast majority of the population from elected office. By not defending the principles contained within these three instances, they have done a disservice to the public and made diversity of views a harder proposition in Thailand.

The all-too-soon skewing of the instruments of reform show that a human rights consciousness must develop within the citizens of Thailand if they are to maintain and extend basic human rights. There need to be more people who will hold the government accountable when it does not implement the letter and spirit of reform. In short, Thailand must embrace the notion of diversity, and the religious, artistic and political freedom necessary to ensure it. Only when a human rights consciousness develops and is manifested will Thailand become a beacon for human rights in Asia.

NOTES

1   United States Government, *Thailand Country Report, Human Rights Practices for 1998 Report*, Released by the Bureau of Democracy, Human Rights, and Labor, US Department of State, February 1999. http://www.state.gov/www/global/human_rights/1998_hrp_report/thailand.html

2   Human Rights Watch, *World Report 1999, Thailand.* http://www.hrw.org/hrw/worldreport99/asia/thailand.html

3   See Amnesty International, *Amnesty International Report 1999: Thailand.* http://www.amnestyusa.org/ailib/aireport/ar99/asa39.htm

4   The Thai Constitution states that '[a] person shall enjoy *full* liberty to profess a religion ...' (Constitution 1997, Article 38 [emphasis added]). A court might hold that the *full* liberty to profess, observe or exercise includes the right to teach others about one's religious beliefs. Or the court might find that teaching is not a protected activity, because the drafters of the Thai Constitution must have known of the international standards, which include teaching, and they did not include it.

5   The Thai Constitution states that '[a] person shall enjoy *full* liberty to profess a religion' (Constitution 1997, Article 38 [emphasis added]). A court might hold that coercive activities by the state, a group or other persons violate the *full* religious liberty of a person. Or the court might not.
6   The Religious Organizations Act of 1969 states that the RAD should recognize a new religion if a national census indicates that such a new religion has at least 5,000 followers, 'a uniquely recognizable theology', and if it is 'not politically active'.
7   Not surprisingly, the abbot and his followers are the exceptions. In June, Dhammachayo filed a civil suit against the Minister of Education, under which the RAD is located, on grounds that there had been 'constitutional violations to deprive him of "human dignity"'. In August, his lawyer argued that 'state authorities had interfered with Dhammachayo's constitutional right to propagate his religion', and he collected between 50,000 and 100,000 signatures so that the case could be brought to the new Constitutional Court (*The Nation*, 18 June, 30 August, 31 August 1999).
8   In May 1999, calls from 209 Buddhist organizations for the abbot to be excommunicated were followed with a rally at Sanam Luang 'aimed at fostering a correct understanding of the religion'. (See *The Nation*, 24 April, 28 May 1999.)
9   Personal confidential contact with persons involved with the National Human Rights Commission.
10   Even one of the leading proponents of the Constitution itself, Dr Prawase Wasi, advocated this solution. (See Prawase 1999: 21–22, and also Stewart 1999.)
11   For a discussion of the significance of the Thammakai phenomenon in Thai 'civil religion', see ibid: 4–5, 40–42).
12   Article 42 of the Constitution of 1997 protects academic and educational freedom: 'A person shall enjoy an academic freedom. Education, training, learning, teaching, researching and disseminating such research according to academic principles shall be protected; provided that it is not contrary to his or her civic duties or good morals'. While the concepts contained in this provision may be similar to the ICCPR protections for seekers and recipients of information and ideas, they are not the same. For example, the rights of teachers and students are not necessarily the same as those of the general public who may listen to the radio, watch television, or attend a movie screening. Furthermore, the ICCPR requires limitations on the seeking, receiving and imparting of views to be provided by law and necessary; the Constitution does not impose the same high procedural standards on actions taken against academic freedom.
13   The Thai Constitution states that 'a person shall enjoy the liberty to express his or her opinion, make speeches, write, print, publicize, and make expression by other means' (Constitution 1997, Article 39). It is interesting that the Constitution protects 'the liberty' of expression, but also 'the full

liberty to profess a religion' (Article 38). A court might hold that interference or coercion by the state, a group, or other persons violates expressive liberties. Or the court might not.

14 Such a case, as improbable as it seems, occurred with the 1996 protests and book burning against an MA student who had said that Ya Mo of Khorat, a local heroine, had been 'created' (in a postmodern sense) by nationalists in the 1930s. The 30,000 protesters demanded the author and her advisors be condemned for *lèse-majesté*, as King Rama III had given Ya Mo a royal title. To question her existence thus insulted the king (see Streckfuss 1998: 1–2).

15 There were a few exceptions. After the movie was banned, two film critics attacked the decision of the Board, accusing it of 'cultural cowardice'. One flatly stated that film censorship had no place in an open society. The critic asked concerning the Board, 'Who are they to decide on behalf of the people?' The public should be able to make up its own mind. He remarked: 'Film is an art form, a showcase of the human imagination. Everyone should be able to judge whether to take it or leave it.' Another said that the decision of the Board was 'clearly a defeat for the country and shows that we prefer to hide in our small world'. (*The Nation*, 30 December 1999)

16 Those persons whose names appeared on the house register for a period of less than 90 days 'shall have the right to cast a vote in an election in accordance with rules, procedure and conditions provided by the organic law on the election of members of the House of Representatives and senators' (Constitution 1997, Article 105: 2). The voting rights of these citizens do not receive the same protection as those of other persons; their opportunity to participate in the democratic electoral process depends on the wisdom and whim of the legislative and judicial branches.

17 See Constitution 1997, Articles 106: 3, 107: 3, 125: 3. The Constitution waives the tertiary degree requirement for those persons who want to be representatives if they have already served as representatives or senators (Article 107: 3). The Constitution does not exempt any group of persons from the college degree requirement if they want to serve as senators (Article 125: 3).

18 For example, naturalized Thai citizens may now vote after five years, instead of ten (Constitution 1997, Article 105: 1; Constitution 1991, Article 109: 1). Thai nationals whose fathers were aliens no longer need to meet additional requirements in order to seek elected office (Constitution 1991, Article 111: 1). Inability to hear and to speak no longer automatically disqualified citizens who wanted to run for a post (Constitution 1991, Article 113: 4).

19 ICCPR, Article 25. The ICCPR also states that these rights may not be restricted on the basis of 'race, colour, sex, language, religion, political or other opinion, national or social origin, property, birth or other status' (Article 2).

20 Committee on Civil and Political Rights (1996, Article 4).

21 If the purpose of the provision is to excuse certain types of Buddhists from the obligation to vote, then the Constitution should contain a provision that permits those persons not to cast ballots.

22 'If there are more than 120 applicants, politicians will be favoured; seats are guaranteed for them', said the Dean of the Faculty of Political Science at Ramkhamhaeng University (*The Nation*, 28 October 1999).

23 Review occurs upon the request of the prime minister or a requisite number of representatives or senators (see Constitution 1997, Article 262; Constitution 1991, Article 205).

24 Review may occur if the constitutional body has not made a decision regarding the challenged law, rule or regulation (see Constitution 1997, Article 264; Constitution 1991, Article 206).

7

DEMOCRATIZATION AND SOCIAL WELFARE IN THAILAND

Johannes Dragsbæk Schmidt

INTRODUCTION

On 2 July 1997 the Thai government was forced to do what it had sworn for months it would never do; it abandoned a steady rate policy in relation to the US dollar, and the baht was subsequently untied from its dollar peg. First the value of the currency fell by more than 20 per cent, then another 40 per cent, and with that started what the international media pronounced the financial crisis in East Asia. However, the background to this crisis was somewhat different to that portrayed by the leading media. The crisis proved to have serious consequences not only in the region, but also in other parts of the world economy.

What is interesting in this connection is that the multilateral organizations before the crisis praised Thailand as 'Asia's Fifth Tiger' and a number of East Asia's economies were held up as development icons for their open economies and high growth rates (World Bank 1993; Bullard 1998). Three years after the onset of the crisis, it was hard to miss the open wounds in Thailand's economy. On Bangkok's Ploenchit Road there was an almost-completed multi-storey building meant to serve as the headquarters of one of Thailand's most aggressive lenders, Finance One. But the company never moved in: its 1997 share price declined to 4 per cent of its 1996 level. A government bailout was priced at an estimated 166 billion baht (US$6.7 billion), or 3.5 per cent of Thailand's GDP.

Once touted as Southeast Asia's fastest-growing economy, Thailand was facing a prolonged period of hardship. The institutions mistakenly appointed to deal with the crisis by international society did not really seek to support maimed Asian economies, but entered Thailand to secure and protect Western investors and banks. One of the reasons why the World Bank and IMF did not react to the considerable incurring of debts was that unlike similar debt crises in most Third World countries – and, as illustrated in the case of Finance One – Thailand's debts had been raised by the private sector, and not by the state.

The genesis of the crisis lay in the way the country had opened its doors to foreign capital. Thailand liberalized by allowing domestic investors access to cheap offshore funds through the Bangkok International Banking Facility (BIBF), launched in 1992. But it made the mistake of keeping the baht pegged to the US dollar. With no concern about currency devaluation, freewheeling Thai speculators borrowed freely and imprudently, without hedging (*Far Eastern Economic Review*, 12 June 1997). Actually the crisis was a result of under-regulation rather than of over-regulation as the spokesmen of globalization claim. Naturally, the crisis has affected Thailand's political economy in a number of ways. This analysis will in particular point to the social tensions and differences of what started as a financial crisis, but which quickly escalated into a structural social crisis. The basic argument is that the so-called financial crisis in Asia has intensified the need for a Japanese-style welfare model rather than proving its disadvantages.[1] Thailand cannot rely on economic growth alone. It has to improve the qualifications of its labour force and its infrastructure. Comparative experience suggests that 'a social security scheme – if it works efficiently – can have a positive impact on the skills and health of the labour force' (Reinecke 1993: 79).

Before the onset of the crisis, Thai policymakers had hoped that Bangkok could become the region's top offshore financial centre, although it remains unclear where the major impetus for the policy of deregulation of the financial sector came from. Under the BIBF, banks could get funding in US dollars at lower US rates and then lend to Thai customers. For domestic borrowers with revenues in baht, there was little currency risk because the baht was pegged to a currency basket, in which the dollar accounted for around 80 per cent. By 1995, BIBF liabilities had soared to more than 25 per cent of Thai GDP, and this wave of money was not spent on increasing productive capacity. The aversion to confronting debtors reflects the close-knit and powerful domestic vested economic interests which had long been actively involved in a politico-bureaucratic alliance.[2]

The economic boom years gave rise to all kinds of speculation, and a growing 'no problem'-cum-repressive attitude on the part of the Thai economic and political elite. As long as the major social contradictions in Thai society could be held at bay by high economic growth rates and foreign capital, democratization and demands for greater distribution of resources and social entitlements could not enter the policy agenda. After the crisis hit Thai society, growing unemployment and its accompanying potential social instability offered scope to break the dominance of Bangkok's big business politician-cum-bureaucrat alliance, and provide greater space for genuine political representation for the working population: the peasantry and the working class.

The absence of social protection and the historically low priority given to social policy expenditures in Thailand, are a reflection of choices about social and economic policy. Thus, as long as sustained economic growth continued, there was a tendency to persist in the belief that poverty would disappear as a consequence of market allocations. This, together with a reliance on traditional support systems through the family and a few royal-sponsored charitable foundations, resulted in limited priority being given to a government-sponsored universal social safety-net based on redistribution and solidarity.

DEMOCRACY AND PATERNALISM

Most definitions of democracy reflect an ideal situation which states and nations strive to attain. Democratization is a never-ending process emanating from below, which is defined as a concept involving power relations and constellations in society and the state. Democratization is concerned with social, political and human rights, the right to free speech, organizational freedom (such as labour rights) and other popular demands directed at the state. In general, democratization – the devolution of state power from military dictators and one-party bureaucracies to civilian democrats – can be seen as a political response to a generic economic crisis. It forms part and parcel of the hegemony of neo-liberalism, as seen in the concerted efforts of state bureaucrats to demilitarize, privatize and demercantilize the state and the economy in order to respond to globalization, resolve outstanding economic problems, and lay the basis for economic growth (Schaeffer 1993: 170).

Instead of presenting democracy as an ideal political system that humans only imperfectly realize, it is the aim here to conceptualize democracy and democratization as a political process that is repeatedly reinvented. Instead of treating the political institutions and practices as exclusively a product of separate national histories and cultures, one aim of this contribution is to add the importance of economic flows across national frontiers and the ways in which those in power in different countries influence one another. Instead of reducing democracy to well-defined routine practices and institutions such as elections and parliaments, it is argued that social movements repeatedly challenge and transform existing institutions.

Democracy carries within it not only the conflicts of the present moment, but is also the legacy of past waves of democratization, which have shaped what is meant by democracy. It is mirrored in any comparison of regime-forms and levels of authoritarianism ('semi', 'soft' and 'hard' authoritarianism, for example), transitions and creation of temporary political pacts. Thailand exhibits quite different patterns of 'democracy' from the mainstream definition.

Thailand has been a political regime in transition since 1932. Until the mid-1970s, the regime comprised a narrow elite drawn from the army officer corps in alliance with senior bureaucrats. Virtually all other sectors were excluded from policy-making, and the regime type was based on paternalism and authoritarianism. Thailand went through three major political events: 1973, 1976 and 1992. Each of them was treated differently by the state. One important reason why Thailand has experienced a switching pattern between democracy and authoritarian regime forms is not only a political, but also a social problem (for details, see Schmidt 1993).

In contrast to Thailand, American democracy was shaped by an English heritage, empty spaces and free land, the absence of an aristocracy, massive immigration, vertical and horizontal social mobility, minimal government, and a pervasive middle-class liberal ethos. No similar combination of factors exists anywhere in Asia (Huntington 1994: 37–38). In fact, permanent democracy is rare. A series of switches in and out of democracy has been the norm, and this underscores the different historical and contemporary dilemma of Thai democracy, based on the interaction of socio-economic and political influences.

The dilemma for Thailand of having to face the external pressures of economic competition at the same time as internal demands for democracy and welfare are growing, is related to its type of economy. Various statistical studies show that much of Thailand's growth has been driven by a massive increase in domestic labour force participation as well as capital, critical parts of which have come from abroad. But these inputs have been difficult to sustain (Asher 1997). This not only implied the levelling off of high rates of growth, but also made a transition to higher levels of social security more difficult, as such a transition could acutely impinge on the international competitiveness of the economy (Asher 1995). Furthermore, economic growth has been characterized as a process of impoverishment, marginalization and increasing inequality in income distribution. Over the past three decades, this transition has led to several important trends, and has primarily meant expansion of industrial output and services. But social welfare and the needs of the rural areas have been largely neglected. In rural areas this occurred through an increase in economic inequality and an uneven distribution of land and other productive assets, an increase in the relative size of the class of agricultural labourers, and stagnation or decline in rural wages. Considerable inflationary pressures have emerged; and, more generally, the relative price of food has tended to rise as growth proceeded.[3] This situation has been even more complicated since the financial-cum-social crisis started in July 1997.

The reasons behind the policy shift to export orientation and deregulation in Thailand have differed in a number of ways from the Korean and Taiwanese NIC experience.[4] In the Thai case,

> the external factors for policy reform were the inflow of international capital and the relocation of light industries into the country. The internal factors were pressure from the local business sector, liberal technocrats and foreign advisors advocating a more liberal development strategy. (Sungsidh and Kanchada 1994: 249–250)

For instance, as early as 1980 a representative from big business, Paul Sithi-Amnuai, tested public response to some elements of future economic policies. He suggested that the traditional bureaucracy–business antagonisms arose from the fact that business activities were historically controlled by the Chinese and Europeans. This distrust had been so traditionally ingrained in Thailand's bureaucratic structure that the image held by officials of the private sector was of a bunch of exploitative middlemen, who needed to be controlled. He then argued that if the bureaucracy and businesspeople were to cooperate, business matters should be decided upon by businessmen or technocrats. His preference was for the appointment of an 'economic tsar from the private sector to run the economy, who could cut through red tape and committees to solve key bottle-neck problems. Another idea was to offer tax incentives for private firms to adopt individual villages, so that 'we would have 1,000 rural villages being helped by private sector entrepreneurs who would not only use their management skills in helping the villages get developed', but also provide the adopted villagers with jobs as 'maids, drivers, guards, factory cleaners [and] messengers' (*Far Eastern Economic Review*, 21 March 1980).

These arguments were echoed after the crisis in 1997 when Democrat MP Supachai Panitchpakdi, who was also a director of Thai Finance and Securities, remarked: 'We have to nurture the private sector because they are in tattered shape'.[5] He compared the 91 troubled finance companies to a convalescing patient and called for a one-off capital injection (ibid., 12 June 1997: 73–74). The often intimate links between the Bangkok polity and big business were one reason why central bank exchange controls were lifted so easily, and why banking deregulation and investment became much easier (ibid., 6 December 1990). However, in order to comprehend the background for this policy shift, it is necessary to understand the labour market and social policy of Thailand, at least as they are seen from the policy and business elite's point of departure, and how they have impacted on the handling of the crisis.

LABOUR MARKET REFORMS AND SOCIAL WELFARE

Labour discipline and peaceful industrial labour are always a prerequisite for export-oriented industrialisation development based on cheap labour. The disciplined labour pool in Thailand since mid-1970s has resulted from the political exclusion of labour through the indirect intervention of the state. First, the state created a legal framework for industrial relations which encouraged weak and fragmented unionism. Second, indirect control of labour was established through institutional conditions for wage negotiation in the labour market. Those are some of the reasons why labour union activity in Thailand in a historical perspective has been weak, and why organized labour has only recently been able to influence the public agenda of social and labour welfare to any significant degree. Although unionization was relatively low, levels of strike activity increased sharply in the period 1995–97, involving between 8,000 and 14,000 workers each year. This overall picture has also had serious implications for the bargaining capacities and wage levels of the working class.

Although repression against workers has been severe, Thailand has several tripartite committees covering a variety of social policy spheres, and having differing degrees of statutory authority, from the purely advisory to actual decision-making responsibility and authority. Tripartism in Thailand must be described as very weak, based as it is on fragile and internally fragmented organizations of workers and employers.

Tripartite instruments and procedures have nevertheless played a role in policy guidance on the economic and social consequences of the crisis.[6] Three initiatives are of particular relevance.

- First, the National Labour Development Advisory Council (NLDAC), an advisory body to the government, established a Subcommittee on the Social Effects of the Economic Crisis in October 1997.

- Second, the labour court system has had an important role to play in safeguarding labour protection amidst worsening economic conditions. By September 1997, the system's nine-month caseload numbered 12,073, already exceeding all annual totals in its 17-year history. Over 80 per cent of the cases in 1997, moreover, concerned severance pay entitlements (in 1985 this issue accounted for 52 per cent of disputes heard).

- The third initiative was the creation in December 1997 of the National Committee on the Alleviation of Unemployment, apparently in response to one of the recommendations of the National Tripartite Forum.

At the root of what may be described as a weak basis for tripartism are the continued constraints on freedom of association. In fact, the credibility of the officially sanctioned and legally recognized national trade union centre is very much eroded now, and workers with grievances – including members of the official unions – are increasingly looking elsewhere for representation. Since recent initiatives to develop independent and democratic trade unions have been contained by government repression, workers' organizations are forced to operate beyond the ambit of the law and often clandestinely; they are effectively unable to criticize government policies and programmes (ILO 1998).

The key problem, no matter how one defines democracy, has been political representation. Labour and other marginalized groups have never had an institutionalized voice in the political arena, except for a brief period between 1973 and 1976. Historical evidence shows clearly that this is not a matter of 'new politics', but is related to repression and outlawing of alternatives to the dominant discourse of neo-liberal growth, exports and elite paternalism.

The investments of transnational companies tend to be less sensitive to social concerns as well as to political pressures of national and regional authorities. Transnational workers in Thailand have in most cases been inhibited from having autonomous workers' organizations defending their standards of living through collective action, and then are almost wholly dependent upon the goodwill of management.

Evidence shows that because of the very few state schemes for improving the income and welfare of employees in order to catch up with inflation, workers' demands initially concentrated on wage increases. But this pattern has been changing. This is clear from the fact that 'major issues of labour disputes from 1987 to 1989 concerned welfare (33 per cent), wages (20 per cent), conditions of employment (18 per cent), and other issues (29 per cent)' (Sungsidh and Kanchada 1994: 241).

The struggle to obtain social security protection in Thailand dates back to the 1950s, but in the late 1980s renewed pressure through public demonstrations and campaigns from the Labour Congress and Trade Union Congress resulted in the promulgation of the Social Security Act of 1990 (Brown and Frenkel 1993: 104). The first phase was implemented in 1992 and covered health insurance, maternity benefit, disability benefit and death benefit. The scheme was financed by employers, employees and the government each paying 1.5 per cent of wages as contributions, but since then a serious debate about the second phase has arisen (Asher 1995: 16). Although labour, comparatively speaking, is weak in terms of bargaining capacity, and not very well organised, it was a major force behind the enactment of the Social

Security Act. Reinecke argues that in the process leading up to the enactment:

1) The labour movement showed more unity and a better long-term strategy in its quest for social security than in the past.
2) The relatively united stand of the labour movement facilitated the cooperation with the professionals. NGOs and academics took part in campaigns for social security, and the press was supportive of the law.
3) The power struggle between the bureaucratic elite and the economic elite forced the latter to accept demands of the labour movement and the professionals in its search for 'coalition partners'. (Reinecke 1993: 90)

After the crisis, in January 1998, a government survey of workers returning to rural (non-municipal) areas placed the figure at 188,000 people. Relative to each region's rural population, the highest proportion returned to the Northeast. This pattern of return migration puts pressure precisely on the weakest parts of the Thai agricultural sector. At the end of 1997, the North and Northeast were hit particularly hard by drought. These regions had furthermore evolved an economy in which remittances from urban areas played a major role in sustaining living standards (ILO 1998). Although circular migration has always been a specific characteristic of the Thai economy, the situation had changed.

In conclusion, there is no institutional apparatus through which dialogue on the consequences of the crisis of enterprise-level adjustment might occur. Of course, the absence of the sort of formal mechanisms for dialogue provided for by labour law does not necessarily mean the absence of dialogue – nor indeed does it imply the absence of good, cooperative labour–management relations. Although well developed, cooperative labour–management relations in a few non-union enterprises do exist, the evidence also suggests that such examples are likely to be in the minority, and slower to diffuse in the absence of a well-developed trade union movement (ILO 1998). This situation begs the question whether Thailand has followed a specifically 'East Asian' social policy and what type of reforms can be expected as a consequence of the crisis.

SOCIAL SECURITY AND WELFARE IN THAILAND

The study of welfare as an aspect of social policy rather than economic policy has been neglected. The concept of social policy should emphasize 'all forms of collective interventions such as fiscal, occupational and social programmes that contribute to general welfare, and focus on the rationale, objectives and social consequences of public policies dealing with welfare – in the how, why and what of social policy (Jayasuriya 1996: 1). What is of importance is to study the impact of the policy instruments on which this chapter concentrates on the link between democratization, labour market reform and social welfare, trying to locate the nexus between the redistributive potential of welfare policies and the level of equality of recipients of welfare. The question is how to define the Thai developmental state in this regard; or, in other words, where does Thailand fit in?

Until the formation of an industrial working class and urbanization, pressures for social protection on Thai governments were limited.[7] Thus policy-makers and élites have been able to interpret the past in order to justify their lack of enthusiasm for Western-type welfare states. In 1983 Prime Minister Prem Tinsulanond expressed Thai conservative elite thinking when he stressed that

> culturally the Thai behaviour and way of life are inactive ... Lack of ambition is the big enemy of the Thai way of life ... The democratic government must take some action by the establishment of the Department of Public Welfare as the tool for action. (Yupa 1985: 357, 363)

Hewison observes that

> King Bhumibol has adopted this perspective. Taking the US as his example, he has argued that millions are spent on welfare, stating that access to welfare is a 'constitutional right' in that country, but that this has several negative aspects:
>
> '[T]hese jobless individuals will not be willing to work; they can apply for public welfare and they get it. These people refuse to work ... The ... individual on welfare will be a useless person for the community and even for himself. Furthermore, he will be a ponderous burden on society.'

Then, turning to Thailand, he argues that to allow the development of a welfare system would cause suffering:

> 'We would be squandering our national budget by giving charity from the money earned by hard-working people from whom taxes are levied, to those who make it a point not to work. Thailand is not like that. Everybody works, some more, some less, but everybody works.' (Hewison 1997a: 66–67)

The implication of this paternalistic ideology of the elite has been a conscious state welfare ideology more inclined to charity than responding to social pressures for public services.

In the beginning of the 1980s, the Thai Department of Welfare (DPW) spent less than 0.5 per cent of the total government budget on social benefits (Yupa 1985: 363). In the 1990s, official social security schemes (covered by the Social Security Act) were available only to formal sector workers in the civil service and those working in enterprises employing ten or more workers. Those working in the informal sector did not receive protection under the labour law, nor were they covered by social security provisions (Pasuk *et al.* 1995: 151). However, as mentioned above, the Thai Parliament did vote in favour of a Social Security Act in July 1990, and the legislation was introduced in March 1991. In its first stage, the scheme covered private enterprises in the non-agricultural sector with 20 or more employers, employees and the government paying each 1.5 per cent of wages as contribution. Four benefits are in force:

- health insurance (medical treatment and 50 per cent of wages);
- maternity benefits (child delivery expenses and 50 per cent of wages);
- disability benefit (medical treatment and 50 per cent of wages);
- and death benefit (lump sum to cover funeral costs). (Reinecke 1993: 78–79)

The consequence of this low coverage and a very ineffective implementation of the new scheme has been that Thailand experiences severe problems of social exclusion due to uneven development and unfair institutional arrangements, such as inadequate provision of basic social goods (Pasuk *et al.* 1995: 159). These comparatively low expenditures on social welfare are not a coincidence, but are closely related to the predominant development model which is based on export. Although the number of insured workers almost doubled in two years, the attitude of the political elite did not change. This was reflected in Deputy Interior Minister Charoenchit na Songkhla's remark that he wanted 'to organize social benefits as well as possible to further reduce the role of the trade unions' (*Matichon*, 16 August 1991, cited in Reinecke 1993: 92).

Turning to the post-crisis context, the DPW had a responsibility for looking after underprivileged target groups, including people with disabilities, women, the elderly, children and beggars. DPW reported that it saw a sharp increase in the numbers of the socially excluded. DPW managed the 2,000 baht grant scheme, as well as the 10,000 baht loan scheme, under which one day of enterprise training was provided for borrowers.[8]

The existing severance pay legislation in Thailand provides for only modest benefits amounting to six months' wages for workers who have been in a job for three years or more. Under a special provision, higher payments are due to workers with six years' employment or more who are made redundant as a result of the introduction of new machinery or technology (ILO 1998).

Thailand's Labour Protection Act, adopted in 1998, provides for higher severance pay for workers with longer periods of employment.

Those who have been in the job six to ten years will be entitled to eight months' pay, and those with ten years, or more service will receive ten months' pay. Although the intention of the legislation was no doubt to provide better protection to workers, it seemed likely that in the short term it would have the perverse effect of encouraging employers to terminate workers' employment before these more costly provisions came into force. Trade unions therefore asked the Ministry of Labour to issue an interim law (ibid.).

In addition to largely urban concerns about inadequate labour rights, educational inequalities are reinforcing the urban–rural divide. Thailand's secondary-school enrolment is the lowest in ASEAN after Vietnam. In 1990, almost half the children who completed primary school did not go on to receive a secondary education. This generation is now entering the workforce, and will be another obstacle to tackling the economic slowdown. Thus low spending on education coupled with increasing unemployment points to new problems in the rural areas, which relate to the long-running debates about land reform and decentralization.

SOCIAL POLICY, THE OBSESSION WITH GROWTH AND THE IMPACT OF THE CRISIS

A papier-mâché dinosaur symbolized the government at a pre-crisis rally in 1997 in Bangkok, where 10,000 poor farmers demanded that the state solve a string of land disputes mostly arising from the seizure of land by the central government. 'It's not just compensation for our land we're after.' Forum of the Poor spokesman Bamrung Koyotha was quoted as saying: 'We are also challenging the political and economic system and demanding more participation for the people.' Their problems were related to the government's resistance to the needs of rural people, which in turn had created more paternalistic bureaucracy. Local officials are only responsible to the bureaucracy in Bangkok. Hence local people have been forced to turn to their MPs, some of whom are engaged in strong-arm tactics and illegal activities. In 1996 the Thai Farmers' Bank Research Centre estimated that as much as 2.6 trillion baht was earned annually in the underground economy, equivalent to roughly 57 per cent of Thailand's official GDP (*Far Eastern Economic Review*, 28 November 1996).

In Thailand 54,000 workers were recorded as retrenched over the period January 1997 to February 1998. Slightly more women than men were made redundant. The actual number of crisis-induced lay-offs is widely assumed to be substantially higher than the official number. Industry associations, for example, reported job losses of some 422,000 to the end of 1997.

With the onset of the crisis, the Ministry of Labour and Social Welfare (MOLSW) created 15 teams of Ministry officials which attempted to assist about 1,000 enterprises in about one year in finding alternatives to lay-offs. The MOLSW prepared a booklet outlining ways in which labour and production costs could be adjusted to avoid lay-offs. Finally, the MOLSW hosted three tripartite seminars in an effort to diffuse knowledge about ways in which employment could be preserved. The Ministry initiatives continued as part of the government's seven-measure programme to address the crisis. While the Ministry's initiatives were clearly positive, there is little information available on their impact.

According to the ILO (1998), due to the impact of the economic crisis and despite a range of initiatives to contain the social costs, the overall picture is that the policy response has been inadequate. In particular, efforts to cater for the large numbers of displaced workers cover only a small fraction of those in need of such relief. In addition, there has been virtually nothing in the way of temporary income support in the form of either unemployment benefits or social assistance to make up for the shortfall in the coverage of direct employment creation measures.

CONCLUDING REMARKS

There are two fundamental reasons why Thailand is in its current state of social distress. The first is the sheer magnitude of the social fallout. This would have put serious stress even on countries with better-developed systems of social protection. The second was the lack of preparedness and underdevelopment of the social protection system itself. Legislation on social security was almost permanently 'in preparation' between 1952 and 1988, without any decisive step being taken towards its implementation (Reinecke 1993: 83). Furthermore, discourses on both the left and right in the Thai political context have relied on the idea that 'civil society' can replace the role of the state.

The basic argument in this analysis has been that 'civil society' (at least in its mainstream understanding) cannot replace the state. Rather, it should put great efforts into pressurizing the state to take up basic responsibilities and enhance developmental and regulatory state capacities and responsibilities in accordance with the country's level of development. There is a great danger that the current over-emphasis on 'civil society' detracts or hijacks the focus away from what is of immediate importance in any country with high levels of poverty, inequality and social crisis. If civil society can include social groupings and strata such as organized labour and the peasantry, it can work more effectively. As recent examples have shown, the labour movement was relatively successful in pushing for the Social Security Act despite resistance from the entrenched politico-business alliance.

Against this background it is important to note that social safety-nets cannot, realistically, be constructed in a short period of time. Similarly, measures such as attempts to save viable enterprises and active labour market policies can achieve only limited results when they go against the grain of macro-economic conditions.

Globally, 'flexibility' has become a buzzword, meaning the dismantling of the welfare state – even the sort of hybrid welfare state that exists in Thailand. However, this issue is apparently being contested from below by demands for democratization and social reforms. The problematique regarding social welfare in Thailand has followed the neo-liberal ideology of globalization, which is essentially a matter of identifying needs, solving problems and creating opportunities at the individual level. The causes behind the need for support are believed to rest overwhelmingly with individuals, on the basis of subcultural defects and dispositions. Responsibility is deflected from states and national economic, administrative and legal organizations to individuals and groups. Little or no attention is paid to the interacting consequences of economic and social change for families, employment, taxation, housing, social security and public services. *Laissez-faire* individualism and the legitimization of discrimination are in fact the intellectual sources of this tradition. This is why the macro-economic dogma characterized by neo-classical and neo-institutionalist explanations claims that high economic growth leads to significant general improvements in the living conditions and incomes of the poor. However, the Thai experience contests the validity of this assertion. Despite high growth rates the reduction in poverty, though significant, has been comparatively modest. The rate of decline has not been enough to bring about any significant fall in the absolute number of the poor.

The particular Thai version of social welfare is in practice closely based on welfare theories about social philanthropy which, implicitly and sometimes explicitly, contradict ideas of democratization from below. It is difficult to discern anything specifically 'Asian' in this theory. Rather, it rests on a particular ideology that is used as a repressive tool to discipline labour's demands for social security and, in general, to limit demands that could humanize and socialize work and living conditions and economic relations. Just as the Great Depression forged a new social contract in many industrialized countries in the 1930s, the post-1997 Asian crisis may serve as an impetus to create a more socially oriented model of development.

NOTES

1 See the discussion about the relevance of the Japanese model to Thailand in Schmidt 1996.

2   This statement is a matter of great dispute; a new body of literature with a neo-institutionalist perspective points to concepts such as 'liberal corporatism' and 'inclusionary institutionalism' to illuminate a growing influence of business coalitions and associations challenging the autonomy of the state. For the most prominent, see Doner 1991; Likhit 1992; Anek 1992a and 1992b. For a discussion of the Korean context, see Wade 1990, 1996, and for an example of an integrated synthesis, see Cotton 1991. For a critique of the neo-institutionalist perspective in the Thai context, see Schmidt 1996.

3   Before there can be income distribution in favour of the rural poor, there has to be a prior redistribution of the income-generating assets, notably land, water rights, productive equipment and livestock. The need for land reform in this broad sense arises both because the present structure of asset holdings may obstruct technological change and because it is the most effective, perhaps the only, instrument of combining growth with the right sort of distributive biases. See also the interview with Ajit K. Ghose and Keith Griffin (*Far Eastern Economic Review*, 13 July 1979)

4   Korea and Taiwan kept foreign capital at bay and only allowed a very small amount of non-national capital acquisition to take place. For a discussion about the role of foreign capital in the Northeast and Southeast Asian NICs and would-be NICs, see Schmidt 1997a, 1997b.

5   Later that year, Supachai became deputy prime minister in charge of economic matters, and was subsequently selected to take over as head of the World Trade Organization.

6   This and the following four instances of tripartism are cited in ILO 1998.

7   For an interesting discussion in a historical perspective of attempts to introduce social policy reforms in Thailand, starting with the Pridi government in 1932 and leading up to the enactment of the Social Security Act in 1990, see Reinecke (1993: 78–115).

8   This and the following examples are adapted from ILO 1998.

PART II

THE POPULAR SECTOR

8

CIVIL SOCIETY AND STREET POLITICS IN HISTORICAL PERSPECTIVE

James Ockey

A new ideal was born, or reborn, in recent decades: Civil Society ... the phrase itself had no living resonance or evocativeness. Rather, it seemed distinctly covered with dust. And now, all of a sudden, it has been taken out and thoroughly dusted, and has become a shining emblem. (Gellner 1994: 1)

The blood and tears of the people, the shouts of dissent and the stout hearts in protesting those things with which the people do not agree have been recorded in the annals of democracy. (*Sanseri*, 23 January 1956)

The sudden emergence in this country of a public opinion having an impact on Government policy and Government unity is the most striking development during my three years here ...There is no doubt that it is here to stay. (British Ambassador Nicholas Gage, 29 May 1956)[1]

22 January 1956 marked perhaps the longest protest march ever held in Bangkok. Thousands marched from Sanam Luang to the parliament, then back to Sisao Thewet and to Ban Manangasila, before marching out to Prime Minister Phibun's residence at Soi Chitlom. The Thai press, in reporting the event, announced that it would be recorded by history, and remembered as a great victory for democracy. Yet, despite this prophecy, the march has been completely forgotten.[2] Why has it disappeared from the record of Thai democracy? And what does its loss teach us about civil society, constitutional reform and Thai politics?

All too often, political scientists write as if the history of Thai democracy began in 1973. Yet if we are to understand the changes in street politics, civil society, and the politics of reform in the 1990s, we will certainly benefit by enhancing our understanding of earlier periods of protest and reform. In this chapter, I shall examine some of the events of the 1955–57 period, paying particular attention to civil society, reform and street politics. I shall attempt to explain the reasons why events of the period have been forgotten. I shall then try to draw some comparisons between politics, civil society and reform in the 1950s and in the 1990s.

As Somchai points out (Chapter 9, this volume), civil society has been defined in a variety of ways in the literature. For our purposes, we can take Somchai's definition of civil society as that sphere between state and economy where people can organize autonomously. In other words, civil society consists of organized groups outside the control of the state. In examining civil society in the 1950s, we shall look at three elements: 1) Do potential groups exist which could be organized? 2) Do organizations exist? 3) Are the organizations outside the control of the state? Of course, important political events may also be largely unorganized, particularly demonstrations and protests. This type of politics I shall call street politics.[3] I shall begin by examining street politics in the 1950s, then turn briefly to civil society before examining the relationship between the two.

THE ORIGINS OF THAILAND'S HYDE PARK

The forgotten protest march had its origins in the round-the-world tour of Prime Minister Plaek Phibunsongkhram, in 1955. It was Phibun's first trip abroad since his student days, some 27 years earlier (Department of State 1989: 807–8). Among the countries Phibun visited were both the United States and Britain. Phibun returned to Thailand in June, apparently determined to accelerate the reforms begun in January, when a bill to decentralize political power and initiate local elections had been introduced. Phibun's decision to promote democracy may have been buttressed by the knowledge that during his absence, his once-loyal follower, Police Chief Phao Siyanon, had planned a coup (primarily against General Sarit Thanarat) and had only called it off at the last minute (ibid.: 827–28; Fineman, 1997: 216). At any rate, Phibun began to pursue reform policies that opened up the opportunity for greater participation in Thai politics. He also contended that coups were out-dated, because of the rise of the media and the development of various 'organizations' in society (*Sanseri*, 20 August 1955).

Among the early reforms, one in particular opened up opportunities for participation. Phibun announced in August that he would allow the establishment of a Hyde Park-style Speakers' Corner at Sanam Luang in central Bangkok. No doubt Phibun knew that a Speakers' Corner would lead to criticisms of the highly unpopular Police Chief Phao. Perhaps he even encouraged some speakers to attack Phao. Yet even Phibun did not anticipate the response to the establishment of the Speakers' Corner. Within six months he was forced to ban the fledgling institution.

Speakers' Corner at Sanam Luang attracted a wide variety of speakers, including opposition members of parliament such as Oraphin Chaiyakan, Thep Chotinuchit and Khlaeo Norapatdi, as well as reporters, the leaders of pedicab (*samlo*) and street vendor groups, provincial politicians, and would-be politicians. Initially meetings were organized almost like forums, with sessions scheduled to discuss topics such as educational policy, the Social Security Act and the role of women in politics. Later a group of regular speakers developed who did most of the speaking. For most meetings during this six-month period microphones and loudspeakers were allowed; crowds were reported to have numbered in the tens of thousands on some occasions, and generally averaged several thousand, rather than the dozen or so listening to each speaker at Hyde Park in London.[4] This, too, when the total population of Bangkok was only about one million.

Although Thailand's Hyde Park began as a discussion forum for government policies, before long it became an avenue for street politics. The first protest march was scheduled for 18 September, in order to protest against the Social Security Act. However, the first march occurred a day earlier, on 17 September, when police decided to ban loudspeakers for the third Saturday meeting of Hyde Park, so that there could be several competing speakers and smaller audiences, just as in London.[5] When police confiscated the microphone, some of the popular speakers from earlier meetings led about 200 listeners to nearby Chanasongkhram police station to protest. The protestors refused to leave until after police met with their leaders and explained the situation. Later in the week, Phibun lifted the ban.

In the ensuing months, the nature of Hyde Park changed considerably. Members of parliament largely disappeared from the platform. Topics began to focus less on policies and more on personalities, particularly Police Chief Phao, and on political reforms, including constitutional reform. And increasingly, speakers and listeners began to make demands and go on protest marches.

Hyde Park at Sanam Luang received a big boost in October, when Phethai Chotinuchit, an opposition MP, returned from London, where he had been studying democracy. Phethai publicly announced that he would speak at Hyde Park, and that he would sacrifice his blood there in order to 'awaken' democracy. The press ridiculed him, saying that this was not the behaviour of 'people who reason'; nevertheless, Phethai remained determined (*Sanseri*, 21 October 1955).

When the day arrived, large numbers of curious listeners turned up. Phethai began by telling the crowd that democracy is government of the people, by the people, and for the people. He then said that Thailand, in the past, had government by the king for the king; later, government was by Phibun for Phibun; currently it was by the Coup Group, for the Coup Group. Never had it been for the people. Phethai called for the dissolution of the Coup Group, and for the government to eliminate appointed MPs and the transitional provisions of the constitution. Phethai led up to his blood sacrifice by stating that when he was abroad, foreigners would ask about the Thai system of government, and when he told them it was democratic with appointed MPs, they would laugh at him. Thai blood, he declared, is as good as foreign blood, and he was willing to sacrifice his blood to sanctify the democracy to come. This, he claimed, would prove his sincerity. He then cut his forearm with a razor to loud shouts from the crowd. Some listeners came forward to dip their clothing in the blood. Some of the blood was collected in a glass. A second speaker then drank the blood from the glass, declaring that it was sacred. Phethai's older brother Thep also offered to cut himself for democracy, but the crowd forbade him (see *Bangkok Post*, 25 October 1955; *Sanseri*, 23 October 1955). Afterwards, the crowd marched to the King Chulalongkorn statue near the parliament in order to show their support for democracy.[6]

The drama of Phethai's speech and 'sacrifice' seems to have attracted people to Speakers' Corner who had never attended before, and for a time, crowd sizes increased. Furthermore, constitutional reform was placed more firmly on the agenda, although attacks on politicians and particularly on Police Chief Phao remained popular. Constitutional reform would be at the heart of an increase in protest activity later in the year.

There were numerous other meetings and protests during this period at Sanam Luang, and various attempts to sabotage Speakers' Corner, particularly by the police. It is within this context of street protest that what may have been the longest protest march in the history of Bangkok occurred. Again events began with an announcement of a blood sacrifice, this time before a crowd at Sanam Luang estimated at over 10,000 by the press. Chan Kratureuk, a retired police captain and a regular speaker, announced on 21 January that he would slash his chest to sacrifice blood in order to oppose a social security law that was awaiting the King's signature prior to coming into effect. This, he said, was necessary because a march would be too risky for the protesters, given past experiences (*Sanseri*, 22 January 1956).

Although the primary target of the demonstrations on this day was the Social Security Act, constitutional reform also was on the agenda. In particular, there was support for Prime Minister Phibun's election bill, which was more liberal than the alternative proposed by the Coup Group. As Chan said in his speech prior to slashing his chest:

This government is not composed of representatives elected by the people. The government controls the Assembly by paying assemblymen 2,000 baht each monthly. That is why the Assembly has been enacting laws against the wishes of the people. (*Bangkok Post*, 23 January 1956)

Shortly thereafter, Chan slashed his chest with a razor and began to collect the blood in a cup, to be used to write posters protesting against the Social Security Act. As Chan was filling a second cup, a young man leapt from the crowd. He shouted out that he was afraid that Chan's blood would be insufficient, and asked that, as a construction worker and a Thai citizen, he be allowed to contribute as well, which he did.

THE 22 JANUARY 1956 PROTEST MARCH

It may be argued that up until that time, much of what had gone on was scripted by people who had been hired by Phibun, though Chan was never accused of being in his employ, and neither Phi nor Thongyu (who probably were in Phibun's employ at that time) played prominent roles on this day. At any event, at that point matters went beyond Chan's announced intention. An occasional speaker, a young woman named Surat Miphakdi, seized one of the banners painted in blood and shouted out, 'Let's march with this to Democracy Monument' (*Bangkok Post*, 23 January 1956). Thus began the march.

Police and the Bangkok mayor, on hand to observe, were apparently taken by surprise, and were not prepared to stop the march. The demonstrators proceeded to Democracy Monument where they performed rites, including circling the monument three times. They then proceeded to the National Assembly. When it appeared that nothing would take place there, someone suggested that the demonstrators take the banners to Ban Amphon, to the King, who reportedly had yet to sign the Social Security Act. Although the marchers knew the King was not in residence, they thought he would return soon, and so they went to Ban Amphon, and gathered on both sides of the gates, leaving a space for the King's car. The King's bodyguard was called out to protect the gates. Eventually the marchers again tired of waiting, and someone suggested a march to Government House. When they arrived at Government House, they found no one there (it was a Sunday), and so they proceeded to nearby Wat Benjamabaphit (the Marble Temple) where more rites were performed. From there, the crowd went to ruling party headquarters at Ban Manangasila, which was also empty. During the march, the crowd chanted, not just the slogans prepared for the day, but of other issues of concern, including demands for the elimination of appointed MPs, calls for Police Chief Phao to resign, and 'we're hungry!' Finally they decided to march to Prime Minister Phibun's residence to take their petition to him personally. By the time they arrived at Soi Chitlom, where the prime minister resided, it was somewhere between 8.00 and 9.00 pm. Some had dropped out during the course of the day, while others had joined. Yet at nearly 9.00 pm, at the end of a long march, the crowd was still large enough to block traffic, and was estimated by the *Bangkok Post*, which generally provided the lowest estimates of crowd size, at 1,500 people. Police met them at the entrance to the street, blocking their way to the prime minister's house. The protesters then decided to sit in until dawn, blocking the road. Despite the calls of one leader for the crowd to return home, they refused. Chan himself reportedly went home at that point, but the crowd stayed on (*Sanseri*, 24 January 1956). The impasse was finally resolved when Phibun arrived on the scene. He inquired about the reasons for the demonstrations, then asked the crowd to return home. They then dispersed (*Bangkok Post*, 23 January 1956; *Sanseri*, 23 January 1956).

THE USE OF HUNGER STRIKES

Before leaving the events of this early period of Bangkok's Hyde Park, one more event should be described. The end of this first stage of the Hyde Park era came a month later. Again, the goal was constitutional reform, particularly the elimination of appointed MPs. This time the technique was a hunger strike, beginning on February 19, led by Thongyu Phutphat. Twenty-three others signed up for the hunger strike. Thongyu and most of the fasters began the day under the makham trees at Government House, the chosen locale for the protest. A few of the fasters began at Sanam Luang, holding the usual speeches in front of thousands of listeners. At Sanam Luang, at 4.00 pm, one of the fasters shaved his head, stating that if the prime minister eliminated the appointed MPs within a week, he would become a monk and offer the merit for his actions to the prime minister. Thereafter, a speaker announced that Thongyu had asked them not to march, fearing that it might lead to a disturbance. This advice was ignored. When Chan told the crowd that there should be no march, but that those who wanted to show support should go on their own, thousands started off down Ratchadamnoen Avenue. The police attempted to block the road with fire engines at several points, but the crowd pushed on through. At about 6.30 pm, the marchers arrived at Democracy Monument, where more speeches were held while leaders met with the police. The police forbade speechmaking at Democracy Monument, but the speaking went on. Thereafter, the police took protest leaders in a police vehicle to Government House in the hope that the march would break up, yet the crowd marched on. At Government House, they shouted out their support for the fasters. Meanwhile the fast was underway at Government House, with Thongyu leading the fasters in Buddhist rites in the evening. He announced: 'The Field Marshal [Phibun] and I once swore an oath together in the House of Representatives. I love the truth, but what about the Field Marshal?' (*Sanseri*, 20 January 1956). Police monitored the fast and limited visitors to the fasters.

The next morning began with a visit from Police Chief Phao, on his way to a meeting at Government House. He checked with the police on duty and was told that the fasters had waited until dark, then had secretly eaten; this was also reported to Phibun and the press, perhaps in an attempt to undermine the efforts of the fasters. Phao mocked ex-police officer Bunyang, saying, 'You are only good at speaking. When matters get serious, you can't succeed (*lue man di tae phut pho oao jinjing ko tham mai dai*)' (*ibid.*). Then he ordered that no further visitors be allowed, so that the meditation of the fasters would not be disturbed, and he left. This ridicule continued when the prime minister had some of his subordinates set up an elaborate feast for the hunger strikers. Deeply offended, they took the food and fed it to a stray dog. When the dog was at first hesitant, one protester exclaimed, 'Look, even the dog has a sense of democracy' (*Bangkok Post*, 21 February 1956).

The fast lasted just one more day. Then on the following day, the fasters were arrested. Public gatherings were banned, not just at Sanam Luang, but nationwide. The Ministry of the Interior report on the incident explained that the arrests and the ban were necessary because some had taken advantage of the democratic initiatives to speak unjustly against the government and to lead the people to favour communism.[7] Thongyu continued his fast during his time in jail and after his release – in all for 24 days. True to his word, he did not re-enter the political arena, and later became a monk for the rest of his life.

Speakers' Corner went through several evolutions after this early period. At one point, it became a platform for hired speakers with specific agendas, most notably *Chang nga daeng*, or Red Tusk Elephant, who spoke on the regicide of Rama VIII. During the run-up to the February 1957 election, political party rallies took over Speakers' Corner, with the regular speakers forming a party of their own, the Hyde Park Movement Party, and holding meetings with the rest. After the election, the Hyde Park Movement Party and some of its socialist allies continued to hold regular rallies. In the final summer of the Phibun regime, students took on a larger role, holding their own Hyde Park meeting at Sanam Luang on one occasion. During the no-confidence debate in parliament in August, a public meeting was held to explain the debate, and the results, to the public. Finally, as the end of the Phibun regime neared, students and Hyde Park regulars combined to support Sarit in his conflict with Phibun and Phao, and marched together to

Government House to call for Phibun to step down. It was this event which helped trigger the Sarit coup. While the role of the students is well known, the Hyde Park speakers have largely disappeared from descriptions of that protest. Why has the Hyde Park movement been so universally ignored, or, when it is discussed, so thoroughly disparaged? And what can we learn of street politics, constitutional reform and civil society in the 1950s and in modern-day Thailand from this depiction?

THE HYDE PARK SPEAKERS

Perhaps the most important reason why Thailand's Hyde Park and the associated street politics have been ignored or even forgotten is the belief that it was a sham, instituted by Phibun for his own purposes. Hyde Park is thought to be a sham as the speakers at Hyde Park were hired by political leaders to promote their own points of view. Therefore, Hyde Park was not about civil society, nor did it represent the views of the people. These contentions need to be analysed in some detail, as they reveal much of the thinking about street politics and civil society.

Were the speakers at Sanam Luang hired by leading politicians? Some almost certainly were. Early on in the Hyde Park era, rumours had become so persistent and so widely believed that Hyde Park speakers all swore oaths that they were not being paid by politicians. The American Embassy believed Thongyu Phutphat and Phi Bunnak were both paid by Phibun.[8] Yet to dismiss Hyde Park so blithely because some speakers were probably paid is disingenuous. While the American Embassy believed that Phi was paid by Phibun, he was accused by fellow speakers of being in the employ of Phao, due to his actions and his willingness to forgive Phao. And in the end, he supported the Sarit coup. He was apparently bitterly disappointed when Sarit turned out to be a dictator rather than a democrat.[9] He may have been paid by all of them at different times, or by none. Thongyu Phutphat may have been paid by Phibun. At the same time, he was a former MP who sincerely believed in democracy. And he ultimately broke with Phibun at the time of the hunger strike, which landed him in jail. Being paid did not necessarily mean that he did not have sincere beliefs of his own. One journalist who covered the movement pointed out that while some speakers were paid, they had first to prove themselves.[10] And proving themselves meant attracting an audience by addressing issues of concern, not just promoting a political agenda.

Of course, paying some speakers did not mean that government leaders were able to control Hyde Park. Phao, Sarit and Phibun were all criticized regularly at Sanam Luang, though Phao bore the brunt of the assault. Phibun was strongly criticized for the order to ban microphones, as this would have diluted the impact of the speakers. Yet he did not give up on his desire to have a Speakers' Corner more similar to that in

England. In December 1955, three months after the attempt to ban microphones, a request was sent to the embassy in London to film activities at Speakers' Corner there so it could be shown in Bangkok. A follow-up was sent in February to determine why no action had been taken. Phibun acknowledged receiving the film in late April.[11] Sarit eventually banned soldiers from the meetings. Phao attempted a variety of stratagems. He tried allowing marches and blocking them. He tried disrupting the meetings. He sent trucks with speakers to circle Sanam Luang and blare advertisements during the meetings. He tried suing speakers. He tried to discredit speakers. And he even tried speaking at Hyde Park to answer his critics. None of these attempts worked. As the American Embassy put it in its report, 'It seems that any control exercised by Phibun, General Sarit, *et al.* is quite loose and that the speakers generally will join in on most themes which seem to strike a chord in the audience.'[12]

Recognizing that some speakers may have been paid and discrediting the entire institution as a result is a mistake. As mentioned above, speakers at Hyde Park included a large number of well-known opposition politicians who were certainly not on the payroll of those in power. These included Khlaeo Noraphatdi, several Democrat Party members, who had their own separate platform on numerous occasions, Oraphin Chaiyakan, and leading members of socialist parties. These politicians spoke to promote their own political agendas. In addition, students held their own Hyde Park session, and occasionally spoke at regular meetings. Large numbers of people, including some who came to Bangkok from the provinces, spoke only once, or only sporadically, and were certainly not paid for their efforts. Dismissing the movement as a whole because some speakers may have been paid ignores all these voices.

THE HYDE PARK AUDIENCE

More fundamentally, dismissing the entire movement as orchestrated by Phibun, or because speakers may have acted out of personal motives is to misunderstand the nature of the movement. The movement was not the product of Phibun, nor was it the product of a few hired or politically motivated speakers. It was fundamentally a movement of the audience. The movement would have been truly meaningless if no one had turned up for the speeches. In other words, we should pay attention not just to the leaders and the speakers, but to the audience, to those who actually made up the demonstrators. They had an impact on the movement, and on politics more generally, in a number of ways. First, they provided tremendous constraints on the speakers themselves. If the speaker was boring, or if the speaker blatantly promoted government policies, the crowd could simply leave. For example, on 24 September, just four weeks into the movement, a platform was organized by some pro-government speakers. Only a small crowd gathered to listen, and after two speakers, the attempt was abandoned. The pro-government speakers could not compete with the speeches at the other end of Sanam Luang, where thousands of listeners had gathered. The regular Hyde Park speakers also competed with Democrat Party speakers on several occasions. Furthermore, on many occasions speakers were booed, even jeered off the platform. In one case, a woman speaker tried two weeks in a row to express an unpopular opinion and was jeered off the platform on both occasions. Third, the speakers often called for 'the voice of the people', asking the audience to express their opinion through applause. The crowd did not always agree with the speakers. Finally, each member of the crowd had to be convinced to join the protest marches. It was much easier simply to go home, rather than march long distances and risk confrontation with the police. Yet, in the case of the march to Phibun's residence, the audience stayed on even after the leaders went home.

So, who made up this audience? Was it civil society? These are perhaps the most intriguing and most difficult questions of all. In paying speakers and competing against one another, Phao, Phibun and Sarit all seem to have accepted that the audience was important – and important enough to risk American displeasure, since much of the rhetoric was anti-American. This alone should call into question the facile dismissals of Hyde Park as a sham. Judging from newspaper pictures, the crowd was made up largely of young men, though there were also many women, older people and even children. This predominance of young men is not surprising, given the dangers of participating in politics at the time. Interviews also indicate that the crowd was quite mixed, and even included people from the provinces.[13] Location certainly played a part in the nature of the audience as well. Speakers' Corner was located just outside Thammasat University, and many students apparently stopped there on occasion to listen to the speeches. Of course, whenever crowds gathered, hawkers and *samlo* drivers were present.

We might get a sense of the existence of civil society at the time by looking at the size of various groups capable of mobilization. If we look to education, we find that there was a potential civil society. Student numbers were rising rapidly, from 27,614 in 1952 to 33,713 in 1957 to 46,552 in 1958 (Wilson 1983: 72–73). In 1952 there were 159,648 monks, declining slightly to 154,487 in 1957. Including novices, there were 245,834 men resident in monasteries (ibid.: 200). While monks in Thailand have seldom been politically active, those who left the monkhood with an education would have been targets of mobilization.

Finally there were conscripts in the armed services who were being provided with some education and exposed to new ideas and places. While active duty soldiers and police were effectively controlled by the state, former soldiers and police were not. The army grew from around 27,000 in 1950 to some 83,000 by 1957, with another 32,000 in the navy and the air force (US Department of State 1989: 834). The police forces also grew tremendously during the period, to about 48,000 (Surachart 1988: 62). Overall, the population was 54 per cent literate (US Department of State 1956: 5). Thus there was a large group of people with some education who could have been mobilized.

Occupationally there were many people who could have been readily mobilized. For the 1960 census there is also a geographical breakdown, so I have included some information from that source as well (see Muscat 1966). Not surprisingly, most of the non-agricultural population (outside the mining sector) was concentrated in Bangkok, with some 590,000 out of 2,155,000 workers there in 1960. Thai middle-class occupations are generally considered to be in commerce and service industries. These totalled 1,434,000, with some 409,000 in Bangkok in 1960. Most of the rest of the non-agricultural labour force were working class. If we break the categories down further, we can see what sorts of occupations predominate. Civil servants, who could be mobilized after work just like any other occupational group, and who could be expected to be interested in politics, numbered 191,434 in 1955, rising to 201,820 in 1957 (Wilson 1983: 304; *Thailand Statistical Yearbook* 23 [1956–58]: 492–493 excludes workers in state enterprises and non-status workers). That these civil servants were seen as politically independent of the state is evident, first in the strong support they had demonstrated for Pridi, even after he was removed from power, and secondly, in that Phibun sought to gain loyalty by conducting psychological warfare among bureaucrats as early as 1952 (King 1954: 173). Retired civil servants make up a related category. In 1955 there were 28,000 people receiving civilian pensions. By 1960 this number had risen to over 46,000 (Wilson 1983: 306). As for labour, in 1957 there were 316,000 workers in Thailand, the number rising to 470,000 by 1960 (Muscat 1966: 180). There were thus many people who could have been organized and mobilized politically, especially in Bangkok.

If we look at actual organizations, there was a wide array in existence. In 1957 there were some 538 registered associations in Thailand, growing to 591 by 1958 (Riggs 1962: 163). For business, there was the Bangkok Chamber of Commerce, with some 300 member firms, and the Thai Merchants' Association, with 1,000 firms. There were associations for rubber, tin and teak exporters, and both rice millers' and rice merchants' associations. There were also a number of small business associations in the provinces (data on associations is from Riggs 1963). There were regional associations for the Northeast, the South and the North. There were a number of professional associations, including those for the medical and legal professions, and associations for artists. Charitable associations included the Thai Red Cross, with some 1,000 blood donors and 250,000 junior members, and the Rotary Club. There was also a large and active Veteran's Association.

Mass-based organizations also existed. There were several youth organizations, the Boy Scouts the largest with some 57,000 members. There were four women's associations: the Thai Women's Cultural Association with 1,130 members in 45 provinces; the Siamese Association of University Women with 600 members; the Women of Bangkok Association; and the Thai Women's Association. There were miners' and fishers' associations. And perhaps most illustrative for further consideration, there were labour organizations.

In the mid-1950s there were two labour federations. The larger was the Thai National Trade Union Congress (TNTUC), established by Phibun through his ally Sang Phathanothai in 1948. By the mid-1950s, it had a total membership of 75,000 (Blanchard 1957: 296), making it the largest labour federation in Thai history. It was not, strictly speaking, a labour union, as it included many workers who were not wage labourers, such as hawkers and *samlo* drivers. The TNTUC received a government subsidy. However, the TNTUC was only loyal to Phibun within limits. After the resignation of Sang in 1953 and after his own resignation from the union leadership at the end of 1955, Phibun's control was much more limited (ibid.: 296). As long as he was a good patron, many workers were loyal. Some groups were more loyal than others. Perhaps the best indication of his limited control was the break-up of the TNTUC after a labour law was passed in 1957, leaving many smaller competing unions (Munithi Arom Phongphanan 1990: 55). The second labour federation prior to 1957 was the Free Workmen's Association of Thailand (FWAT) under the patronage of Police Chief Phao. It had a membership of 14,000 workers, about 60 per cent of them Chinese (Blanchard 1957: 299). Thus labour was well organized, but organized and supported by the state.

Finally, it is worth considering the urban–rural divide. The Hyde Park movement, like the 1973 and 1992 uprisings, was primarily a Bangkok phenomenon. Yet it also had an impact on the countryside. Shortly after Speakers' Corner was initiated in Bangkok, Phibun ordered all provincial governors to establish their own sites for public speaking. Meetings were held in many provinces; especially active were Thonburi, Chonburi, Phetburi and Chainat. Topics were mostly local, but sometimes included national politics. Crowds were sometimes estimated in the thousands, a surprisingly high number for 1950s provincial

Thailand. Radio and newspapers also served as sources of exposure to the events and the ideas of the Hyde Park movement. In addition, once electioneering began in late 1956, politicians from the Hyde Park Movement party were active in the provinces. At least one speaker, Phi Bunnak, had made enough of a name for himself in his Hyde Park activities that he was invited to run in Suphanburi, where he won a seat for the Hyde Park Movement Party.[14] Perhaps most importantly, there was during this period considerable migration into the city from the Northeast, some of it temporary, some permanent. In either case, immigrants kept in touch with their relatives back home. Bangkok grew by an estimated 7.1 per cent annually during this period (Siffin 1962: 135), and a drought in 1956–57 meant even more extensive temporary migration as job seekers flooded the cities. Finally, it is worth noting that leaders at the time did not think the people in the countryside were incapable of political mobilization. The psychological war against the Communist Party was almost entirely focused on the countryside, and included speeches from makeshift platforms which were deemed 'effective'.[15]

HYDE PARK AS CIVIL SOCIETY

Did this constitute a 'civil society'? A number of factors must be considered. First, there was a potential civil society in place. There were certainly enough people capable of acting politically to place major constraints on the actions of the government, and to support democracy. Many of them felt strongly enough about democracy and constitutional reform to join demonstrations at considerable personal risk. Second, there were a number of organizations in existence, including business and labour organizations, women and youth organizations, professional organizations, and some very large charitable organizations. Third, many of these organizations were outside of the control of the state, such as the business and professional associations, and the Thai Red Cross (under the patronage of the Queen). Others, particularly women's associations and labour organizations' were more problematic. It is not enough simply to state that the labour federations were organized and subsidized by the state. The provincial chambers of commerce so often held up as evidence of the development of civil society in the provinces in the 1980s (see Anek 1992a) resulted from a specific government policy calling on provincial governors to create them. Similarly, while the government initiated Speakers' Corner, and leading members of the government probably bought off some of the speakers during some periods, it did not control events there. Indeed, events so escaped the control of the government that it constantly sought to limit activities, by banning microphones, by moving the venue, by arresting speakers, by refusing permission to march, and even by closing Hyde Park down entirely. Control is a matter of degree. As Kasian (1992: 271–272) pointed out, the left worked through the official labour movement, and even took over some of the unions late in the Phibun period (see also Munithi Arom Phongphangan 1990: 51–57). And even to the degree that labour federations were controlled, control was fragile, maintained only by granting patronage. The labour movement was able to obtain higher wages, observation of May Day, and a labour law that included the right to strike during this period. Thus state 'control' should be considered in a more nuanced way.

So, what happened to this budding civil society? Leftist intellectuals were arrested and labour unions and political parties dissolved. Sarit then sidetracked the political impulses of civil society by refocusing them on development, not just for the countryside, as has often been noted, but for themselves. By emphasizing private enterprise, he took the state out of economic competition with civil society. By bringing in huge amounts of American rest and recreation money and foreign investment, and encouraging civil society to compete for it, he effectively depoliticized civil society. Sarit also raised the salaries of civil servants and increased educational opportunities. Furthermore, for those interested in promoting development of the countryside, he provided a direction, one that clearly placed the Communist Party of Thailand as the enemy. Thus the discontent that would erupt in 1973 may be better classified as a return to politics by civil society rather than attributed to an entirely new actor on the scene. This allows us to understand that democracy was possible in Thailand well before the 1970s. It should refocus our understanding of Thai politics of the 1950s and earlier. Certainly there is a need for the re-evaluation of civil society not just today, but in the past.

CONCLUDING REMARKS

We can draw a number of lessons from the 1950s that enrich our understanding of civil society, street politics and reform, and especially civil society in the 1990s. Setting aside the question of whether civil society is a useful concept at all, it is clear that we need a more nuanced view of civil society. This is true in at least two ways.

First, it is not enough simply to consider civil society as comprising organizations independent of state control. Control is not a dichotomous variable, but is a matter of degree, and must be examined carefully. Examining only who organized a grouping and then allocating it to the state or to civil society is even more problematic. It would seem far more useful to examine who organized which groups and why. Why is it, for example, that in the 1950s government leaders organized labour, while in the 1980s they organized provincial business? Why was provincial business left to organize itself in the 1950s? Why was labour left to organize itself in the 1990s? And what are the implications of this switch in focus?

Second, civil society changes considerably over time. All too often studies of civil society in Thailand treat it as something that emerged in the late 1960s and has remained much the same since that time. And yet more years have passed since 1973 than passed between 1955 and 1973. The disappearance of the student movement and the left after the bloody crackdown in 1976 (leaving only elite-led civil society through the 1980s and early 1990s) and the rise of the Forum of the Poor in the late 1990s (perhaps signalling the reappearance of the lower classes in the form of street politics) mark two important shifts in the nature of civil society since 1973. Certainly a careful examination of how civil society has changed over time is needed.

As for street politics, we see a strong tendency to consider not the crowds, but only the leaders. The Hyde Park movement is often dismissed because some of the leaders may have been paid. Similarly, in 1992, Chamlong Srimuang felt compelled to deny any political ambitions, and to promise to retire from politics in order to lead the democratic uprising (McCargo 1997: 269–270). Leaders are not allowed to benefit in any way from their movement, or the whole movement is considered tainted. Thus the most important democratic voices may be lost, as they are not allowed to continue in politics. As for the crowds, their views are assumed to be imposed upon them by their leaders. It is assumed that Hyde Park demonstrators could not have had real grievances because some leaders were paid by politicians. In 1998, in the midst of the drought and the economic crisis, Northeastern farmers protested. Rather than consider their genuine concerns, the press claimed the protests were just the result of ousted former premier Chavalit Yongchaiyudh stirring up trouble. The press and politicians frequently have tried to determine who is behind the Forum for the Poor, as if somehow that is more important than the actual grievances articulated by the movement. In other words, leaders are expected to be free of self-interest, and crowds are assumed to be controlled by their leaders, with no genuine interests of their own.

Finally, as Somchai (Chapter 9, this volume) and McCargo (1998) have pointed out, there is a focus on elite civil society in the political reforms of the 1990s. Furthermore, much of the academic and nearly all of the media discourse on the uprisings of the 1970s and 1990s credits the middle class exclusively (see Ockey 1999). Civil society in Thailand is generally concerned with middle-class organizations, and not with labour or peasant organizations or slum community organizations. Conceiving of civil society as elite, or as middle class, has actually eroded democracy, as the poor have been left out of the democratic process. Nowhere is this focus on the elite and the middle class more marked than in the 1997 constitution, where only those with a university education will be allowed to run for parliament. Labour and peasant leaders are very unlikely to satisfy this requirement. Naruemon (Chapter 12, this volume) provides some hope that NGOs are organizing and leading some of these marginalized groups back into participation in civil society. Yet the Forum of the Poor has reacted to its marginalization from the post-reform institutional politics of elite civil society by taking to the streets. We might expect to see more street politics in the future from marginalized groups, and conflict between street politics and the now institutionalized elite civil society. Perhaps this is also a reason why civil society and street politics in the 1950s have largely disappeared from the discourse. The Hyde Park movement was not middle class oriented. In slashing forearms and painting posters with blood, it catered to an entirely different audience. Yet this audience was powerful enough that Phibun, Phao and Sarit all competed for its support. And the urban component of that audience has grown since then. Perhaps it will not always be possible to ignore this audience, or to buy it off at election time.

ACKNOWLEDGEMENT

I would like to thank Suphot Chaengraeo for his help with the research for this chapter.

NOTES

1   See FO371/129611, Gage to Selwyn Lloyd, 29 May 1957. This was Gage's 'valedictory address'.

2   There are several sources on this period, including Kobkua (1995), Fineman (1997) and Darling (1965). All discuss the Hyde Park movement in general, but not in detail, and none mentions this particular march.

3   By street politics, I mean something quite different from McCargo's (1997: 16–17) 'rally politics'. While we both refer to non-institutionalized politics, McCargo associates rally politics with strong leadership. I associate street politics not with leadership, but with the crowd. There was no single strong leader at Thailand's Hyde Park, but rather a number of 'stars' (*dara*). Different speakers 'led' different protests and marches, to the degree that anyone led at all, and none of the 'stars' was particularly prominent or successful in politics without the crowds at their backs. The implications of considering protests in terms of crowds rather than in terms of a strong leader are addressed briefly below.

4   Press reports of the period vary considerably in their estimates and reports were often sensationalized. Still, an observer from the American

Embassy estimated the crowd on one occasion at 20,000. See US Embassy to Department of State, January, 1956, 792.00/1-56.
5   Loudspeakers were allowed only with a permit, which the organizers of that Hyde Park forum had already obtained (*Sanseri*, 19 September 1955).
6   US Embassy to State Department, January, 1956, 792.00/1-56.
7   [3]so ro. 0201.6/36 box 3 'The urgent arrest of eaters and fasters' no. 4431/2499.
8   US Embassy to State Department, January 1956, 792.00/1-56
9   Interview, Chaiwat Bunnak, 13 August 1998.
10 Interview, Prachuab Amphasawat, 20 August 1998.
11 [3] so ro. 0201.53/47 'Filming the speakers at Hyde Park in London'.
12 US Embassy to State Department, January, 1956, 792.00/1-56.
13 Interview, Prachuab Amphasawat, 20 August 1998.
14 Interview, Chaiwat Bunnak, 13 August 1998.
15 FO371/123643, forwarded from Kelso, Australian Embassy, 16 January 1956.

9

CIVIL SOCIETY AND DEMOCRATIZATION IN THAILAND: A CRITIQUE OF ELITE DEMOCRACY

Somchai Phatharathananunth

Since the overthrow of the military-backed government in May 1992, political reform has been an important item on the agenda of the democratic movement in Thailand. The economic crisis in mid-1997 turned political reform into a wider public debate. All sides of the debate agree that even though Thailand has been ruled by a parliamentary system, the country's politics have been dominated by old-style politicians and money interests. There is a consensus among social activists and academics that major political change is needed to overcome such problems. However, different groups still hold different ideas on how to improve the existing political system. The differences centre around the question of how to initiate such political change. Should it be implemented from above, should it be based on pressure from below, or both? The purpose of this chapter is to demonstrate the inadequacy of the elitist perspective, which relies on the state and elite for the success of democratization. It is argued that only popular participation from below can lead to significant change in the Thai political order.

THE PROBLEM OF ELECTORALISM IN THAILAND

Electoral politics and democracy

After the victory of democratic forces over a military clique in 1992, some authors commented that 'in Thailand the process of democratic consolidation seems well under way' (King and LoGerfo 1996: 102). The reason for their optimism was the absence of any forces advocating non-parliamentary rule. This interpretation conformed to Schumpeter's ideas, which defines democracy in a narrow sense. According to

Schumpeter, 'the democratic method is that institutional arrangement for arriving at political decisions in which individuals acquire the power to decide by means of a competitive struggle for the people's vote' (Schumpeter 1976: 260). This idea has become the dominant definition of democracy. Regular elections with honest and fair competition are seen as amounting to democracy. Some even view the mere fact of elections as a sufficient condition for the existence of democracy, even though a significant proportion of citizens cannot freely participate. This kind of idea has been branded 'electoralism' (Schmitter and Karl 1991: 78). As Fox points out, electoral politics should not be confused with political democracy (Fox 1994: 151). Elections form only one part of democracy. According to Held, democracy should include equal rights for all citizens:

> Individuals should be free and equal in the condition of their own lives; that is, they should enjoy equal rights (and, accordingly, equal obligations) in the specification of the framework which generates and limits the opportunities available to them, as long as they do not deploy this framework to negate the rights of others. (Held 1987: 271)

For Beetham and Boyle (1995: 31–33), there are four main components of democracy:

1. *Free and fair elections*: Competitive elections provide the platform for popular control over government, electoral choice between candidates and programmes, and equality between electors.

2. *Open and accountable government*: This kind of government will guarantee the public accountability of officials. The accountability of government to citizens depends on two principles: the rule of law upheld by independent courts, and decision-making that is responsive to public opinion.

3. *Civil and political rights*: Such rights encompass freedom of expression, association, movement, and so on. These rights enable citizens to express divergent or unpopular views, to create an informed public opinion, to associate freely with others, and to find their own solution to collective problems.

4. *A democratic or 'civil' society*: In a democratic society, state power needs to be countered by independent social associations of all kinds. In addition, democracy will have a strong basis when such associations (family, school, church, workplace and voluntary associations) are not only independent from the state but also internally democratic. The democratic experience in these associations will make its members active citizens who feel responsibility for their society at large. (Beetham and Boyle 1995: 31–33)

From these points of view, democracy may be seen as consolidated only when the population can fully enjoy their socio-economic and political rights, beyond simply casting their votes.

Thai electoral politics

In Thailand electoral politics are completely different from democracy as defined above. At best, Thai electoral politics can qualify as a democracy in form only. From the point of view of almost all Thai politicians, involvement in politics is the best way to access wealth. Therefore, for them competing in elections, or 'playing politics' as they refer to it, has become a kind of business activity. It is a special kind of business that can make one rich in a short period of time. Frequent elections do not mean democratic progress, but as Neher commented on the 1995 elections, 'rather than moves toward more progressive democracy ... elections set back the clock with the re-emergence of old style politicians and money interests' (1995: 435). The same held true of the 1996 elections.

To win elections, politicians spend a lot of money on vote-buying. For example, during the July 1995 elections, candidates and parties spent almost US$700 million in election campaigns, much of which went to buy votes (King and LoGerfo 1996: 115). According to Pollwatch documents, one MP from central Thailand bought more than 200,000 votes for US$2.4 million, including payment to canvassers of about US$2 per vote, and US$40,000 for travel costs. In the general election of November 1996, politicians handed out more US$ 1 billion to buy votes (Vatikiotis and Fairclough 1996a: 16–17). In certain provinces, for example in Sri Sa Ket, some candidates donated large sums of money to organizations such as housewives' groups, youth clubs or temples (Callahan and McCargo 1996: 387).

Such expensive elections require substantial fundraising. It has been shown that much political funding, especially in rural areas, comes from illegal and untraceable sources. For example, in Chiang Mai, the biggest city in Northern Thailand, one MP reportedly owns a major illegal gambling den. To fund their campaigns, other politicians rely on underground lotteries, drug trafficking and oil smuggling (Vatikiotis and Fairclough 1996a: 18). Two senior politicians, Vattana Asavahame and Narong Wongwan, have been suspected of involvement in drug trafficking by the United States (Neher 1995: 437).

After winning elections, politicians use their power to reap rich rewards. Corruption is widespread and lucrative. When the military seized power in the February 1991 coup, they set up an Assets Examination Committee to investigate corruption charges against thirteen high-ranking politicians. The Committee found that they were 'unusually wealthy', their unexplained wealth ranging from more than US$24 million in the case of a former minister of commerce to about US$13.24 million for a former communications minister and about US$9.04 million for the former prime minister (Neher 1995: 435). From the 1970s onwards, the number of MPs who came from the business sector increased steadily, from 29.4 per cent in 1976 to 45.55 per cent in 1992 (Sombat 1993: 169–170). As a result of the penetration of electoral politics by business groups, government policy represents the interests of the business sector more than the interests of the population as a whole.

Electoral politics and popular rights

In the late 1980s Thailand experienced rapid economic growth. Between 1987 and 1991 the country's GDP increased by 10.5 per cent annually. According to Hunsaker, the source of economic dynamism came from the ability to gain access to foreign markets, foreign direct investment, and 'the conversion of Thai natural resources into exportable goods' (Hunsaker 1996: 1).

Thailand's modernization drive has been based on the exploitation of the countryside. The wealth created by the agricultural sector has been channelled to finance industrialization and growth in Bangkok (Missingham 1996: 193). According to Medhi, since the first economic and development plan, the agricultural sector has been the source of cheap labour, cheap food supply and revenues. However, the most important role of agriculture in industrialization has been foreign exchange earnings, which are necessary to purchase technology and industrial inputs (Medhi 1995b: 43–50). It is not surprising to discover that after more than three decades of development the income of the agricultural sector lags far behind that of the non-agricultural sector. In 1990 the ratio of non-agricultural income to that of agriculture was 11:2. Moreover, in 1992 Thailand ranked sixth among the countries with the worst income distribution in the world (Pasuk *et al.* 1996: 12–14).

Unequal development not only resulted in extreme economic disparities between urban and rural areas, but also environmental degradation and conflict. Economic growth led to conflicts in the countryside over natural resources between farmers, on the one hand, and the economic sector and the state, on the other. Ubonrat Siriyuvasak (1991: 299) noted that disputes over the rights to control the use of land, forests, rivers and waterways have become the focal point of conflicts. In the early 1980s there were only two protests concerning environmental issues. However, after the economic boom accelerated in 1987, the number of such protests increased sharply. In 1990 the numbers of conflicts over natural resources rose to 58 cases. Between 1994 and 1995 there were 1,742 protests in Thailand, of which 610 cases involved the use of natural resources. In Isan alone there were 187 conflicts over natural resources during this period (Praphat 1998: 30, 39–40). Politicians, bureaucrats, the police and business interests try to suppress popular protests by using force or intimidation (Fairclough 1996: 20). Between 1993 and 1996, ten protest leaders were killed and nine protesters were injured. In addition, 20 NGO and village leaders were arrested (Naruemon *et al.* 1996: 31).

Factory workers faced similar problems to those of farmers. The government has always sided with employers to quell protests. Successive Thai governments and the business community have prevented the creation of an organised labour movement. Legally, workers in the private sector have the following rights:

- to form and join unions;
- to express their views without government or employer interference; to form confederations with other unions;
- to receive protection from discrimination, dissolution, suspension or termination by any outside authority because of union activities (Amnesty International 1985: 728).

But in reality, union leaders are often fired and put on black lists. If workers join a union, they are likely to experience problems such as trouble with management, or being assigned unpopular shifts. As a result, Thai unions remain weak, and less than 2 per cent of the country's industrial workers belong to unions. Most of the unions represent workers in a single factory, and coordination among them is weak (Fairclough 1997: 81).

It is not only economic interests that cause the elected government to act in anti-democratic ways, but also national security sentiments which linger on from the Cold War period. Elected governments have accepted the military's idea that human rights are a threat to national security. For them, human rights do not form an integral part of democracy. For example, on 29 March 1993 at the Asia-Pacific Regional Conference on Human Rights in Bangkok, Prime Minister Chuan Leekpai argued that the universality of human rights would be better promoted if there were a clear recognition of differences between societies. Governments have always accused social movements for human rights in Thailand of being foreign agents, and have viewed pressures from the international community as acts that violated Thai sovereignty (*Thai Development Newsletter 1993*: 67–68). Such attitudes are reflected in the country's laws. The Thai constitution recognized socio-economic and political rights of all citizens, but with reservations. The constitution states that no one can exercise such rights in the way that is harmful to national security, religion or the monarchy. However, harmful actions can be interpreted broadly. Practically all actions can be interpreted as endangering national security, religion or the monarchy. Furthermore, specific rights are subject to a number of restrictions (Viboon 1985: 97–99).

One such restriction is the Anti-Communist Law. Introduced in 1952, the law allows broad powers of arrest and detention without trial. The police or military authorities can detain anyone for an initial period of one month without recourse to the courts. With approval from the director-general of police, the detention period may be extended to seven months. Article 20 of the law allows police or military officers from the rank of sub-lieutenant and above to make an arrest without a warrant. In addition, in some rural areas, battalion commanders may declare martial law in areas under their command. Even after the collapse of the Communist Party of Thailand, the government continued to use this law as a mechanism to control democratic movements. In early 1995, five school teachers who helped local farmers organize a protest against land appropriation in the northeastern province of Ubon Ratchathani were accused of behaving in violation of anti-communist legislation (Vatikiotis 1996: 23, 26).

Although the last military-backed regime was overthrown in 1992, democracy in Thailand is still far from consolidated. Electoral politics have been dominated by money interests, and corruption has reached an unprecedented scale. Furthermore, the state still has not fully acknowledged the basic rights of the people. As a result, the civil and political rights of ordinary citizens have often been violated.

DEMOCRATIZATION FROM ABOVE

Deepening democracy has become an important demand of Thai democratic movements in recent years. Generally, before the mass uprising against the Suchinda government in May 1992, hopes for any kind of democratic change among Thai social activists and progressive intellectuals rested on popular initiatives from below. However, after the popular victory in May, political reform came onto the national agenda, and genuine democratic change carried out by the state seemed a real possibility. In this optimistic atmosphere, some progressive intellectuals have begun to propose the concept of democratization from above.

The modernization theory of political corruption

The first concept of democratization from above that will be discussed here places emphasis on the positive effect of modernization on democracy. This theory was proposed by Anek Laothamatas, a political scientist from Thammasat University. According to Anek, modernization was a crucial element for democracy. For him, backwardness and democracy were incompatible. 'A dependent and backward agriculture and countryside', argues Anek, 'is unable to form the basis for democracy', because 'democracy is a part of urbanization and capitalism' (Anek 1995: 73, 84). As a result, 'democracy within the nation-state can be materialized ... only when the nation is urbanized and industrialized' (ibid.: 62). He justified his idea by arguing that in the present day most underdeveloped countries, except India, have been unable to 'maintain' and 'develop' democracy. On the contrary, the countries that had successfully consolidated democratic rule were industrialized nations, in which the majority of the population lives in towns and cities. In addition, those third world countries that had succeeded in making transition to democracy in the previous decade were the countries which had succeeded in urbanization and industrialization (ibid.: 61).

Why did modernization occupy such an important position in the democratization process? Because, argues Anek, it created the middle classes, who act as a bulwark of democracy. For him, the failure or success of democracy depends on the size of the urban middle class, which in turn depends on the transformation of the countryside. From his point of view, the Thai middle classes, especially in Bangkok, viewed democracy according to a 'Western standard'. They believed that democracy was first of all a political system that emphasized policy, ideology and the merits and abilities of political parties and politicians in administering the country. Moreover, in elections, the middle classes vote as free individuals who make their voting decisions independently. Such political attitudes are quite different from those of their rural counterparts. Villagers, who according to Anek live in a backward society, viewed elections as a chance either to find new political patrons or show their allegiance to old ones. Most important factors that influenced their voting behaviors were *bunkun*, indebtedness to the benevolence of others, and rewards which they expected to gain in the future. As a result, when farmers cast their votes, they seldom think that they are independent individuals, who are free to vote as they want without taking *bunkun* and rewards into consideration (ibid: 7, 8).

For Anek, since farmers form the majority of the population in Thailand, such patterns of voting behaviour led to the dominance of corrupt politicians in the Thai political order. How to overcome such a problem? Anek proposed that in the short term there should be institutional changes, for example, electoral reforms, decentrali-zation and promotion of direct democracy in the villages. The first measure is designed to increase opportunities for the middle classes to influence the country's politics. The second and third measures are meant to help to undermine patron–client relations in the countryside (ibid.: 12–21, 35–53). However, as Kasian has pointed out, for Anek, 'the long-term survival of Thai parliamentary democracy depended on the gradual and protected urbanization of the countryside' (Kasian 1996: 36). To guarantee the success of democracy, he called for Thailand to transform itself from a country consisting of the capital city and a backward countryside into a country dominated by small and medium sized towns in the provinces (Anek 1996: 75).

> If the middle classes are true to what they pledge – to establish a democracy ruled by leaders with integrity and competence – they must earnestly lend support to a rural development which will turn patronage-ridden villages into small towns of middle-class farmers or well-paid workers. During the last two decades several battles have been dramatically fought on the streets of Bangkok for the cause of democracy, but the one, and the only one, that delivers a long lasting victory for democrats will take place in the rural areas in the form of protracted and perhaps uneventful socio-economic transformation. (Anek, cited in Kasian 1996: 36)

Anek's view can be dubbed the 'modernization theory of political corruption' for he believes that a more developed economy will lead to less political corruption. In such a society, voters will be interested in 'issues' rather than 'access', and will base their decisions on individual choice, which will eliminate corrupt politicians from Thai electoral democracy. Such a concept clearly suffers from an economic deterministic view of democracy. Capitalism, as Calhoun (1994: 310) has rightly warned, is not 'somehow by itself an adequate support for democracy'. Even though there is a positive correlation between development and democracy, other factors such as social and political structure also influence the course of democratic development. As a result, social change does not occur in a unilinear manner. Development can also generate new forms of patron–client relations and encourage corruption (see Surin and McCargo 1997: 132–148). Moreover, it is the very same middle classes who have emerged from the modernization process that engender and often benefit from corruption. As Huntington has pointed out:

> Modernization also contributes to corruption by creating new sources of wealth and power, the relation of which to politics is undefined by the dominant tradition norms of the society and on which the modern norms are not yet accepted by the dominant groups within the society. Corruption in this sense is a direct product of the rise of new groups with new resources and the efforts of these groups to make themselves effective within the political sphere. (Huntington 1993: 379)

Political changes in Thailand in recent years have shown that a more developed economy did not result in a better political system. For example, more modernization in the provinces, both in villages and towns, generated higher levels of corruption. It must be noted that the middle classes in such areas, who Anek argues base their electoral decisions on ideology or policy, do not demonstrate a voting behaviour different from that of farmers; they also vote for corrupt politicians. If we compare MPs from constituencies in the countryside and MPs from provincial towns in which the middle classes formed the majority of voters, we shall find that there is no difference in political 'quality' between them. In addition, the middle classes not only vote for corrupt politicians, but many of them also act as the 'election staff' of such politicians, and play an important role in helping them to win elections. Anek's hope for the progressive role of middle-class businesspeople in the provinces also has not materialized. He urged provincial businesspeople to act as the front line of democratic change in the provinces. Anek was committed to such an idea because he believed that provincial businesspeople were close to the Bangkok middle class economically, socially and culturally, and so would be able to understand the Western-style democracy imagined by Bangkokians (Kasian 1996: 37). In reality, provincial businesspeople have generally preferred to involve themselves in money politics rather than building democracy in the countryside.

The idea of elite civil society

The second concept of democratization from above, the idea of elite civil society, has been proposed by a group of leading Thai public intellectuals, most prominent among whom is Prawase Wasi. Their idea is similar to the concept of 'state-led civil society' elaborated by Frolic in his study of civil society in China. According to Frolic, by 'state-led civil society' he refers to those organizations and groups created by officials to 'serve as support mechanisms to the state' (Frolic 1997: 56).

> State-led civil society is a form of corporatism. The state determines which organizations are legitimate and forms an unequal partnership with them. The state does not dominate directly. It leaves some degree of autonomy to these organizations, but it does demand a disciplined partnership based on cooperation within specified sectors, usually in tripartite arrangements among business, labor, and the state. (Ibid.: 58)

For Frolic, 'state-led civil society' in China contains the following features. First, it is not riven by clashes between social organizations and the state. Since these organizations formed a part of the state, they are not against the state: 'It is a marriage of convenience rather than a catalyst for citizen resistance.' Second, the state uses them as a mechanism for the development of civic consciousness. Third, they perform as mediators between state and society. Fourth, both state and social organizations recognize the strengths and weaknesses of each other: it is a trade-off between them. While 'the state perceives the need for change and regards social organizations as functionally useful, without threatening the state's hegemony', the actors in those organizations 'perceive a slightly weakened state, but are more interested in short term economic gains than individual autonomy at the expense of state power' (ibid.: 58).

The elite civil society concept shares main assumptions with the idea of state-led civil society. For its advocates, 'civil society' is not 'a sphere of society which organizes itself autonomously, as opposed to the sphere that is established and/or directly controlled by the state' (Lummis 1996: 30). On the contrary, both the state and social organizations are the components of 'civil society'. Civil society, argues Chai-Anan Samudavanija, is a partnership of the state, the private sector and the popular sector (Chai-Anan 1998: 41).

Similar to the idea of state-led civil society, the elite civil society concept used in Thailand also emphasizes cooperation between state and social organizations. However, the theorists of this line of thought do not believe that it is necessary for social organizations to cooperate with the state because the state was weak. On the contrary, because the state is very strong, it is impossible to achieve any meaningful change without state cooperation (Prawase 1998: 5). For them, the state must play a key role in the efforts to construct *prachakhom* or 'civil society' in Thailand. As a result, advocates of this view reject the idea of excluding the state from civil society, and they also believe that building civil society from below has no future in Thailand. According to Prawase, such ideas will lead to conflict, hate and rivalry, which will weaken the efforts for a better life within society. For him, endeavours to strengthen civil society should be based on 'love' and 'cooperation'. To avoid confrontation, Prawase proposed that the state, the business sector, NGOs, local elites and intellectuals, should form a 'partnership' and work together to solve the country's social and politico-economic problems. Such a partnership, which includes all parts of society, will create a powerful and sustainable civil society that is able to solve all kind of problems (ibid.: 22–26).

In the early stages, Prawase proposed the idea of partnership to build 'local civil society' in the provinces. His idea was incorporated into the Eighth National Economic and Social Development Plan. However, after the economic crisis in the late 1990s, he developed such ideas into the concept of 'good governance'. According to Prawase, to overcome the crisis, Thailand needed politico-economic and social reforms to achieve 'good governance'. Such reforms would strengthen Thai society in every aspect, intellectually and materially, and would create transparency, happiness and new prosperity within the country on a stable basis (ibid.: 22).

Prawase's ideas are similar to those of Thirayuth Boonmi, another theorist of 'good governance'. For Thirayuth, 'good governance' is the interactive relation between the state, the private sector and society which would lead to a transparent, efficient government and economic sector, and at the same time increase popular partici-pation, reduce state power and strengthen civil society (Thirayuth 1998a: 12; Yod 1998: 62–70). To carry out reforms, Prawase and Thirayuth proposed the setting up of a committee, which would comprise 'good' and 'capable' elites from various groups such as political leaders, army officers, government agencies, business-people, academics, media practitioners, religious leaders, and the leaders of urban-oriented NGOs, to carry out reforms (Ji 1998: 169; Prawase 1998: 21, 33–34).

However, Prawase differs from Thirayuth on one point: he is more concerned about the rural community than is Thirayuth. As a result, his ideas have been called the 'communitarian version' of good governance by some critics. There are still other versions of 'good governance', for example, the authoritarian version of the army, and the liberal version of the business sector (Kasian 1998: 26). The common point of these versions is that the reforms necessary for 'good governance' should be carried out by the elite.

Problems with the elite view

The efforts to build civil society discussed above suffer from a number of problems. First, the elite civil society line of thought is quite similar to the idea of democratic elitism, which argues that the threats to democracy come from the masses because 'they are prone either to take direct action against democratic institutions and value, or provoke counter-elites to engage in antidemocratic action'. Therefore, the survival of democracy depends upon 'the leadership of "an enlightened elite" to shape and direct policy aimed principally to keep the masses politically quiescent' (Bachrach and Botwinick 1992: 22–23).

Second, they are reforms carried out by elites, who aim at preserving the existing structure. Such reforms, as Saneh Chamarik has pointed out, assume that *prachakhom* and 'good governance' have to be built from above and led by capable elites. Any change in society must confine itself to the improvement of the existing structure without a change in the status quo. It means that there will be no change in the unbalanced relationship between the state and economic sectors on the one hand, and society on the other. They are reforms designed to perpetuate the rule of the elite over common people. Such reforms will never generate democracy but the domination of the elite (Saneh 1998: 8). Since this kind of change does not restructure the existence politico-economic structure in any fundamental way, it may be described at best as 'conservative reform'.

Third, it is difficult to find any evidence to support the view that the state interested in democratic development at all. On the contrary, the state often acts against efforts to strengthen civil society. Elite civil society theorists naively believe that if social organizations give up their activities against state oppression, in return, the state will change its anti-democratic policies to democratic ones. In other words, they treat the state as something that can be manipulated easily. In reality, as Chai-Anan has argued, the Thai state is difficult to change 'because of the longstanding and deeply ingrained authoritarian, centralist, clientelistic and corrupt tradition of its bureaucracy' (Kasian 1996: 47).

Fourth, the arguments against the independent struggle of the grassroots movements advocated by the concept of elite civil society supplied ammunition for the state to de-legitimize the activities of democratic movements. The Thai state, as mentioned above, frequently accuses popular movements of being 'trouble-makers', whose activities threaten national security. To argue that the struggle against state oppression was improper because it caused conflict within the nation was easily exploited by the state to support their 'trouble-maker' allegation, in order to isolate the movements from the rest of society. Such an accusation is a form of what Therborn called 'ideological excommunication'. According to Therborn, the victim of such an accusation will be 'excluded from further meaningful discourse as being insane, depraved, traitorous, alien, and so on'. The excommunicated person, argues Therborn, 'is condemned, temporarily or forever, to ideological non-existence: he is not to be listened to' (Therborn 1988: 83).

Fifth, the idea of 'partnership' proposed by the elite civil society theorists also helps to strengthen the state's position vis-a-vis civil society. It invites the state to become involved in a wide range of activities which were formerly carried out independently by social organizations. As a result, instead of reducing the power of the state, the creation of 'partnerships' will help state agencies to increase their control over society. In theory, forming a partnership assumes that all members are equal, but in reality the state is stronger than other groups. The strength of the state is further enhanced by the insistence of elite civil society advocates that conflict with the state is undesirable. Furthermore, since the state is generally the main source of funding, it can influence, neutralize, depoliticize, and manipulate the activities of the partnership. This fear has been confirmed by the activities of the partnership over the past two years. The state dominated the partnership from the beginning. *Prachakhom* bodies were set up at the provincial, district and sub-district level on the instructions of the Interior Ministry, and approved sub-district *prachakhom* were provided with a budget of 10,000 baht (Crispin 2000: 21). In the view of officials, *prachakhom* should not act as a pressure group, but should adopt principles of responsibility, order and discipline, and should help to preserve the prosperity and unity of the country (Rattana 1999: 14). Social organizations that joined the *prachakhom* did not challenge such attitudes, because they were afraid that otherwise the state would not support their *prachakhom*. According to Dr Vanchai Vatanasapt, the chairman of the *prachakhom* in Khon Kaen, the partnership should refrain from activities that might lead to conflict with government officials, 'in order to gain credibility, respect and cooperation from the government' (ibid.: 15). As a member of the *prachakhom* in Khon Kaen has pointed out, since it was founded two years ago, *prachakhom* has been 'a tool for the government to co-opt and control civil society' (Crispin 2000: 21). Under such conditions it is not difficult for the state to dominate the partnership, and turn it into state corporatism. Cooptation has already begun to appear among some social organizations that receive funds from the government. Because of their reliance on government funds, some existing organizations have given up their anti-government activities, and new ones have refrained from involvement in such activities.

Sixth, avoiding conflict with the state means that the partnership has to ignore the violation of human rights by the state. As mentioned earlier, many policies of the Thai state have violated the rights of the underprivileged masses, especially in rural areas. In some cases they threaten their survival. However, a partnership is unable to take any action against the state because such action will lead to conflict with the state. As a result, partnership activities tend to be confined to 'non-political' issues such as the problem of refuse collecting in towns. Furthermore, grassroots organizations, which actively protect the rights of large strata of the population, have been excluded from the 'partnership' arrangement.

Finally, elite civil society theorists tend to forget that most conflicts have been generated by state policies. To avoid conflict within Thai society means that the state has to stop violating the rights of the population. If the state remains committed to such undemocratic policies, conflict will not only exist but intensify.

It is clear that the democratization from above fails to provide mechanisms to generate significant democratic change that will lead to democratic consolidation. If we hope to make any democratic progress, we should address the problem from a different angle.

CIVIL SOCIETY, RADICAL DEMOCRACY AND DEMOCRATIZATION

To find the way for democratic progress in Thailand, we can start by looking back at the root meaning of democracy, its 'radical' meaning. As Levine has pointed out, 'historically, "democracy" meant rule by the 'demos', the people, the popular masses in contrast to elites' (Levine 1995: 158). In other words, democracy means that the people are empowered. It is, according to Lummis, democracy 'in its essential form, democracy at its root' – radical democracy (Lummis 1996: 25). This is the starting point for further progress towards democratization in Thailand.

Radical democracy is a political form of popular empowerment. There are two elements which are crucial for radical democracy. First, radical democracy must be based on a lively civil society. Civil society is a complex concept, which has different meanings for different people. Civil society is the sphere of society situated between the state and the economy in which the population can organize itself autonomously. This is the definition of civil society set out by Gramsci (1971), Harbermas (1996), and Cohen and Arato (1994). Instead of becoming part of the state and helping the state to expand its functions as proposed by elite civil society theorists, civil society, as Lummis suggests, must play a role in transforming the state, and radically reducing its power, restructuring it by 'eliminating functions that have been made redundant by the autonomous organization of the civil society itself', and 'reforming or establishing new government institutions appropriate to the new situation' (Lummis 1996: 37).

Second, another crucial element for radical democracy is popular empowerment through political participation. In addition, theorists of radical democracy argue that the empowerment of the subordinate classes plays a special role in the democratization process. Democracy is unthinkable without active popular participation. As Bachrach and Botwinick pointed out, 'widespread mass participation is an indispensable component of a healthy democratic polity. In its absence, leaders become unresponsive to the needs of the people'. In addition, a 'democracy' that prevents widespread mass participation denies the majority of the population 'the multiple benefits derived from political participation – and thus undermines its principal reason for being, namely, to promote the well-being of all the people' (Bachrach and Botwinick 1992: 32).

More important, the participation of the poor is crucial for democratization. According to Rueschmeyer *et al.* (1992), social class is a central category to the analysis of democratization. For them, class and democracy are interrelated: 'Those who have only to gain from democracy will be its most reliable promoters and defenders', while 'those who have the most to lose will resist it and will be most tempted to roll it back when the occasion presents itself' (ibid.: 57).

> Democratization was both resisted and pushed forward by class interest. It was the subordinate classes that fought for democracy. By contrast, the classes that benefited from the status quo nearly without exception resisted democracy. (Ibid.: 46)

Therefore, in the process of democratization the strength of subordinate classes is critically important for the advance of democracy. Subordinate classes can strengthen their position by social mobilization and by the development of relative autonomous groups within civil society. For Rueschemeyer et al, the density of these autonomous groups is important in three different ways:

> as a way in which the empowerment of subordinate classes is realized,
>
> as a shield protecting these classes against the hegemonic influence of dominant classes, and...
>
> as the mode of balancing the power of state and civil society. (Ibid.: 49)

In the Thai context, popular empowerment within civil society, if strong enough, has the potential to contribute to the deepening of democracy in five different ways. First, civil society promotes popular participation. The importance of civil society for democratic development in Thailand is more pronounced because of the exclusionary nature of 'Thai democracy'. Even though electoral democracy is gaining increased significance as a legitimate form of political rule in Thailand, large strata of the population remain excluded from meaningful political participation. Surin and McCargo have pointed out that: 'Politicians are becoming increasingly arrogant, believing that elections give them a form of absolute legitimacy.' [They]'regard all extra-parliamentary political activity as illegitimate' (Surin and McCargo 1997: 148). As a result, for Thai political leaders, popular participation has been confined to merely casting votes. To overcome electoralism, it is necessary to open up political space in order to increase democratic participation. However, since there is no channel for increased political engagement within electoral politics, civil society has become the major base of the struggle for popular participation. From there, the masses can push the democratization process further, and expand the scope of participation beyond elections by organizing themselves into different kinds of social organizations in order to enhance their bargaining power with the state. As Linz and Stepan have noted, a robust civil society has 'the capacity to generate political alternatives and to monitor government and state'. It can also help 'transitions get started, help resist reversals, and help deepen democracy' (Linz and Stepan 1996: 9).

Second, participation in civil society organizations will provide an opportunity for the masses to learn about democracy through their experience. Within electoral politics, democratic participation involves only voting on election days. The masses, especially in the countryside, have no chance to engage in other democratic activities. However, when they join grassroots organizations, they are able to learn how a democratic system works, and how to act democratically. Through work within organizations, they learn to work in groups, which is a crucial skill for democratic development in any society. In addition, they have a chance to engage in debate in meetings in which they can express opinions, as well as having to abide by majority rule. The more they are involved in the activities of the organizations, the more they will deepen their understanding of democracy. These are the most valuable experiences which it is impossible for the poor to gain from other sources. More important, since the activities of the grassroots organizations are related to their survival, such participation makes democracy an integral part of their lives.

Third, the empowerment of civil society organizations will undermine patron–client relations. One reason for the existence of patron–client relations is that members of the underprivileged classes are unable to rely on themselves, and so they have to find someone to help or protect them. The empowerment of grassroots movements changes such a situation. According to Bachrach and Botwinick, the struggle to increase the political participation of the poor will 'nurture and heighten group identity ... sharpening awareness of the individual self', and 'engender a transformation from a sense of powerlessness to power' (Bachrach and Botwinick 1992: 30). As a result, instead of relying on political patrons, they rely on their own strength and collective action.

Fourth, civil society organizations are the most important mechanism for protecting the rights of the underprivileged classes in rural areas. In recent years, the rights of the rural poor in many areas have been violated by the elected government. Frequently such violations threaten their survival. The government has sometimes used force to evict farmers from their land for dam projects and agri-business plantations. The only way for farmers to protect their lives from disaster was to organize themselves against state intrusion. Grassroots organizing is a weapon of the weak, in a society in which the violation of human rights has been conducted in the name of the law, development and the national interest.

Last but not least, the activities of civil society organizations will generate counter-hegemonic ideologies which are crucial for democratic development. Such ideologies are a product of the struggle, and they develop among the members of organizations via participation in practical activities. By engaging in collective action, the masses will view their relationship with the state from a new angle.

One of the most important features of the Thai dominant ideology derives from the Buddhist idea of karma. It is believed that one's status in society results from karma accumulated in past lives in the form of merit (*bun*) and demerit (*bap*). According to Chai, 'the degree of "highness" or "low-ness" of an individual's status is believed to vary according to his store of *bun* and *bap*: the more *bun*, the higher one's status' (Chai 1998: 40). In other words, those who are rulers are so because of their *bun*. As a result, the differences between the ruler and the ruled are perceived to be natural and appropriate. Such a belief implies that the existing socio-political structure is unchangeable, and therefore the ruled have no choice but to depend on the ruler (Sombat 1998: 72). This is the ideological basis of patron–client relations in Thai society. Such an idea prevents the subordinate classes from acting in their own interests. It obstructs them from developing into what Marx called 'class for itself' (Kolakowski 1981: 356). As Scott and Kervliet note on peasant consciousness, 'as long as a peasant sees his relation to agrarian elites as one of legitimate dependent – as long as he feels himself part of a vertical community – peasant "class-consciousness" is unlikely' (Scott and Kerkvliet 1977: 439).

The empowerment of the subordinate classes through collective action undermines such ideas. The poor realize that if they act together, they have the power to bargain with the state, and may sometimes be able to force the state to comply with their demands. They are increasingly convinced that it is possible to change the relationship between dominant and subordinate groups. As a result, they stop viewing government officials as 'masters' whom they dare not to challenge. Furthermore, they see their struggle as a struggle for better lives, not as trouble-making. In sum, instead of accepting the existing socio-political structure as a manifestation of karma, they will criticize its injustices and aim to change it.

CONCLUSION

It is difficult to find evidence to support the view that democratization from above will succeed in Thailand. On the contrary, in the last three decades the two major democratic transitions – the October uprising in 1973 and the May bloodbath in 1992 – were initiated from below. This is also true for constitutional reform in 1997. Even though the new constitution was passed by Parliament, such moves were not initiated by the state (see McCargo 1998: 6–9). Only continued pressure from below made the government give up its attempts to block the draft charter. As senate president Mechai Ruchuphan pointed out, if the attempt to pass the draft charter had failed, there would have been social turmoil. People saw constitutional change as Thailand's last hope for reforming its corrupt political system, and a precondition for economic recovery following the July 1997 collapse of the baht (*The Nation*, 24 August 1997).

It must be noted that the arguments against top-down democratization made here do not mean that all initiatives from above are useless. But we should place them in the proper context of our attempts to promote democratic development. Manoeuvres from above can play only a supporting role to endeavours from below. If we make top-down efforts into the most important mechanisms for democratization, our democratic struggle will rest on fragile foundations. In sum, both forms of democratic effort are desirable, but with the right priority given to grassroots efforts.

To emphasize pressure from below does not means that we underestimate the difficulty of building a strong civil society in Thailand. Social organizations in the country are still weak, and there is a lot of work to do before we can achieve the aim of strengthening them. However, it is surely a mistake if we view the development of social movements separately from politico-economic changes in society. As has been shown by the October 1973 and May 1992 events, tiny movements can be transformed into strong mass movements within a short period of time when the window of opportunity opens to them.

However difficult it may be, struggle from below is indispensable for democratization in Thailand. Without active popular participation from below, substantive democracy will have no chance to materialize.

10

RESPONDING TO ECONOMIC CRISIS: THAILAND'S LOCALISM

Kevin Hewison

The 1980s and 1990s saw remarkable political, economic and social change in Thailand. The collapse of the military-backed regime in 1992 under the weight of widespread popular opposition marked an important step on the path to political reform. It also marked the emergence of non-governmental organizations (NGOs) as significant political actors in the movement for reform. As other chapters in this volume show, the role of NGOs is now broad-ranging and NGOs exhibit an ability to influence the political agenda and promote reforms and issues in both national and local contexts. They have tended to be amongst the more radical elements of those promoting political reform (see McCargo 2001).

When the economic crisis struck Thailand in July 1997, NGOs played a significant role in challenging the mainstream policy responses of both the Thai government and the International Monetary Fund (IMF). As will be indicated, the NGO response was both populist and nationalist. It also linked with a broader international NGO protest regarding the impact of neo-liberal globalization.[1] This international response was most clearly evident in demonstrations in Seattle in December 1999, at the meetings of the World Trade Organization.

The significance of the ability of NGOs to mobilize opposition against global capitalism and the expansion of global finance is now clear. However, there have been few attempts to assess the alternatives to neo-liberal globalization articulated by its opponents. This chapter will examine the alternative offered by one group of NGOs and related intellectuals, identified in this chapter as constituting a localist response and alternative. It will outline localism's main elements and detail an assessment of its political and economic viability. Before doing this, however, it is first necessary to provide some background on Thailand's economic boom and bust and some brief comments on the political background of the country's NGOs.

BACKGROUND

If there were league tables for economic growth, Thailand would have been near the top for much of the four decades from 1957 until mid-1997. The uninterrupted growth of this period is a unique economic performance. Perhaps more remarkable was the unprecedented boom over the final decade of this period. In some years Thailand's growth exceeded that of all other similar economies. Real growth was in excess of 10 per cent in each of the years 1988, 1989 and 1990. Thailand achieved these remarkable results through an ability to attract pro-digious amounts of foreign capital, especially from East Asia, and a capacity to mobilize domestic funds for capitalist industrialization.

But a focus on this period as an economic phenomenon would miss the deep processes of social and political change that have also taken place over this period. The boom brought rapid change that transformed Thailand from a rural, overwhelmingly agricultural society, to an urbanizing society where non-agricultural pursuits predominate. Employment opportunities grew and absolute poverty declined during the boom. Thailand has been undergoing a capitalist revolution.

The results of the transformation were spectacular. In 1960 agriculture accounted for about 40 per cent of GDP, most exports, and employed more than 80 per cent of the population. By 1997 just 48 per cent worked in agriculture, some 35 per cent of GDP was attributable to manufacturing, and industrial growth saw manufactured exports expand from 1 per cent of total exports in 1960 to 80 per cent by the mid-1990s (Economic Section 1998: 9; Mingsarn 1998: 3–4).

The success of capitalist development brought great optimism regarding the future. Business confidence was especially strong, and was bolstered by a process of political liberalization. Thailand's new magnates, seemingly created overnight, wanted to do everything on a grand and ostentatious scale. They bought only the most expensive cars and consumer goods, they wanted to construct the world's tallest buildings and imposing shopping centres, and began to look outside Thailand for newer, better and bigger opportunities. The government was keen to support them.

All of this saw most of the social and political debates of the 1970s and 1980s become far less significant. At the time, prior to the end of the Cold War, society had been polarized. Students, workers and intellectuals had been radicalized by the increasingly violent events of the 1973–76 period which saw military dictatorship overthrown, only to be replaced by a new authoritarianism three years later following a bloody coup. Many joined the clandestine Communist Party of Thailand (CPT), while others went into exile in the West. They continued to be interested in rural development, uplifting the poor, opposed the military and bureaucratic authoritarianism, and challenging capitalists and their close links with the state. They opposed the imperialism of Japanese and American investors, drawing heavily on dependency theory's images of the rich sucking out surpluses from the poor.[2] They considered their society corrupt, hierarchical, authoritarian and stifling, and believed that its economic and political leaders were the tools of capitalist and foreign interests.

Within a few years, however, such attitudes were changing. The CPT's Maoism was seen as too rigid, and its structures and decision-making as too hierarchical, while its strategies, focused on rural revolution, seemed less relevant for a rapidly industrializing Thailand. In addition, splits between communist parties in the region were demoralizing. Those in US and European exile were exposed to new theories and critiques of Soviet communism. At the same time, the government moved away from its extreme authoritarianism and appeared more conciliatory to those who had fled. Further, new state development policies also seemed better focused and open to local participation (Prudhisan and Maneerat 1997: 198–199).

When some returnees found that they were not subject to repression, others followed. This movement took place in the first half of the 1980s. While many returned to their studies or previous work, others found opportunities as academics, in business and in NGOs that were developing following the end of heavy state repression. They had returned just as the economy and society were about to enter their boom decade, coinciding with a political reformation. Conservative and authoritarian forces remained strong, but there was a transformation to a system where the constitution is more significant and elected civilian politicians rule. The period also saw civil society flower, with the media and various NGOs coming to play significant roles in challenging various policies of both military-dominated and elected governments. They have targeted corruption and abuses of power, and have been in the vanguard of democratic forces (see Hewison 1997a).

For the radicals of the 1970s, many of whom became the intellectuals of the boom era, the approaches, theories and ideologies they had learnt in the 1970s seemed anachronistic. Many of these intellectuals reflected the optimism of the boom. Some argued that the forces unleashed by globalization were unstoppable. They predicted that globalization would sweep aside much that was anachronistic in society. The ideals and concerns of the 1970s were 'solved' or simply bypassed as the economy boomed and transformed society.

THE ECONOMIC MELTDOWN

But something went wrong. In July 1997 the Bank of Thailand embarked on an expensive, ill-advised and ill-fated venture to shore up the baht. Concerted attacks on the currency in May and June depleted official reserves from about US$38 billion to just US$2.8 billion by the 2 July unpegging of the baht (Bello 1998: 14; Chalongphob 1998: 3–4, 8). When the crisis bit, foreign investors dumped the baht, and residents with unhedged foreign liabilities rushed to cover them, putting further pressure on the currency. The resulting economic firestorm engulfed the country. By August 1997 the government had no choice but to go to the IMF for a bailout.

The contraction of the economy that followed the devaluation was spectacular. Bangkok Bank (1999) figures show an economic contraction of over 11 per cent in 1997 and 1998. Whole business empires collapsed and bankruptcies doubled as thousands of companies closed in 1998, and hundreds more followed in 1999. Investment fell significantly, especially in the property, construction and manufacturing sectors, and the resulting record levels of unemployment approached 2 million. This had a significant impact in rural areas due to the strong links between rural incomes and urban employment. The poor saw incomes reduced by up to 25 per cent while the cost of living rose by as much as 40 per cent (*The Nation*, 26 September 1998, 22 March 1999). In education, the crisis saw dropout rates increase substantially (*Bangkok Post*, 18 February 1999). The downturn meant that many of the income and other gains of the boom were rolled back. A massive restructuring of business has occurred, with a large part of the domestic capitalist class struggling to retain its position. Foreign capital has made large gains, increasing investments in a range of sectors (Hewison 1999b: 31–33).

The initial IMF-organized response was focused on economic and fiscal targeting. While more attention was given to social safety-nets as the recession deepened, the strict controls demanded by the IMF became the target of intense criticism. Part of this reflected a nationalist response to increased foreign ownership, Western triumphalism that blamed the crisis on Asian social, economic and management 'sins', and the arrogance of international financial institutions in dealing with local agencies. National pride was threatened.

Significant disillusionment emerged. The advantages that many had felt would emanate from liberalization and globalization were seen to have been negated by the crisis. This paper will examine discontent regarding the liberalization and globalization, and assess the strength of its critique. The discontents, especially those representing significant elements of NGOs, social movements and intellectuals, were vigorous in their rejection of liberalization and globalization, and proposed an alternative rural localism.

OPPOSING NEO-LIBERAL GLOBALIZATION

Following a brief period when the government led by Chavalit Yongchaiyudh demonstrated its inability to respond to the crisis, a new coalition led by Chuan Leekpai took office in November 1997. At that time, Thailand announced its commitment to the IMF's economic programme. It accepted the IMF diagnosis of the economy's problems, and its emphasis on the need to restore investor confidence through tight monetary and fiscal policies, increased financial liberalization, greater economic openness and foreign investment, and the reform of public and private governance. In short, Thailand's government accepted a neo-liberal response to the crisis. Despite debate with the IMF, the Chuan government has generally adopted a recovery strategy that favoured further liberalization.

Opposition to this approach emerged from a number of groups. Elements of big domestic business were, for a time, critical of the IMF programme for its negative impact on liquidity. Even so, the relationship between the Chuan government and big domestic business was maintained. Small and medium business was less sanguine, reflecting the differential negative impacts of the crisis and the measures for amelioration. A more vociferous reaction emerged first as a desire to 'save' the country, and especially from foreigners who appeared to be gaining concessions and advantages. This involved some business leaders and NGOs criticizing IMF policies and opposing the government. Buddhist monks became involved in collecting gold and cash 'for the nation'. Workers opposed privatization; and a shelf of anti-IMF publications came off the presses. For a time it looked as though this movement was gaining strength, but its intensity soon waned. However, an NGO-social movement-intellectual opposition remained active. This opposition has been most coherent in developing and sustaining an alternative discourse of localism.

LOCALISM

Emerging alongside and associated with the nationalist reaction, localism distinguished itself from simplistic nationalism by denigrating the capitalist triumphalism of the boom and by drawing attention to perceived weaknesses in the country's development path from the mid-1950s. Pasuk (1999: 1) characterized this as a 'localism discourse' because it asserts the significance of the rural community as an opposition to economic growth, urban and industrialism.

It is important to recognize that localism is not simply an opportunistic response to the crisis, for it builds on several earlier debates. First, it links with discussions in the mid and late 1980s regarding NGO development strategy and ideology, much of it related to the cultural development perspective (*watthanatham chumchon*; henceforth CDP) on village development (see Chatthip 1991; Rigg 1991; Hewison 1993a). At the time some NGO activists considered this perspective conservative, as it did not directly address issues of state repression. Their criticisms reflected radical positions generated in the 1970s and early 1980s, and there were some deep and angry divisions in NGO ranks. However, the opening of the state to NGOs, brought by democratization and the move by development agencies to incorporate NGOs, saw the less confrontational CDP gain adherents and funding.[3]

The recent discussion has been more diverse than the earlier CDP debate. While not all NGOs, social movements and intellectuals have been a part of the localism push, the impetus has been driven by a significant section of them. Localism gained particular poignancy with the impact of the crisis. It also drew together the strands of earlier NGO and intellectual debates. Briefly, the crisis seemed to resurrect discourses from the 1970s. The catchwords of that period, such as 'imperialism', 'neo-colonialism', 'dependency' and 'domination', re-entered political debate. The crisis made rural localism a radical alternative. Where the CDP had been criticized as backward-looking, now it was taken up in the broader populist debate that opposed the IMF and the government. Conservatives and radicals were drawn together in their opposition to globalization, neo-liberalism and capitalist industrialization.

This process was significantly enhanced by the strategic intervention of King Bhumibol Adulyadej. The carefully-crafted image of the King has long advertized his concern for the rural poor. Part of this image presents him as a practical and skilled scientist seeking solutions to improve their welfare. In recent years the King's influence has grown dramatically, so that governments await each piece of his 'advice' and need to be seen to be responding.[4] The King's birthday speeches have played an important role in this. These events are now televized, and the King speaks at length on matters that interest him to an assembled audience of the powerful and wealthy.

In December 1997 part of the King's wide-ranging, even rambling speech included observations on the crisis. These drew on his so-called 'new theory' of self-sufficient agriculture meant to help people make a living at a level close to subsistence, and being content with this, bringing new direction and hope to their lives (Chai Pattana Foundation 1995, 1997).[5] He pointed to agriculture, arguing for the importance of 'having enough to eat ... enough to get by on' (Bhumibol 1998: 4, 7). This was a powerful message to government, and assisted in bringing conservatives and radicals together. He returned to this theme in subsequent speeches, 'clarifying' the meaning of *setthakit pho phiang*,[6] and reinforcing the 'alliance'.

With this context, it is now appropriate to turn to a discussion of the defining elements of this alternative localism, each to be discussed below: self-sufficiency, self-reliance, the rejection of consumerism and industrialism, culture and community, power, rural primacy, and nationalism.[7]

Self-sufficiency

Like the CDP before it, the new localism advocates rural self-sufficiency in basic needs – food, health care, housing and clothing. An important element in this is the view that production for family and community consumption meant that farmers would not be reliant on the market. The market is viewed as a major source of exploitation. By becoming more self-sufficient, the potential damage accruing from the vagaries of domestic or international markets is reduced. In this perspective, self-sufficiency denotes a 'moral economy' (*Bangkok Post*, 2 February 1998; Sungsidh 1998a: 42). Dr Prawase Wasi[8] (1999a: 5) argues that self-sufficiency involves the economy, but that it also should include compassion, wisdom, co-operation, stability and the environment. He also makes the point that self-sufficiency can apply as much to a nation as to individuals and families (Prawase 1999a). The suggestion is that a self-sufficient nation does not need to focus on the outside world. Rather, it may be selective in choosing its links, thereby avoiding being 'forced' into international markets and trade and the risks this entails.

Self-reliance

Self-sufficiency is meant to build self-reliance. It does this by constructing strong communities with the confidence to resist external and market pressures. Self-reliance is the ability of a community to take control of its destiny by making informed decisions about the future (Seri 1989: 4–5). This approach can apply to individuals as much as to communities. Prawase (1999b) argues that self-reliance entails being able to stand on one's own feet, and achieve sustainable development deriving from personal initiative. This perspective can be anti-development, suggesting that farmers de-link from the market economy and return to subsistence (see the discussion in Chatthip 1991: 124). The idea of de-linking is based on the assumption that it is indebtedness that prevents farmers from overcoming their poverty. The proposed answer to this problem is to cut the rural community's ties to the 'mainstream economy' (*Bangkok Post*, 24 May 1999).

Localists often define self-reliance in Buddhist terms. Prawase (1999a, 1999b) makes this connection most explicitly. He suggests that the greed inherent in modern development has led to chaos, and that solutions need to be grounded in Buddhist teaching. It is for this reason that Prawase pays particular attention to the elements that he identifies as the bedrock of Thai culture and values – Buddhism and agriculture (Kitahara 1996: 92–93). Prawase's vision of self-reliance is seen as a 'middle path', built on a society that emphasizes virtues such as truth, honesty, love and justice (Prawase 1999a: 3–4).

Consumerism and industrialism rejected

A strong message in localism is that liberalization and market economics have failed. The economic crisis and recession are seen as evidence of this failure (Sungsidh 1998a: 33). The market, consumerism, materialism, urbanism and industrialism are seen as the interconnected outcomes of rampant capitalist development, and each is identified as injurious for rural communities. 'Modern agriculture' is regularly blamed for having destroyed the assumed abundance of the past. Production for the market and export, the introduction of cash crops, land clearing, the use of chemicals and fertilizers and the impact of Western concepts in farming systems are held responsible for 'food shortage, low production, financial loss and indebtedness' (Ruang 1996: 24–25). That such Western methods have been attractive to farmers is seen to be driven by the desire to consume all kinds of goods that were seldom available in villages in previous decades. Indeed, rural malaise and the economic crisis itself are seen to derive from rural people's false and created need for consumer goods (Set Sayam 1997: 52). This perspective can also include a deep suspicion or even rejection of development approaches that promote industrialism and urbanism (Sanitsuda 1998).

Prawase (1999a: 18) argues, following the King, that Thailand's salvation is not in the export and industrial economy, but in 'reversing into the canal'. His argument is that Thais need to return to the values that provide strength to communities, rejecting the consumerism and the individualism of modern society. For localists, the antidote to this 'lust for consumption' is the self-reliant economy. Once established, its proponents argue, peace and happiness will emerge in rural communities, and the problems of 'migrant labour ... crime, narcotics and gambling ... [will] become less severe' (Sungsidh 1998a: 45). For many, this involves the end of the market, for where there is no cash economy there can be no greed and no debt (Kitahara 1996: 93).

Culture and community

Localism sometimes indicates an antipathy to urban life. Because it emphasizes values that are said to derive from rural communities, their culture and religion, these will often be portrayed as opposites of urban life and values. There is a tendency to view rural society as having been 'full of generosity, compassion, and mutual assistance, which are all disappearing' in the modern urban world (Rewadee 1996: 22). When localists examine rural society, they often find the values of the past have deteriorated, and they argue the need to reinvigorate or rediscover community values.

Where the romanticism of such perspectives on the past is recognized, localists will argue that the point is to create appropriate values that are seen to characterize the self-sufficient and self-reliant community. Whatever the perspective, 'community' is given significance as a term imbued with particular values. These include solidarity, equality, ruralism, popular wisdom, environmental concern and the like.

The enemies of these values and of community are money, trade, the market and commerce. These are features associated with urban life, industrial development and capitalism, and are seen to be rapacious and predatory of rural community values. For localists the community is not simply a source of empowerment for really existing villagers. Rather, the community is an ethical construction. The community and its values become a means of resistance to neo-liberal globalization and for reasserting values identified as appropriate. Indeed, this ethical or moral community is seen as the rootstock for a new, self-reliant, self-sufficient society (Pasuk 1999: 6–7, citing Saneh Chammarik, a respected activist and academic).

Power

The localist analysis of power places great emphasis on these rural–urban dichotomies. As noted above, it is urban culture, capitalism and consumerism that are identified as responsible for the destruction of the rural community and local cultures (see *Thai Development Newsletter*, 34, 1997: 49). In this, industry is identified as a 'curse', having 'dis-integrated communities, broken family ties, and destroyed the very root of the rural society' (*Bangkok Post*, 24 May 1998). Much is made of the fact that capitalists and powerful political elites have squeezed the village economy. It is argued that farmers must work hard just to survive, and that the exploitation of agriculture has meant that farmers have been made labourers and are pushed into cities in search of work (Chang Noi 1997: 44; Chatthip 1991: 131). Of course, this to the detriment of the village and further exacerbates the power of cities over villages.

Industry is seen to have provided few benefits for the agricultural sector. This is because industrialists and urban classes have grown wealthy while the peasantry has been left in poverty (Sungsidh 1998b: 52). For some, the cause of poverty is the rapaciousness of urban exploiters. Recent political conflicts tend to reinforce this picture. For example, several administrations have been keen to build dams in rural areas, ostensibly for irrigation, but principally for hydroelectricity to be consumed by industry. When villages oppose such 'public' works, as in the case of the Pak Mun dam, they are harassed and mistreated. The Chuan government was particularly unsympathetic to the Pak Mun protestors (see *Bangkok Post*, 30 July 2000) and to the plight of villagers in general. This reinforced the localist perspective that urban interests dominate Thailand's political economy.

Rural primacy

As should be clear in the foregoing discussion, rural society is central to the localist analysis. The exploitation of that society derives, in part, from the neglect of agriculture in state development strategies that emphasize urban enterprise and society. According to localists, this results in a fundamental ignorance of the economic potential of the countryside and its significance in the development of modern Thailand (Saneh in Pasuk 1999: 9). Hence localists call for a return to basics through an increased emphasis on agriculture. For some, agriculture and small community businesses are considered the only economic sectors that are 'real'; certainly, finance and big business are seen as somehow above the fundamental level of the economy (Prawase 1999a: 13).

Nationalism

The CDP included nationalist elements, but also reflected a suspicion of state nationalism, born of the political struggles during the 1970s. State nationalism was associated with the political right. The new localism, coming to prominence during the economic recession, has been far more responsive to a vocal nationalism. In part, this drew strength from public and intellectual oppositions to the liberalizing reforms demanded by the international financial institutions and implemented by the Chuan government. The government was seen as 'selling out' the country to foreigners, at the behest of the IMF (*Bangkok Post*, 8 and 14 March 1999). It also reflected the intellectual development of localism, where great emphasis was being placed on the local as unique and distinctively Thai. The privileging of things Thai and local meant that the gap between localism and nationalism was narrowed.

This resulted in sweeping statements that Thais had been misled by the West, and made slaves of financially strong countries. This slavery was evidenced in 'false' desires to consume all that emanated from the West (*Thai Development Newsletter* 1997: 49). Director of the important NGO, the Project for Ecological Recovery, Srisuwan Kuankachorn (1998) argues that the model of development adopted by Thailand has been 'wrong'. Rapid, large-scale development dependent on foreign capital had led Thais to a development dead-end. This model was foisted on Thailand by the US, which, through aid and education, brainwashed the elite and technocrats to implement an American development model. This approach encouraged resource destruction, brought no benefits to the majority, and entrenched consumerism. The IMF and World Bank are seen as reinforcing this model, threatening 'Thailand *as a culture*' (Pasuk 1999: 12).

In this context, globalization is perceived as a particular threat for it emphasizes money and capital 'at the expense of the nation and nationalism' (Sungsidh 1998a: 34). Globalization is often used as shorthand for Westernization and its associated negative outcomes for Thailand. For example, well-known rationalist Buddhist and human rights campaigner Sulak Srivaraksa uses 'globalization', 'consumerism' and 'Westernization' interchangeably, with the latter identified as a new colonialism (*Nation*, 21 March 1999). This colonialism threatens Thai values, resulting in a call to protect Thai culture, and especially rural life and agriculture.

Self-styled nationalists have been strong in their criticism of liberalization as a tool of rapacious foreigners keen to gain advantages in Thailand. This makes nationalists and localists allies in their opposition to further liberalization.

ASSESSING LOCALISM

In the 1980s the lengthy debate regarding the efficacy of the CDP revolved around its appropriateness as an approach to village-level development. For example, Rigg (1991) criticized the CDP for being an approach that was alien to most villagers, unrealistic, and which privileged an elite and misconceived the cultural picture of the village. He argued that the CDP was populist and backward looking. While Rigg's critique was not unchallenged (see Hewison 1993a), the nature of the new localism suggests a need to revisit his analysis.

In this section an assessment will be made of Thailand's contemporary localism. In the wake of the massive demonstrations at the 1999 Seattle meeting of the World Trade Organization, where neoliberal globalization was the subject of remarkable criticism, it is important to assess NGO and social movement alternatives. To be taken seriously, such alternatives should offer a realistic interpretation of the threats and negative impacts of liberalization and globalization. They should also provide a feasible alternative to the mainstream approach of governments, international business and financial institutions. These alternatives will need to be robust in their political and economic analysis. To begin this assessment, attention will be paid to the populism of the localism discourse.

Despite being a most imprecise term in the social sciences, populism has been a major theme of development theory and practice (Kitching 1982). The main elements of populism are:

1. a reverence for tradition;
2. a preference for organic models;
3. a conservatism where change is seen to derive from the inner growth of community institutions and practices;
4. the past is seen as a 'golden era', with modernization having diluted the idyllic village and its traditions;
5. agricultural development is privileged;
6. if industrialization is even considered, then it must be labour intensive;
7. justice, equity and equality are considered central aspects of society; and
8. outsiders are seen as exploiters, and urban-based exploiters are held responsible for removing the rural surplus.

If one examines these characteristics in relation to Thailand's localist discourse, then it is clear that it falls into the populist category.

In a paper sympathetic to the localist approach, Thailand's leading political economist, Pasuk Phongpaichit (1999: 13–14) notes that localism has been the subject of considerable criticism. As well as challenging its assumptions, logical inconsistencies and conservatism, there have been three major criticisms of the localist approach in Thailand. First, critics suggest, viewing the community as a source of morals and values is a 'hopeless idealization'. If there ever were such a moral community, it has been irreversibly transformed. Second, rural community values, rather than being based in egalitarianism and co-operation, derive from the patronage system. It is patronage that has permitted the political and economic exploitation of the rural community. Third, the salvation of the rural community is not to be sought through a reactivation of local wisdom but through a more thoroughgoing transformation of the community and countryside. These are important criticisms, hotly debated by the localists, but they do not exhaust the problems associated with this new populism. Here we can outline seven further points.

The first relates to the 'anti-capitalist' nature of the populist localism. Opposition to capitalism is an element that draws together the disparate group in the localist camp. It draws heavily on the dependency approach and like that approach, localism often misconceives capitalist society and economy. For example, Pasuk (ibid.: 15) argues that the localism discourse has gained currency because 'of the social division and environmental damage which are features of the development of urban capitalism all through history and all around the world'. Capitalism is therefore conceived as an imposition on, and thus external to, rural areas. But this is not the trajectory of a capitalist system that has a relatively short history and is only now becoming universal. As Pasuk has shown in her important studies of Thailand's development, rural areas have been critical for the emergence of capitalism (see Pasuk and Baker 1995).

This position also suggests that any analysis of exploitation must be based on a rural–urban dichotomy. Most analysts of capitalism would locate exploitation in the relationships between the owners of capital and others. While such relationships may exist between rural people and those in urban areas, this is not the only site of exploitation. It is also apparent that some localists draw on emotions that derive from debates that began during the nineteenth century in Thailand. These debates argued that middlemen who worked with very large margins in trading rural products exploited farmers. Often including a racial element – most of these traders were ethnic Chinese – such perspectives tend to conflate trade and capitalism. Implicit also is a privileging of a particular kind of work – agricultural production. As an editorial in the *Bangkok Post* (23 June 1998) observed, the 'farmer may be the backbone of the nation but is no more important than the truck driver, the computer programmer, the doctor and the business executive'. This anti-urban bias can and does preclude political alliances across the supposed rural–urban split. It is especially dismissive of the potential of a political role for organized labour. As Ungpakorn (1999) has indicated, to ignore labour – most of it urban-based – is to misunderstand its significance in the Thai political economy.

Second, it needs to be remembered that 'community' is a product of modernity, created as a reaction to modernization (Kemp 1996). 'Community' and 'modernity' are thus constructed as opposites, with 'community' defined in functionalist terms, where the organic whole is composed of essentially inseparable parts (Kitahara 1996: 77–78). This approach reinforces the conservatism of localism. It also suggests that it is essentially grounded in a romantic construction of an imagined past. Further, these constructions of community also ignore stratification, exploitation and power operating in villages. Such conservatism is not suggestive of a dynamic alternative vision of social or economic organization that challenges the dynamism associated with neo-liberal globalization.

A third point of criticism derives from the observation that discussions of community are a mixture of empirical description and normative positions (ibid.: 16). Thailand's localism is essentially normative. In response to empirical criticisms, localists have argued that their position on community is not a description of any reality, but an ethical proposition (Pasuk 1999: 15–16). However, such a defence does not cover localist critiques of modernity. It is noticeable that in their opposition to industrialism, many urban-based intellectuals ignore the positive outcomes of industrialization. Certainly, Thailand's development has created a most inequitable society and destroyed resources at a tremendous rate. At the same time, however, there have been remarkable gains in health, productivity and wealth (see Hewison 1993c). It has yet to be demonstrated that such advances are possible without industrialization and accompanying urbanization (Kitching 1982: 2–3).

The broad area of representation is a fourth issue for Thailand's localists. In his critique of the CDP, Rigg (1991: 204) argued that this approach was both externally constructed and elitist. He suggested that 'selective notions of village self-reliance, cooperation and participation have been coopted by academics (and then by the state) and placed within an entirely new, alien framework.' In response, it was possible to argue that the CDP had emerged from NGO experiences in village communities and that this meant that the CDP maintained strong links with the grassroots. In examining the new discourse, this argument is not so easily made. It is noticeable that the impact of intellectuals on the localist discourse has been rather more significant than in the case of the CDP.

The economic crisis prompted a number of intellectuals to take up the localism cause. The problem is that some of these intellectuals have tended to alienate the CDP from its roots in village-level development practice. They have re-established it as a localist discourse in a context where it offers little that is different from past forms of populist rhetoric. A variant of this approach sees academics and intellectuals as playing a critical role in establishing self-sufficiency. For example, Prawase (1999a: 8–9) makes much of the role for universities, the media, lawyers and other professionals and policy-makers in supporting and promoting self-sufficiency. He also argues that 'carefully thought-out' research should be funded to examine the potential for self-sufficiency in villages, and that research should be well organized.[9] Finally, he suggests the need for the government to appoint an 'economic tsar' to oversee the support of the 'fundamental' economy in agriculture and community business (Prawase 1999a: 17).

Such views appear to confirm Rigg's view that localism has a tendency to elitist prescriptions. In some formulations it also appears to favour a technocratic approach. It may be concluded that, when localism becomes an intellectual discourse and is removed from its grassroots, it is likely to promote backward-looking strategies.

The fifth issue for localism relates to the involvement of state officials. When they take up localist notions, 'self-reliance' and 'self-sufficiency' are transformed into elements of a top-down state development discourse. This sustains Rigg's criticism that localism is an alien framework masquerading as village-based, and is little different from orthodox development strategies. Such tendencies are especially noticeable when the King's ideas are included. The King's image as a reformer, scientist, philanthropist and remarkable Renaissance man has been so carefully crafted and marketed that no government can ignore his 'advice'. This usually means that some effort will be made to promote the King's ideas, even if this is only a matter of being seen to be responding. The problem, however, is that this approach tends to bring out the worst in government implementing agencies. Localism was taken up, most clearly in the Ministry of Interior, where sympathetic academics were influential as ministerial advisers. The Ministry (1998: 15–30) managed to make ideas of self-sufficiency fit its top-down approach, while academics produced development blueprints that reproduced all of the elements of state paternalism (see Mongkol 1998).[10] In other words, the coopting of the discourse by the state, while welcomed by those localists who saw an opportunity to promote their cause, was more likely to herald the decline of the approach as a development strategy.

Sixth, the linking of localism, populism and nationalism, noted above, suggests some unlikely relationships. Thai nationalism has usually been identified with the authoritarianism of monarchs and the military. There have been challenges to this state nationalism, and various political groups have attempted to adopt the symbols of nationalism. However, at least since the demise of communism, it is official nationalism that has pervaded Thailand's political space. Since the crisis began, localists and their intellectual allies have developed a discourse that now includes all the elements usually associated with the right-wing nationalist shibboleth of 'Nation, Religion and Monarchy'.

According to Pasuk (1999: 1), a groundswell of support for self-reliance grew from the King's birthday speech. Almost every piece of intellectual support for localism draws on the King's position.[11] Given that some of these intellectuals suffered at the hands of royally sponsored fanatics in the 1970s and 1980s, their adoption of royal positions is surprising. Of course, some intellectuals have long supported the monarchy. A good example is Prawase Wasi. He cultivated links with NGOs in the late 1980s, and especially with those favouring localist and Buddhist approaches. The crisis and the prominence of localism allowed him to promote his agendas, stating that

> I am of the view that the profound and incisive thoughts of His Majesty [on self-sufficiency] are true. Let the Thai people study and understand what His Majesty has had to say and we shall be able to turn the country around ... and protect ourselves from the suffering of future economic crises. (Prawase 1999a: 8)

Localism's emphasis on community has privileged religion. As mentioned above, Buddhism is seen as a critical element of Thai, especially village, culture. This has seen localism associated with Buddhism. Religion has thus become an element of what Prawase (ibid.: 1) refers to as 'national correctness', where self-sufficiency and self-reliance are seen as Buddhist traits. This approach tends to imbue localist rhetoric with considerable Buddhist chauvinism.

While the emergence of nationalism is understandable in the context of the severe economic downturn and in the face of the IMF's unpopular remedies, it is not simply an outcome of the crisis. For example, Chatthip (1991: 133) argues that the 'community culture discourse' is 'unique to Thailand'. Here he nationalizes a populist discourse that has been a common historical reaction to the inequalities associated with capitalist industrialization in a range of historical settings.

Nationalist rhetoric was especially popular amongst a group of politicians, most of them unelected senators, who opposed the IMF and the Chuan government. They were keen to adopt localism in support of their cause (*Bangkok Post*, 12 March 1999). In discussing this group, Thitinan (1998) contends that 'it was not surprising that the very same individuals and coalitions who earlier pushed for financial liberalization were now trying to erect nationalist fences to shut out foreigners', and he observes that many of those who opposed further liberalization were responsible for Thailand's economic problems. He warned that 'NGOs and pro-democracy groups ... should not allow their hardship and disenchantment to be manipulated and co-opted'. He added that for NGOs to allow their hardship and disenchantment to be manipulated and co-opted was naïve politics, for the real 'enemies' in the economic crash were not outsiders.

Finally, it is important to examine the economic potential of populist localism. It is obviously critical that this potential be established if the approach is to be considered a viable alternative to capitalist industrialization and neo-liberal globalization. It is recognised that the economic model at the heart of populist localism does not necessarily reject notions of material progress. Rather, it sees progress as deriving from agriculture based in smallholder production and the values associated with the community of smallholders. There is no place for large-scale industrialization or urbanisation. Rural society and culture must be maintained and, if necessary, recreated.

In his analysis of similar approaches, Kitching argues that there is no example to support the thesis that living standards can be raised and inequality reduced while maintaining the rural family household as the basic production unit. Further, it seems that there may be a limit to the levels of welfare that can be expected from agricultural production (Kitching 1982: 136, 180). While there are arguments against this, the localist's tendency to see the market and trade as necessarily exploitative demands that agriculture be small-scale.

Populist localism provides a vision of equality and freedom from the ecological destructiveness and human exploitation of global capitalism. But it presents few insights as to how this vision could be implemented through localist development strategy. As Kitching (1982: 180) argues, an 'attractive utopian vision is not an adequate basis for a theory of development, nor does the desirability of a state of affairs guarantee its possibility'.

CONCLUSION

Thailand's localism offers a moral critique of capitalist industrialization, liberalization and globalization. It has a powerful appeal because it challenges neo-liberal development dogma. In addition, the recognition that the rural sector has been ignored and exploited is a useful corrective to the capitalist triumphalism associ-ated with the economic boom. As Pasuk (1999: 16) notes, during the crisis, localist criticisms have seen some state and society 'initiatives to moderate free-market liberalism', and the localism discourse has been a 'source of hope' for some. While this may be sufficient in itself, if Thailand's localism is to provide an alternative to the neo-liberal vision, then it needs to go further. It would need to disentangle itself from past populisms that have been singularly unsuccessful.

At present, however, localists are not able to offer any politically sound or economically viable alternative. Thailand's localism has not wrenched itself free of the influence of the dependency perspectives of the 1970s and 1980s. This prevents it from accurately locating the causes of exploitation in capitalist processes. As a populist discourse it remains bedevilled by the issues that have been a feature of populist politics everywhere; it is reactionary, romantic, anti-urban and chauvinist. In any case, where populist ideology has been converted into national development practice, the outcomes have been poor (see Kitching 1982: Ch. 5). While it is true that there are gross social and economic injustices involved in Thailand's development, the localist alternative appears no more viable than any of the previous forays into populist theory and practice elsewhere.

To reject populism is not to condemn the poor to the worst excesses of capitalist exploitation. The point is to note that populist development ideas are a frequently seen response to industrial development and the expansion of capitalist methods of production. But their alternatives have been found wanting, politically and economically. This is not to suggest that localist approaches to village-based rural development have no merit (see Hewison 1993a). But where localism becomes a national development strategy or a political discourse, an approach, once firmly rooted in development praxis, it is transformed into a middle-class intellectual exercise.

That the dominant neo-liberal development perspective needs to be challenged for its neglect of equity and other negative outcomes is clear. That NGOs and social movements should have a significant role in this challenge is not in doubt. Not all challenges will be realistic, and Thailand's localism indicates this in its reliance on utopian visions. While offering succour for some, such approaches represent a limited political strategy and risk diminishing the impact of NGO and social movement critiques of the dominant neo-liberal orthodoxy.

ACKNOWLEDGEMENTS

This paper is based on my contribution to a paper presented with Malcolm Falkus at the Seventh International Conference on Thai Studies, Amsterdam, 4–8 July 1999. His contributions to that paper are gratefully acknowledged. Discussions with Apichart Thongyou, Nicola Phillips, Richard Higgott, Shaun Breslin, Chris Baker, Pasuk Phongpaichit, Michael Connors, Duncan McCargo and Ji Giles Ungpakorn were most useful, as was the research assistance provided by Scot Barmé. I am grateful for the support of the Centre for the Study of Globalisation and Regionalisation at the University of Warwick, where some aspects of the paper were re-examined.

Earlier and shorter versions of parts of this paper were presented in Hewison 1999a; 2000.

NOTES

1   For a detailed discussion of neo-liberal globalization, see Gill 1995 and MacEwan 1999.
2   On dependency theory and Thailand, see Hewison 1989: 13–16.

3 This is not to suggest that the CDP did not bring development benefits in practice. See Hewison 1993a for examples.
4 For a general discussion of the King's role, see Hewison, 1997a.
5 While the King pointed to agriculture, he also directed his comments to factories, where self-sufficiency was seen to involve reduced wages and benefits for workers during the crisis.
6 This term is best translated as 'self-sufficient economy'. However, since at least 1998, the King has insisted that it be rendered 'sufficiency economy'. It might be argued that his 'clarifications' represent an attempt to remove some attention from notions of autarky implicit in terms like 'self-reliance' and 'self-sufficient economy'. This fits neatly with the King's long interest in fostering conservative notions of order based on concepts of moderation and morality. While the King's penchant for embedding his meanings in anecdotes and obscure examples means that it is sometimes difficult to discern his exact message, it seems that on this occasion he was reinforcing his conservative message of the need for people, especially those in rural areas, to be content with their lot, so long as they could get by.
7 In the discussion of the concepts involved, the sources utilized will include materials produced prior to the economic crisis, but which reflect the localism discourse.
8 Dr Prawase Wasi is a respected medical doctor, rationalist Buddhist, author, commentator, political reformer and human rights campaigner. While not a political radical, Prawase has a strong record of anti-authoritarianism. This has allowed him long-established links to NGOs. In recent years he has been invited to advise and work with government, most importantly in developing the 1997 constitution. For comments on this latter role, see McCargo (1998: 11–27). Since 1997 he has been a leading advocate of the self-sufficient economy, providing a link between NGOs and the King's approach.
9 Among areas suggested for research is 'culture', including: Thai food, fruit and vegetables, traditional medicine, Buddhism, local woven cloth, music and the performing arts (Prawase, 1999a: 25–27).
10 There is considerable opposition to the perceived opportunism of the Ministry of Interior in its adoption of self-reliance and self-sufficiency (Pasuk 1999: 14–15).
11 Many intellectuals have been very enthusiastic about the King's ideas. While the *lèse-majesté* law might prevent any serious and critical analysis of the King's 'new theory', if intellectuals were not keen on the King's ideas, they might have just ignored his interventions.

11

POLITICAL REFORM THROUGH THE PUBLIC SPHERE: WOMEN'S GROUPS AND THE FABRIC OF GOVERNANCE

Philippe Doneys

INTRODUCTION

Much of the recent literature on political reform has been influenced by the concept of good governance, borrowed originally from economic management theories and applied by the World Bank to public institutions. This appropriation, however, repeated the management discourse of the 1980s, with downsizing and institutional restructuring as central features, and so the concept was used mostly endogenously to the state. Paradoxically this state-focused interpretation of governance was either ignored by civil society theorists who dismissed any reference to the state (hence avoiding state reform altogether) or encouraged by those who claimed that civil society has a beneficial effect on the state, increasing both transparency and accountability in decision making.[1]

This chapter supports the second view, but also argues further that any political reform should articulate the institutional linkages that would combine state and non-state actors for effective reform. It attempts to reconcile discussions of civil society within a political reform agenda by using the concept of the public sphere, and by presenting a case study to show how this sphere institutionalizes itself vis-à-vis the state, and therefore redefines the scope of reform itself. Such changes go beyond the watchdog role that we ascribe to non-state actors since, as this chapter suggests using the concept of the public sphere (Habermas 1989), organizations such as women's groups in Thailand demonstrate the quiet changes taking place whereby non-state actors affect both policy and the structure of decision making itself. This is done by prying open and reconstructing the legitimate sphere of political debate and normalizing a public sphere where new actors contribute opinion, judgement as well as expertise, and are encouraged to develop contentious strategies.[2] Non-state actors' political role must therefore be located in the transformation of the political through the public sphere.

As political power is increasingly shifting from material and militaristic forms to communicative and informational ones, according to Keohane and Nye, the role of non-state actors in decision making will grow rapidly (Keohane and Nye 1998). Already, one would be at pains to understand the political reforms taking place in Thailand since 1991–92 (such as decentralization and autonomy of the judicial system), without looking further than state institutions and traditional power holders like the military, the bureaucracy and the business sector. This loss of sovereignty, whereby sheer force cannot on its own overcome popular discontent, must lead us to re-evaluate the legitimate location of political power. Or, as Rosenau and Durfee put it:

> To challenge the authority of the state and then to redirect legitimacy sentiments toward supranational or subnational collectivities is to begin to deny that the state has the ultimate decisional power, including the right to resort to force. (Rosenau and Durfee 2000)

This 'relocation of authority', however, is often the result of much less conspicuous trends at work, trends that are nevertheless important to our understanding of political change. The public sphere can be a useful tool in understanding new forms of political engagement at the base of any successful reform. This paper first starts with an explanation of the public sphere, followed by an evaluation of its use for political reform and the presentation of an especially relevant application in terms of gender relations in politics. It will then focus on the role of women's groups during successive constitutional and electoral periods in Thailand, and considers how women's groups used an extensive network – spanning grassroots, human rights, development and research organizations as well as foreign support agencies – in combination with opening up a discursive process as a legitimate domain of political activity and participation, to influence legal changes and the 1997 constitution-drafting process. It concludes that women's organizations occupy a new strategic position in this public sphere within the larger structure of traditional Thai power relations and that reform, to be effective, should be able to tap strength from such activities.

The case of women's groups is especially interesting, considering, for instance, the low ratio of women sitting on the Constitutional Drafting Assembly and yet the realization of many objectives set by women's organizations in the constitution. The large number of women's groups and their activism is in contrast to the low ratio of women in the parliament or in higher governmental positions. The concept of public sphere may provide clues to this paradoxical situation. The central argument is therefore not to test the appropriation of political power by non-state actors but to demonstrate how specific legal and political projects were either designed or shaped through a subtle but marked participation by non-state actors in the public sphere.

THE PUBLIC SPHERE AND REFORM IN A THAI CONTEXT

Habermas uses an historical approach to describe the rise and fall of the public sphere in Western Europe. He locates the rise of the public sphere at the point where the production of a bourgeoisie was accompanied by a sphere of discursive relations based on communicative reason.[3] The word 'public' is used in a specific form, one in which discourse in civil society took on a political shade based on public opinion. In that sense, the word 'public' is not associated with state institutions. Yet, it cannot simply be opposed to 'private', since Habermas places the public sphere outside state boundaries but also distinguishes it from public forms of association (hence our opposition later between 'unpolitical' public space and the more 'political' public sphere).[4] Therefore, as will be shown, women may take a public role by engaging in philanthropic activity, remaining nevertheless outside the public sphere. This semantic distinction has a determinant influence in understanding the public space women were afforded until recently, and helps frame the private/public divide, and later the public space/sphere divide, in surprisingly clear gender terms.

More generally, the concept of the public sphere could help us understand the link between the rising bourgeoisie in Thailand, and the creation of a critical discursive sphere that presented itself in words that were admissible by the authorities. In this way, the public sphere, in its expanding phase, may provide a stepping stone into the political sphere by remaining within the bounds of what is acceptable, or what is perceived to be non-political. This is especially relevant for women who were excluded from the political world of men in pursuit of power. For instance, it allowed women's groups to receive assistance denied to them in the political sphere through close networking with foreign organizations. This would also help to explain how the rise of a discourse among non-state actors labelled as 'unpolitical' was present in a public sphere that reinvented the political scene in everything but its name. Hence NGOs in Thailand came out relatively unscathed from the state repression of the late 1970s and early 1980s.

It also refines our conception of civil society by locating actions in relation to other spheres while articulating its structural dimension.[5] It approaches civil society without forgoing the state or opposing it to the state, a simplification common to civil society theorists. The importance of all this for reform is that political institutions are less clearly demarcated outside society.[6] If that is so, cannot society and the state blend together for future reforms? According to Habermas, however, whatever the extent of linkages between them, these actors should remain distinct as, ultimately, the source and responsibility for actions (and hence reparation or compensation) must be clearly located (Habermas 1993).

Keck and Sikkink's (1998) conceptualization adds a practical and actual viewpoint to that of Habermas, by showing how the different 'politics' used by non-state actors are increasingly embedded in the state's procedures, policies, discourse or behaviour. Their four political tactics (information, symbolic, leverage and accountability politics) have all been comparative advantages of non-state actors in Thailand, including women's groups. These advantages flow first from the perceived lack of self-interest of non-state actors, where both the Thai state and business organizations are marred in the public eye by having self-seeking motives, then from the multiplicity of actors which force alternative forms of information, and finally from non-state actors' specialization, whereby these actors can choose an area of support, ignored by the state, without the need for reallocation of resources. This chapter will cover examples of every one of these tactics. Keck and Sikkink also identify five stages of influence. Of these, women's groups have been particularly efficient at (1) issue creation and agenda setting, and (2) influence on discursive positions (2). They also at times influence (3) institutional procedures,[7] (4) policy changes,[8] and in rare cases, (5) state behaviour.[9]

WOMEN THREADING THEIR WAY THROUGH PUBLIC 'SPACE'

Thai women are often described as enjoying more freedom than women in other Southeast Asian countries, especially when they venture outside the private world of the family. While traditionally Western women were kept out of both political and business sectors, Darunee Tantiwiramanond argues that women in Thailand could not afford to remain on the fringe of the economic sector since they had to 'invest' in the Buddhist orders (Darunee 1997: 171). Men, however, could choose to earn merit by entering the monkhood. Moreover, during the corvée era, women had to become self-sufficient while their husbands were away for several months of the year (Juree 1994: 523). More recently, as men migrated to work in the cities and abroad, women became the main actors in local economies. As a result, women have entered the business field, and are today even favoured by employers over their male colleagues for reasons ranging from being less troublesome to being more productive (*Bangkok Post*, 12 November 1998). In 1997 women made up more than 45 per cent of the labour force, the highest percentage in Asia (compiled from NSO 1997: 40).

The emergence of women in the economic arena has been called by some as a 'quiet, yet powerful revolution'.[10] Nevertheless, this foray out of the private realm of the home has not translated into an equivalent expansion into the political field. Indeed, in the 1998 Human Development Index, Thailand ranks third behind Barbados and Bahamas for the ration of women in economic activity compared to men, but is down at number 28 for the number of women in government out of a total of 34 developing countries included in the high human development group (four Islamic states do worse, as well as Argentina and Uruguay) (UNDP 1998b).

Although women were given the right to stand for election in 1932, when Siam became a constitutional monarchy, between 1992 and 1993 women made up a minuscule 2.7 per cent of all MPs and only 2 per cent of senators (calculated from Suteera and Thomson 1994: 11). Today women still make up only about 6 per cent of the parliament (UNDP 1998a). In the bureaucracy, women make up the majority of employees (51.8 per cent in 1995) but only as a result of their dominance of the bottom three ranks (out of eleven) in the civil service (Suteera 1995). The top three ranks comprise less than 10 per cent women. This lack of representation has had significant consequences. Women, for instance, could not become local government officials such as *phuyaiban* (village head) or *kamnan* (subdistrict head) until 1982, and, as a result of this low representation, many labour and family laws are still discriminatory. As Pasuk and Baker remark (1996: 114), 'Most women work. A few manage. None govern.'

Traditionally, however, for women to enter a public space was hazardous territory. When women voiced political demands, they were branded as unwomanly and accused of endangering the unity of the family, similar to the suffragettes in early twentieth-century England. Fishel adds that, if anything, the 'notion of a distinction between public and private spheres' that accompanied the centralization of the bureaucracy under the reign of King Chulalongkorn 'further marginalized women, as decision-making and administrative work moved from the home and into public offices' (Fishel 1997: 455).

As in nineteenth-century England, women in Thailand could venture into public roles so long as they remained within the bounds of domesticity (Yeo 1989). Thus, despite having open access to economic activities outside the home, when women ventured into the public eye their roles remained identified with the virtues of caring and devotion associated with motherhood. As in England, Thai women of aristocratic descent created various philanthropic organizations for the care of war-wounded, the young and the disabled. Indeed, they were the first indigenous non-state philanthropic agencies to be established apart from Chinese secret societies.

It is therefore not coincidental that the first non-governmental organizations that gave women a public space were philanthropic in nature. Already in 1893, Thanphuying Plien Pasakornravongs, one of the Ladies of the Royal Thai Court, proposed the establishment of the Sapha Unalom Daeng (which is now the Thai Red Cross) with the consent of King Chulalongkorn.[11] Sapha Unalom Daeng was created to care for wounded soldiers and the sick, as well as to provide medical supplies (TDN 1995: 49). After the 1932 coup, a female editor of *Ying Thai* magazine set up the Samakhom Satri Thai Haeng Sayam (Women City Club), a social service association, and in 1943 the wife of the premier created the Women's Cultural Club (WCC) to care for those in need (Amara and Nitaya 1997: 29). By 1956, the WCC was present in almost every province and became the National Women's Council of Thailand. Amara and Nitaya describe the organization as a coalition of associations consisting 'of upper class people who provide social services to the poor or destitute' (ibid.: 30).

This public activity, however, created an alternative public space where femininity was further 'domesticated' (Yeo 1998: 3). Yet other obstacles delayed women's entrance to the male-dominated public sphere. Darunee, for one, argues that the tradition of servitude was undepinned by the Brahmanist forms that Buddhism assumed in Thailand (Darunee 1997: 169, 173). This influence was also present in the judicial system, which was based on Brahmanism right up to 1932. Accordingly, up to the end of the nineteenth century a woman was a man's asset and therefore was not a legal entity, effectively removing her from public forms of engagement. Bencha Yoddumnern-Attig argues that, in the household, historically, the man was 'responsible for dealing with outsiders, particular officials and upper class people' (Bencha 1992: 32).

Furthermore, women are considered 'merit deficient' (Darunee 1997: 171 calls them 'merit clients' to male 'merit patrons') and for this reason would constantly need to 'make merit'. The highest form of merit for a woman according to Juree is earned through a man, when her son enters the monkhood (Juree 1994: 522). Thus, the most enviable position for a woman is not only to serve, but to be the mother of a son.

Another traditional hindrance to women entering the public sphere was the recognition of the female sex as a polluting agent (on this topic, see ibid: 522–523). Hence, when a woman entered a public space, she ran the risk of draining strength and power from men.[12] As a consequence, until the twentieth century women were excluded from the only avenue to literacy, the Buddhist monasteries.

Women's entrance in a public space, and then into the public sphere, must be understood with this knowledge. Effectively, women had to thread their way carefully into the public sphere. The 'domestic ideology' was therefore both a blessing and a curse. It allowed women to venture into a public space but it effectively changed the nature of what was 'public' by creating an alternative public space, one that was gendered on perceived female traits. This is not to say that women have never tried to enter the public sphere, but that it was only well into the 1970s that women ventured out of the charitable field (public space) into more political activities on a wide scale (public sphere). The reasons for this are diverse, but one reason in particular came from the charitable work itself, the realization that no amount of care would be enough to improve women's conditions without a more political approach.

INTO THE PUBLIC SPHERE AND TOWARDS POLITICAL REFORM

A few women's civic groups have been around for a while in Thailand. The Association of Women Lawyers, for instance, dates back to 1947. Yet, only with the 1973 change from a military to a civil government did women's groups become more active and political. The 1980s saw the NGO sector mushroom, and this growth was also reflected in the number of women's groups. Many of these organizations, such as EMPOWER and Friends of Women Foundation (FOW), started as charitable organizations geared to protect and help disadvantaged women in the rural sector and in prostitution, but later felt the need for political change. This change of approach is also consistent with Korten's (1990) typology of NGOs, in which they evolve from mostly charitable to more structural activities. This evolution happens when humanitarian organizations learn from grassroots experience that structural factors need to be altered for an effective and sustainable improvement in standards of living. Muller (1989: 59) sees this evolution as a displacement in the strategic response from a technical option of intervention towards a more ideologically based motivation.

The 1980s witnessed the coalescence of various groups around specific issues. Thus the reform in 1982 of the Local Administration Act (1914) helped trigger a movement for the inclusion of women as village and district chiefs. Organizations like the Friends of Women Foundation both campaigned on specific issues – such as the treatment of women in police custody – and worked with government agencies in producing surveys and framing possible areas of state intervention (or agenda setting, in Keck and Sikkink's framework). The late 1980s saw the creation of more politically active organizations which viewed the political system less as institutions to oppose but as targets to include in a wider framework for political demands concerning women's rights.

Suteera Thomson remarks that the first women's organizations did not aim at increasing awareness of women's issues.[13] They came to realize, however, that such a limited approach was dwarfed by a larger political structure. And as men dominated these institutions, a policy of increasing women's representation in these agencies became a priority for many women's organizations. Ruengrawee Ketphol, of the Asia Foundation, adds further that from satisfying practical needs, women's organizations were led into political issues and ultimately to amending or changing the constitution.[14]

This change also reflected the willingness of foreign donors to fund programmes and projects that aimed at educating the population politically and organizations that were involved in more political work. Many foreign aid agencies such as CIDA (Canada) or DANIDA (Denmark), as well as NGOs such as NOVIB (Netherlands) the Asia Foundation (USA) and CUSO (Canada) have specific guidelines regarding the inclusion of women, and some, such as CIDA, clearly state the need for political change in that regard.[15] Therefore local groups have also developed horizontal links across national divides. Transnational organizations, whether governmental or non-governmental, offer both guidance and assistance that may be difficult to get internally. This is an important development which provides these groups with a support network which movements such as the suffragettes did not have in their time. Without conflating the importance of these links, they provide resources, information and networking which strengthen the movements by making them more autonomous from domestic pressures.[16] Regional organizations such as the Centre for Asia-Pacific Women in Politics (CAPWIP), or the Asian Cultural Forum on Development (ACFOD), build their power on the exchange of similar experiences across countries. This opening of NGOs, including women's groups, to both larger political structures and the funding from foreign donors that accompanied such change, has unwanted consequences. Already the Thai government has accused local NGOs of being pawns in the hand of foreign agencies (the infamous *mu thi sam* or 'third hand'). This very accusation, however, as Callahan argues, indicates that NGOs are *ipso facto* political actors (Callahan 1993).

Thus groups like the Association for the Promotion of the Status of Women (APSW, created in 1974, registered in 1982), the Gender and Development Research Institute (GDRI, established in 1990), the GenderWatch Group (GWG, created by GDRI in 1993) and the Women in Politics Institute (WPI, established in 1993) were created with the objective of empowering women by making the political system more democratic and more decentralized, and by encouraging women to become candidates in local and national elections. According to Dr Pusadee, director of WPI, women's groups see the constitution as an important tool to change labour and family laws that are discriminatory towards women.[17] Besides women being barred from certain government positions, quotas existed until very recently in universities.[18] Moreover the Family Law still allows a man to divorce on grounds of adultery – a right not extended to his wife (unless the husband openly admits that he has another partner), a situation that the Council of State explains by reference to 'men's and women's nature as well as the traditions of Thai society'.[19]

These groups claim that leadership positions in the government are a necessary step towards increasing women's rights in the long term, and it is through the public sphere that such schemes are encouraged.

WOMEN'S GROUPS AND ADVOCACY

The 1974 constitution was the first constitution in Thailand which stated that 'men and women have equal rights. Any action limiting equal rights and freedom is unconstitutional and not permissible' (Suteera and Maytinee 1996: 3).[20] At the time, only one woman sat on the drafting committee, and according to one male member, those provisions would not have been included in the constitution without the female representative. The 1974 constitution was abrogated with the military takeover in 1976, and many of its progressive elements were then lost. The 1978 charter omitted the specific reference to women on equal rights (stating 'all persons have equal rights ...'). However, building on the contribution of the Women Lawyers' Association to the 1974 constitution, and the campaign that led to the amendment of the Local Administration Act in 1982, the women's movement became more cohesive in the late 1980s and early 1990s.

Since that period, the Thai women's movement has clearly illustrated the 'politicization of social life' implied in the concept of the public sphere, where reform is shaped from outside the state. The struggle to end discrimination has been carried into the media, and the discursive mechanisms used (such as conferences, hearings and seminars) were combined with an increasing array of democratic mechanisms ranging from lobbying, collaborative tactics and mobilization. Women's groups have rallied around specific campaigns, and have proved capable of changing state policy on occasion. One example was the Prevention and Suppression of Prostitution Act (1996), which transferred criminal responsibility from the prostitute to the customer and to sex trade establishments.

A rational approach underlies two currents in the movement which formed the basis of action prior to the 1997 constitutional changes.[21] On the one hand, women's groups fought for greater decentralization and representation of women in state agencies, especially at the local level. One of the main obstacles was the 1978 cabinet resolution that barred women from the position of deputy district chief, effectively removing the main access to the positions of district chief and provincial governor. Women's groups such as the APSW and the Women Lawyers' Association (WLA) started campaigning in 1990, and the ban was finally abolished in early 1993. Two weeks later two women were promoted to the positions of governor and deputy governor (TDN [22] 1993: 1; TDN [19] 1991: 54).

Meanwhile, other organizations began preparing women for local political office. For example, the Gender and Development Research Institute (GDRI) and the Women for Democratic Development Foundation prepared the ground for the Subdistrict Council and Subdistrict Administration Organization (SAO) Act of 1994. The GDRI trained women both on democratic institutions in general and specifically on the new Act, and encouraged them to file candidacy for the first SAO elections. In total 547 women were specially trained concerning SAOs. From this group, 126 women stood as candidates in May 1995. Sixty-four women who had been trained eventually won their elections. These training programmes in effect created links and institutional support for local women leaders, people's organizations and non-governmental organizations. Although some observers, such as Juree Vichit-Vadakan, admit that there are limitations to changing society through laws, such legal opportunities allow women to demonstrate their capacity to perform and thus foster a normative dimension not necessarily induced by regulations.[22] In a sense, the law in itself does not change political culture, but creates institutional arrangements that may contribute to internalization and build a foundation for further reforms.

The second issue of campaign regards legal discrimination, both in ministerial regulations and in the constitution. As soon as the military-led government submitted its new charter in 1991, women's groups used the ratification by Thailand in 1985 of the UN Convention on the Elimination of all forms of Discrimination Against Women (CEDAW) to push for changes in the constitution.[23] A movement formed around the GDRI to amend Article 24 of the 1991 charter, which stated: 'Persons are equal before the law and shall be granted equal protection under the law.' The proposed additional sentences were: 'Women and men have equal rights. Any action limiting equal rights and freedoms is unconstitutional and not permissible.' The GDRI co-organized conferences in July 1993 on the topic, along with the GenderWatch Group and the Female Parliamentarians Group, and invited the chairperson of the Constitutional Amendment Committee. The GenderWatch Group used its grassroots bases to organize public meetings with local MPs. A petition was also launched with the signature of about 3,100 prominent citizens, amongst whom were 90 MPs (Suteera and Maytinee 1996: 14). Since 316 votes were needed in parliament, the GDRI added a postcard-writing campaign using the network of women that it had used since it began working on local government. According to Suteera Thomson, the Minister of the Interior admitted that many MPs had never previously received this sort of mailing, and therefore were worried about women's support in the coming election.[24] The amendment was unanimously passed in October 1994.

Aside from the issue of evaluating whether the campaign was effectively responsible for the overwhelming support in parliament, it brought together different actors of civil society that ultimately were to meet again in subsequent campaigns.

THE CREATION OF THE 1997 CONSTITUTION

For the first time, as Klein argues, the 1997 Constitution is not a subservient tool to established laws and regulation (Klein 1998). It states clearly that 'the constitution is the supreme law of the State. The provision of any law, rule or regulation which are contrary to or inconsistent with this constitution shall be unenforceable' (OCS 1997: 3, Article 6). Given the more visionary scope of the new constitution, women's groups were aware that if they could influence the drafting committee into including a reference to equality, this could open the door to a general abolition of existing organic laws and regulations.

By the time the Banharn administration decided on 17 May 1996 to amend Article 211 of the constitution to allow the drafting of a new charter, women's groups had developed into an effective movement that could reach directly to the grassroots level, gaining the attention of the national media, as well as contacting key state officials. According to Ruangrawee Ketphol of the Asia Foundation, much of that process was opened up following the Beijing Conference in 1995.[25]

Thus, women's organizations decided to create the Women and Constitution Network (WCN), a coalition of 54 NGOs, to influence more efficiently the new charter-drafting process under an umbrella organization. The first goal of the organization consisted of getting as many women as possible to apply for candidacy to sit on the Constitutional Drafting Assembly (CDA). After all the male-dominated drafting committees of previous charters, the WCN wanted to make sure that this time around women could influence the process. As Klein argues, however, women's groups were victims of their own success as the mass campaign to fill the list of ten representatives per province was replicated by other organizations (Klein 1998: 12). Out of 10 people elected for each of the 76 provinces (elections took place within the group of people who applied if there were more than 10 candidates), one was to be selected by the parliament. Even though in the end only six women – out of the 6,789 female applicants and 64 women elected – were among the 76 candidates picked by the parliament, the process succeeded in creating links with organizations and individuals throughout the countryside to monitor the CDA and participate in public hearings (ibid.: 12).

The coalition used a twin strategy of direct pressure on the constitution-drafting process and indirect influence through education and mobilization. On the one side the WCN lobbied the drafting members directly, and submitted its own 'handbook' indicating what to add or change in the constitution. The network had a close relationship with the drafting members, especially through the six female CDA members. According to Dr Pusadee Tamthai, the six members were constantly briefed by women's groups and given important information, such as research findings, to pass on to the drafting sub-committee (made up of academics). These research findings are often only avail-able through women's groups. Prapapan Udomchanya, for instance, a judge on the central juvenile and family court, remarked that she often cites information obtained from the GDRI to advocate law amendments (GDRI 1996: 17). Moreover, Naiyana Supapung, the current WCN co-ordinator, points out that women's groups were aware that many people sitting in the assembly would eventually present their candidature as MPs or senators, and so they used election campaign strategies to win over CDA members.[26]

Another strength of the non-state sector could be seen in the use of specific case studies. According to Jiraporn Uafua and Nawyeat Yotying-Aphiram of the Foundation For Women (FFW), NGOs found that these studies offered an effective support to advocacy work, as the studies showed first-hand the shortcomings of existing regulations.[27] Organizations such as the Friends of Women Foundation have carefully documented police treatment of rape victims, for instance. This research is used to argue for legal and political change, but even more importantly, to check whether existing programmemes are being implemented, which can be a powerful form of accountability politics.

To what extent these efforts were decisive in influencing the drafting assembly is hard to evaluate. Dr Somkit Leutpaitoon, one of the legal experts of the CDA, said that important information was conveyed by these organizations that may not have been included otherwise.[28]

Moreover, specific points raised by women's organizations were eventually written into the constitution, including the important Article 30 which states that men and women enjoy equal rights, Article 53 which ensures that youth and family members are protected and cared for by the state (an article which Dr Suteera Thomson of GDRI said was the proposal of women's organizations), and Article 80, which states that the state shall promote equality between women and men. Article 78, which stresses decentralization, was also an objective, but one shared with numerous other organizations.

The second strategy was based on engaging the public at large in the process. Public hearings and seminars were organized throughout the country with the help of the GenderWatch group and the Women and Constitution Network, and the information gathered was passed on to the CDA, MPs and other NGOs. A training programme on political institutions and processes organized by the WCN reached a few thousand women. According to Dr Pusadee Thamtai, the Women in Politics Institute (WPI) also organized a Master Trainers programme to develop a network of women responsible for educating local women on the constitution-drafting process, and on the possibilities of participation.[29] The Women Lawyers' Association published a set of five booklets on the constitution and issues related to women in politics, which had a large distribution. These organizations believed that lobbying would not be enough, and thus dedicated much time to informing a population that would both participate in public hearings and pressure the assembly and the parliament through mobilization. Women's groups also organized press conferences to reach a wider public and to explain the benefits of the proposed changes. For this purpose, one strength of NGOs was their recognition of the media as a critical intermediary between their work and public opinion. Sanitsuda Ekachai, an FAO award-winning columnist with the *Bangkok Post*, remarked that as the media searched for other sources of information besides public authorities, they found an increasingly professional NGO sector that understood the need for research and information.[30] She explained that many reporters, because of their urban upbringing, could not find proper sources at the grassroots and rural level. NGOs provided a neutral source, as they were not associated with state agencies or with political parties.[31] For women's groups, as with other NGOs, the media is a crucial ally for the success of both accountability and leverage politics (the recent focus on corruption is a clear example of both).

This co-operation is an example of a symbiosis found in the 'institutional configuration' of the public sphere (Dahlgreen 1994: 249). It is by understanding the links between various institutions and how debate is created, disseminated and mediatized that we may, according to Dahlgreen, evaluate whether such configurations ultimately encourage the democratic participation of citizens. In the process, the media in collaboration with non-state organizations contribute to the political normalization of these discursive tools.

The merging of these two approaches, with both state and public as targets, was an objective in itself. According to Dr Pusadee Tamthai, women's groups were adamant about gaining some kind of legally recognized participation in decision making.[32] Article 190 ensures that no less than one-third of ad hoc committee members appointed by the House of Representatives are from private organizations concerned with the substance of the bill under consideration. The much-quoted Article 170 also provides the right to submit a draft law if 50,000 eligible voters sign a petition under the proposal. Women's groups, under the leadership of the WCN, have already started working on an Anti-Discrimination Act in accordance with this article. This institutional recognition of non-state actors is the next stage of influence in Keck and Sikkink's (1998) typology, as procedures themselves are altered by non-state actors. It also legitimizes the public sphere in decision-making, an indication that this sphere is becoming indivisible from that of governance.

Although the drafting process allowed different groups to interact with the state, it also absorbed foreign actors within its debate. Indeed, non-state organizations such as the Asia Foundation and the Friedrich-Ebert Stiftung were involved in the constitution-drafting process, as well as foreign development organizations such as the Canadian International Development Agency through the Women's Investment Fund (WIF). The Asia Foundation, according to James R. Klein, representative of the Foundation in Thailand, even provided MPs and senators with their own staff, hoping to influence the process through their 'women in politics' programme.[33] The WIF, according to its coordinator Suzanne Thibault, spent most of its funding in 1996 and 1997 on supporting seminars and training both to the women in local administration campaign and the constitution drafting process.[34] Moreover, many women's organizations in Thailand receive support from abroad because, according to Dr Pusadee Thamtai, it is difficult to get funds for women's rights within Thailand.[35] The WPI, for instance, was set with funds from the International Republican Institute (IRI), an organization supported by the US Republican Party. This raises the interesting question of whether the public sphere is really constrained by the bounds of the state.

The lessons learned (and linkages fostered) during the drafting of the constitution continue to be used for other campaigns. After the charter was passed, the WCN, sponsored by the Asia Foundation, organized more than 50 workshops across the country on gender issues and the constitution (*Bangkok Post*, 29 April 1998). Much of the work nowadays consists therefore of this twin strategy of directly lobbying state institutions, and providing public education in order to urge MPs to repeal discriminatory laws in accordance with the new charter. According to Naiyana Supapung of the WCN, women's groups have also been busy getting a good representation of women judges on the Human Rights Commission.[36] They have also lobbied MPs and senators, pressing for the legal use of maiden names after marriage.

The example of women's groups during the 1997 drafting process indicates two fundamental changes in the public sphere. First, many of the arguments put forward during these seminars highlight the appropriation of a 'communicatively generated rationality' that undermines both the legitimacy of male leadership and the virtual demarcation ascribed between the private and public domains (Eley 1992: 290). Women were described as 'sin fearing' and thus less prone to accept bribes or build infrastructure solely for the sake of re-election (*Bangkok Post*, 19 July 1998; 24 October 1996). Using this approach, stereotypes are turned upside down, and what are considered 'male' tendencies towards corruption, intimidation and opportunism are presented as examples of non-rational traditional behaviour.

This chapter does not argue that women are less prone to corruption. Nevertheless, the process shows how a group traditionally defined by men as irrational and thus unable to contribute to political deliberation and decision making, reverses the discourse against those who hold it by using symbolic tools available in the public sphere.[37] This is an example of 'issue creation' and 'influence on discursive positions' by way of 'symbolic politics' as the link between corruption and gender became a topic of public discussion since, according to Vitit Muntabhorn, many people believed that the 1997 economic crisis was triggered by the embedded corruption within the political system (*Bangkok Post*, 10 June 1998).

Another important achievement of the public sphere was to force the state to recognise that matters previously considered to be within the private sphere of the family were actually legitimate areas of public concern. More than any other groups in society, women's groups successfully brought private matters into public scrutiny. Article 53, for instance, states that 'family members shall have the right to be protected by the state against violence and unfair treatment' and Article 80 decrees that the state shall 'develop family integrity' (Office of Council of State 1997: 17, 23). Many women's organizations believe that the division between the private and public sphere is a male construct. They want debates on issues such as rape, abortion laws and domestic violence.[38]

The constitution-drafting process provided a platform to introduce these issues to a wider audience. This is important since although the law may be changed, the authorities may not necessarily enforce them. According to Khun Thanawadee Tachin, director of FOW, 'women's groups tried to make the police understand that violence against women is not a personal issue but a social one'.[39] The Foundation therefore trains police officers on sexual harassment and domestic violence. Here it is not the scope of these programmemes that is interesting, but the very fact that government agencies accept non-state training on a topic once considered to be outside the state's concerns. Today, women's groups have effectively changed 'institutional procedures' and 'state behaviour', at least at the departmental level.

CONCLUSION

There is no shortage of activism in the public sphere. Why therefore, compared with the diversity of the women's movement, do so few women sit in parliament or occupy high positions in the government? And what does that say for future reforms? The question is ambitious but indicates that culturalist arguments fall short of explaining this anomaly. Two surveys conducted during the constitution-drafting process suggest that urban Thai men are by a large majority in favour of equality, or recognize at least that women have a role to play in politics.[40] This suggests that beyond discrimination, there might be other reasons for the low numbers of female politicians. Perhaps male politicians fear the loss of their entrenched power base. Those women who dare enter the political sphere find it difficult, as Juree Vichit-Vadakan argues, because:

> the modus operandi or the rules of the game for all important conduct of political networks, alliances and exchanges, set up by men who dominate the political process, strongly favour 'old hands' and seasoned players and nurture the character of 'an old boys' club'. (Juree 1997)

As Juree further points out, few women have been assigned to important parliamentary committees or to high positions within them.

It may be too simple, however, to conclude that because the Thai political system is based on patriarchal rules, future changes may only come about through struggle. Part of the answer may be found in the paradox itself. Many women considered political institutions to be male-dominated and felt intimidated about entering a world traditionally closed to them. One of the most common reasons given to GDRI staff by local women for a reluctance to enter local politics was the view that politics is a man's world, both in terms of its male domination and the nature of its activities. This is also the conclusion of Rosa Linda Miranda of the Centre for Asia-Pacific Women in Politics, who argues that the low participation of women in politics may also be due to 'low self-esteem, lack of confidence in understanding national and global issues, and a sense of inability to communicate, lead and manage people' (*The Nation*, 5 May 1997). She remarks further that from a study conducted with women, it was clear that women associated political participation with the act of being elected.

This means that over and above legal changes, much work needs to be done to educate and train men and women, as well as to increase women's self-confidence in both the public and political spheres, in order to ensure full participation in the formal political process and the peripheral activities that make the process more democratic. It also confirms that the strategy of informing and reaching women at the grassroots level is an important public precondition for women's entrance into the political sphere, and to reform a political system dominated by men.

Much of the basic work happens, as we saw, in the public sphere. The constitution-drafting process was an opportunity to expand a public sphere based on communicative reason to reach a much wider audience. It also brought politics home. The state is not simply an institution to oppose, but an institution to reform, and to link with. Since effective reforms cannot be built out of a vacuum, women's groups are precisely the type of organizations that state planners must consult, and accept as partners in governance, for broad-based political reforms. Even if we accept Habermas's statement that state structures must be separated from the non-state sector to provide responsibility for political decision making, the fabric of governance is nevertheless increasingly shaped by non-state actors such as women's groups.

AUTHOR'S NOTE

This paper is a revised version of the one presented at the Seventh International Conference on Thai Studies, Amsterdam, 4–8 July 1999 under the title 'Non-State Actors and Political Reform: Women's Groups and the Use of the Public Sphere in Thailand'.

NOTES

1 The definition of governance given by the World Bank has shifted over time to include civil society as a state-monitoring mechanism, as the second group suggests (see World Bank 1989: 60; World Bank 1997: Ch. 2).

2 A very good introduction to ways non-state actors acquire political significance can be found in Keck and Sikkink (1998). Although they mainly cover transnational coalitions, Keck and Sikkink's panoply of tactics and stages of influence explain to a large extent NGOs' role in domestic politics.

3 Habermas centres his argument on a strong differentiation between communicative reason, based on a minimum of common understanding, and practical or instrumental reason which is based on achieving successful ends. This distinction can be found, for instance, between the Seventh and Eighth National Economic and Social Development Plans in Thailand. While the Seventh Plan was based on technocrats' perceptions of good technical ends such as GDP, growth and other statistical targets, the Eighth Plan stressed a communicative reasoning process that led to less quantifiable targets of human and holistic development.

4 According to Nancy Fraser (1992), parliament is a strong form of public.

5 There is a rich literature in Thai conceptualizing the political significance of civil society. Among some of the best-known studies are those of Chai-Anan Samudavanija, Prawase Wasi and Thirayuth Boonmi. Chai-Anan (1997) argues in his three-dimensional state model that Thailand has focused particularly on the security and development dimensions of governance (security being a primary objective), and needs to provide space to the participation dimension – see especially Chapter 1. Prawase Wasi (1996) and Thirayuth Boonmi (1998a) have also stressed the importance of a strong society (*sangkhom khemkhaeng*). According to Prawase, society in Thailand is atrophied compared with the state and business sectors. Society would act as a monitoring device if it were nurtured to become a strong civil society. Thirayuth (1998a) argues that a strong society is a precondition to more effective governance in policy-making.

6 Other theories that focus on society either stress the non-contentious communicative role of local groups (social capital) or else the agonistic member-based nature of non-formal groupings (social movements and collective action). However, NGOs are either too formal in their approach or too institutionalized to fit these analytical frameworks.

7 For example, their contribution to the 1997 constitution, and the Eighth Plan with its focus on gender, holistic development and decentralization.

8 Such as the amendments in 1982 of the Local Administration Act B.E. 2457 (1914), and the new Prevention and Suppression of Prostitution Act B.E. 2539 (1996).

9 For example, police treatment of victims, and sexual harassment.

10 This increasing presence of women in the economic field is nevertheless to be contrasted with figures from the Department of Industrial Promotion, quoted from the same article, which show that women represent 60 per cent of employees in small and medium industries but only 18 per cent of managers. See Atiya 1998.

11 For details see the website: http://www.redcross.or.th

12 This partly explains why even today women and monks should avoid any physical contact.

13 Interview with Dr Suteera Thomson, Gender and Development Research Institute, 17 November 1998.

14 Interview, 19 November 1998.

15 Interview, Suzanne Thibault, coordinator, Women's Investment Fund, 17 November 1998.

16 These agencies can, however, bully local organizations to follow their agenda.

17 Interview, 20 November 1998.

18 These quotas were repealed in 1998 in accordance with the 1997 constitution.

19 Sanitsuda Ekachai 1997. Breach of betrothal is another example. A man can sue the lover of his fiancée but a woman cannot sue the lover of her fiancé. See *The Nation*, 8 March 1999.

20 The charter also 'required that all sexually discriminatory laws be revised within two years' (Flaherty and Filipchuk 1994: 41).

21 Hence the use, by women's organizations, of empirical studies (number and level of women in state agencies), the use of comparative analysis across states (the importance of UN figures and treaties such as the UN Convention on the Elimination of all forms of Discrimination against Women, CEDAW) and the central place of logical arguments in debates with state officials and in public seminars (the link between gender and political misdeeds).

22 Juree Vichit-Vadakan argues that using the law to change the status of women is unrealistic since many women-related private issues 'fall outside the direct domain of law; the changes in family relationships are not directly determined by, nor are they likely to be altered by, law' (Juree 1994: 523). This is no longer entirely true, as Article 53 of the 1997 Constitution specifically recognizes the right of family members to be protected by the state.

23 On this topic, see Suteera and Maytinee 1996. On CEDAW see ibid: 8.

24 Interview, 17 November 1998.

25 Interview, 19 November 1998.

26 Interview, 30 May 2000.

27 Interview, 7 June 2000.

28 Interview, 19 November 1998.

29 Interview, 20 November 1998.

30 Interview, 20 November 1998.

31 Sanitsuda was one of the first reporters to be sent to the rural areas for a feature story. NGOs offered to take the reporter on a tour of their work and

projects in the countryside. Dej Phoomkhacha, Director, Thai Volunteer Service, interview in Bangkok, 4 March 1998.

32 Interview, 20 November 1998.

33 Interview, 3 March 1998.

34 Interview, 17 November 1998.

35 Interview, 20 November 1998.

36 Interview, 30 May 2000.

37 Even such respected figures as Prawase Wasi and Mechai Veravadya now claim that women should be appointed to ministerial posts to curb corruption and 'clean' national politics. See Nattaya Chetchotiros, 'Women seen as best remedy for corruption' *Bangkok Post*, 19 July 1998. Mechai Veravadya, for instance, argues that his 'experience in rural development tells [him] that men's ideas of development are no good (Sanitsuda 1996).

38 For instance, according to Thai law, a man may not be convicted of raping his wife. Rape is also not possible if the victim is male, thus boys are not protected by the law. See *Bangkok Post*, 29 April 1998.

39 Interview, 24 May 2000.

40 An Assumption University Research Centre poll conducted in 1997 revealed that 88 per cent of the 1,519 respondents said that men and women should be equal before the law. Most agreed that women were still discriminated against. A Suan Dusit poll conducted with 3,470 people, found that close to 80 per cent of the respondents believed that women and men should enjoy absolute equality. Note, however, that the respondents were from the Bangkok area.

12

NGOS AND GRASSROOTS PARTICIPATION IN THE POLITICAL REFORM PROCESS

Naruemon Thabchumpon

INTRODUCTION

By linking with community groups and people's organizations, NGOs in Thailand have filled a vacuum created by the inability of political parties, trade unions and peasant associations to expand popular participation. Through a strategy of articulating issue-based platforms, NGOs have proved able to expand their role in the sphere of civil society. In the view of NGOs, a strong civil society has four important characteristics:

1. The poor are organised and politically influential.
2. Voluntary associations are politically independent of the state.
3. A culture of tolerance exists.
4. Substantive equality of access prevails for all groups, without discrimination.

For NGOs, a real democratic society is one within which all basic human rights are implemented and fully respected, and ordinary people at grassroots level are given an opportunity to participate in the political arena (*Our Voice* 1993: 99).

To promote genuine participatory democracy, Thai NGOs have proposed the empowerment of the people. In their view, a formal democratic political system is more concerned with representation and political institutions such as political parties, elections and legislatures, than with citizen participation. However, they argue that elections are meaningless unless people are aware of the real choices and the meaning of those choices, as well as having full information concerning policies that will affect them. For NGOs, democracy will be reached only through the activity of communities, particularly at the grassroots level.

Therefore, progress towards democracy means strengthening civil society organizations, the expansion of democratic space, popular participation, effective control of the public agenda, and just distribution of resources.

One issue being put forward by NGOs to create a participatory democracy is 'substantive' political reform. In the Thai context, however, political reform is narrowly defined as 'procedural' political reform – the process of creating the legal mechanisms required for a better political system, chiefly by means of constitutional reform. By calling for substantive political reform in Thailand, NGOs have played a key role in the process of widening political participation. For them, substantive political reform demands good governance, freedom from corruption, and the accountability of the state and other authorities to the people. It is intertwined with issues of social justice. By pushing for substantive political reform in Thailand, NGOs may help create a wider and deeper democratization in Thai civil society.

Throughout this chapter, I shall argue that the grassroots participation of local non-governmental organizations in the democratization process is very important. By advocating people's participation and empowerment, grassroots NGOs may be in a position to expand the scope of democracy, from mere representative government to a deeper participatory democracy. In the Thai case, however, the possibility of success will depend upon whether NGOs are able to establish a linkage between 'elite-urban' and 'rural-popular' elements in Thai civil society today. The key question is whether or not grassroots NGOs are able to add a concept of grassroots democracy to Thai civil society, and create an enhanced form of participatory democracy in Thailand?

CIVIL SOCIETY, DEMOCRACY AND NGOS

Civil society has been strongly emphasized as an element of the democratic process even though its meaning remains unclear. Most authors agree that civil society is very important for democratization, both as a counterweight to state power, and as a means to greater democratic legitimacy and effectiveness (Baker 1998). However, the proper role of civil society in the process of democratic consolidation is still imprecise. Diamond, for example, views the role of political parties as the key element in the consolidation of democracy, rather than civil society. After the end of authoritarian rule, according to Diamond, the single most important and urgent factor in the consolidation of democracy is political institutionalization, not civil society (Diamond 1994: 15). He reasons that strong political parties and effective state institutions are important for implementing market-oriented policies, in order to reduce levels of poverty, inequality and social injustice.

In contrast with this 'elitist democracy' viewpoint, Cohen and Arato single out social movements as a key feature of a vital, modern civil society, and an important form of citizen participation in public life. In their view, the independence of civil society provides the impetus for democratic deepening generally, as society acts upon itself in a self-reflexive way while protecting the boundaries of the 'lifeworld' from the intrusion of economic and bureaucratic power. They argue that social movements keep a democratic culture alive because 'movements bring new issues and values into the public sphere and contribute to reproducing the consensus that the elite model of democracy presupposes but never bothers to account for' (Cohen and Arato 1994: 19).

The concept of civil society also emphasizes the political role of voluntary organizations in the process of democratization. The advocacy role of grassroots NGOs in the democratic process is a key element that links the democratic potential of civil society with people's participation, particularly at the local level. Grassroots NGOs can address the methods of achieving community-based and people-centred citizen engagement in public policy through their political activities with local communities and people's movements. In connection with civil society organizations, NGOs can facilitate the process of generating informed public judgements and encouraging a politically active citizenry. In developing countries, NGOs include academic think-tanks, the church, developmental agencies, philanthropic foundations, and other organizations focusing on issues such as the environment, indigenous peoples, gender, agricultural development, health and social welfare (Clarke 1995: 1). Currently, many authors have categorized NGOs as a 'third sector' standing alongside the state and private sector (Tandon 1994: 128). In the case of Thailand, NGOs are 'private, non-profit organizations with a substantial degree of independence from the government and concerned with public welfare goals' (Rüland and Ladavalya 1993: 60).

WHAT IS GRASSROOTS DEMOCRACY?

There is a growing interest in new sites for democratic activities and in new ways of participating. Democracy is not just about states; it is also about civil society, villages, firms, people's organizations and action groups. It is not only about voting, but also about face-to-face involvement, active participation, debate and discussion. However, democratizing the state is quite different from democratizing civil society. At the level of the state, problems of democracy are primarily focused on institutional designs, such as how to ensure accountability, and how to balance the rights of citizens with those of effective government. At the grassroots level, however, democracy needs ways of raising people's awareness, ways of empowering those who have never had a voice, and methods of ensuring the involvement of everyone. Grassroots groups also deal with organizational problems, such as how to make effective decisions, how to survive without resources, and how to overcome the hostility of the elite and threats of physical reprisals. According to Blaug (forthcoming), grassroots democracy sees the primary source of legitimacy as coming from 'its capacity to secure the informed and free agreement of actual participation'. He stresses the importance of involving people in meeting face-to-face, and of their informing themselves through discussion and debate. For him, the most important theoretical development of grassroots democracy has focused on the quality of discussion which precedes decision-making within such groups. Grassroots democracy, when conceived as being based on fair discussion, is strong in its moral clarity and its capacity to involve participants. Therefore, grassroots democracy entails maximizing fair and effective participation in public groups at all levels, including local and community-based groups.

THE POLITICAL ROLE OF NGOS IN THE DEMOCRATIZATION PROCESS

There are two broad views about the political role of NGOs as a dynamic element of civil society. The first stresses the role of NGOs as an agent for 'democratization' and a component of a 'thriving civil society'. Since the practice of democracy is not limited to elections, NGOs are seen as an important force for the establishment of checks and balances on the exercise of state power, and for increasing representation of the views of the people. According to Fowler, NGOs can counteract state power by 'strengthening and linking people's organizations, grassroots movements and other community-based organizations into 'people's movements'. Such actions not only strengthen civil society, but also encourage good governance which 'increases the scope for holding governments accountable for the management of public resources and limits the arbitrary exercise of power by upholding civil and political liberties' (Fowler 1991: 61).

The second view stresses the socio-economic role of NGOs as a political mechanism of grassroots organizations in solving economic and social problems. According to this view, poverty arises because people do not have access to power. According to Bratton, the poor experience great difficulty in making decisions about their lives because they have little or no control over the material and institutional conditions under which they exist (Bratton 1989: 569). For NGOs using this approach, democracy means not simply procedural representative democracy – where people vote every five or six years to elect their rulers who take decisions on their behalf – but is it also fundamental to justice, to equality and to a 'sustainable society'. They therefore argue in favour of 'grassroots level, participatory democracy in which people decide the fate of their communities, in which they take a fair process of collective decision making about their resources' (Bhasin 1992: 35). In the case of Thailand, however, grassroots NGOs still share several common objectives, such as building community-based organizations as the basis of a 'healthy' civil society and as a counter-balancing force to the state. Many are also searching for new strategies to deal with structural changes that cause disadvantage and powerlessness. They also share a strong belief in popular participation in 'defining and implementing' programmes (Naruemon 1999: 315).

THE POLITICAL ROLE OF NGOS IN THAI CIVIL SOCIETY

In Thai civil society, there is a contrasting picture between the 'elite-urban civil society' found mainly in Bangkok, and the 'rural-popular civil society' of the provinces (Vitit and Taylor 1994: 47). As a result of 30 years of national economic development policy, elite-urban civil society – including progressive civil servants, the business community and the middle class – is growing and gaining more political power. Its supporters have demanded political reform in order to achieve a better standard of efficiency and 'rational' administration, and to replace old-established corrupt and paternalistic ways following the 1997 economic crisis. This elite-urban group is concentrated in Bangkok and certain regional cities. By contrast, economic development has not helped to foster political participation among peasants. Rather, development has contributed to the concentration of economic and political power in the hands of a few, and has caused marginalization and disempowerment among the villagers (Suthy 1995: 97). As a result, grassroots NGOs have established themselves as a popular voice of conscience in Thai civil society. These organizations can be seen as the core of rural-popular civil society, as they have been at the forefront of popular democratic struggles against authoritarian rule and military politics. They have tried to establish a linkage between 'elite-urban' and 'rural-popular' elements and to push forward grassroots democracy in Thai civil society.

Most NGOs in Thailand are non-registered organizations, since they try to circumvent state control by avoiding official registration. According to the 1942 National Cultural Act, any non-governmental organization wishing to register as a legal foundation or organization had to state that it had no political objectives and 'will not be involved in political activities'. This restriction was lifted after the May 1992 events, but foundation applicants must have sufficient funds to cover a deposit of between 200,000 and 500,000 baht, and submit annual financial and activity reports to the Interior Ministry. NGOs – most of which are not registered – take on a variety of forms, such as group, project, society, network, forum, assembly, federation, confederation, association and foundation. These organizations are working in areas such as rural development, children and youth development, education, women's issues, human rights and advocacy, environment, slum development, social services, consumer protection, appropriate technology and democracy (Dej 1995: 89).

Focusing on their political role, there are three broad types of NGO activities in Thailand. The first emphasizes a politics of cooperation. In this case NGO activities are confined to influencing government policy, but not intervening in the political process. The so-called 'non-political approach' is designed to 'give confidence to the people that NGOs are neither an agent of the government nor biased in favour of any political or religious group' (Eldridge 1995: 37). The work of such NGOs is closely linked with state agencies and/or policies in many areas, including social welfare, public health and other issues related to the official national social agenda. NGOs working with the National Economic and Social Development Board (NESDB) and the Social Investment Fund (SIF) represent this type of NGO. Examples of NGOs in this category include the Population and Community Development Association, the National Council on Social Welfare of Thailand and the National Council for Child and Youth Development.

The second political role emphasizes a politics of grassroots movements. NGOs in this category are more explicitly critical of government development policy. They actively organize people at the local level to support campaigns at the national level. NGOs in this pattern usually avoid collaborating with government officials. They try to monitor the implementation of state policies at the grassroots level instead. Those working with villagers affected by state policies, farmers, workers and marginalized groups are included in this type of NGO. These NGOs try to highlight economic and social problems as issues that need to be dealt with in the political sphere, as political issues, and not as the product of economic conditions alone. Some examples include the Campaign for Popular Democracy, the Union for Civil Liberty and the Forum of the Poor.

The third category of NGOs emphasises political empowerment from below. These groups of NGOs believe that social and political change depends more on strong self-reliant groups than on policy reform by the government. They concentrate their work on 'building awareness of rights' and 'building up confidence and skills among the people' to help them solve their problems by themselves. NGOs working at the community level, searching for self-sufficiency and acceptance of popular wisdom represent this type of NGOs. For these NGOs, 'solutions are in the villages' remains the major slogan of their activities. Examples of NGOs in this category are the Village Foundation, the Traditional Medicine in Self-Curing Project and the Community Forest Project. The rest of this chapter will deal primarily with the political role and impact of the second and third types of NGOs, since they are examples of NGOs working on grassroots democracy.

Since the 1980s, NGOs have begun to pay attention to alliance formation with other social groups in Thai civil society, in order to gain wider support and legitimacy for their movements. They have started to develop linkages with other sectors, including the media and the middle class, in order to co-ordinate and strengthen their activities. Umbrella groups have formed as single co-ordinating bodies to assist grassroots organizations pursuing specific issues such as the environment, public health or human rights. Networks are created as these groups launch campaigns to criticise a state policy or put forward specific initiatives. During this process, grassroots NGOs have received some support from 'elite-urban' civil society, such as academics, media people and a few government officials (Banthorn 1993: 7). Some NGOs have used tactics ranging from maintaining positive relationships with socially-concerned government officials, to receiving technical and information support from academics and the urban middle class, and creating public forums to inform and open dialogue with other civic groups, in order to maintain popular support within civil society (Gawin 1994: 148).

THE ECONOMIC CRISIS AND ITS POLITICAL IMPACT

The economic crisis of 1997 has had several direct political consequences. It has intensified the debate among academics and competing civil society groups over the most appropriate development paradigm for Thailand. The crisis also generated more conflict between the state and the 'rural popular' side of civil society, particularly the NGOs.

In the wake of the crisis, the number of unemployed increased from 697,000 in February 1997 to 1,613,000 in August 1998 (UNDP 1999: 126). This was a record for Thailand. The crisis also had a substantial impact on the poor. According to Kakwani, the number of 'ultra poor' with incomes below 80 per cent of the official poverty line increased from 3.7 million in 1996 to 4.3 million in 1998 (*NESDB Newsletter*, 1999). As the average per capita real income of the Thai population in 1998 was 3,753 baht per month, the 'ultra poor' were actually living on less than 100 baht, or around 2 US dollars a day. These people had benefited little from the boom, and were among the first to suffer from the bust. They were affected particularly by higher inflation, with some basic foodstuffs going up by more than the overall inflation level of 9 per cent, and the staple food, rice, approximately doubling in price. Dr Prawase Wasi, a prominent NGO leader, described Thailand's economic crisis as something worse than the sacking of the ancient Kingdom of Ayutthaya by the Burmese in 1767. He said the government alone was inadequately equipped to fend off the threat posed by foreigners, and suggested that people should join with the government in protecting their interests and in putting pressure on the IMF. According to Prawase, the slump was an opportunity for the people to demand social reform (*TDN* 1997: 21).

Dr Narong Phetprasert, however, predicted that there would be a polarization, particularly between the urban rich and the rural poor. He argued that those living upcountry would reject Bangkok people for being overly concerned with the country's industrial and financial economies instead of its agriculture. In the end, this would lead to the rejection of the state:

While we were focusing on industrial development, we never looked at the farmers and the agricultural sector. When we were talking about the country's financial problems we should ask whose finance it is. We are more concerned about the banks and finance companies for the rich, but what about finance for the poor? (*Bangkok Post*, 6 May 1998).

Due to the cause of the crisis, NGOs associated with the rural-popular side of civil society argued that the crash of the Thai economy was not only the result of mismanagement, but also inherent weaknesses in the country's economic condition. Under elitist guidance, they argued, people had not been encouraged to boost their capabilities and discipline to build a stronger economy. The majority of leaders in both government and finance also lacked the honesty, professionalism and longer-term vision to cope with rapid changes on a global scale. In the NGOs' view, development policy needed to pay proper attention to building up a domestic capital base for sustained business development, rather than focusing largely on foreign investment.

As a result, many rural-popular civil society groups were formed to represent their points of view on macro-economic policies and models of development. For example, the People's National Liberation Alliance (*Neao rom prachachon ku chat*) made up of 30 rural NGOs, state enterprise trade unions and people's organizations including the Forum of the Poor, was formed in 1998 to propose alternative ideas of rural-popular civil society organizations about the impact of the IMF bail-out package. It demanded that the government reconsider its priorities and focus on solving the long-term problems of the poor rather than those of the financial institutions. For example, the PLA urged the government to review its support for the Financial Institution Development Fund (FIDF) since it benefited only a small number of people in the financial sector. It proposed a five-year debt moratorium for poor farmers instead. Its recommendations to the government were as follows:

- to make public the agreement and conditionalities which the IMF had made with the Thai government;
- not to set conditionalities which affected the poor and marginalized sectors that had not been involved in causing the debt;
- not to make opportunistic use of periods of economic difficulties in Thailand to set conditionalities that interfered with and manipulated the Thai economy and politics; and
- that any kind of development assistance should be based on the principles of social justice, morals, sustainable society, global concern and equality which would bring peace to the community. (Watershed 1998: 21)

Another group established at around the same time was the National Restoration Civic Group (*Prachakhom kob ban ku muang*). This group can be seen as a elite-urban civil society organization because its components were more from affected business leaders from both the public and private sectors; and those involved in organizing civic groups network. During the campaign, the group came out in support of a self-sufficient economy, an idea inspired partly by the King's 1997 birthday address (for a discussion, see Hewison, this volume). The group also organized a series of forums as a way to create social communication with the public, without pressuring or accusing any particular groups or individuals. It also proposed the idea of a 'Thai people's share-owning democracy' to encourage people to buy shares in the government-owned Bangchak Petroleum Company, because of Bangchak's excellent reputation for supporting local communities (Naruemon 1999: 315).

Following the stabilization program proposed by the IMF, members of the Thai elite-urban civil society started talking about 'good governance'. According to Thirayuth Boonmi, a student activist leader from the 1970s, good governance – involving transparency, accountability and citizen participation – was a way to help Thailand survive the economic crisis (see Thirayuth, this volume). For him, the economic crash of 1997 was essentially a crisis of political governance. The causes of the crisis were to some extent the result of deficiencies in government management mechanisms, and public policy and administration, as well as corruption in the public services. To solve the problems, therefore, competent ministers or administrators would be necessary to guide government policy. The good governance concept has been supported by bureaucrats, academic groups, businessmen and capitalist leaders, including former Prime Minister Anand Panyarachun. In 1999, for instance, the office of the prime minister issued a regulation on good governance which included six rules: the rule of law, the rule of integrity, the rule of transparency, the rule of participation, the rule of accountability, and the rule of value for money (Office of the Civil

Service Commission 1999: 1). It also proposed that the cabinet designate the creation of good governance as a national priority in order to ensure the better performance of state agencies. Even the 1999 Human Development Report of Thailand addressed good governance, as a way to build a more open and democratic society (UNDP 1999: 9). However, this approach was criticised by some NGOs working with the rural-popular side of civil society for ignoring the inequality between different sectors, particularly marginalized groups. According to Nitirat, the key issue concerning good governance was the question 'whose governance is it?' (Nitirat 1997: 57).

SOCIAL CAPITAL AND THE POLITICS OF THE SOCIAL INVESTMENT FUND

Debate among NGOs grew when the government used US$600 million in World Bank loans to provide direct assistance at the village level. Some 16 billion baht were administered by government departments, and 4.8 billion by civil society organizations. The reason for using civil society organizations as a channel reflected a recognition that the crisis had not only demonstrated the robustness of traditional coping mechanisms, but had also fostered greater self-reliance and self-sufficiency among local communities in both urban and rural areas. This was reflected in many initiatives in the area of group saving schemes, which were supported by NGOs and government agencies in order to respond to the needs of returning migrants. During that time, NGOs used a strategy of cooperation, and proposed that the country needed to re-examine its development path, which had traditionally seen social capital subordinated to the needs of financial capital. For them, to develop social capital meant re-establishing the ties that had traditionally bound together families and communities, the strength and importance of cultural heritage, and the value system of the society. An emphasis on social capital had to include more efforts to develop social safety-nets and social security systems, the importance of which had been highlighted by the World Bank. As a result, a former secretary-general of the NGO-CORD set up an organization named the Social Investment Fund (SIF) for administration of the 4.8 billion baht. Its objective was

> to revive the intermediary web of relations, which the organisers believe was a basis for stronger communities, and thus it will not only ensure the well-being of the poor or those affected by the economic downturn, but also reduce their dependence on government money. (*TDN*, July–September 1998: 62)

In Anek's view, NGOs needed to play a positive role in helping the state to reduce the impact of the economic crisis. However, radical NGOs working with the rural-popular side of civil society argued that the World

Bank should acknowledge its responsibility for social problems facing Thailand at the time, and should provide social investment funds to Thailand free, instead of as a loan (ibid: 63).

CONFLICTS BETWEEN THE CHUAN GOVERNMENT AND NGOS

In spite of formidable economic and social problems, Chuan Leekpai's second government (1997–2001) initially gained strong support from a public tired of the indecisiveness and internal bickering of its predecessor, headed by Chavalit Yongchaiyudh. The Chuan government, however, found it difficult to avoid the charge levelled by NGOs that it was unsympathetic to the poor, particularly for its use of public funds to pay off debts accumulated by government institutions that had loaned money to the private sector. Even though the government tried to set up a committee to look into the social impacts of the crisis, it was still perceived as having made no sincere and concrete initiatives to solve the problems of the poor. The Forum of the Poor, for instance, criticized the government for seeking to increase its reputation among the middle and upper classes, by concentrating on solving the problems of the financial sector while ignoring the problems of the poor. The Assembly also reported that in 1997–98, only one of the 104 problems of the poor acknowledged by the Chavalit government in 1997 had been resolved. The Chuan government had also revoked most of the agreements that the people's groups had reached with the previous government. As a result, concerned agencies had not been enthusiastic in working out solutions.

The relationship between state and the rural civil society organizations deteriorated, as the Chuan government used its sanctions and power to apply a 'divide and rule' strategy. The aim was apparently to destroy the people's movement by supporting the non-political activities of urban groups, but condemning any protest rally as a threat to economic recovery and political stability. As Wanida pointed out, 'whenever there was a protest rally by villagers and supported by NGOs and people's organizations, these sympathizers of the villagers would be branded by the government as agitators' (*TDN*, July–December 1998: 42).

Even before the crisis, the annual 'dry-season' campaigns of farmers from 1994 to 1999, involving demonstrations or public rallies in Bangkok and other major cities, had seen a progression from invasion to siege, to treaty negotiations. However, the Chuan government seemed to want to roll back this development. Unlike Chavalit, Prime Minister Chuan never personally met with protesting villagers. He preferred to address farmers' concerns through legislation and governmental regulations, and to form high-level committees. The Democrat government sought to return to a model where villagers stayed 'out there', and were looked after by paternalistic state officials. However, the rural-popular movement argued that the economic crisis had already led to a questioning of the mainstream development path that depended upon an export-oriented strategy. The crisis had contributed to a positive revaluation of the role of agriculture and rural areas in the national development strategy, as a way to restore the well-being of a nation that was still predominantly rural. When agriculture was returning to the top of the national agenda, why was the government still reluctant to consult regularly and seriously with farmers, in the same way it dealt with bankers and businessmen?

However, the government claimed that grassroots movements and mass rallies were 'not representative', that some rallies were 'politically motivated', and that demonstrations damaged Thailand's image (*TDN* 1999: 21). It also accused opposition parties of orchestrating an anti-government campaign (*Bangkok Post*, 6 August 2000). As a result, strategies of mass protest seemed to be unpopular among the middle classes, even though they might disagree with the government. For example, pro-democracy NGOs tried to mobilize a protest rally when the government gave an honorary military award to General Thanom Kittikachorn, a former dictator and prime minister. Even though the Democrat Party came under strong attack by the media, only a few people turned out for the demonstration.

NGOS AND POLITICAL REFORM IN THAILAND

Since the May 1992 events, Thai civil society has engaged in discussions of political reform, particularly through the concept of constitutional reform, good governance and civil society participation. To strengthen democratization, the political system has to move beyond electoral politics, which is monopolized by traditional politicians and bureaucrats. However, civil society groups during the 1997–2000 period lost both trust and confidence in the government and political institutions. The new constitution has contributed to political reform, and facilitated the restructuring of the relationship between state and civil society. Ideas surrounding political reform in Thai civil society, however, are dependent on the political context, and the role of key players in politics including the elite-urban and the rural-popular sides of civil society. Their different agendas on political reform will be explored in the following sections.

From the rural side of civil society, grassroots NGOs have participated in substantive political reform in the areas of decentralization, participation and empowerment. They have pushed for people's participation and empowerment in many ways, particularly at the local level. For grassroots NGOs in particular, political reform will only begin to function meaningfully through an active process of public dialogue. Through such dialogue, speakers from the grassroots can have the opportunity to voice their grievances and express their ideas on how their problems ought to be handled. Their concrete measures would need to be included in the new constitution and related public laws. During their constitutional reform campaign, rural NGOs used a strategy of networking with other groups, including the elite-urban civil society organizations. They were able to create a national network which included pro-democracy groups, people's organizations, trade unions, women's groups, civic organizations, some progressive businesspeople and elements of the middle class to campaign on constitutional reform.

By strengthening their network of people's organizations and grassroot movements, NGOs have tried to put pressure on the government to recognise the concept of community rights over natural resources. They have proposed the idea of decentralizing power to communities, which in essence means giving local people the right to self-government, and the right to manage local resources at all stages of the development cycle. In the 1997 Constitution, as a result, the concept of these frameworks deals with the basic rights of the people, and their right to participation in the political decision-making process by guaranteeing individual freedom and fundamental rights in the public laws (1997 Constitution: Articles 46, 59, 60 and 76).

On the positive side, the economic crisis did not bring about a *coup d'état* as it might once have done. Instead, it brought about a silent revolution that may prove even more significant in the long run. While the crisis undermined the traditional authority of the state, it reinforced demands for greater openness, greater participation and people's empowerment. That made the civil society movement gain more strength from the crisis, and this strength is reflected in the pursuit of the political reform agenda established by the new Constitution. Through the process of people's participation in constitutional reform, NGOs have played a key role in strengthening civil society by building democracy at the grassroots level, and providing necessary forums for the 'voice of the people' to be expressed and taken into account by government. However, the question was how far this process could be institutionalized, and be further developed once the immediate crisis was over. The 1997 constitution sought to establish a broader political system than the one that had long been monopolized by traditional politicians and bureaucrats. Substantive political reform had to be seen through greater openness, greater accountability, more participation and the empowerment of local communities in the process of legal implementation.

Since the crisis, civil society institutions have continued to play an influential role in political reform in different ways. While the efforts of rural groups can be seen through the search for an alternative development strategy, urban groups maintained pressure on the government to focus on issues of sustainable development, good governance and opposition to corruption. From the rural side of civil society, for example, 29 villagers from Kud Chum district in Yasothon province began trading in 'bia', an interest-free community currency on 29 March 2000. Their aim was to reduce the number of things villagers bought from outside the community to encourage the support of locally produced goods and services. Even though the project was finally stopped because of objections from the Bank of Thailand, this proposal can be seen as an alternative way of reducing the shortcomings of economic dependency, and strengthening local communities (*Bangkok Post*, 8 April 2000).

From the urban side of civil society, however, the political reform agenda emphasized opposition to corruption. Amongst new provisions addressing these issues were requirements that elected officials and their families had to declare their assets before and after taking office, provisions allowing citizens backed by at least 50,000 signatures to petition a new anti-graft commission to investigate officials suspected of corruption, and an independent election commission that would oversee the electoral process to ensure its integrity. For instance, the right of 50,000 electors to impeach officials perceived to be corrupt was invoked in relation to a scandal over public medical purchases involving ministers and senior health ministry officials. Threats of a similar petition in relation to other scandals – over illegal logging early in 1998, and government purchase and distribution of vegetable seeds in 1999 – put pressure on the government, and in the latter case led to the resignation of the deputy agriculture minister. In May 2000, the Constitutional Court decided that Major-General Sanan Kachonprasart – the interior minister and party secretary-general who had orchestrated two Democrat-led governments – had lied about his assets declaration to cover up an unusual increase in his wealth. This was an example of a successful case organised by the urban side of civil society organization against political corruption, following a parliamentary no-confidence debate allegation (*Bangkok Post*, 21 May 2000). During the process, the media played an important role, highlighting and investigating a number of notable scandals.

GRASSROOTS PARTICIPATION IN THAI POLITICAL REFORM: CHALLENGES AND OPPORTUNITIES

For Thai NGOs, the term 'grassroots democracy' means a democratic system that responds to the needs and aspirations of the people at the grassroots. It requires wide-ranging reform of the bureaucracy and decentralisation of power to allow more autonomy for local communities and people's organizations to take part in decision-making processes affecting their economic and cultural life – as well as to restore their rights to manage local resources. Since poverty was a politically constructed problem, exacerbated by public policies, it had to be solved by political means. Examples include the campaign on community rights, public participation in natural resource management, people-centred development policy and political reform (*Bangkok Post*, 2 May 2000).

From the urban side of civil society, grassroots participation could be seen in the 70 per cent voter turnout for the senate election on 4 March 2000. For 60 years, the Senate had been viewed as 'the house of bureaucrats', consisting merely of elite members whose job was only to scrutinize laws written by the government or by the lower house. The impressive turnout suggested that these senate elections were one of the most significant developments in Thai democracy since the abolition of absolute monarchy in 1932. After the new constitution was first promulgated on 11 October 1997, Thai civil society groups had felt that they had achieved what they had fought for, and interest in political reform subsided. Three organic laws governing the election of MPs and senators, political parties and the Election Commission failed to live up to expectations. There were several shortcomings in these laws that could be exploited by unscrupulous people, while some regulations were not workable. Even on the senate election day, Bangkok people were generally happy with the results in the city, yet reports of irregularities were still rampant in the countryside (*Bangkok Post*, 12 March 2000). Many people were optimistic that Thailand's first democratically elected senate would usher in a new era of clearer government. In reality, however, the efficacy of electoral reform remained unclear.

From the rural-popular side of civil society, grassroots NGOs have emerged to defend the rights of local communities by undertaking policy advocacy work, as well as bringing the plight of affected people into the realm of public debate. To achieve their demands, rural NGOs used a strategy of mass mobilization in pressing the government to accept a new policy. However, this strategy had no effect on the Chuan government. For example, article 46 of the new Constitution stated that local communities have the right to protect and manage their natural resources. The Community Forest Bill was introduced after 1997. The bill proposed by the Royal Forestry Department (RFD) sought to recruit local farmers to grow tree plantations in forests under the supervision of the RFD. The purpose of the RFD proposals was to relocate hilltribe people and other poor farmers living in forest conservation areas, and to ensure that the RFD had power to control forestry management policy.

The Forum of the Poor and its allies then used Article 170 of the new constitution to propose their own version to Parliament. They argued that forestry problems would never be solved if the RFD ignored the participation of local people in managing the forest. The two versions were then integrated into one bill (based on the RFD version) for deliberation in a special committee of the House. Yet in late 2000, the RFD was continuing to evict hilltribe people from forest areas citing measures which purported to protect the ecosystem, even when those evicted could prove they were living there before the passage of the National Forest Act. The proposed Community Forest Bill was an example of a public law that contradicted the spirit of the new constitution, and the concepts of citizen participation and decentralization.

Also in 2000, the Forum of Poor demanded that the government revoke the 30 June 1998 cabinet resolution on land claim verification. According to the Forum, this resolution effectively cancelled two cabinet resolutions issued by the Chavalit administration which had allowed villagers to live in the forests while their claims were being verified by witnesses. The 30 June Cabinet resolution required verification only by aerial photos that would be interpreted by the RFD. The government, however, disagreed with the Forum's demands, arguing that it needed to protect forests in the national interest. The RFD continued to arrest and use violence against villagers who resisted its orders and who tried to remain in forest conservation areas (*Bangkok Post*, 9 August 2000).

To promote grassroots democracy in Thai civil society, NGOs need to advocate the concepts of people's empowerment and participation. However, the question is whether the NGOs will be able to democratize Thai civil society, especially around the idea of participatory democracy. Since the crisis, conflicts over resource management have been intensifying, particularly at the grassroots level. Mass rallies by people suffering long-standing problems are becoming more common. This kind of situation has been described as a 'warless war' (*The Nation*, 23 June 1998). The two sides are fighting for territory not on any geographical battlefield, but on the field of national public discourse. Victories are not by body counts but by public-sympathy points. Any display of violence concedes territory to the opposing side. The interesting point is whether NGOs are in a position to establish a linkage between 'elite-urban' and 'rural-popular' civil society through their political participation. Since the crisis, it has seemed that NGOs remain unable to broker an effective concept of grassroots democracy in Thai civil society.

CONCLUSION

Thai civil society is the public sphere standing between 'political society' (the state and political parties) and economic society. In Thailand, civil society is the most important factor not only in the transition from authoritarian rule, but also in the consolidation of democracy. The most active groups behind Thai civil society are NGOs, particularly those working with the rural-popular side of civil society. These organizations have played a crucial role in defending popular rights. The reason is that they view Thailand's human development as the key to the country's overall development. This idea has led them to advocate the basic rights of the poor.

One issue that has been put forward by NGOs and civil society organizations is substantive political reform. Through the participatory role of NGOs in political reform, Thai civil society is more engaged in political discussions and is increasingly involved in the political arena. By advocating people's participation and empowerment, the NGOs have helped push forward the democratization process in Thai civil society by providing citizens with opportunities to engage in the policy-making process. They have promoted a participatory democratic society by bringing the 'voice of the voiceless' into the public debate. However, substantive political reform in Thailand seems unlikely to be created in the current situation.

By developing their ability to challenge the government's previous virtual monopoly on information and resources, NGOs appear to be building up the idea of grassroots democracy. In Thailand, however, a key challenge for the grassroots movement is to bring together such ideas into an attractive strategy for change that is both visionary and pragmatic. The greater challenge is how to formulate a political strategy that can bring all groups, social strata and classes negatively affected by the economic crisis into a broad alliance for change, and thereby establish a deeper form of Thai democracy. Since the crisis, it remains to be seen whether the role of NGOs can aid a wider and deeper concept of grassroots democracy in Thai civil society.

PART III
ELECTORAL REFORM

13

THE 1997 CONSTITUTION AND THE POLITICS OF ELECTORAL REFORM

Sombat Chantornvong

INTRODUCTION

By the time of the January 2001 general election, it was more than three years since the new constitution had come into effect. Even though the new provisions for running general elections had yet to be tested, the public had generally been led to believe that Thailand had finally come up with truly workable monitoring mechanisms which would effectively control corruption and limit the influence of money in politics. The drafters of the new constitution[1] appeared to be convinced that they had solved the problems of legitimacy and efficiency which had long destabilized the Thai political system.[2] The practice of vote-buying by competing politicians was the source of many of these evils. The new charter sought to minimize this practice by introducing compulsory voting, in the expectation that the resulting high turnout would discourage vote-buying. The electoral system was also changed to help reduce vote-buying, and to make MPs more accountable to the electorate. Under the 1997 Constitution, members of the House of Representatives comprised 400 members to be elected on a single-member constituency basis and another 100 elected nationwide on a party-list basis. It was argued that these smaller, single-member constituencies would allow candidates to establish close contact with their supporters, without having to resort to bribing or intimidating potential voters.

The party-list method was clearly designed to deter vote-buying and to strengthen the party system, since parties gaining less than 5 per cent of the total number of votes throughout the country would not be eligible for any party-list seats at all. This system was designed to undermine the proliferation of small parties, so reducing levels of political instability. The party-list system was also supposed to encourage better-known and more respectable personalities to enter politics with a national mandate. It was further expected that political parties would place prospective ministers on their party-lists, since all ministers must relinquish their parliamentary seats on taking office. While party-list MPs who become ministers are simply replaced by the next party candidate on the list, a new election is required for ministers appointed from the constituency seats.

Under the new Constitution, 200 senators from 76 provinces (including Bangkok) are directly elected by the people. The new senate is much more powerful than the appointed one under previous constitutions. It is entrusted with the power to recommend the removal of persons holding political posts, ranging from the prime minister and his cabinet members down to individual MPs. Equally important is its power to recommend the appointment – and removal from office – of members of all monitoring bodies and other independent agencies. While its main function is to make politicians and public officials more accountable to the public, the senate also has wide-ranging political responsibilities. It may censure the government by calling a debate without a vote. Apart from filtering legislation, the new senate deliberates jointly with the House on various important issues. Clearly, the charter writers wanted the new senate to be completely free from politics. Candidates are prohibited from engaging in election campaigning. They are only permitted to 'introduce themselves' to the public, while the state will impartially arrange for each candidate to appear on different media channels. Senators must not be party members, nor can they receive financial support from political parties. Once elected, members of the senate may serve only one term of six years. They cannot become ministers while in office, nor assume ministerial posts within a year of leaving the senate. There is little doubt that the reform of the senate was meant by the drafters of the new constitution to be a significant milestone in the modern political history of the kingdom.

In order to build a system that allows clean elections to take place, an independent Election Commission was formed. Gone were the days when the administration and supervision of local and general elections were undertaken by the powerful minister of interior. The new election system was designed to sever the crucial ties that exist between politicians and the civil servants responsible for administering elections. The Election Commission was expected to organize free and fair elections, and to take action against all kinds of irregularities and fraud that had long plagued Thailand's electoral process. Thus, it has the power to conduct investigations concerning poll fraud, and can bring offenders to court. If necessary, it may even call for new elections. It was hoped that overall this new body would significantly reduce vote-buying and other abuses of the electoral system.

The new charter also sought to reduce the political instability produced by coalition governments, in which cabinet seats were generally allocated according to the number of MPs in each coalition party. In nominal parties dominated by powerful factions, the allocation of ministerial posts was based on a nominee's financial power, and his ability to control his faction of MPs within the party. This system produced factional infighting within parties, leading to frequent party-switching by groups of politicians. A government may find itself at the mercy of cliques of rebellious MPs, especially during regular but crucial no-confidence debates. After every dissolution of Parliament some parties break up and new ones are formed, as many MPs will move to new homes, looking for better political and financial deals.

The writers of the 1997 Constitution seemed to be well aware of the above problems and so imposed new requirements for political appointees. From now on future MPs and members of the cabinet must have a bachelor's degree. Academic qualifications were thought to ensure a certain level of calibre and character. This provision assumed that both supporters of the government and members of the opposition parties would at least be academically qualified to function intelligently. However, this requirement simply excludes 95 per cent of the rural population, and over 99 per cent of those in the agricultural sector. The stability of the government was further strengthened by the provision under the new charter which limits no-confidence motions by the opposition to only one per year; and further requires those proposing motions of no confidence in the prime minister to nominate an alternative backed by two-fifths of the House. Stability may be further enhanced because the prime minister can easily neutralize any possible rebellious ministers by reshuffling the cabinet: the separation of legislative and executive functions means that, once removed from their cabinet posts, former ministers lose their parliamentary positions. Having no parliamentary seats to return to, members of the cabinet will have to think twice before going against the leadership of the premier.

For their part, constituency MPs will be discouraged from switching from one political party to another at election times by the requirement that a future candidate has to be a member of his party for at least 90 days before he can run for a seat. The 2001 general election was therefore the last chance for MPs to switch party easily: henceforth, they will have to to resign their seats well before a dissolution of parliament if they plan to defect. MPs under the new Constitution can now choose the prime minister by an open vote in the House. There is no longer any need for the speaker of the House to sound out party leaders' opinions searching for a suitable candidate for the post. This practice, argue the drafters of the new charter, was too susceptible to manipulation and wheeler-dealing by party bosses.

GROWING DOUBTS

By the second half of 2000, a feeling that the drafters of the 1997 Constitution may have been overly optimistic and idealistic was beginning to surface. The stipulation that voting was a duty, and that any eligible voter who fails to vote (without giving authorities involved good reasons) is liable to punishment was the first case in point. Parliament itself desperately avoided having to be the one to impose such penalties by assigning this responsibility to the Election Commission. The Election Commission, in turn, referred the matter immediately back to Parliament. In the end it was agreed that non-voters should be deprived of the following rights guaranteed under the new constitution for five consecutive years:

- the right to challenge election results (national and local); the right to challenge election results (village and district);
- the right to run for office in the House of Representatives, the Senate, and local assemblies;
- the right to run for the office of village head (*phuyaiban*) or subdistrict chief (*kamnan*);
- the right to co-sign a legislative proposal and the right to co-sign a local ordinance;
- the right to co-sign a petition to the senate seeking the removal of political appointees; and
- the right to co-sign a petition seeking the removal of a member of a local assembly or local administrators.

Unsurprisingly, these punishments were not strong enough to encourage most voters to go to the polls.

The 1997 Constitution not only makes it a duty for all eligible voters to go to the poll but it also for the first time gives the right to vote to those Thais living abroad. Yet, despite an extensive publicity campaign, only 26,592 Thais – representing just 3 per cent of the total 757,655 eligible citizens residing overseas – had registered to vote for the 4 March senate election (*Bangkok Post*, 22 April 1999). The high cost of organizing voting overseas (estimated to cost 57 million baht for just the first round of polling) prompted a member of the Election Commission to propose an amendment to the Constitution allowing expatriates the right to vote only for party-list candidates. Such a call for constitutional changes can certainly be justified by the low level of interest among overseas voters. But since the new Constitution expressly states that

Thais have the right to vote, such a change is not possible. Furthermore, the charter has also stipulated that within five years after the initial adoption, the Election Commission may not submit any recommendation for the amendment of the Constitution.

THE MIXED OUTCOME OF THE 2000 SENATE ELECTIONS

The idea that the senate could be free from ordinary politics has not been realised. Growing concerns that the new senate might be dominated by political parties were voiced earlier by several observers, including the former senate president Meechai Ruchuphan (*Phujatkan Daily*, 30 July 1996). The 200-strong senate is directly elected by the people from 76 provinces all over the country. An entire province represents a single constituency, and each voter is allowed to choose only one candidate even if the province is qualified to have more than one seat in the senate. Bangkok, for example, has 18 senate seats with about 3 million eligible voters. Those who believe that the Upper House can be insulated from political influence have argued that because each constituency is going to be very big, it would be difficult for any political party to interfere in senatorial elections. Yet the 4 March 2000 senate election saw large numbers of former politicians and relatives, children, wives and aides of established politicians including the spouses of former Interior Minister Sanan Kachornprasart and Justice Minister Suthas Ngernmuen among those candidates competing for seats in the senate. And since the law bans senate hopefuls from campaigning, several candidates reportedly turned to canvassers of political parties for help. Many of these senate candidates simply went beyond the limits of the law by throwing feasts for their canvassers, handing out cash and food to potential voters and pledging favours.

From the very beginning the election was thus plagued with complaints of outright fraud and allegations of vote-buying in all its ugly guises. Vote-buying and irregularities were so rife that the Election Commission suspended 78 winners from 35 provinces in the 4 March poll, and call for a second round of voting. Not surprisingly, many of those suspended turned out to be local influential figures running shady businesses or having questionable backgrounds. As also anticipated, many were relatives, wives and associates of national politicians. But despite the suspensions, electoral fraud was still widespread in the second round of the senate elections: suspended candidates who were allowed to run again became even more sophisticated and more subtle in their illegal methods of winning votes, leaving little or no evidence or leads. Quite embarrassingly for the Election Commission, those whom it suspended were re-elected in droves, including the self-confessed gambling tycoon Chatchawal Khong-udom of Bangkok.

The Election Commission, which won public praise after disqualifying 78 of the 4 March winners, began to feel the heat as people became more frustrated with the seemingly endless elections. Voter turnout nationwide had already dropped substantially from a record high of 72 per cent[3] in the first senate election to 52 per cent the second time around. Still, strong evidence of electoral fraud and vote-buying was found in the third round election as voter turnout fell to 41 per cent.

Yet probably even more disheartening was the ruling by the Constitutional Court that the Election Commission's rule empowering itself to disqualify candidates suspected of campaign frauds from further contest was unconstitutional. Having no power to disqualify candidates or winners who cheated, all the Election Commission could do was to order a fourth round of senate polling in four northeastern provinces. Needless to say, in the provinces where only one seat remained available, some candidates became bolder and more inventive in their efforts to win at any cost. Eventually, it took almost five months – at a cost of around 2.3 billion baht – before all 200 senate seats could be filled.[4] Wives, children and associates of politicians managed to win no less than one-third of the 200 senate seats, while a further third of the senate seats were won by former or retired government officials. The background of most senators leaves much to be desired, to say the least. The new Upper Chamber is unfortunately dominated by entrenched power groups – something quite different from what it was originally supposed to be.

The first senate meeting which was held to elect the speaker and his two deputies illustrates the above observation. For weeks prior to the election of the speaker, potential candidates for the post were attacked by anonymous, often scandalous leaflets. Intense lobbying, including reports of money changing hands in the media, led the public to question whether the senate could truly serve as a counter-force to the old kind of politics. Charges of interference and vote-buying by political parties surrounding the election of the senate speaker have forced outside observers to wonder if anything much has changed in Thai politics. Equally frustrating to reformers was the fact that even before the speaker could be elected, senators with political links were also busy jockeying for the chairmanships of the 16 senate standing committees. In short, the way the new senate elected its speaker and committee chairmen left the public with the clear impression that the Upper House was already polarized and dominated by voting blocs. It came as no surprise therefore that an opinion survey carried out in early August 2000 showed that most Bangkokians were doubtful about the efficiency and impartiality of the newly elected senate (*Bangkok Post*, 7 August 2000). The new Upper House was not something the people could trust and be proud of after all. Even after 145 days, 2.3 billion baht and five rounds of voting, Thai voters still had to return to the polls once more in eight provinces on 21 April 2001. 10 senators faced reruns following complaints filed against them by failed candidates, and the Speaker himself was among those who lost his seat.

The Election Commission's first task of organizing the senate elections drew both criticism and praise from the public. Despite being named the Best Government Reformer by *Asiaweek* magazine (18–25 August 2000), the Commission was not without its own critics. The five members of the Election Commission seemed to find difficulty in working together, and their preparedness and competence were, to say the least, questionable. Its first big blunder came when the Commission decided to disqualify 43 senate hopefuls, many of them apparently honest and capable, on the grounds that they were 'other state officials' and thus ineligible to run. This ruling affected prominent candidates serving on various state councils, boards and committees such as the Law Society of Thailand, the Islamic Committee of Thailand, the Council of Rajabhat Institutes, state enterprise boards and the Science and Technology Institute of Thailand. Moreover, the ruling came long after their candidacies had been initially approved by the registering election committees. When some of the disqualified candidates challenged this decision in the civil courts, the Election Commission suffered its first setback; the courts ruled that the Commission was not empowered to disqualify candidates seven days after the registration had closed. One of its members resigned accordingly (*Bangkok Post*, 5 February 2000). Then the Constitutional Court struck a final blow by its ruling that most of the senate candidates barred by the Election Commission were not 'state officials'.

Another example of the Commission's lack of readiness was the fact that most ballot boxes used in the senate poll were cardboard boxes instead of standard metal boxes, because 80,000 metal ones ordered by the Commission could not be delivered in time (*Bangkok Post*, 23 February 2000). Meanwhile, provincial election panel members did not fare any better. As expected, they were accused of political partiality. Provincial branch officials of the Election Commission were often reported to be biased against certain candidates. But that was not all. Their handling of witnesses who volunteered to testify against senatorial candidates in electoral fraud cases also left much to be desired. The most tragic incident involved a witness in Mahasarakham province whose identity was publicly revealed. As a result the witness received death threats from local law enforcement officials, and committed suicide shortly afterwards. Thereafter there were growing reports that the Election Commission was examining the conduct of provincial members nationwide, and up to 20 of the 434 provincial election panel members were expected to be dismissed for lack of political neutrality (*Bangkok Post*, 3 September 2000).

However, much more crucial than poor preparedness and lack of organization was the credibility of the Election Commission itself. When PollWatch and other non-governmental organizations which were supposed to be working closely together with the Election Commission accused it of having failed to disqualify many dishonest candidates, especially in the later rounds of polling, the public became very annoyed. PollWatch and its allies claimed that the Election Commission ignored information given to it that implicated some winners in voting fraud, and that some Election Commission officials informed suspected senators-elect about the charges against them in advance so that they would be better prepared to defend themselves. Eventually PollWatch and its allies managed to come to terms with the Election Commission, but it could not be denied that the credibility of both sides had suffered significantly in the preceding bickering.

REVIEWING THE ELECTION LAWS

The debacle of the Senate elections heightened the need for an amendment of the election laws. Insisting that issuing an executive decree was not a proper way to amend electoral laws, the Chuan government appointed a committee headed by Meechai Ruchupan, the former senate speaker, to put forward amendments to the electoral laws. Central to the Meechai draft was the transfer of powers to bar suspected cheats from the courts to the Election Commission. Interestingly enough, this was done in a rather ingenious way. To recall, the Election Commission had earlier issued a rule empowering itself to bar poll winners suspended twice for electoral fraud from contesting re-elections. However, the Constitutional Court later decided that such a rule was unconstitutional. According to the Meechai draft, the Commission would have the power to revoke for one year the election rights of those caught cheating. The Commission was also to be empowered, for example, to dissolve political parties whose leaders or executives were found guilty of making false accusations of poll frauds against candidates of other parties. It would also be empowered to enter and search residences without warrants and to impound evidence of fraud.

The government-sponsored election amendment bill, however, met with strong opposition in the House completely dominated by the government's own MPs. While the whole point of amending the election laws was to strengthen the hand of the Election Commission, most MPs seemed to try their best to disarm the Commission in their own interests. Instead of giving the Commission sole power to disqualify cheats, they wanted to give the Supreme Court the final say on the eligibility of candidates. Critics quickly pointed out that without the power to disqualify candidates, the Commission could never achieve what it had set out to do. For one thing, the court, as a rule, has to adhere to the principle of substantial evidence to decide a case. Thus the judicial process has all along proven ineffective in convicting politicians of electoral fraud, since in a vote-buying case it is almost always impossible to obtain 'clear evidence'. The Buriram vote-buying scandal of 1995 should serve as an excellent example. In that case, 1 million baht in small denomination notes was seized from a canvasser's home with campaign flyers of certain candidates already attached to the money: yet the court failed to link them with the notorious MPs behind the wrongdoing. On the other hand, the standard used by the Election Commission in its ruling against cheats is different from that of a court. All that the Commission needs to disqualify candidates suspected of electoral frauds is any 'convincing evidence'. Obviously, in proposing to take away the Commission's power to red-card vote buyers, politicians were afraid that they themselves could fall victim to the Commission in the coming election.

Apart from trying to neutralize the Commission's power, practising politicians also demanded that the Election Commission file a criminal lawsuit against every disqualified candidate. Again, critics argued that the differences in criteria and process used by the two bodies would enable cheats to escape punishment. For one thing, people generally fear the influence of political figures, and very few would dare to testify against them in a court of law. Moreover, should the court rule against the Commission's decision, then, the Commission itself would run the risk of being sued by the disqualified candidates for malfeasance. In the end, the bill as passed by the House to the Senate required that all disqualifying rulings be screened by a special committee of 11 chief law councillors of the Council of State, which is officially under the Prime Minister's Office. The Commission was also required to file criminal charges against any cheats that it disqualified. The senate added a further stipulation that any constituency MP chosen to become a minister (and thereby forfeiting her or his constituency seat under the terms of the constitution) would become liable for the costs of the resulting by-election. This had the effect of firming up a strong distinction between the two types of MP; in the event, all ministers in the new Thaksin government came from the party-lists.

Another potential time bomb planted by the 1997 Constitution was the provision which guaranteed the right of MPs to vote freely and openly in the nomination for the premiership. Article 156, which clearly states that MPs are free and are not bound by party resolutions or any other obligation in a vote to approve a political office, has caused some leading politicians to worry about the future development of the party system itself. Such concerns received serious public attention once the Prachakorn Thai Party failed in its attempt to oust its own 12 rebel MPs who in defiance of the party resolution switched their support for the premiership from Chatichai Choonhavan (the late Chart Pattana leader) to Chuan Leekpai of the Democrat Party (*Matichon*, 12 February 1999). The leadership of the Prachakorn Thai Party was expecting that the expulsion of the rebellious MPs from its party would cause them to lose their House seats. The Constitutional Court's decision to throw out the party's expulsion order on some legal technicalities, however, enabled these MPs to retain their House seats although they had to join a new party within 30 days. After this ruling, many observers expressed their fear that from now on MPs may be encouraged to think that they could break ranks with their parties without fear of losing their House seats. Some even speculated that once MPs were allowed to defy party decisions, there would be nothing to prevent candidates for the premiership from buying support from some House members.

It is probably fair to say that most veteran politicians had some reservations about the 1997 Constitution. Leaders of small parties naturally criticized the party-list system, arguing that large parties stood to gain the most from it while smaller ones were clearly discriminated against. Some found the academic qualifications required of all parliamentary candidates unfair and undemocratic. The requirement for cabinet ministers to have at least a bachelor's degree was another sore point for those senior MPs who found going to college at an advanced time of life quite difficult; although Ramkhamhaeng University helpfully opened a special programme that was designed specifically to help politicians or 'experienced professionals' who did not have a bachelor's degree to gain one within a very short period of time (*Bangkok Post*, 19 February 2000). A few politicians found the provision giving 50,000 eligible voters the right to hold elected politicians and public officials accountable highly offensive.

ATTEMPTS TO DISCIPLINE CONSTITUTION VIOLATORS

As the new constitution becomes institutionalised, Thai politicians will adapt and adopt whatever strategy they find most suitable for their own political survival. After the censure debate in late 1998, the New Aspiration Party (NAP) lost no time in requesting the Constitutional Court to decide whether the prime minister and the minister of finance were guilty of constitutional violations. The premier and the minister of finance, alleged the opposition, had submitted letters of intent (LOI) which required legal enactment and should have been treated as 'treaties' to the International Monetary Fund (IMF) without parliamentary endorsement (*Bangkok Post,* 9 April 1999). The NAP also sought to impeach the prime minister and other ministers for abuse of authority by lodging a motion with the senate and subsequently with the National Counter Corruption Commission (NCCC). Although in the LOI case the Constitutional Court ruled in favour of the government (*Bangkok Post,* 26 May 1999), the Court revealed certain weaknesses that in the long run may undermine its own authority. Only six out of 13 judges explicitly ruled in favour of the government, whereas two voted in support of the opposition parties. The remaining five judges declined to deliberate, since they were of the opinion that the Court should have declined the petition from the very beginning. In the face of a growing number of cases being referred to the Constitutional Court for review, apparent indecisiveness or unreadiness on the part of the Court to play its proper role raises doubts about its political impartiality (*Thai Post,* 11 June 1999).

Another most striking example was that of Nevin Chidchob, the deputy minister of agriculture, who was found guilty in a libel suit by the Buriram Provincial Court, and given a suspended six-month jail term. According to Article 216, argued the President of the Constitution Association, a minister loses his post when he is sentenced by a court to prison no matter if the sentence is suspended or not.[5] The government was forced to take the matter up to the Constitutional Court – but the Court, true to form, again procrastinated before finally producing a verdict that drew sharp criticism from all sides.[6]

The NAP, however, did manage to land a mortal blow to the Democrats in the censure debate of December 1999, when one of its members claimed that Major-General Sanan Kachornprasart, the deputy prime minister and the interior minister, had faked debts in his assets and liabilities report to the National Counter Corruption Commission (NCCC) in order to launder ill-gotten wealth. In March 2000, the nine-member NCCC unanimously ruled that Sanan's loan documents were false and that he was lying to mislead the Commission. Sanan immediately resigned as deputy prime minister and interior minister. His case was next referred to the Constitutional Court for further review. Sanan was then barred from holding any political position for five years when the Constitutional Court overwhelmingly ruled in August 2000 that he had fabricated a 45-million baht-loan in his declaration of assets. Sanan was forced to resign as Democrat secretary-general. To some observers, the fall of Sanan – who up to a few months earlier had been one of the most powerful men in the country – marked a watershed in Thai politics. To others, it was too soon to rush to such a conclusion. The case brought against Sanan, they reasoned, involved a relatively minor charge and Sanan was simply too careless in handling it.

DILEMMAS OF POLITICAL PARTIES

From the viewpoint of a political party, the 1997 Constitution seems to present different parties with different problems depending basically on their respective size and potential. The very survival of a small party such as the Prachakorn Thai Party may be at stake, because as a Bangkok-based party with little support outside the capital, it cannot realistically hope to gain any MPs from the party-list system: it would face enough difficulties simply to come up with a respectable list of up to 100 candidates, as required by the law. But even medium-sized parties such as the Chart Thai Party or the Chart Pattana Party were threatened by the new political game. If a major party like the Democrats realistically felt that only the first 30 names on its party-list were a sure bet, then a middle-sized party would not find it an easy job to recruit a respectable person who was willing to have his or her name placed lower than number 12 on its list.

As a matter of fact, the selection of a hundred respectable and well known personalities to be candidates on the party-list proved a difficult task even for the major parties. For one thing, certain parliamentarians resented the idea of the party-list MPs, seeing them as 'parasites' who would do nothing except depend on the campaigning efforts of ordinary MPs. Only a few faction leaders or influential figures in the party were entitled to have their names put among the very first of the list. A few party-list seats were also set aside to accommodate these MPs whose new constituency boundaries overlapped with each other. This was to avoid having equally strong MPs who used to belong to the same party compete against each other for the same constituency seats in the coming election. By arranging to put some on the list, and encouraging others to contest the district seats, the parties stood to gain from the sure victory of its candidates. The same kind of accommodation was also made for MPs from other parties who decided to join up with the new party as a group. Naturally, a few party-list seats had also to be reserved for those businessmen who had faithfully supported the party, financially and otherwise. Having the names of other well-known, respectable personalities in different areas who could make the list of the party more attractive was also important. Yet in the event there were hardly enough seats left for people belonging to this last category.

Because future cabinet members were expected to come from party-list MPs, the process of ranking the party-list candidates, especially the very top ones, was a very sensitive one for various faction leaders within each party. Moreover, the fact that the number of ministers under the new constitution was now reduced from 49 to 36 made this political dealing much more difficult. Some hard political bargaining had take place among formal and informal leaders and supporters of the party regarding future political responsibilities. For example, medium-sized parties with no potential for further expansion found it practically impossible to satisfy the political ambitions of all their leading members. Merger with a larger party was the best solution, but the merging of parties rarely runs smoothly. Each party, therefore, had to decide whether to put most big names on the party-list – as expected by the public – or risk losing out in the constituency contests.

Another unforeseen factor in Thai politics occasioned by the 1997 Constitution was the mass switching of parties in the run-up to the 2001 elections. The Thai Rak Thai Party (TRT) was by far the largest beneficiary, while almost all political parties were destabilized as a result of the mass defections of their incumbent MPs to TRT. The New Aspiration Party (NAP) suffered the most: about two-thirds of the party's former strength of 125 MPs defected to TRT. Politicians with divergent backgrounds who used to be at one another's throats, all of a sudden found themselves in the same party. For example, Sanoh Thienthong, the former secretary-general of the NAP, defected to the TRT only to be joined by his old adversary Jaturon Chaisaeng, who had previously replaced him as the NAP secretary-general.

All in all, Thaksin Shinawatra's Thai Rak Thai Party managed to draw about 110 incumbent MPs under its wing, making it the largest in terms of current and former MPs. Needless to say, reports of MPs being offered huge sums of money to change parties were widespread. Although the TRT leadership consistently denied that it had offered bribes to members of other parties to join it, citing instead the new rules of the constitution which made it more difficult for MPs to change party in the future to explain the mass defections, the criticism continued. In sum, there can be no denial that money politics has long been and still is an integral part of the Thai political system. A war of words between key members of the Chart Thai Party – deputy leader Boonchu Trithong and Jongchai Thiengtham, the Chart Thai deputy transport minister – serves as the best illustration (*Bangkok Post*, 7 July 2000). In this case, Boonchu who was defecting to the TRT, accused Jongchai among other things of trying to sell him his deputy labour portfolio for 50 million baht. Jongchai, in turn, accused Boonchu of trying to buy a portfolio for 100 million baht. In the course of their heated exchanges, it was revealed that the Chart Thai Party secured the loyalty of its MPs by paying them 30,000–50,000 baht a month. The monthly allowance had since been increased to 100,000 baht. There were also reports that those MPs who threatened to defect to another party would be paid double. One can only guess as to how much those MPs who joined TRT were being paid for their new loyalty.[7]

WORKING THE SYSTEM: SURVIVING AS AN MP

The attention paid to policy platforms by Thai Rak Thai and the Democrats prior to the 2001 elections was evidence that certain provisions of the 1997 Constitution and crucial political issues of the day had conditioned major parties to think and function more as national institutions than they had done previously. But the same thing definitely cannot be said about individual MPs. Under the new constitution, MPs were being pushed to become more parochial and in some cases more independent of their parties. The new election system's smaller constituencies favoured those candidates who are more closely associated with the local people. As a result, the new system of single-member constituency made the competition for a House seat very fierce. Under the old system of multi-member constituencies, prominent candidates could always work out an agreement among themselves, regardless of the parties they belonged to, so that the two or three most powerful politicians from the same area could emerge as winners.[8] Under the new constitution, such a compromise was no longer possible: winning had become a matter of 'do or die' for each candidate.

The shape of things to come could be clearly seen in the Samut Prakan municipal elections. On 2 May 1999, an election was held for the 24 seats on the municipal council of Samut Prakarn province, a city on the outskirts of Bangkok. The competition between the team led by a son of Vatana Asawahame, a deputy minister of interior (whose command of a faction of 12 rebel Prachakorn Thai party MPs had made it possible for Chuan to become prime minister) and another team also led by a relative of Vatana, turned out to be the dirtiest election in modern Thai history. Outrageous tactics such as using fake ballots, stuffing the ballot boxes with the pre-marked ballots, and tampering with lists of eligible voters, took place in broad daylight in front of TV cameras and in the presence of policemen. Evidence showed that at least 20 of the 44 polling centres were rampant with all kinds of election fraud.[9]

The first three months of 2000, which saw a series of local elections for provincial administration organizations, municipalities and the senate election, also witnessed 35 cases of murder believed to be related to political rivalry (*Thai Rath*, 7 April 2000). Even the police attributed the rise in local murders to the fact that as local administrative bodies gained greater freedom to manage their internal affairs, the bigger budgets funded either by the government or by the collection of local taxes had induced conflicts of interest among local politicians across the country (*Bangkok Post*, 12 June 2000). The intensification of contestation for parliamentary seats seemed likely to precipitate violence, fraud and intimidation on a formidable scale. Such a fight-to-the-death kind of competition can be very costly at times when a party cannot be of much help. Often, the credit for winning a provincial house seat in the next election will be rightfully claimed by individual MPs or their faction leaders. Those who have managed to secure more or less safe seats have not normally done so through the popularity of their parties. Groups of MPs led by Kamnan Poh of Chonburi or Newin Chidchob of Buriram, for example, are willing to pay for their own campaigns.

Moreover, while trying to make electoral politics more attractive to competent and promising people who usually would not have been interested in entering the political arena, the new constitution may actually end up making it even more difficult for these new faces to do so. Before the 1997 Constitution it was already a common practice among veteran politicians to recruit their children or close associates into politics. Chart Thai Party leader and former premier Banharn Silpa-archa of Suphanburi serves as a good example. Before the resignation of his younger brother Chumpol, who later became a Bangkok senator, three out of five MPs from Suphanburi belonged to the Silpa-archa family: Banharn himself, Chumphol, and Banharn's daughter Kanchana. With his rebellious brother Chumphol out of the picture, Banharn's only son Worawuth ran in Suphanburi. The case of Somchai Kunpleum, better known as Kamnan Poh or the so-called 'Godfather of the East', was no different. Kamnan Poh himself (the mayor of Saensuk municipality) did not stand for election but three of his sons, two whom were already MPs, did so.

It is, of course, also possible that the new election system's smaller constituencies may result in making urban voters in some municipal areas dominant forces in those new constituencies. If so, former municipal politicians will naturally have advantages over other candidates and they can become new faces in the House. Yet, it is often the case that members of the House and municipal politicians belong to the same group or share the same interests. As such, it would seem that a single-member constituency system will strengthen the hands of the old guard in politics even more. Take, for example, reports that local politicians competing in the 1999 municipal council election at Ubon Ratchathani were all connected to current MPs and their parties (*Matichon*, 21 June 1999). With the introduction of the elected senate and the party-list system, powerful politicians may have even more opportunities to expand their political power bases. As already mentioned, many former MPs have successfully run for the Senate. Also a good number of senators are either relatives or the wives of politicians. Now, it has become common practice for MPs of some status to run on the party-list system and to let their brothers or sister or spouses run in constituencies. At least 40 MPs planned to field family members in their constituencies in the general election, while they themselves would contest in the party-list election (*The Nation*, 11 October 2000). While many new faces entered the political arena, the 2001 Parliament also partly resembled a politicians' wives' club, or an assembly of political clans or dynasties. Clearly on the rise was the trend towards family-based politics, and alliances between veterans and local politicians. Despite all the talk about reform, the body politic remained more or less the same.

CIVIL SOCIETY AND PUBLIC AWARENESS OF POLITICAL RIGHTS

It has often been argued that over the last decade the political scene has evolved significantly. Rural politics has become much more assertive. Organizations have spread. The broadening of democracy is everywhere to be seen. Indeed, the new constitution should be viewed as part of a series of changes spearheaded by civil society activities that had so forcefully emerged in Thailand by the year 1997 (Prudhisan 1998). Clearly, Thai politics was no longer the exclusive domain of bureaucrats and politicians. So-called Thai 'civil society' – exemplified by grassroots level activities – had begun to make its influence felt. Yet a fundamental question remained as to whether the Thai social and political structure had *essentially* changed since the promulgation of the 1997 Constitution. With the new constitution now formally enacted, can one assume as a matter of course that politics will be cleaner and politicians will be better, despite the fact that even before the 1997 Constitution, there were already laws against vote-buying and corruption in place? Is it not a fact that the underlying causes of many of the problems that reformers set out to solve through the process of constitutional reform were actually the result of economic inequalities which separated wealthy politicians from poor villagers (King 1992: 1119)? If so, how could any political reform ever be achieved, as long as these economic problems remain unsolved? By the end of 2000 Thailand remained economically vulnerable, as the country was still facing a huge amount of non-performing loans, high public debt, estimated to be around 2.6 trillion baht, and a weak currency. Three years after its return to power, the Chuan government, which had promised to nurse the economy back to health, had failed to stimulate the economy and address other woes. According to the National Economic and Social Development Board, the number of Thais living below the poverty line (defined as an income of less than 886 baht per month or 10,632 baht per year) was now close to 8 million (or about 13 per cent of the total population). Furthermore, the latest labour surveys by the National Statistical Office indicated that around 6.8 million Thais had a monthly wage of only 750 baht. The worsening income distribution situation was also reflected in the fact that only 1 per cent of the population, or 650,000 people, had a monthly income of more than 20,000 baht (*Bangkok Post*, 1 June 2000). The slow recovery of the economy coupled with alleged widespread corruption among politicians had made both the rural poor and the more affluent urbanites increasingly impatient with the government.

Despite all the bad news about the economy, could observers still count on the better understanding and democratic awareness of the people to make reforms a reality soon? Did the reformed constitution not make any difference at all? That the framers of the 1997 Constitution had tried their best to provide the people with all possible opportunities to hold politicians and public officials accountable was obvious. Yet whether or not the 'public' was ready for it is another matter.

Consider, for example, the concept of 'public hearing' spelled out in the present constitution to guarantee transparency in government. In April 1999 a group of mass communication academics and consumer advocacy NGOs had called for a 'public hearing' to review the price increases made by a cable TV operator. Such a change, they claimed, was unfair to its subscribers as it should first go through the process of 'public hearing' (*Bangkok Post*, 10 April 1999). It was very disappointing to observe that even academics did not realize that what goes on between a pay TV owner and his customers was a matter of private concern, which should not be confused with the idea of 'public hearings' mentioned in the constitution.

Even more shocking was the fact that this kind of confusion could take place while the very same 'public' seems to tolerate other outright violations of basic human rights. Consider, for example, the case of the official licence to be on the air. The Department of Public Relations, the public relations arm of the Thai government, had for years exercised its tight control over the media personnel by devising the rule that any television and radio announcer or commentator, before he or she can go on the air, must first acquire a certificate of Thai language proficiency. This requirement that to be able to talk on the air entails passing a pronunciation test authorized by the Department, is based on the grounds that the airwaves, considered to be state property, should be used by only those who can speak Thai properly. Standard 'Thai' in this case, however, turns out to be the central or Bangkok version which naturally discriminates against other regional 'accents'. Obviously, this autocratic decree can also be used to silence or make harder the lives of those who dare challenge the political views of the state. Strange though it may seem, most people working in television and radio have slavishly conformed to this demand. Even now under the new constitution which is supposed to grant more freedom of expression and more freedom to mass media, the media community (especially those in the press who have switched over to the radio and television business) have failed to challenge this ridiculous government decree. The lesson is clear: one should not expect the public or even the media always to come to the rescue of the cause of political reform.

As is often the case, political enthusiasm on the part of the public can also be very short-lived, especially when there is no concrete or material gain at stake. Politicians and government officials, on the other hand, can always count on time being on their side. Hence apart from a basic understanding and awareness of the issues involved, the public, as an active political actor, also needs to be very energetic and persistent in the pursuance of its goals. Here the corruption allegations made against the former health minister, his deputy and the permanent under-secretary of the public health minister by an alliance of thirty NGOs appear to be a case in point. When the health minister and his deputy finally resigned in September 1998, it looked as if at last the people could really check the conduct of administrators and politicians. However, months passed before any action was finally taken by the investigating committee. In the end nothing was said about the role of the politicians responsible. A few public health officials were fired. The permanent under-secretary was not found guilty and was not subject to any further investigation. Most important of all, although in the past three years the government has been upset by series of corruption scandals and relentless negative comments from all sides, yet so far not a single politician has been found guilty of any crime. Even disgraced former Interior Minister Sanan Kachornprasart was able to get off free when the National Counter Corruption Commission, citing technicalities, decided not to pursue criminal action against him (*The Nation*, 4 October 2000). And Thaksin Shinawatra won a sweeping election victory despite the fact that the Thai Rak Thai Party leader was subject to investigation by the National Counter Corruption Commission for his role in the dubious transfer of the ownership of stocks in companies in his business empire.

CONCLUSION

In conclusion, it was hardly surprising that the January 2001 elections were characterized by much the same features as the pre-reform elections. Money continued to play a crucial role, and there was evidence that the new electoral system resulted in more intensified political competition and more election-related violence. Intimidation is nothing new in Thai politics. In spite of the new constitution, traditional practices would not go away.[10] When the key drafters of the 1997 Constitution gathered to mark its third anniversary, they grudgingly admitted that the political reform had failed to produce new choices for the people (*Bangkok Post*, 12 October 2000). Money, candidacy and party (in that order) were the factors deciding the election outcome in most parts of Thailand. Major parties, despite their national economic platforms, continued to be divided along regional lines. Naturally, rural voters and the Bangkok voters remained worlds apart. The absolute freedom which MPs now enjoyed in nominating the prime minister simply meant that the number of actors in this crucial political bargaining would increase almost indefinitely. While at one point the six former coalition partners – the Democrats, Chart Thai, Chart Pattana, Seritham and Rassadorn – publicly affirmed their intention to stick together beyond the general election after having made the assessment that their combined seats could form majority control in the House of Representatives, the idea of a 'grand alliance' soon collapsed. Meanwhile, most political observers expressed doubts about Thaksin's wisdom in taking a short-cut to government leadership by bringing in MPs with different backgrounds from several parties. It was certainly not clear how the TRT leader could manage to keep his party from disintegrating, because by bringing in MPs from all sides, he was evidently repeating the very same mistake as General Chavalit's ill-fated 1996–97 administration.

In short, the 1997 Constitution, extraordinary though it may be, will not be able to alter the nature of the Thai politics in any significant way, at least not in the foreseeable future.

NOTES

1 While materials on the development of the 1997 Constitution can be found, what is really needed is a piece on the politics of the constitutional drafting itself. It is interesting to note that a list of candidates supposedly approved by the government to be on the Constitution Drafting Assembly (CDA) had already appeared in the newspapers days before the parliamentary selection took place. Most of the people on that list were actually selected by the Parliament to be among the members of CDA. This fact alone seems to indicate that political parties and politicians hardly stood idly by as the 99 CDA members, including some former MPs, set out to reform the Thai political system.

2 Almost all publications by the Constitution Drafting Assembly (CDA) and its political allies explicitly voice this sense of optimism and idealism. See, for example: CDA 1997c: 36–37; Committee on Development Promotion and Dissemination 1998. Most writings by former CDA members strongly support the Constitution. See, for example, Kanin 1998 (Kanin was a former member of the CDA from Chonburi province).

3 This massive 72 per cent voter turnout may be misleading, since at the time of the 4 March election many people did not understand that they

would only lose certain minor political rights by not voting. Fear that they would be deprived of other essential rights – the right to renew their driving licences, for example – drove voters to cast their ballots in unprecedentedly high numbers.

4   Ubon Ratchatani was the only province that had to go to a fifth round of voting. Interestingly enough, the winner in the end was the very same candidate who had been suspended in the second and fourth rounds, and won in the fourth round. The final voter turnout was lower than 30 per cent.

5   Interestingly, Newin claims the charges were a conspiracy by former drafters of the constitution to retaliate against his father, MP Chai Chidchob who has accused the writers of the new charter of mismanaging their expense accounts while serving on the Constitution Drafting Assembly (CDA) (*The Nation*, 30 April 1999).

6   On 10 June 1999 the Constitutional Court called a meeting to deliberate on this matter – only to postpone the announcement of the verdict on the grounds that there was not enough time for all the judges' statements to be read (*Thai Post*, 11 June 1999). When the Constitutional Court finally announced its verdict in favour of Newin by a vote of 7 to 6, it drew fierce criticism from everywhere, especially from the leading members of the CDA. What made the whole business look so bad in the eyes of the public was that the verdict was reported in the newspapers one day before the formal announcement by the court. Accusations were also made against a member of the Court who voted with the majority, of having a conflict of interest in making such a judgement (*Matichon*, 20 June 1999).

7   It is interesting to note, for example, that even the NAP has reportedly increased the monthly pay of its MPs from 200,000 baht to 500,000 baht. The pay hike was obviously aimed at stopping the mass defection of its MPs to other parties (*Bangkok Post*, 27 August 2000).

8   In 1986, three leading candidates from different parties competing in the same constituency in Pitsanulok province had their pictures and numbers, along with a common slogan, appear on the same billboard. All three were elected (Sombat 1997: 102).

9   It is interesting to note the explanations given by government officials and politicians involved in this Samut Prakarn incident. The governor of Samut Prakarn first explained away the poll frauds by accusing the losing party of committing fraud in the hope that there would be a new election (*Bangkok Post*, 6 May 1999). The interior minister simply said he had no authority over municipal elections.

10 Yuwarat Kamolvej, the only member of the National Election Commission with some experience in supervising elections, was of the optimistic opinion in mid-1999 that the next general election would be at least 50 per cent cleaner (*Matichon*, 29 May 1999).

14

POLITICAL REFORM AND CIVIL SOCIETY AT THE LOCAL LEVEL: THAILAND'S LOCAL GOVERNMENT REFORMS

Daniel Arghiros

INTRODUCTION

The decentralization and devolution of administrative and fiscal powers to elected bodies is increasingly seen as a panacea for reforming over-centralized and unresponsive states. Thailand is an excellent case in point. Unusually for a development policy, it has won support from those on the left and right of the political spectrum. Neo-liberals see decentralization as a means of cutting back corrupt and inefficient states while those on the left applaud its capacity to counterbalance state power by redistributing power to 'civil society'. Where decentralization involves the devolution of power at the local level to elected bodies, it is seen as a means of facilitating good government. It is argued that a positive relationship between governance and economic performance exists: after years of focusing just on the economic underpinnings of growth, influential organizations such as the World Bank have come to the conclusion that good government creates the conditions for growth. Theoretically, local good governance is achieved by extending political participation to the mass of the population, formerly excluded from government. When taken together, decentralization and democratization 'are seen as a way of reducing the power and size of swollen central state bureaucracies, and of improving accountability for development planning and spending at a more local level'. In theory, taking fiscal and administrative control from non-elected, centrally located bureaucrats and giving it to elected local residents makes the development process more effective and efficient. Crook and Manor call this form of decentralization 'democratic decentralization' – a term that I have adopted in this paper.

Democratic decentralization is also credited with providing the conditions for invigorating 'civil society'. Opening up opportunities for the masses to participate in the political life of the nation is thought to support the growth of civil society. In turn, the growth of civil society is thought to strengthen and deepen democracy. As an advisor to USAID argues, 'decentralization provides incentives and opportunities for local CAOs (civic advocacy organizations, the building blocks of civil society) to engage in resolving local problems'. There is little agreement over what does and does not constitute civil society. All commentators tend to agree that civil society is to be found in the realm of social or associational life that lies between the household and the state. There is also agreement that the activities of voluntary associations that make up civil society should be autonomous from the state and, furthermore, in some way limit the power of the state.[1] Political parties are excluded because they aim to win and exercise state power rather than to influence it from outside. The most restrictive interpretation comes from more naïve practitioners in the development community, who tend to equate civil society with NGOs. Interventions that emanate from this school of thought generate programmes and projects that amount to little more than the sponsorship of NGOs. Civil society groups do not necessarily have a liberal or pro-democratic agenda. However it is defined, civil society is seen to benefit from democratic decentralization.

There are a variety of reasons why democratic decentralization fails to deliver on its promises in any given context. Particularly in societies with little experience of democracy, the formal electoral process often yields representatives who are only a little more accountable than non-elected civil servants: patronage and mutually helpful relations between bureaucrats and a commercial elite can mean that power remains concentrated within this sphere. At the local level decentralization is prone to lead to the extension of bureaucratic power into local communities – the bureaucratization of rural communities and the deconcentration rather than devolution of central authority. Ironically, reforms can give the state an entry point through which to exert more rather than less influence over local communities. Even under favourable conditions in which there is relative political freedom, robust economic growth and a state apparatus self-confident enough to relinquish some powers, the benefits of democratic decentralization at the community and provincial levels tend to be captured by 'local powers' (Turton 1989). These 'local powers' tend to become new and alternative patrons to bureaucrats: indeed, at least in Thailand, as councils obtain greater influence there is often a reversal in status between members and bureaucrats. Council members may emerge the superior party. Such a scenario tends to arise where a nascent rural stratum of capitalists exists but where otherwise there is little by way of 'civil society'.

However, these tendencies do not necessarily constitute an argument against deploying democratic decentralization as a policy instrument. However imperfect the result, democratic decentralization is still often an improvement on the monopolization of power by unelected state officials. It is also possible to see the pre-eminence of 'local powers' as a transitional scenario – and one that will evolve as the electorate becomes more demanding and discerning. Likewise, in the short term decentralization may lead to greater state penetration of local communities while in the longer term locals can turn these institutions around to serve their own needs and interests.

This chapter examines the extent to which the institutions and reforms created in Thailand to bring about democratic decentralization have been successful. My aim is partly to show how Thailand's ongoing experiment with institutional reform is beginning to work out on the ground. But it is also to indicate the extent to which the obstacles that undermine the effectiveness of reform can and cannot be avoided by better planning and legislation. It looks at policy and practice at the provincial and subdistrict level, and highlights state–civil relations and the question of bureaucratization; it examines the role of local elites and the conduct of elections. Some of the barriers restricting the achievement of democratic decentralization are due to political interference at the planning stage and could be counteracted by better legislation backed by political will; others arise from the wider political, economic and social context in which the reforms are being implemented, and are thus even more difficult to counteract. Barriers at this level demand gradual change in socio-political structures and culture. The chapter draws on fieldwork that I conducted in a central Thai district of Ayuthaya province, which I call 'Klang', between 1989 and 1998. It also draws on data gathered from elsewhere in provincial Thailand while conducting research on other issues.

DEMOCRATIC DECENTRALIZATION AT THE SUBDISTRICT AND PROVINCIAL LEVELS IN THAILAND

Compared to many others, the Thai state is extremely strong and has effective reach into all provinces and districts, no matter how far they are from Bangkok. Although Thailand was never colonized, its provincial administration is reminiscent of the colonial apparatus of administration established by the British in India and the French in Indochina. It was designed to ensure effective central control of rural areas, and through the 1890s until the early 1900s the Thai state launched a programme of what some have called 'internal colonization'. This heritage goes some way to explaining why, despite never having been colonized, Thailand's experience with democratic decentralization shares so much in common with former colonies elsewhere. The problematic aspects of Thailand's experiment with political reform share many features with former colonies such as India, Nepal and a number of African states.

The Ministry of Interior controls all aspects of not only provincial and district administration but also the branch of the civil service with responsibility for mainstream development, the Community Development Department. The Ministry's long-standing preoccupation has been with national security. Through the 1970s and 1980s this was a response to internal communist insurgency and a perceived threat from neighbouring socialist and communist states (Vietnam, Cambodia, Laos and Burma). Given this heritage, it is not surprising that the Ministry of Interior has long resisted any reforms that would loosen its grip over the provinces. Opposition was so entrenched that USAID terminated a decentralization programme in the early 1980s due to inadequate support from the Thai government. It has also fought hard against recent reforms that promised to curtail its control over newly empowered local government. The current push for democratic decentralization is largely an internally driven programme, and is the brainchild of Chuan Leekpai's reform-minded but short-lived government of the early 1990s. This contrasts with the largely donor-driven decentralization programmes of African states – programmes that are to governance what structural adjustment programmes are to the economic arena.

Civil administration outside of urban areas is concentrated at the provincial level: no regional apparatus exists. Provincial governors, who are responsible to the Ministry of Interior, administer provinces. In turn provincial governors oversee the field officials of central ministries that have provincial level branches. Local government at the provincial level takes the form of the 'Provincial Administrative Organization' (PAO). Despite its name, the PAO should not be confused with the non-elected provincial administration. Districts are administered as subdivisions of the province and are not independent of the provincial administration. Mirroring the organization of provincial administration, the district officer oversees the work of de-concentrated field representatives of various central ministries and departments. There is no provision for district-level local government. Districts are divided into subdistricts. Until 1996 all subdistricts had a very partial form of local government, namely the 'Subdistrict Councils'. These councils have now been replaced by Subdistrict Administrative Organizations (SAOs, *ongkan borihan suan tambon* or OBT). Administratively defined villages are grouped into subdistricts. Villages are administered by elected locals, 'village heads'; the head of a subdistrict is elected by residents from among the village heads. Subdistrict and village heads – though locally elected – are answerable to the District Office.

One cannot fully appreciate the ways in which democratic decentralization has worked out on the ground without appreciating the impact and ongoing influence of national electoral politics. Politicians have become more directly involved in controlling rural votes, and their campaign strategies have filtered down to dominate practices at the local level.

Prior to a student uprising in 1973 the bureaucracy, in its military and civilian components, controlled the Thai state and its apparatus. In an arrangement that could be a description of contemporary Cambodia, the bureaucracy maintained control over the political arena by forming a 'government party' and gaining appointment to the Upper House. Until the 1970s government parties could rely on the control of the Ministry of Interior to win elections and the government party directed local state representatives to mobilize rural voters on its behalf. District officials used local leaders, subdistrict and village heads, as canvassers and the latter in turn used their influence over villagers. At this time vote-buying was largely absent and local leaders exerted a strong influence over villagers' voting behaviour. As one old villager in 'Klang' district reflected:

> In the past it was not necessary to buy votes ... the candidate would go to see the *kamnan* [subdistrict head] and he would call his villagers together and say 'vote for number one and two [candidates]' – in those days people were easy to speak to. We listened and believed.

The legislature gained influence relative to the military during the 1980s, prompting individuals and interest groups that had never done so before (notably, the military) to seek national political office. Competition for membership of the National Assembly increased as it became the new locus of power. An associated change has been greater direct involvement of capitalist interests in national electoral politics. One ramification of intensified competition for National Assembly seats, from among both military and business, is the greater use of vote-buying as a means of winning electoral support. The practice was common even in the 1970s, but became more widespread in the mid to late 1980s. Material patronage, the giving of goods to communities, is also a method of choice. Indeed, until recently, MPs had at their disposal large personal development budgets (20 million baht, or approximately US$800,000) which they used to win favour within their constituencies. The crucial point here is that the electioneering methods first developed by candidates in national elections have now been adopted by candidates at the provincial and subdistrict levels. Vote-buying is now endemic to elections at these levels. The outcome of democratic decentralization is deeply coloured by national political processes.

DEMOCRATIC DECENTRALIZATION AND THE SUBDISTRICT ADMINISTRATIVE ORGANIZATION

Let us first look at structures designed to promote democratic decentralization at the subdistrict or *tambon* level. Subdistrict councils charged with enhancing participation in development planning have been active since the mid-1970s. However, reforms that came into effect in the mid-1990s have transformed these organizations into local government bodies, Subdistrict Administrative Organizations (SAOs), with greater powers. This section firstly depicts the features of these earlier councils, and then identifies the barriers that limit the effectiveness of the latest democratic decentralization reforms.

Subdistrict councils were criticized on several grounds. Some criticisms continue to be applicable to the new Subdistrict Administrative Organizations and it is worth reviewing them. Among the main objections was the fact that restrictions on the powers invested in Subdistrict Councils meant that they were weak relative to the state administration: they served as vehicles of bureaucratic power rather than media for local governance. Furthermore, control at the local level has often been concentrated in the hands of a local elite, negating the rhetoric of participatory planning.

Subdistrict councils were established early this century but only came to have a meaningful developmental role in the 1970s. They were presided over by the subdistrict head (*kamnan*) and made up of village heads plus one other representative from each village. Councils were first allocated discretionary funds for local development in 1972. Then, in 1975, the Tambon Development Act institutionalized the decentralization of decision-making, ostensibly putting control into the hands of villagers and increasing their political participation. This was an early attempt to reverse the entirely top-down structure of Thai development administration. Councils were allocated central funds for local development projects, a change that was subsequently extended by the Fifth National Economic and Social Development Plan. This accorded councils the power to write and implement five-year development plans for their subdistricts.

Subdistrict councils were, however, only partially a structure for local government: although members were elected and had the authority to administer and implement local development plans, the council was firmly under the authority of the provincial government and did not have any law-making powers. Councils lacked the authority to make independent financial decisions and were given relatively small grants. Councils' development plans had to be passed back up the administrative hierarchy for approval. It was also common practice for subdistrict heads and council members to receive kickbacks on contracts for work they commissioned. Perhaps rather cynically, Morell and Chai-Anan refer to the 1975 legislation as producing 'decentralized corruption'. Furthermore, it was common for powerful subdistrict heads to determine the use of development funds in ways other than those decided by the council. Within individual subdistricts there was frequently a 'gap between the rhetoric of participation and the reality of exclusion': council members did not consult villagers, who were completely ignorant of the workings of the council.

In principle recent legislation should enable the successors to subdistrict-level councils to function as genuine forums for local interests. Legislation that came into effect in early 1996 has replaced each of the country's 7,000 Subdistrict Councils with a Subdistrict Administrative Organization (SAO). The new SAOs have a broader representative base than the old Subdistrict Councils with two rather than one elected villager representing each village. In its original form the SAO legislation stipulated that all seats should be contested in local elections and none was to be reserved for existing subdistrict and village heads. However, aware that they stood to lose a key source of influence and kickbacks, the country's subdistrict and village heads aggressively lobbied the minister of interior, Chavalit Yongchaiyudh, to change the proposed legislation. Subdistrict and village heads have for several decades been the primary linkage between the state and the rural population. They have occupied an ambiguous position between serving as villagers' representatives and being quasi-civil servants under the Ministry of Interior. Latterly, as competition has become increasingly dominated by money, they have tended to serve their own interests and those of the state before the electorate. While until the early 1990s these positions were held until retirement, they are now subject to five-year terms. In view of the fact that subdistrict and village heads are the all-important grassroots canvassers for electoral candidates at all levels, Chavalit threw his weight behind them and forced this aspect of the reform to be altered. Chavalit became Thailand's prime minister in November 1996; it goes without saying that he and his party received overwhelming support from subdistrict and village heads in the preceding general election. Subdistrict and village heads enjoyed reserved seats in the SAO until 2001 and the subdistrict's *kamnan* lost their positions as SAO presidents in 1999. They lobbied vigorously, but ultimately unsuccessfully, to try to ensure that these provisions were upheld in perpetuity.[2] On an individual basis, *kamnan* and village heads have also promoted the election campaigns of their relatives to ensure that they can wield influence over SAOs that they do not formally dominate.

The new SAOs also have at their disposal vastly increased financial resources – comprised of government grants and returned local taxes – and, more importantly, they have been granted legal status: they are juristic persons. Their powers and jurisdiction are, on paper, extremely broad ranging and ill-defined. Their 'general duties' are to 'develop the subdistrict economically, socially and culturally'. Their mandatory duties include the provision and maintenance of waterways and roads; health care; relief regarding public hazards; the promotion of education, religion and culture; the promotion of the development of women, children and youth, the elderly and disabled; and the protection of natural resources and the environment. Their legal status allows them to execute development projects themselves and SAOs can enter legally binding contracts with outside service providers without deferring to the District Office for either funds or approval. These new organizations are now better equipped to develop local facilities that central government has neglected. SAOs can use their own considerable funds to establish or improve agricultural infrastructure, public water supplies, nursery and primary schools, and roads. If they wish they can draw up local poverty reduction projects, such as providing free school meals or selling rice at subsidized prices. They are also now empowered to impose local by-laws and are thus able to ban from their subdistricts economic activities and enterprises (such as sand extraction, rock blasting, polluting industries) that undermine local residents' livelihoods and quality of life. However, despite their new powers and financial resources it is unlikely that SAOs will approach meeting their mandate or using their powers in the near future.

There are several obstacles hindering SAOs from fulfilling their mandate:

- The country's authoritarian bureaucracy is reluctant to recognise the autonomy of SAOs and is attempting to incorporate them within the existing administrative structure.
- The rise of a new rural elite and the pervasive use of vote-buying in elections is distorting SAO membership to represent minority interests.
- Male prejudice against women holding political office virtually excludes one of the sexes from participating in the organizations.
- There is a simple lack of local experience and expertise to ensure that SAOs use their powers effectively.

These factors combine to restrict the extent to which Thailand's new decentralization policy can generate broad-based participation in planning and implementation of local development. Let us examine each of them in more detail.

There is a strong risk that the implementation of the decentralization reforms will result in the systematic bureaucratisation rather than the empowerment of local communities. The bureaucratisation of local development processes is a relatively common outcome of local-level decentralization reform in Southeast Asia.[3] Thailand's traditionally authoritarian bureaucracy is finding it very hard to accept the autonomy of the new SAOs. Instead, the Ministry of Interior treats SAOs as vehicles for extending its administrative reach into rural communities – it views them more as mini District Offices than as independent local institutions. Considerable statutory powers are still vested in the district officer, who is empowered to dissolve an SAO; and shortly before SAOs were introduced the Ministry of Interior tightened the supervisory relationship between subdistricts and the District Office by assigning a deputy district officer to oversee each one. As high-ranking local state officials, these individuals carry a lot of weight with the villagers who sit on SAOs.

The District Office is able to exert a great deal of influence over the nature and scope of activities undertaken by SAOs and to oblige them to implement national policies. The District Office's line of command is through the 'SAO deputy', the '*palat* OBT'. The deputy of the SAO is head of the administrative arm of the SAO and answers to the District Office, though his salary is paid by the SAO. The SAO deputies attend a monthly meeting with the deputy district officer at which they are issued with directives on programmes that they should ensure their SAOs undertake. At a meeting I attended in Klang district in August 1998 the deputy district officer issued SAO deputies with a document that formed the basis of the agenda for subsequent SAO meetings. This represents a continuation of previous practice in the district when subdistrict council meeting agenda were produced and distributed in mimeo form by Community Development Department officials at the district office – local issues were dealt with under the heading 'any other business'. For example, in this meeting SAO deputies were told to ensure that their SAOs were implementing projects that complied with the government's new policy of encouraging community economic self-sufficiency – a rather ill-defined policy in reaction to the economic crisis. Another more petty example is that the next SAO meeting was required to discuss its plans for celebrating national Mothers' Day. Clearly SAO meeting agenda are dominated not by local concerns, but by the preoccupations and priorities of the state.

Of course, it is necessary to ensure that excesses of SAOs are tempered with counterbalancing controls and that they operate within their mandate: the District Office has a legitimate interest in ensuring that abuses do not occur. According to the deputy district officer of Klang, he spent much of his time in the first few months of their operation telling SAOs they could not use funds to buy mobile telephones for members, or buy pick-up trucks for their use. The problem is, however, that the District Office still has direct control over SAOs and this tends to preclude the capacity for SAOs to act as forums for local interests.

The central bureaucracy's reluctance to see SAOs as independent bodies is also reflected in the way officials expect SAOs to adopt the forms and practices of the bureaucracy. This can be taken to extreme lengths. One deputy district officer of Klang district advised a new SAO president to have wooden name plaques engraved and placed in front of members at meetings, despite the fact that members were all village neighbours. In the SAO handbook no less than 12 pages depict the cut and style of the quasi-official uniforms that village members are expected to wear. It also devotes several pages to identifying officially sanctioned colours that an SAO may paint its workplace.

However, the influence of officialdom over SAOs is more insidious than these fairly transparent efforts to extend central control over SAOs. The goal of making SAOs a participatory forum is undermined by the fact that village-based SAO leaders have taken on board the bureaucracy's hierarchical and non-participatory institutional culture. While SAO leaders are *kamnan* and village heads, official practices and cultures are replicated within the new organizations. In particular, meetings and decision-making within the SAO mirror the methods of the district administration – to which subdistrict heads have long been exposed. Whether this will change now that *kamnan* and village heads have lost their membership rights remains to be seen. If SAOs are to perform their intended role, then they will need to assert their autonomy from the district administration; but, and this is the more difficult task, they will also need to reject the official institutional culture they have adopted for a more egalitarian and participatory one.

The second major obstacle preventing SAOs from realizing their potential as institutions for participatory rural development is the ease with which local economic and political elites can dominate SAO membership. Subdistrict Councils have long been run by local political elites, subdistrict and village heads, who occupied the majority of seats by right of position. Subdistrict and village heads had at least three years (1996–99) to fill village representative positions on the SAO with their supporters or family members. But why should one be worried that subdistrict and village heads will continue to dominate SAOs? After all, these people were themselves elected by villagers in secret ballots. The problem is that the outcomes of elections for these positions are increasingly determined by vote-buying. Recently elected subdistrict and village heads are either local economic elites who won office because of their own purchasing power, or they are appointees whose funds come from higher-level politicians seeking dependable local canvassers. Given the importance of money as a campaign instrument, the poor are excluded from even attempting to compete for these positions. Either way, the subdistrict and village heads who dominate SAOs have little or no popular basis of support, and are unlikely to be answerable to the local population in a meaningful way.

Vote-buying is such a pervasive and effective canvassing tool in contemporary Thailand that there are already indications that control over SAOs is passing to wealthy, vote-buying candidates. There are reports of vote-buying in elections for SAO village representatives, and I witnessed this myself in elections in a Klang subdistrict in 1997. In the second round of SAO elections in mid-1999, vote-buying was so widespread it led commentators in the Thai national press to despair that vote-buying was starting to dominate yet another level of election.[4] Because of the importance of money as a campaign instrument, the poor are easily excluded from attempting to compete for these positions. Seats on an SAO enable members to contract out the construction projects that the organization commissions to their or their associates' businesses. The decentralization of fiscal and administrative control to provincial councillors described in the next section provides a glimpse of what may befall SAOs: elected members of PAOs are overwhelmingly individuals with an interest in the construction industry. The danger is that SAOs will evolve in a similar way. This fear has even been expressed by the former minister of interior who supported the campaign by subdistrict and village heads to be given ex officio positions in the new organizations. Anticipating what might befall SAOs, then Prime Minister Chavalit is reported as saying: 'What I'm afraid of is that the *kamnan* and village headmen may all become construction contractors when the power is delegated to them'. This outcome will only be avoided if villagers act collectively to resist vote-buying and elect community-oriented representatives.

One obvious consequence of the domination of SAOs by local economic elites with interests in the construction industry is that a majority of projects will be infrastructural ones. These are often of no particular benefit to the poor. Moreover, when an SAO is controlled by village elites, the majority of villagers are not given the opportunity to participate in drawing up its plans. Little of what the SAO does is a result of consultation with villagers, and residents of the poorest neighbourhoods remain entirely voiceless.

A major obstacle preventing SAOs from becoming effective vehicles for popular participation is the fact that they will inevitably fail adequately to represent the interests of women. Politics is, as elsewhere, seen as a man's world, and this is true of community-level as well as national-level Thai politics. Despite lobbying by women's groups at the drafting stage, the decentralization legislation failed to establish a quota of women members – the aim had been to reserve one of the two village seats in an SAO for a woman. Without positive discrimination, however, it is exceptionally difficult for women to get elected onto an SAO, partly because of male prejudice but also because they lack the kinds of vertical patronage relationships that male candidates tend to enjoy. In one typical province, for example, two-thirds of the 134 SAOs surveyed had no women representatives, and women constituted only 2 per cent of members.[5] A number of Thai NGOs are trying to support women's efforts to stand in SAO elections and it remains to be seen how successful they will be. But the problem is not just one of numbers. If a woman does manage to get elected onto an SAO, she will have to struggle to establish a meaningful role for herself: she will be expected to serve refreshments to male members and will have to operate in an unashamedly sexist environment where drinking and gambling are the staples of socializing. Had they been allocated half of village seats, women would have formed a critical mass on SAOs and would be well placed to pressure them to address social as well as economic development needs – to channel funds toward health care and education as well as toward road-building.

Because SAOs are often dominated by local economic and political elites who run the organizations in the image of the central bureaucracy, local NGOs active in rural areas tend to work around them and not through them. This means that NGOs, as well as women, are not in a position to draw SAOs away from their predilection for highly visible, construction-related infrastructure projects, and another opportunity to mobilize SAOs' considerable funds for more socially meaningful projects is lost.

Finally, the capacity of SAOs to fulfil their mandate is limited by the capacity of members to execute their responsibilities. The organization of the SAO and the procedures that govern it are highly complex and, for many members, confusing. This tends to increase the reliance of SAOs on the SAO secretary, and on government officials such as Community Development Department field staff. This increase in dependency in turn heightens opportunities for the District Office to impose its will upon SAOs. Training for SAO members provided at the district level is typically non-participatory and fails to impart and test the transfer of key competencies.

Better planning and legislation could have avoided some of the obstacles undermining the effectiveness of Thailand's new decentralization policy. If subdistrict and village heads had not been initially been given privileged positions on the SAOs and if women had been guaranteed seats, the organization would probably have a much broader popular base than is now the case. Amending the decentralization legislation to give women a quota of seats could still bring about the desired effect. Those problems that are part and parcel of the Thai political and socio-economic context, however, cannot be solved so easily. SAOs themselves will have to assert their autonomy from the district administration if they are to serve villagers' interests, and avoid being reduced to the status of subdistrict-level government offices. They will also need self-consciously to reject the bureaucracy's authoritarian institutional culture for a more participatory one. And villagers themselves will have to take a keen interest in their SAOs to ensure that the organizations do not become mere instruments of vote-buying local elites and political appointees. To be effective, decentralization policy requires not only exemplary legislation but also sustained, critical interest from the people it is supposed to empower.

DEMOCRATIC DECENTRALIZATION AND THE PROVINCIAL ADMINISTRATIVE ORGANIZATION

The Provincial Administrative Organization (PAO) is a body designed to facilitate democratic decentralization at the provincial level. However, it is far from being an effective vehicle for popular participation in local government, and is perhaps even further from achieving its mandate than SAOs. This is due to a combination of factors. The reluctance of the state to devolve substantive powers is the most important. Almost as important, however, is the fact that the executive arm of the PAO, the Provincial Council, provides members with privileged access to development budgets. This has resulted in the widespread domination of councils by local capitalists, whose economic interests are closely related to infrastructure 'development' – such as the construction of roads, dams and irrigation channels. These 'local powers' win elections using strategies that include vote-buying, deployment of material patronage and intimidation. Their business interests are often part legal, part illegal. Councils made up of such individuals demonstrate little capacity to represent the needs of the provincial electorate. Arguably, the political importance of Provincial Councils rests on something other than their status as local government bodies, as it is from within Provincial Councils that MPs recruit the district-level vote brokers upon whom they rely in general elections. It may not be an exaggeration to say that Thailand's recently emerged electoral clientelism hinges on this service provided by provincial councillors to MPs.

Provincial Councils that had only a consultative role were established in 1933, soon after the abolition of the Thai absolute monarchy in 1932. The Provincial Administrative Act of 1955, which has been superseded by an Act of 1997, gave councils autonomy and control over budgets by creating the Provincial Administrative Organization (PAO). The executive branch of the PAO is the Provincial Council. This council comprises members elected from each district that makes up a province. Elections are held simultaneously in each province every five years. Aside from municipal councils, the Provincial Council constitutes the only avenue for formal representation available to residents of a province. Otherwise, all authority is centralized in the provincial administration. The state unambiguously presents provincial councillors as the democratically elected representatives of the populace at the provincial level.

Historically, the major constraints on the ability of Provincial Councils to serve as effective forums of local government have been those imposed by central government. Power has remained concentrated in the hands of provincial representatives of the central bureaucracy. Of course, this is a very familiar scenario in developing countries with highly centralized state administrations. For example, the Thai case is similar to that of Ghana, where a military regime was unwilling to risk permitting the growth of power independent from the government. In the context of Nepal's rather young democracy (dating from around 1990) the civil administration's resistance to relinquishing powers to the equivalent of the PAO made a mockery of democratic decentralization from the outset. The roles and duties of the PAO are so circumscribed that in practice the organization has little influence over either provincial development or the work of the provincial administration. Central government has consistently maintained a high degree of control over the procedural and law-making functions of local government. It has also limited local government's autonomy by exercising strict financial control: tax structures have been too narrow to allow the PAO to take on a meaningful role, and the bulk of provincial budgets pass through the line departments represented at the provincial and district levels. A further limiting factor is that the personnel with responsibility for the functioning of the PAO are officials from the provincial administration. Until the ratification of the PAO Act of 1997, the PAO was chaired by the provincial governor, a reflection of the control held by the central bureaucracy. This seat is now occupied by an elected member of the council: the impact of this change has yet to become apparent. Despite some support for a move to make the position of provincial governor an elected one, the government has consistently refused to back this proposal – and civic advocacy groups have voiced concerns that if the position were an elected one, it could be dominated by 'godfathers'. By consistently refusing to decentralize substantive powers, the state has ensured that the provincial council continues to be 'window dressing'.

Reforms contained in the 1997 Act do not appear to have strengthened significantly the capacity of PAOs to act as effective local government bodies. Nelson argues that PAOs have been ascribed fewer rather than more responsibilities. They are still charged with policy formulation, supervision of the general administration of the province, passing legislation and approving the provincial budget. As part of their representative role, councillors are theoretically empowered to scrutinize the use provincial and district officials make of the portion of development funds derived from local taxes. A council may meet three or four times a year, at which time the provincial governor may be questioned. It is rare for a councillor to use this power, since both parties are likely to cooperate in abuse of such funds. As Nelson suggests, 'it is certainly not an exaggeration to say that the provincial administration can work undisturbed by local councillors' criticism' (ibid.: 14). But the most significant activity performed by councils relates to their role in approving and allocating infrastructure development budgets in the province. This is reflected by the fact that commentators as well as provincial councillors themselves have seen the recent diversion of PAO development budgets to SAOs as a threat to the very existence of the PAO. The concern was that PAOs would be without a role. The change led to widespread protests from provincial councillors and their federation. It does seem that the empowerment of SAOs has been at the cost of PAOs. The respective roles and responsibilities of these bodies are still not sufficiently differentiated to avoid confusion and conflict. In particular, provincial councillors resent the power that SAOs have to hire their own contractors and source materials – a major source of revenue for provincial councillors under the former system.[6]

Notwithstanding the recent partial withdrawal of PAO funds, the PAO and its council have increased in importance since the early 1980s. Provincial businesspeople tend to monopolize elected positions on the PAO's council. Provincial councillors are often drawn from commercial and bureaucratic interest groups. Landowners do not figure significantly among members, which is largely a reflection of the general stagnation of the Thai agricultural sector.[7] Nationally, around 65 per cent of councillors are businesspeople, as opposed to around 17.5 per cent who are categorized as farmers. Moreover it is so common for officeholders to operate construction contractor businesses that councils are often known locally as the 'contractors' council'. Official figures fail to define the business sector of incumbents and do not indicate the proportion of contractor-councillors. However, in an interview with me in February 1997 the director of the division responsible for national policy toward PAOs acknowledged that between 80 and 90 per cent of all provincial councillors are contractors. Council members are able to exclude outsiders from bidding for contracts to undertake local development project contracts. They allocate contracts among themselves. Before the introduction of SAOs they benefited from development grants allocated to Subdistrict Councils, either extracting a percentage or demanding contracts where they were able to influence allocation. It is taken for granted among the electorate that councillors use their positions to promote their own economic interests.

Provincial councillors are frequently seen as synonymous with 'godfathers' (*jao pho*). This term, which gained currency in the 1980s to refer to provincial businessmen who have wealth and power but operate above the law, is an increasingly appropriate term for provincial councillors. It is common for councillors' business interests to draw them into conflict with villagers. Where this is the case, councillors use their status and contacts to defuse opposition. For example, a provincial councillor who is the owner of a paper mill in Khon Kaen province has been able to use his position to prevent bureaucrats acting upon the opposition of villagers affected by pollution downstream of the factory. Similarly the opposition of villagers in Saraburi and Surin provinces to rock-blasting near their homes yielded no results as the businesses are owned by provincial councillors.[8] Occasionally provincial councillors will support villagers against local business interests: one of the provincial councillors in Klang district lent his support to workers striking outside a textile factory that had a particularly poor labour rights record. The provincial councillor stood to lose little, however, as the factory owner was not a local.

The degree of accountability demonstrated by Provincial Councils and individual members to the electorate remains extremely poor. Councils tend to serve the collective and individual interests of members more effectively than those of the electorate. They are insulated from citizens' pressure groups – pressure from 'civil society' – to a large extent. Obviously there are exceptions to this generalization. However, Murashima's assessment of the council he studied in Central Thailand more than a decade ago remains accurate: provincial councillors were 'primarily interested in maintaining their own vested interests and not in drawing up and executing policy'. There are no forums for provincial councillors to listen to the concerns of their constituents – they do not maintain offices in their districts or hold weekly 'surgeries'. It is rare even for a provincial councillor to attend District Office meetings at which he could address all the district's subdistrict and village heads. The only time when there is any contact between a councillor and villagers is around elections. However, when their village heads and subdistrict heads cannot help them, villagers will go to provincial councillors for assistance – often to ask them to mediate between themselves and bureaucrats (notably the police). Provincial councillors have also been the first port of call for subdistrict and village heads who seek development grants. Councillors can be petitioned either to support local applications for PAO funds, or to appeal to MPs on behalf of village and subdistrict heads. In effect provincial councillors are the new patrons of rural Thailand.

During national elections provincial councillors play a crucial role that lies entirely outside their formal role. They are the primary vote canvassers of national politicians. Candidates in general elections recruit provincial councillors to canvass on their behalf in the districts that they represent. MPs will often bankroll the campaign of a provincial council candidate. They do this on the understanding that provincial councillors will then mobilize the lower-level voter networks that they established for their campaigns:

> Of the new provincial councillors, many are 'vote brokers' of MPs. They received both open and covert support from MPs who wanted to take care of, and expand their voting base for use in future elections.
> (*Thai Rath*, 28 October 1990)

Many provincial councillors use their district-level canvassing networks to launch careers into national politics. There are grounds, therefore, for competition between national politicians and provincial councillors. Nevertheless, to date the majority of such relations are symbiotic and collaborative rather than antagonistic. When in early 1997 provincial councillors protested to parliament against local government reform that transferred control of development funds from the Provincial Administrative Organization to the Subdistrict Administrative Organization, provincial councillors petitioned parliament and won significant concessions from the government. National politicians lent their support in the knowledge that they stood to alienate their primary canvassers. This state of symbiosis may change, however. It is likely that the 1997 Constitution, with the definition of smaller, single-member constituencies, will make it easier for provincial councillors to propel themselves into national politics since they will already have established voting bases in a significant proportion of the new constituencies. We may thus see more provincial councillors launching national political careers, and we may see more antagonistic relationships and less co-operation between national and provincial politicians and government. If competition from provincial councillors becomes a real threat, we may witness a reversal of existing democratic decentralization reforms, as occurred in Kenya in the late 1960s. The authority of local councils was curtailed there because national politicians were concerned that local councillors would soon prove effective competitors in national elections. Local councillors had developed patronage networks using council resources.

The strongest argument in favour of democratic decentralization is that local government transfers power from unelected civil servants to representatives of the people. Elections are the mechanism by which the people's representatives are chosen. Elections are opportunities for civil society, in the form of voluntary associations, NGOs or unions, to participate in local government. The paragraphs below reveal that the quality of political participation in provincial level elections is far from being capable of yielding effective representatives. Campaigning relies heavily on material rewards, and campaigns are won on the basis of short-term exchanges of money or material for votes. The account draws on research I conducted on two consecutive Provincial Council elections in Klang district (1990 and 1995) in Ayuthaya province.

It would be a mistake to assess the quality of political participation by voter turnout alone. In Ayuthaya province there has been an increase in voter participation in provincial councillor politics over the last 15 years. Voter turnout in 1980 was 29 per cent, 40 per cent in 1985, 44 per cent in 1990 and 54 per cent in 1995. It would be unwise to assume from these figures an increase in interest in the provincial council and greater responsiveness of councillors. The increase in voter turnout can be attributed to greater vote-buying. Vote-buying is now endemic in provincial councillor elections but the outcome of elections cannot be reduced to just a battle with money. Other factors are important.

The success of a campaign hinges on both the effective deployment of vote-buying money and the candidate's record of bringing grants to an area (new candidates are at an obvious disadvantage). Candidates rarely distribute elaborate election manifestos: their appeals go no further than to claim good 'work records' and to be 'approachable' and 'serviceable'.[9] Village-based votes are delivered with the help of subdistrict and village heads. In both 1990 and 1995 money played a major part in contests in Klang, but so too did the strategic giving of goods to communities. Candidates still found it necessary to establish reciprocal relationships with villagers by making communal gifts to temples, schools and hamlets – the latter often in the form of temporary road surfacing (laterite). Candidates also visited funerals and donated money to the families of the deceased; they were guests of honour at temple festivals and made generous donations. The support of religious leaders was an important factor in both elections, as was the support of MPs who provided direct and indirect assistance. Candidates portray themselves as 'taking care' of the electorate: they project a persona of a generous patron, willing to help villagers in need. Successful candidates, once elected, cannot afford to ignore the electorate and must take care of the electorate between elections. In the words of a Klang councillor who won a seat in the 1990 and 1995 elections:

> If you're a provincial councillor ... you've got to behave so that people give you their trust. Then in the next campaign you'll be able to canvass – but it's still not easy. Money plays a part. We take money and distribute it to buy votes ... But going to see the people creates a bond: it makes people say 'he's elected but he still comes out to see his kinspeople'. Every time I go into the subdistricts I meet the people and say 'How are things grandpa and grandma, uncle and aunt, cousins? What are your problems?' And they say 'The road is no good, the electricity doesn't work, we don't have water'. So I've got to find a grant – from the PAO, the MPs' development fund, or whatever.[10]

This is an ideal representation of the behaviour of a provincial councillor that few provincial councillors live up to.[11]

A vicious cycle dominates the conduct of provincial councillor elections. This cycle undermines any basis for accountability between the electorate and councillors. Following the introduction of vote-buying by aspirant MPs, candidates in provincial councillor elections distribute money in exchange for votes. Candidates who wish to exploit office for commercial gain often have few other bases for appealing for support. The electorate appreciates that candidates exploit office for their own gain and increasingly wants compensation for in exchange for votes. As a villager noted, provincial councillors 'give us one baht but get two baht back'. Villagers see their votes as helping the candidate gain access to the fruits of office. The electorate increasingly wants to be compensated in advance of polling. They do not trust that if they give a candidate their vote freely, they will be rewarded after polling: it is a common assumption that politicians disappear after elections. Candidates are thus obliged to distribute money 'up front' and have no opportunity of winning if they do not. All successful candidates will therefore exploit council membership to recoup and gain an increment on their campaign expenditure. Politics has become a commercial enterprise and vote-buying is spoken of as 'investing' (*long thun*).

Few positive indicators of democratization can be drawn from the conduct of Provincial Council elections in 1990 and 1995. There were no signs of the electorate becoming more demanding or of candidates becoming more 'service-oriented'. This is despite a nationwide democratization programme implemented in the early 1990s.[12] There is one noticeable trend, however, that could be read as a positive sign. Village and subdistrict heads have found it progressively more difficult to command their villagers' votes on behalf of provincial council candidates.

Whereas in the past local officeholders could and did effectively determine whom 'their' villagers voted for, this is no longer the case. This is a common cause for complaint among canvassers. One headman-canvasser spelled out how persuasion rather than coercion is the most productive approach: 'We've got to think a little bit democratically. You can't force people, and you can't speak too strongly – you've got to speak softly and gently.' Some people even see vote-buying as a consequence of villagers' ability to choose, and the inability of village and subdistrict heads to command votes. One canvasser noted: 'It's a fully fledged democracy: they want money.' Candidates and their canvassers also complained that the electorate no longer so readily vote according to how they are paid. More independent-minded villagers are starting to accept vote-buying money and proceed to vote according to their personal preferences. It is gradually becoming more expensive to buy votes: 'yields' are getting smaller. These two developments could be seen as grounds for optimism. In the longer term vote-buying may become an increasingly inefficient and expensive way of securing votes. Similarly intimidation – whether subtle or overt – is becoming increasingly counterproductive. If these trends continue, then candidates will base their campaigning more heavily on their capacity to serve the electorate: councillors will play the role of representative for more than the few days surrounding elections. There is a long way to go, however.

CONCLUDING REMARKS

The failings of Thai democratic decentralization at the subdistrict and provincial level recounted in this chapter make for rather dismal reading. For both the SAO and PAO there is a very low level of accountability towards the electorate. Neither demonstrates much capacity to express or represent public demands because there is an absence of contact and consultation between electorate and representatives. Moreover, the public have little knowledge or interest in local government, particularly at the provincial level. In other words, popular participation in SAOs and PAOs is very low indeed. Furthermore, elected representatives do not effectively express popular demands through policies and projects once they are in office – too often they are preoccupied with winning large-budget infrastructure projects. The bond of accountability that theoretically should run between representatives and electorate is largely broken by the use of money in elections. In the crudest terms, having bought the votes of the electorate, representatives are no longer answerable to them. These weaknesses on the part of SAOs and PAOs are compounded by the consistently overbearing and centralist attitude of the administration. Reluctance on the part of district and provincial administrations to cede control to elected representatives is in danger of delivering the stillbirth of devolved government.

Wherever it is implemented as a development policy, decentralization raises an inescapable dilemma. If democratic decentralization is not pursued, then power remains concentrated in the hands of non-elected state representatives who undeniably lack the capacity to serve effectively the development needs of local communities. But, if power is devolved it seems almost inevitable that – at both higher and lower levels – decentralized powers will fall directly into the hands of 'local powers' of one kind or another. This is nowhere truer than in contemporary Thailand. In the vast majority of provincial areas there is simply an absence of appropriate civic advocacy organizations able or willing to increase the accountability of local government. The capacity of 'local powers' to represent the needs of the electorate may not be much of an improvement on the performance of state officials. The majority of the population have as little influence over the decision-making of councils controlled by local or provincial commercial elite, as they do over the decisions made by bureaucrats.

One might then ask whether, given all the criticisms that can be levelled against democratic decentralization when it is put into practice – it is fine in theory – it is worth supporting as a policy instrument. There is indeed a compelling argument for promoting democratic decentralization, despite its myriad problems. Without decentralization no possible advance can be gained in local governance. Democratic decentralization is a necessary first step. While today elected councils may be controlled by 'local powers', in five or 15 years they may be more representative. Democratic decentralization at least gives local people opportunities to capture some decision-making power. Without decentralization policies this potential would never be allowed to develop. But the outcome of reform is largely indeterminate. Outcomes differ not only between countries but also within a country from province to province and from subdistrict to subdistrict.

There is, though, a possibility, albeit rather remote, that a combination of the economic crisis and the creation of SAOs will stimulate positive change in the composition of provincial councils. It is possible that PAOs will gradually be filled with provincial councillors more accountable to the electorate. Provincial councillors whose livelihoods depend upon contracting businesses are the very group who have been hardest hit by the economic crisis that struck Thailand in mid-1997. The first industry to suffer the effects of the crisis was the construction industry – building projects shuddered to a halt, government infrastructure grants shrunk, and many businesses went bust. If it proves difficult for councillor-contractors to earn profits – because budgets have constricted within the PAO and a reduction in building activity in the economy at large – then individuals with interests in the construction industry may think twice before launching expensive election campaigns. The loss of budgetary control to SAOs also further restricts provincial councillors' opportunities for graft – and there is even less likelihood that members will be able to recoup campaign expenses. It is thus possible that local capitalists will lose interest in provincial-level political office, just as at the subdistrict-level economic elites will lose interest in the positions of *kamnan* and village head as new rules of SAO membership come into effect, and spaces may open up for more community-minded candidates. Such candidates exist but have simply been squeezed out by the domination of money politics. But we should probably be sceptical rather than hopeful. If PAOs are able to work with SAOs to distribute the spoils of infrastructure projects to their mutual satisfaction, then it is unlikely that the pattern will change. Furthermore, we should also remember that the problems that have beset PAOs are in effect being 'localized' to SAOs. Ironically this was accelerated by the economic crisis: in an attempt to create employment opportunities for redundant labour, the World Bank and Asian Development Bank directed huge sums through the Ministry of Interior to the country's SAOs to support infrastructure projects. We are probably going to witness another round of 'decentralized corruption', as first observed by Morell and Chai-Anan in the 1970s.

It is possible to measure how effective democratic decentralization is in delivering the tangible ouputs of 'development' – better local infrastructure and so on. However, it is not so easy to measure whether democratic decentralization is worthwhile in terms of its potential to stimulate that chimera, 'civil society'. Will we see associations and organizations increasingly use SAOs and PAOs to represent their needs? We have certainly seen the formal Association of Local Officeholders (village heads and *kamnan*) and PAO members petition government, but their aims have mainly been to limit the effectiveness of decentralization reforms. These reforms will not suddenly lead to an efflorescence of civic activity. An evaluation of the value of democratic decentralization programmes for sowing the seeds of 'better' governance can perhaps only be made over the long term. As a note of caution, however, it is easy to claim too much for democratic decentralization programmes. One is forced to agree with Crook and Manor that 'democratic decentralization should not be seen either as a catch-all "solution" to wider problems of poverty, social inequality or economic stagnation; nor is it likely to be a catalyst for any marked degree of change'. If they are anything, democratic decentralization programmes are experiments in socio-political change. And in Thailand we should not expect too much from this experiment.

AUTHOR'S NOTE

This paper is based on fieldwork conducted between October 1989–December 1990, July 1995–May 1997 and July–August 1998. The second period of fieldwork was conducted whilst holding an ESRC Research Fellowship [H52427004094] and two British Academy Research Awards. Research in 1998 was funded by a Faculty of Social Sciences Research Award, University of Hull. Research was conducted with the kind permission of the National Research Council of Thailand and whilst I was affiliated to Chulalongkorn University Social Research Institute. Pseudonyms have been given to all local place names and to all individuals except national politicians no longer politically active.

NOTES

1 Political scientists such as Rodan argue for a more discriminating interpretation. He argues that the term 'civil society' should be reserved for groups who undertake 'regular attempts to advance the interests of members through overt political action' (1997: 162).

2 The campaign of village heads and *kamnan* was in full swing in mid-1998. *Kamnan* and Village Heads Associations throughout the country gave their support to a petition to oppose the removal of these officeholders from the SAO. The president of the *Kamnan* and Village Heads Association in Klang district was assiduous in getting the signatures of all the district's officeholders. The general view among these officials was that once they lost their rights to SAO membership their positions would become less desirable: they would lose power over budgets and their main duty, as one village head put it, would be 'just to look after villagers'.

3 The Indonesian state, for example, in a putative attempt to further rural development by 'increasing participation (*partisipasi*), preparedness (*prakarsa*) and self-reliance (*swadaya*) of village society', introduced legislation that succeeded in freezing in place 'a top-down administrative structure', exacerbating 'the lack of communication between the central government and the Indonesian population' and 'threatened to undercut long-evolved and highly effective mechanisms for community co-operation'. Similarly, in the Philippines state reform led to the undermining of indigenous institutions, organizations and capacity.

4 The government made a special though fruitless effort to prevent electoral fraud following particularly public instances of fraud in municipal elections in the province of Samut Prakan (*The Nation*, 16 July 1999). There were many reports of vote-buying and influence-peddling in the 617 subdistricts in which SAO elections were held on 18 July 1999 (*Matichon*, 10 July 1990; *Thai Rath*, 20 August 1999).

5 These figures refer to SAOs that had been established in the Northeastern province of Nakhon Ratchasima by 30 September 1996. From

the 134 SAOs there were only 75 women of a total of 3,326 members. The figures for Ayuthaya province are a little more positive. Up until 1996 there were 12 SAOs in Ayuthaya: of these only half had at least one female member. In absolute terms, women amounted to 7.8 per cent of members (12 women of 153 total SAO members) (ibid.: 361–362).

6   Interview with PAO deputy, Ayuthaya province, 14 August 1998.

7   Murashima notes that 'the membership of local representative councils and assemblies is composed mainly of wealthy, urban merchants and businessmen; large landowners are not present' (1987: 384).

8   These data were gathered during research in 1997.

9   In the only policy statement of any length that I encountered the first-time candidate promised not to act as a contractor: 'I am neither a merchant nor a capitalist ... I will not be a contractor. It is being a contractor that leads to dishonesty among provincial councillors. When a provincial councillor is a contractor you lose out: completed projects end up half-measure' (candidate's campaign letter, Klang district, October 1990).

10 Interview, 20 September 1995.

11 Ironically, the provincial councillor who made this statement could be considered a typical example of a 'local power': he is a former policeman who owns the district's largest construction contractor business and building supplies retail store. In 1990 he cooperated with his running mate in an unsuccessful attempt to assassinate his chief competitor in the election.

12 In 1992 vote-buying and the influence of 'dark powers' (*ithiphon muet*) were recognised as problems of national importance. The state launched a spate of anti-vote-buying and democracy education programmes. However, they were run by the Ministry of Interior, whose local officials often collude with candidates, and as subdistrict and village heads were the local project coordinators, the programmes tended to ring rather hollow. One reason for the effectiveness of vote-buying is the fact that, upon receipt of a candidate's money, villagers feel a sense of indebtedness and tend to vote 'honestly' for the candidate who pays them: many people, particularly the elderly, consider it 'sinful' to do otherwise. For a more detailed analysis, see Arghiros (1995).

15

THAILAND'S JANUARY 2001 GENERAL ELECTIONS: VINDICATING REFORM?

Duncan McCargo

The first general election under the 1997 Constitution was held on 6 January 2001. From the outset, there were two clear front-runners: the incumbent Democrat Party – led by twice-prime minister Chuan Leekpai – and the new Thai Rak Thai Party (TRT), led by the fabulously wealthy telecommunications magnate Thaksin Shinawatra, a former deputy PM and foreign minister. While the Democrats insisted that their coalition administration (backed primarily by the Chart Pattana and Chart Thai Parties) had successfully restored international confidence in the Thai economy after the 1997 meltdown, Thaksin invoked populist nationalist rhetoric (implicit in the title of his party, 'Thais Love Thai') to argue that the Democrats had neglected ordinary Thais in their over-enthusiasm to please the IMF. TRT made various expensive and uncosted election pledges, offering to give every village in Thailand a 1-million-baht development fund, to offer a debt moratorium to farmers, and to provide medical treatment to all-comers for a token 30 baht fee. While the Democrats sought to cling to the moral and political high ground, accusing Thaksin of seeking to buy his way to the premiership, it did not help when several key Democrat party figures were themselves implicated in scandals. Democrat secretary-general and interior minister Sanan Kachornprasart – the power-broker who had stitched together the ruling coalition – was barred from political office for five years on asset concealment charges in 2000. The popular perception that the Democrats were somewhat cleaner and more professional than other parties was seriously tarnished accordingly.

If one important aim of the political reform process embodied in the 1997 Constitution was to transform electoral politics in Thailand, the outcome of the first general election under the new arrangements was not a resounding success. The elections of January 2001 failed to realize the hopes and promises of the political reform movement in a number of ways; yet in certain respects, the reform agenda appeared to be advanced. The political reform movement was too complex a set of processes to be evaluated on the basis of a single general election. Even the prime movers behind the 1997 Constitution could not have expected it immediately to re-engineer the Thai electoral system. What may have been more important than the actual results of the 2001 election was the extent to which battles were now being fought, questions were being asked, and new pressures were being felt.

The election resulted in a landslide victory for Thaksin Shinawatra's Thai Rak Thai Party. While the original election results suggested that TRT might receive more than 250 of the 500 parliamentary seats, these expectations were undermined by the outcome of electoral reruns on 29 January. Reruns were held where candidates accused of vote-buying and other transgressions were given 'yellow cards' (invalidating first round results) or 'red cards' (disqualifying them from standing). TRT finished up with 248 seats. Yet even this was not a final result, but one repeatedly modified by subsequent reruns.

Thai Rak Thai formed a coalition administration with the New Aspiration and Chart Thai Parties, while also absorbing the small Seritham Party (which formally merged with TRT in October 2001). The Democrat and Chart Pattana Parties comprised the main opposition, while those smaller parties that contested the election were virtually wiped out. As discussed in the Introduction, the most widely shared aims of the reform process were improving the quality of elected politicians, and reducing the influence of money in the electoral process. Reformers had sought to promote these goals through two main methods: by changing many of the rules of the electoral game, and by introducing new bodies such as the Election Commission to manage and referee the game more effectively. This chapter will offer a preliminary sketch of some issues raised by the 2001 elections.

SELECTING POLITICIANS

In theory, the electoral reform was supposed to allow 'good and capable' people to enter politics by dividing elected representatives into three categories: senators, party-list MPs (from amongst whom ministers would be chosen) and constituency MPs. Senators would serve as the 'great and the good' of Thai society, occupying an exalted position above the cut-and-thrust of daily politics. Party-list MPs were to be highly respected individuals well suited to ministerial office. Constituency MPs, who would form the bulk of parliamentarians, would in effect be 'lower quality' politicians who were debarred from substantive influence, and confined to representing the views of their local areas.

Yet an article in *Thai Post* (21 January 2001) clearly demonstrated the extent to which there were overlapping linkages and interconnections between the three kinds of politicians. Political families around the country sought to place members of their own group into all three levels of parliamentary representation. No less than 50 close relatives of senators stood for the Lower House, including a brother and a nephew of the then president of the Senate, who became Thai Rak Thai MPs; 28 of them were elected, including 22 who were members of the new TRT-led coalition. The list published in *Thai Post* may not have been exhaustive, since it mainly listed those parliamentary candidates who shared the same surnames as senators. It seems very likely that some other candidates with less direct relationships to senators also stood for parliament. As the author noted, whilst relatives of senators were entitled to stand for elected office, any suggestion that senators and MPs were collaborating along political lines could provoke a crisis of public confidence in the integrity of the senate, especially if doubts emerged about its transparency in making appointments to the supposedly neutral bodies that were meant to monitor the political process.

Nor were all of the fresh faces elected in January 2001 especially new. According to *Krungthep Thurakit* (19 February 2001), there were 200 newcomers out of 400 constituency MPs, and 36 new faces out of 100 MPs from the party-list system. However, the *Nation Sudsapda* (15 to 21 January 2001) reported that while 60 out of 136 MPs from the Northeast were newcomers, a closer analysis reveals that 95 per cent of these so-called 60 'new faces' are actually family members, relatives or former canvassers of current MPs (including local politicians). Only 5 per cent of them were really new in the sense that they unexpectedly won by riding along the Thai Rak Thai bandwagon.

CURTAILING ELECTORAL ABUSES

A report issued on 22 January 2001 by a Senate working group to summarize information about the election results concluded that out of the eight underlying causes of electoral irregularities in the 6 January parliamentary elections, five reflected clear procedural weaknesses for which the Electoral Commission had responsibility (*Krungthep Thurakit*, 25 January 2001). The causes were as follows:

1. Treating good ballot papers as spoilt. The number of spoilt ballot papers was very high in this election, as a result of a combination of irregularities by officials and ignorance of proper procedures. In too many cases, members of the local election commissions were partial

to one or other candidate; in other cases, the training of those in charge of counting was inadequate, and confusion was rife.
2. Unusual similarities in the numbers of votes cast in different categories: there was an extraordinary correlation between the numbers of votes for constituency candidates and party-list votes, which cast doubt on the integrity of the voting process.
3. Extensive use of fake ballot papers.
4. Mixing up of ballot papers for different constituencies. In some places where there had been shortages of ballot papers, papers from other constituencies were used instead.
5. Dishonesty of polling station and vote-counting officials.
6. Over-intensive counting: in most places, vote-counting went on for 2, 3 or 4 days without a stop, leaving counting teams exhausted. There needed to be two counting teams who could work a shift system.
7. Vote-buying and gift-giving. The Electoral Commission centrally assigned so much importance to this that they neglected other issues of electoral abuse.
8. Yellow and red cards were handed out to candidates against whom there was evidence of vote-buying, but in other cases no reruns were ordered. Perhaps this was because the Commission did not have enough time to investigate all the allegations properly.

Most of the abuses noted by the Senate working group arose from the machinations of sleazy candidates, who were often able to outmanoeuvre the electoral commissioners. There were a number of positive changes brought about by the new system: the use of central vote-counting made the process much more secret, liberating voters to pick candidates of their choice; crude ballot-stuffing was more difficult; and some old gangs were split by the new single-member constituencies, resulting in former allies fighting each other for many seats.

Nevertheless, the general elections of January 2001 seriously undermined the standing and credibility of the Election Commission. There is some evidence that candidates switched their energies away from risky vote-buying activities, preferring where possible simply to buy local election commissioners. Even the five national commissioners were not above suspicion (Crispin 2001b). In the days after 6 January, there were complaints, protests, demonstrations and even mini-riots across the country precipitated by allegations of vote-buying and vote-rigging. While vote-buying was often investigated by the Commission, vote-rigging allegations were largely ignored, even where the evidence was overwhelming – such as video footage of one counting official pocketing handfuls of ballots, shown on Channel 11 on 8 January. It was impossible to tell how many of the challenges to election results were genuine complaints by voters, and how many were orchestrated by the candidates or parties who had lost. There was also ample evidence that some of the challenges to election results came not from disgruntled voters or candidates, but from gambling syndicates; enterprising gamblers bet not simply on the poll winners, but also on margins of victory and a wide range of other variables, and so had a great deal invested in very obscure aspects of the outcomes.

The principles of accountability and transparency enshrined in the new constitution gave new scope for questioning the integrity of the way elections were managed. Given the widespread abuses of the process, many of these questions were justified: why, for example, were 33 per cent of the votes cast in one Chiang Mai constituency declared invalid (Crispin 2001b)? The ethos of the new constitution encouraged a healthy trend of challenging apparent irregularities and abuses. Yet the extent of the challenges also threatened to undermine the legitimacy of the election process as a whole. The five successive reruns held for the Senate elections in 2000 had tried the patience of the electorate, degenerating gradually into farce (see Nelson 2000; Sombat, Chapter 13, this volume). In the light of the Senate fiasco, the Commission faced greater checks and balances concerning the use of its powers. The Council of State, a conservative pre-reform legal advisory body, now had oversight of the Commission's use of 'red cards' (Crispin 2001b). Nevertheless, Nelson (forthcoming) argues that the Election Commission emerged from the Senate controversy with an amended election law giving it an enhanced range of powers to deploy. When the Election Commission began to run into difficulties during January 2001, there was some resort to old measures: for example, military cadets were brought in to help with vote-counting in places where counters were exhausted. Officials from the Ministry of Interior, who had lost their powers to supervise elections under the new constitution, could hardly conceal their *schadenfreude* at the troubles faced by the Commission. All the old allegations of corruption and bias formerly levelled at district officers, provincial governors and Bangkok bureaucrats were now being applied to those working for the Election Commission.

THE CHANGED ELECTORAL MAP

To some extent, the reformed political process was successful in ousting old-style politicians. Some of what Chang Noi calls 'the old baronial families' were badly damaged, including the Asavahames in Samut Prakarn, the Anginkans in Petchaburi, the Manasikarns in Phitsanulok, the Iasakul in Nong Khai, the Jurimaks in Roi Et, and the Yoobamrungs in Thonburi (Chang Noi 2001). The old-style godfathers extensively discussed by commentators in the late 1980s and early 1990s (for the best summary, see Sombat 2000) seemed to be losing their previous political clout.

Yet there was a danger of overstating the case for a substantive realignment. Shawn Crispin, who kept a close eye on the Samut Prakan elections, has argued that Thai Rak Thai thrashed the Asavahames' Rassadorn Party simply by outspending it, offering 300 baht per vote instead of 200 (Crispin 2001a); if so, this was less a triumph of the popular will, and more the result of a particularly well-funded auction. Old-style political families such as the Thienthongs in Sa Kaew, the Silpa-archas in Suphanburi, and the clan of godfather Kamnan Poh in Chonburi, survived virtually unscathed, while the Chidchobs of Buriram retained ten seats in their sphere of influence, despite the failure of leading scion Newin Chidchob to gain a party-list seat. In these provinces, the political dynasties had combined despotism with paternalism, making sure that their constituents received more than their rightful shares of government largesse.

Chang Noi observed that the election results divided the country at a line he calls the 'Bangkok Fault'; south of Bangkok, the Democrats were overwhelmingly dominant; north of it, with the exception of some pockets controlled by the Democrats and by smaller parties, Thai Rak Thai ruled supreme. He further noted that Thai Rak Thai effectively comprised two different parties of almost equal size: new faces with an average age of 38, and defectors from other parties (led by the Sanoh Thienthong faction) with an average age of 55.

LANDSLIDE OR REALIGNMENT?

Did the 2001 elections mark the usual replacement of one dominant party with another, or was a sea change taking place in the nature of Thai politics, a boost in the quality of the process? Commentators were divided here. Broadly speaking, three explanations were advanced for the Thai Rak Thai landslide: voter rejection of the Democrats; the spending power of the Thaksin campaign; and the attractive policy platform of Thai Rak Thai. For some, the electoral defeat of the Democrats was primarily a routine punishment beating by the voters. Thongchai Sunitvong (*Krungthep Thurakit*, 15 January 2001) argued that the Democrats lost because of voters' 'boredom' with the Democrats' inability to organise themselves, their lack of teamwork and their failure to address popular concerns. Kasian Tejapira suggested that the Democrats had sealed their own destruction by becoming the unpatriotic choice, the party that failed to pay attention to the needs of society, and had paid a very high price accordingly (*Matichon*, 13 January 2001).

KPI researcher Michael Nelson has argued that there are many similarities between Thaksin's *ad hoc* Thai Rak Thai Party (created solely as a vehicle to deliver him the premiership) and the Samakkhi Tham Party set up for the same purpose by Suchinda Kraprayoon and his NPKC allies in 1991–92. Both Thai Rak Thai and Sammakhi Tham based their core electoral strategy on buying up electable candidates, or 'MP buying' (Nelson, forthcoming). The analogy is a compelling one, since in many respects the political reform process of the 1990s was driven precisely by an attempt to avoid the emergence of Sammakhi Tham-style parties that were merely collections of *phuak*, interest-based cliques. The logic of Nelson's argument was that political reform had completely failed. Indeed, it is hard to argue that electing one of Thailand's richest men prime minister really reduced the importance of money in politics, which was one of the original aspirations of the reformists. The Election Commission confirmed that this was the dirtiest and most expensive election in Thai history.

However, a page three column in *Matichon* (24 January 2001) questioned whether even someone as wealthy as Thaksin could simply 'buy' the entire electorate; to suggest as much was to look down on the Thai people as a whole. The author noted that Thai Rak Thai had received 11,634,142 votes under the party-list system, or 40.64 per cent of all votes cast – around four million more than the Democrats. This could not be dismissed simply as the result of money politics, but was also testimony to the popularity of the TRT manifesto. For Attachak Satyanurak, writing in *Krungthep Thurakit* (15 January 2001), the success of TRT reflected its policy platform, its ability to present itself as a 'catch-all party' embracing the aspirations of widely divergent sectors of the electorate. Other parties such as New Aspiration, Chart Thai and Chart Pattana had continued to rely on paternalism and personal connections, but were eclipsed by TRT's platform policy approach, while the Democrats bureaucratic approach was clearly losing impact outside their home territory in the South. For Attachak, Thai politics was explicitly moving in the direction of greater popular responsiveness.

An article in *Krungthep Thurakit* (23 January 2001) argued that the victory of Thai Rak Thai was not a matter of chance, but of strategic planning in a variety of areas, including presentation of the party leader, policy platform, election campaigning and careful candidate selection. Thaksin had used his business experience to develop his political organisation, bringing in a team of advisors who had worked for ex-US president George Bush. He made extensive use of the latest technology, using clear principles to select ministers, and targeting the Science Ministry for special attention. Given the political realities which actually underlay Thaksin's cabinet formation, some of this article can safely be dismissed as Thai Rak Thai 'spin': for example, the science and technology ministry was eventually given to a Chart Thai nominee, Sonthaya Khunpleum, the son of the famous Chonburi 'godfather' Kamnan Poh.

WEIGHING UP THE ELECTION

According to *Phujatkan Daily* columnist Samart Mangsang, the changed electoral arrangements under the new constitution had both positive and negative effects (16 January 2001). On the positive side:

- There was an increase in party voting based on policies.
- Some old-style politicians lost out despite winning many times before.
- The party-list system meant that people had to choose parties, and were less inclined to support parties with fuzzy or unattractive policies or images.
- This held out the prospect of a reduction in the number of parties in the future, a trend that would reduce the level of party-switching by MPs and help parties become better institutionalised.
- Ultimately, Thailand will have a single party government, which will lead to better quality administration and an end to negotiating benefit-sharing between parties.

On the negative side, the level of complaints all over the country about the counting procedures and irregularities in the voting process created a negative image concerning the reformed election procedures, which had the potential to lead to widespread protests and political chaos. Nevertheless, Samart felt that on balance the election had more positive than negative outcomes, and was a good beginning for the political reform process, so long as all sides involved could work together to improve matters, and to address problems that had arisen.

Some old-style politicians thrived under the new rules. They were the ones who had picked the right strategies: those who defected to Thai Rak Thai in plenty of time; those who contested constituency seats they had nurtured carefully for years; those who had secured high places for themselves on the party-lists for major parties. Those who had expected to win party-list seats under the banner of smaller parties, leaving their safe constituency seats to relatives and subordinates (like Newin Chidchob) saw cousins elected in their stead. Vattana Assavahame could probably have been elected if he had concentrated his resources in one key Samut Prakan constituency, instead of assuming that his Rassadorn Party would sweep the province. In part, the 6 January 2001 elections were a learning process for politicians. The likes of Newin and Vattana would not make the same mistakes twice. The new rules did not debar old style politicians, but simply made it tougher for them to win through.

'Thaksin fever' was eventually bound to abate, and many familiar faces were likely to return to Thai politics before very long.

GOVERNMENT FORMATION

Many international commentators assumed that Thaksin would seek to create a coalition with the smallest possible number of partners, or even to establish an unprecedented one-party administration. TRT could certainly have gained a pretty strong parliamentary position with just one coalition partner. Thaksin's preference for bringing in three partners showed that Thai politics remained a politics of benefit-sharing, under which it was far better to bring potential opponents into the fold than to leave them out in the air-conditioned cold of the opposition benches. Ever sensitive to criticism, Thaksin was eager to coopt and to neutralise prospective dissenters wherever possible. From the outset, it was clear that the Democrat Party would form the sole real opposition to TRT, and that all other parties were ready, willing and expecting to join the government. Thaksin's challenge was to bring most of them on side, and secure their loyalty at the lowest possible price.

Even prior to the second round of voting, Thaksin had announced an alliance with the New Aspiration Party (NAP), led by former Prime Minister Chavalit Yongchaiyudh. In some areas, the two parties pooled resources to help ensure that their candidates were elected on 29 January. While TRT and the NAP nominally appeared to be separate parties, Thaksin served briefly as a deputy prime minister under Chavalit, and TRT sources were widely believed to have part-funded the NAP during the 2001 campaigning. Thus Thai parties remained essentially loose affiliations of factional interest groups, with no ideological baggage to speak of, and there was no essential difference between Thai Rak Thai and New Aspiration. The inclusion of the New Aspiration in Thaksin's coalition was therefore a foregone conclusion.

CHOOSING GOOD MINISTERS

Despite Thaksin's overwhelming electoral mandate and his oft-repeated insistence that he would ensure that only well-qualified individuals were appointed to cabinet posts, in practice he demonstrated that he remained captive to a quota system of ministerial allocations. Thaksin ought to have been well-placed to form his cabinet according to criteria of his own choosing, since his party had a formidable and unprecedented parliamentary mandate, and his coalition partners were much smaller and lacked credible leadership. Furthermore, the new constitution made it easier to appoint ministers from the 100 party-list MPs rather than the 400 constituency MPs, and the party-lists were supposed to contain respectable senior politicians.

In fact, however, this election involved an exceptionally protracted period of haggling for cabinet positions. On 12 February – more than a month after the shape of the new coalition was clearly visible – Thaksin submitted a ministerial list to the cabinet secretary for vetting (under the terms of the 1997 Constitution, ministers must meet no fewer than 30 different criteria in order to be eligible for office). Yet this was simply a list of individuals, with no portfolios specified. Thaksin subsequently announced that he planned 'minor reshuffles' to the list before presenting the final version on 17 February, just prior to the inaugurations by the King the following day.

Controversy raged over several appointments. Chavalit Yongchaiyudh was the first former premier to return as a mere minister. His assumption of the defence portfolio alarmed those who felt that his previous term of office in this post (in 1995–96) had seen a re-politicization of the military, and an emphasis on potentially commission-yielding arms and business deals. Somkid Chatusripithak, an academic with a background in marketing, was given the finance portfolio – but the appointment was heavily criticized by voices calling for a professional banker to be chosen. Surakiart Sathirathai was named foreign minister despite an undistinguished political career, including a troubled spell as finance minister in 1995–96. Chucheep Harnsawat became agriculture minister in spite of near-universal disapproval. Nathee Klibthong was nominated by Chart Thai for deputy agriculture minister, in the face of vociferous criticism that he was the stooge of notorious power-broker Newin Chidchob, who had failed to be elected.

Some of these controversies reflected the fact that ministerial portfolios were assigned in line with party and factional quotas: Thaksin remained the creature of a collection of grubby factional interests. Where he did control appointments, he generally preferred yes-men to well-qualified and substantial figures. For all his image as the omnipotent CEO who could make quick and effective decisions, Thaksin was not able to use the six weeks that elapsed between the election and the cabinet inauguration to resolve differences about key portfolios. While the final line-up contained a couple of interesting choices, it was scarcely more impressive overall than the cabinet of the outgoing, 'pre-reform' Chuan Leekpai administration. At least, however, ministers were drawn largely from the ranks of party-list MPs, and problematic individuals such as Sanoh Thienthong, Chalerm Yubamrung and Newin Chidchob were not given cabinet posts.

CONTINUING ELECTORAL PROBLEMS

The months following the January 2001 elections saw a rash of new problems emerge. After the fifth round of Senate elections, out of the 54 senators who were investigated by the Election Commission, 9 senators from 7 provinces including the then president of the Senate were disqualified. At about the same time the vice-president of the Senate was forced to resign after being caught having sex with a minor. A sixth round of Senate election was held for 10 senators in 8 provinces on 29 April. The former president of the Senate was one of those who failed to be elected. In an extraordinarily ironic twist of fate, Manoon Ruepkajorn, the former Young Turk who had led two abortive military coups in 1981 and 1985, became the new president of the Senate. A seventh round of senate elections was held on 26 May in Srisaket. These year-long shenanigans substantially discredited the supposedly apolitical upper house.

MPs were not to be outdone. Second round elections were quickly held in 62 constituencies of 29 provinces; a third round of voting in 7 constituencies took place in June, and a fourth round was held in 2 constituencies as late as 18 August 2001 (Nelson, forthcoming). This still left the Election Commission with the task of assessing outstanding complaints against winners in a further 275 constituencies.

The term of the Election Commission expired on 26 May 2001; and the political parties lobbied furiously to ensure that sympathetic candidates were appointed to the new Commission, mindful of the fact that the Commission could only act on the basis of unanimous decisions. The first round of nominations generated a list of ten candidates, most of whom had little public credibility, and the process of appointments to the Commission became intensely politicised. When the final names were announced on 4 October 2001, there was considerable criticism of the selection procedures and their outcome. General Sirin Thoopklam, who was named chair of the Commision, had been dismissed as a Lopburi senator by the previous Election Commission on grounds of cheating. Another new commissioner, Parinya Nakchatree, had been investigated on charges of involvement in the printing of fake ballot papers (*Bangkok Post*, 7 October, 13 October 2001). There were calls from a group of 38 senators for an investigation into the handling of the selection process. Whatever criticisms had been raised concerning the performance of the first team of commissioners, it seemed certain that the incoming team would be far more controversial.

CONCLUSION

The January 2001 general election was a trial run for Thailand's reform process, producing a mixture of positive and negative developments. In many respects, the second election under the new arrangements will be more significant, as politicians learn the many and varied lessons of the first. Money will form a major part of the Thai electoral process for the foreseeable future; yet insofar as the 2001 general election suggested the growing importance of policy agendas and party voting, and the rise of challenges to subversion of the electoral process, there were encouraging signs of positive change.

Nevertheless, the election did raise serious questions about the integrity and authority of the new bodies created to monitor Thailand's power structures. Not only did the Election Commission turn in a disappointing performance; Thaksin himself fought the election under the shadow of an investigation by the National Counter Corruption Commission of his alleged non-disclosure of assets, allegations which had the potential for the Constitutional Court to debar him from holding political office. Thaksin adopted the stance that his landslide election victory gave him a popular mandate to govern, effectively overriding any outstanding legal and constitutional niceties. While the election itself offered some good news for reformers, the capacity of prominent politicians to disregard both the letter and the spirit of the 1997 Constitution appeared to bode ill for the project of political reform.

Thaksin's acquittal by the Constitutional Court on 3 August 2001 appeared to suggest that the new 'rules of the game' established by the 1997 Constitution could be applied selectively. The judges ruled in Thaksin's favour by a narrow margin of 8–7. Four of those who acquitted him did so on a legal technicality: they argued that Article 295 of the constitution did not apply to Thaksin, since he had not been in public office on 7 November 1997, the day he submitted the fateful assets declaration (*Bangkok Post*, 4 August 2001; for a fuller discussion, see Nelson, forthcoming). The narrow verdict was widely questioned; the *Bangkok Post* cited one source as saying that two of the judges who had acquitted Thaksin had done so the day before the vote 'at the request of a person who has considerable clout'. It quoted one of these judges as saying 'I was forced to swallow my blood while writing this' (*Bangkok Post*, 4 August 2001). Thaksin himself behaved with bad grace after his controversial reprieve. He first thanked only those judges who had found in his favour (rather than the court as a whole), and then told reporters at an informal meal the following day:

> It's strange that the leader who was voted by 11 million people had to bow to the ruling of the NCCC and the verdict of the Constitutional Court, two organizations composed only of appointed commissioners and judges, whom people did not have a chance to choose. This is a crucial point we have missed. (*Bangkok Post*, 5 August 2001)

Thaksin was not alone in making this argument. Many commentators, including some of the architects of the reform process, had called for him to be acquitted in the national interest. Some even argued that no one else was suited to serve as Thailand's prime minister. Yet they had apparently lost sight of the original point of political reform: the 1997 Constitution had subordinated elected politicians to a rules-based system, designed to ensure the integrity of the political process. Electoral success was not a higher form of validation than constitutional legitimacy. Independent institutions were essential to monitor electoral politics. As Crispin and Tasker noted:

> Those institutions were widely seen as vital pillars of political stability to mediate between competing elite interests once King Bhumibol Adulyadej's all-steadying influence eventually passes from the scene. (Crispin and Tasker 2001)

The Thaksin verdict left the National Counter Corruption Commission completely emasculated, and substantially undermined the credibility of the Constitutional Court.

Less than four years after the promulgation of the widely-heralded 'people's constitution', the institutions of political reform had largely lost their way. Thai politics had been fundamentally altered by the new constitution, and 'civil society' (however defined) now had much greater political space. The popular sector had been empowered and emboldened, and there could be no simple return to the top-down approaches dominant before 1997. Yet the image problems of bodies such as the Constitutional Court and the Election Commission had seriously eroded public faith that legal mechanisms could provide an effective and neutral check on the activities of businesspeople-turned-politicians. Thai politics was once again at a difficult juncture.

AUTHOR'S NOTE

I should like to thank Michael Nelson for his extremely meticulous comments on a draft version of this chapter.

16

CONCLUSION: ECONOMICS, POLITICS AND CIVIL SOCIETY

John Girling

Neither economics, nor politics, nor civil society exists in a vacuum. It is for purposes of analysis that each can be treated separately – as in this book – that is, abstracted from its environment. But in real life they are intricately related and it is my task, in conclusion, to recognise this: to show how the parts relate to one another and to the whole.

Consider, for example, how a large enterprise contributes funds (openly or surreptitiously) to a major political party for its electoral campaigns. The party, in turn, targets various constituencies – the youth vote, or that of women, trade unions, professionals and so on, in other words, 'civil society'. But the funding enterprise, like any well-run business, expects to get a satisfactory return on its expenditure. This may be either in terms of general policy promoting economic development, or one that favours a particular industry: 'What is good for General Motors is good for America' is one memorable attempt at justification.

Evidently the policy of a major political party is thus being influenced in the interest of one of its constituencies (business) at the expense of others – since public money is limited – for the others do not have the same clout, even if they are a majority in society. This may not matter so much in a 'developed' country, where there are sufficient resources to be widely distributed throughout society (and where capitalism is to some extent regulated), but it does matter in a developing country, where public policy may be seriously distorted by powerful economic interests (national and global) at the expense of ordinary people.

That is why a civil society is needed, that is strong enough to stand up to economic demands and to bolster political resistance. The latter is especially important because without pressures from civil society, politicians succumb all too easily to economic inducements. The relationship between civil society and political institutions – in the context of economic development – is therefore a key factor in determining the success or failure of responsible 'modernization'.

Yet another interrelated factor is important. For it is customary, especially since the end of the Cold War, to claim that the market economy and democratic politics are the two essential conditions of a modern developed nation. In each case there is freedom of choice – as customers or as voters. Moreover it is freedom with equality: each political 'unit' – whether male or female, rich or poor, young or old – is equal to all the others. Similarly, each economic unit is equal: the dollar owned by a poor person is worth neither more nor less than the dollar owned by a rich person. Yet, as the eminent sociologist Max Weber, who can by no means be accused of radicalism, has pointed out:

> It is the most elemental economic fact that the way in which the disposition over material property is distributed among a plurality of people, meeting competitively in the market for the purpose of exchange, in itself creates specific life chances. (Weber 1970: 181)

According to Weber, these chances for 'supply of goods, external living conditions and personal life experiences' are 'determined by the amount and kind of power, of lack of such, to dispose of goods or skills for the sake of income in a given economic order'. This 'mode of distribution', he goes on, favours the owners over the non-owners of economic power: 'It increases, at least generally, [owner's] power in price wars with those who, being propertyless, have nothing to offer but their services ... in order barely to subsist'. He therefore concludes that 'the kind of chance in the market is the decisive moment... for the individual's fate' (ibid.: 181–182).

It is, of course, another 'elemental economic fact' that the equal unit (money) is essential for the exchange of goods and services in the market. But the economic reality of market transactions obscures the social reality that those who 'transact' – that is, people – are not equal. And it is this that matters, and not abstract equality, in determining people's fate. Here again, the missing factor – civil society – is essential to improve the 'balance of power' (economy, politics, society) in favour of ordinary people.

In conceptualizing this triangular balance, three theorists of civil society are particularly important. First, Antonio Gramsci, who envisages civil society as the creation of 'citizens' demanding a voice in the formulation of public policy affecting their lives – and livelihood. Second, Alain Touraine, who focuses on specific elements of civil society – such as trade unions, environmentalists and the women's movement – considered as 'social movements'. Each unites particular interests with a 'universal' culture; but to be effective each must cooperate with as well as contest the power of state and economy. And finally Pierre Bourdieu,

CONCLUSION: ECONOMICS, POLITICS AND CIVIL SOCIETY

with his radical theory of 'symbolic power'. For example, when male values determine different kinds of behaviour by men and by women and are internalised by women so that the difference between them appears to be 'natural' – this is the effect of 'symbolic power'.

Each theorist privileges one side of the triangular balance. Gramsci emphasises the autonomy of politics, aiming at the establishment of 'hegemony' (government by consent) through civil society. Bourdieu, on the other hand, considers the economy ('economic capital') to be the major factor in the division of labour in society between the dominant and the dominated classes. Touraine, in turn, champions civil society, in the form of social movements, as the only way to regain true modernity (and rationality) in a society threatened by the abuse of power by the state and the economic system.

Is Thailand in this sense – in these senses – a civil society? The answer, to my mind, is yes: for two reasons, one theoretical, and the other empirical. From a theoretical perspective, all the elements considered above are evident in Thailand: social movements, women and environmentalists in particular, are active; there is symbolic power, because 'male domination' as well as economic and political 'elitism' still characterize society; while 'hegemony', which prevailed in the era of the 'bureaucratic polity', is now being re-created through a civil society that is largely shaped by the interests and values of the growing middle class.

Empirically, too, civil society has passed the test of two major crises, political and economic. In 1992 it was civil society – especially younger middle-class professionals – which successfully resisted the military attempt to restore the bureaucratic polity. Again, in 1997, civil society survived the devastating impact of the economic crisis, as discussed in the chapters by Johannes Schmidt and Kevin Hewison. With the support of civil society, the political system was enabled to carry out its proper democratic role: to replace a (discredited) government with one that enjoyed popular support.

Nevertheless, questions remain. They are raised precisely by the ambiguous attitudes of the Democrat-led government of 1997–2001: that is, how to satisfy the global economic requirements of capitalism in order to regain the confidence of national and especially international investors; and, at the same time, how to defend the interests of the poor and precarious in Thailand, who are most at risk from economic forces outside their control?

The very interesting contribution by Kevin Hewison considers the populist reaction to the devastating effects of the recent economic crisis. The previous euphoria over economic growth soon changed into massive disillusionment. One of the forms this took was a retreat into 'localism', that is, an 'alternative discourse' based on the presumed strengths of rural community culture – turning away from what are felt to be the evil consequences, as well as the failures, of capitalism and market forces. Yet, as Hewison concludes in his careful assessment of localism, it rests on a 'romantic construction of an imagined past': whatever one's sympathy for its proponents, it does not provide a politically sound or economically viable alternative.

Thirayuth, the influential advocate of 'good governance', has criticised the Chuan government for using public funds to pay off debts accumulated by government institutions that had loaned money to the private sector. Moreover, in its concern for the financial establishment, as Naruemon points out, the government seemed indifferent to the problems of the poor. Thirayuth's intriguing support for good governance urges the interaction of civil society and political institutions to produce practical reforms, which is precisely in line with Touraine's strategy for social movements. But he couches his arguments in Bourdieu-like terms, envisaging changes in the roles of social, cultural and political 'capitals' in order to strengthen economic capital – although without succumbing to Bourdieu's deterministic stance. To the contrary, Thirayuth's list of 'duties and responsibilities' makes a good case for social activity and public understanding.

Such are the implications of 'Thai-style development' as outlined by Johannes Schmidt: global economic constraints have an adverse effect on social policy, resulting in cheap labour, weak trade unions, large-scale unemployment and low social welfare. He is correct. But another factor should also be taken into account: unless resources are generated by economic development, facilitated by government policies, there will not be sufficient funds available to sustain effective social programmes in the first place. This, I believe, is an area where political reform (emphasized in Duncan McCargo's introduction) backed by civil society, can do much to harmonize the requirements of capitalist accumulation and the need for social legitimacy.

What is the evidence of political reform? Despite the moral inspiration of Prawase Wasi, the context of 'money politics', with its perversion of institutions and corruption of politicians, weighs heavily on the valuable reforms that are apparent in the 1997 Constitution (note, however, Kobkua's positive assessment of the real and not just constitutional powers of the present monarchy). As for Sombat Chantornvong's scepticism, it no doubt reflects his experience of scholarly investigation of political parties. 'It does not take much to imagine', he infers from the 'outrageous tactics' of one recent election, 'how nasty a future [general] election can be'.

Despite the liberal phaseology of the 1997 constitution, David Streckfuss and Mark Templeton are as sceptical as Sombat about the practical outcome. Human rights still have a long way to go. Old laws and attitudes still triumph over such crucial democratic issues as freedom of religion and freedom of expression. The weight of official sanctions – by the Buddhist hierarchy, the Ministry of Education and by national security officials – against the assumed 'heresy' of a dissident abbot are indeed disturbing. Perhaps even more so is the fact that few intellectuals came to his defence. Freedom of expression too suffers from the draconian laws protecting the monarchy – in this case, the banning of the film *Anna and the King of Siam*. What seems scarcely credible, however, is that the Film Censorship Board even rejects scripts that are critical of past dictators, arguing that they are defamatory. In theory, the authors conclude, the National Human Rights Commission Act has created a powerful organisation for promoting social, political and cultural freedoms. But, in practice, 'it will be impossible to determine how effective the Commission will be'.

Even more critical of the established order is the vigorous radical interpretation by Michael Connors of the (admittedly heterogeneous) political reform movement, which aims to combine an elitist order with popular democracy – but in the overall interest of the capitalist system. 'Good governance' – in a very different sense from Thirayuth – becomes a catchword to regain the confidence of international investors. Accordingly, it seems somewhat optimistic for Connors to conclude that the reform process, despite the power of vested interests, has the potential 'radically to alter the nature of Thai politics'.

The rural–urban divide is at the heart of many of Thailand's problems. It is a commonplace that urban voters are more concerned with issues (but see Jim Ockey's fascinating early example of 'street politics' populism in Chapter 8 of this volume) while rural voters consider their interests. Given the great disparity in urban and rural incomes and the fact that most constituencies are rural it is not surprising that country people vote with their pockets. Vote-buying reflects the peculiar fusion in the provinces of patron–client relations, 'raw' capitalism and power politics. The 'new men', benefiting from lucrative (part-legal, part-illegal) ventures, act as brokers between villagers and local administration, as entrepreneurs providing new forms of employment, and as politicians linking regional and national levels.

The political effect of these socio-economic forces at the provincial level is particularly well brought out in Daniel Arghiros's study of local elections. As he notes, the benefits of 'democratic decentralization' tend to be captured by 'local powers', acting as patrons, who now displace the formerly important bureaucrats. Vote-buying is rampant, the construction industry (as always!) is well represented, and 'male prejudice' virtually excludes women from holding political office.

Under such conditions – the 'dark side' of patron–client relations – social movements have limited options. They may decide, in view of the abuses of economic and political power, that confrontation is the only way to help ordinary people: Somchai, for example, insists that this is essential for 'radical democracy'. Naruemon, however, argues that NGOs adopt different strategies according to their objectives. One group seeks to influence government policy and even to cooperate in the field of social welfare and public health. Another group, in her view, is 'more explicitly critical' of official development policy. It actively organises people at the local level and tries to highlight economic and social problems that need to be dealt with politically. It is the third group (as with Somchai) which strives for 'political empowerment from below' as an authentic form of 'grassroots democracy'.

Social movements have indeed been effective – using one or other of these strategies – in environmental campaigns and in rural empowerment; but the labour movement (immature, divided and often co-opted by powerful 'patrons') remains a weak link. Perhaps it is the women's movement, well reviewed by Philippe Doneys, that is the major cause for optimism in the arduous task of civil society to tilt the balance of economic and political power in favour of ordinary people.

BIBLIOGRAPHY

Amara Pongsapich and Nitaya Kataleeradabhan (1997) *Thailand Nonprofit Sector and Social Development*. Bangkok: Chulalongkorn University Social Research Institute.

Ammar Siamwalla (1997) *Thailand's Boom and Bust*. Bangkok: TDRI.

Amnesty International (1985) *Amnesty International Country Report 1985*. London: Amnesty International.

Amorn Chandara-Somboon (1994) *Constitutionalism: thang ok khong prathet Thai* [Constitutionalism: The Solution for Thailand]. Bangkok: Institute of Public Policy Studies.

Anderson, James (1982) 'Rapid Rural "Development": Performance and Consequences in the Philippines', in Colin MacAndrews and Chia Lin Sien (eds), *Too Rapid Rural Development*. Athens OH: Ohio University Press, pp. 62–87.

Anek Laothamatas (1992a) *Business Associations and the New Political Economy of Thailand*. Boulder, CO: Westview Press.

—— (1992b) 'The Success of Structural Adjustment in Thailand: A Political Explanation of Economic Success', in Andrew J. MacIntyre and Kanishka Jayasuryia (eds) *The Dynamics of Economic Policy Reform in South-East Asia and the South-West Pacific*. Singapore: Oxford University Press, pp. 32–49.

—— (1995) *Song nakhara prachatippatai* [A Tale of Two Democracies]. Bangkok: Matichon.

—— (1996) 'A Tale of Two Democracies: Conflicting Perceptions of Elections and Democracy in Thailand', in Robert H. Taylor (ed.), *The Politics of Elections in Southeast Asia*. Cambridge: Cambridge University Press, pp. 201–223.

Anuraj Manibhandhu (1992) 'The Monarchy: the King Defusing the Tension', *Catalyst for Change: Uprising in May. A special publication of the Bangkok Post*. Bangkok: Post Publishing, pp. 27–28.

Arghiros, Daniel (1995) *Political Structures and Strategies: A Study of Electoral Politics in Contemporary Rural Thailand*. Occasional Paper 31. Hull: Centre for South-East Asian Studies.

—— (1999) 'The Temple, Money and the Polling Station: Rural Monks and Thai Electoral Politics'. Paper presented at the Seventh International Conference on Thai Studies – Buddhism, Cults and Popular Culture Panel, 4–8 July, Amsterdam.

—— (2001) *Democracy, Development and Decentralization in Rural Thailand*. London: Curzon/NIAS.

Asher, Mukul G. (1995) 'Social Security Systems: A Regional Challenge'. *Bangkok Post*, 18 May.

—— (1997) 'ASEAN Countries Must Adjust to a Globalized Economy'. *Asia Times*, 8 January.

Atiya Achakulwisut (1998) 'Working Women', *Bangkok Post*, 12 November.

Bachrach, Peter and Areyeh Botwinick (1992) *Power and Empowerment: A Radical Theory of Participatory Democracy.* Philadelphia: Temple University Press.

Baker, Gideon (1998) 'Civil Society and Democracy: the Gap between Theory and Possibility'. *Politics,* vol. 18, no. 2, pp. 81–87.

Bangkok Bank (1999) 'Economic Indicators', http://www.bbl.co.th/eco_inc/4_gdp.htm.

Banthorn Ondam (1993) 'Ongkonphatthana-ekkachon kab prachatippatai Thai' [NGOs and Thai Democracy] in Sungsidh Piriyarangsan and Pasuk Phongpaichit. *Chon chan klang bon krasae prachatippatai Thai* [The Middle Class and Thai Democracy]. Bangkok: Political Economy Center, Chulalongkorn University, pp. 317–321.

Batson, Benjamin A. (1984) *The End of the Absolute Monarchy in Siam.* Singapore and New York: Oxford University Press.

Beetham, David and Kevin Boyle (1995) *Introducing Democracy: 80 Questions and Answers.* Cambridge: Polity Press.

Bello, Walden (1998) 'From Miracle to Meltdown: Thailand, the World Bank and the IMF'. *Watershed,* vol. 3, no. 2, pp. 17–21.

Bencha Yoddumnern-Attig (1992) 'Conjugal and Parental Roles: A Behavioral Look into the Past and Present', in Bencha Yoddumnern-Attig, Kerry Richter, Amara Soonthorndhada, Chanya Sethaput and Antony Pramualratana (eds), *Changing Roles and Statuses of Women in Thailand: A Documentary Assessment.* Salaya, Thailand: Institute for Population and Social Research, Mahidol University, pp. 25–35.

Bhasin, Kamala (1992) 'Celebrating Democracy and Human Rights', in National Organizing Committee of the People's Plan for the 21st Century (PP21), *People, Participation and Empowerment.* Bangkok: Union for Civil Liberty, pp. 28–43.

Bhumibol Adulyadej, King (1998) 'Phraratchadamrat yutlak setthakit baep pho phiang' [Royal Speech on the Self-Sufficient Economy], in Ministry of Interior, *Setthakit chumchon phung ton eng: naeo khwamkhit lae yutthasat* [The Self-Sufficient Economy: Thoughts and Strategies]. Bangkok: Ministry of Interior, pp. 2–14.

Blanchard, Wendell (1957) *Thailand.* New Haven, CON: HRAF Press.

Blaug, Ricardo (forthcoming) 'Engineering Democracy'. *Political Studies.*

Borwornsak Uwanno and Wayne Burns (1998) 'The Thai Constitution of 1997: Sources and Process'. Online Thailand Law Journal, http://members.tripod.com/asialaw/articles/constburns1.html

Bourdieu, Pierre (1998) *La Domination Masculine.* Paris: Seuil.

Bratton, Michael (1989) 'The Politics of Government–NGO Relations in Africa'. *World Development,* vol. 17, no. 4, pp. 569–587.

Brown, Andrew (1997) 'Locating Working Class Power', in Kevin Hewison (ed.), *Political Change in Thailand: Democracy and Participation.* London: Routledge, pp. 163–178.

Brown, Andrew and Stephen Frenkel (1993) 'Union Unevenness and Insecurity in Thailand', in Stephen Frenkel (ed.), *Organized Labor in the Asia-Pacific Region: A Comparative Study of Trade Unionism in Nine Countries.* Ithaca, NY: ILR Press, pp. 88–106.

Bullard, Nicola with Walden Bello and Kamai Malhotra (1998) *Taming the Tigers: The IMF and the Asian Crisis.* Bangkok and London: Focus on the Global South and the Catholic Aid Agency.

Calhoun, Craig (1992) *Habermas and the Public Sphere.* Cambridge, MA: MIT Press.

—— (ed.) (1994). *Social Theory and the Politics of Identity*. Oxford: Blackwell.
Callahan, William A. (1993) 'Year Later, May Questions Still Rankle', *The Nation*, 17 May.
—— (1998) *Imagining Democracy: Reading the 'Events of May' in Thailand*. Singapore: Institute of Southeast Asian Studies.
Callahan, William A. and Duncan McCargo (1996) 'Vote-Buying in Thailand's Northeast: the Case of the July 1995 General Election'. *Asian Survey*, vol. 36, no. 4, pp. 376–392.
Catley, Bob (1999) 'Hegemonic America: The Arrogance of Power'. *Contemporary Southeast Asia*, vol. 21, no. 2, pp. 157–175.
CDA (Public Relations Committee) [Khanakanmathikan prachasamphan supha rang ratthathammanun] (1997a) *Preliminary Framework in Drafting the People's Constitution* [Krop beuangton rang ratthathammanun chabap prachachon]. Public Relations Committee, Constitutional Drafting Assembly: Bangkok.
—— (1997b) 'Raingan khong khana thamngan rapfang khwamkhithen khong ongkon thurakit lae ongkon ekkachon' [Constitution Drafting Assembly, 'Report of the Public Hearings Committee of Business and Private Organizations']. Mimeograph.
—— (1997c) *Prachachon cha dai arai chak ratthathammanun mai* [What Will the People Get from the New Constitution?] Bangkok: Constitution Drafting Assembly.
Chai Pattana Foundation (1995) 'New Theory', http://www.kanchanapisek.or.th/articles/new-theory.en.html.
—— (1997) 'New Theory: New Life in Korat', http://www.rdpb.go.th/chaipat/journal/dec97/eng/ntheory.html.
Chai-Anan Samudavanija (1997) *Trailaksana rat kap kanmuang thai* [The Three-Dimensional State and Thai Politics]. Bangkok: Institute of Public Policy Studies.
—— (1998) 'Interview', in Chuchai Sobpawong and Uwadee Kadkarnkai (eds), *Prachasangkhom* [Civil Society]. Bangkok: Matichon, pp. 39–52.
Chai Podhisita (1998) 'Buddhism and Thai World View', in Amara Pongsapich (ed.), *Traditional and Thai World View*. Bangkok: Chulalongkorn University Press.
Chalongphob Sussangkarn (1998) 'Thailand's Debt Crisis and Economic Outlook'. Paper presented to the conference 'The Asian Crisis: Economic and Market Intelligence'. University of Melbourne, 8 May.
Chang Noi (pseudonym) (1997) 'The Countryside Will Save the Day'. *Thai Development Newsletter*, no. 33, pp. 43–45.
—— (2001) 'The New Political Map of Thailand'. *The Nation*, 22 January.
Chatthip Nartsupha (1991) 'The "Community Culture" School of Thought', in Manas Chitkasem and Andrew Turton (eds), *Thai Constructions of Knowledge*. London: School of Oriental and Asian Studies, pp. 118–141.
Christensen, Scott and Ammar Siamwalla (1993), 'Beyond Patronage: Tasks for the Thai State'. Paper presented to Thailand Development Institute 1993 Year End Conference 'Who Gets What and How? Challenges for the Future'. Chonburi, 10–11 December 1993.
Chulalongkorn University Social Research Institute (CUSRI) (1989) *Directory of Public Interest Non-Government Organizations in Thailand*. Bangkok: CUSRI.
Clarke, Gerard (1995) 'Participation and Protest: The Roles of NGOs in the Philippines'. Unpublished PhD dissertation, University of London.
—— (1996) *Non-Governmental Organisations (NGOs) and Politics in Developing World*. Swansea: Centre for Development Studies, University of Wales.

Cohen, Jean and Andrew Arato (1994) *Civil Society and Political Theory*. Cambridge MA: MIT Press.

Committee on Civil and Political Rights (UN Human Rights Committee) (1996) 'The Right to Participate in Public Affairs, Voting Rights and The Right of Equal Access to Public Service' (Article 25). 12/07/96. *CCPR General comment 25*. General Comments: Fifty–Seventh Session.

Committee on Development Promotion and Dissemination (1998) *Leuaktang Thammai* [Why Vote?]. Bangkok.

Connors, Michael (1997) 'When the Dogs Howl: Thailand and the Politics of Democratization', in Phillip Darby (ed.), *At the Edge of International Relations: Postcolonialism, Gender and Dependency*. London: Pinter, pp. 125–147.

—— (1999) 'Political Reform and the State in Thailand'. *Journal of Contemporary Asia*, vol. 29, no. 4, pp. 202–226.

—— (2000) 'Subjecting Citizens: Democracy, National Ideology and the Doctrine of Political Development in Thailand.' Unpublished PhD dissertation, University of Melbourne.

Constitution of the Kingdom of Thailand (1974) Bangkok: Office of the Council of State.

Constitution of the Kingdom of Thailand (1991) Bangkok: Office of the Council of State.

Constitution of the Kingdom of Thailand (1997) Bangkok: Office of the Council of State.

Cotton, James (1991) 'The Limits to Liberalization in Industrializing Asia: Three Views of the State', *Pacific Affairs*, vol. 64, no. 3, pp. 311–327.

Crispin, Shawn (2000) 'Uncivil Society'. *Far Eastern Economic Review*, 31 August.

—— (2001a) 'Twilight of a Godfather'. *Far Eastern Economic Review*, 25 January.

—— (2001b) 'Reform: at Death's Door'. *Far Eastern Economic Review*, 8 February.

Crook, Richard C. and James Manor (1995) 'Democratic Decentralisation and Institutional Performance: Four Asian and African Experiences Compared'. *Journal of Commonwealth and Comparative Politics*, vol. 33, pp. 309–334.

—— (1998) *Democracy and Decentralisation in South Asia and West Africa: Participation, Accountability and Performance*. Cambridge: Cambridge University Press.

Dahlgreen, Peter (1994) 'L'espace public et les médias'. *Hermès*, no. 13–14, pp. 243–262.

Darling, Frank (1965) *Thailand and the United States*. Washington DC: Department of Public Affairs.

Darunee Tantiwiramonond (1997) 'Changing Gender Relations in Thailand: A Historical and Cultural Analysis'. *Indian Journal of Indian Gender Studies*, vol. 4, no. 2, pp. 167–198.

Dej Poomkacha (1995) 'And Then What Next Thai NGOs?', in *Thai NGOs: The Continuing Struggle for Democracy*. Bangkok: Thai NGO Support Project, pp. 88–96.

DDC (Democratic Development Committee) (1995a) *Khosanoe kropkhwamkit nai kanpatirip kanmuang Thai* [Proposed Conceptual Framework for Reforming Thai Politics]. Bangkok: Thailand Research Fund.

—— (1995b) *Kho sanoe nai kanpatirup kanmuang Thai* [Proposals for Reforming Thai Politics]. Bangkok: Democratic Development Committee.

Dhani Nivat, Prince (1954) *JSS Collected Articles of HH Prince Dhani Nivat*. Bangkok: Siam Society.

Diamond, Larry (1994) 'Rethinking Civil Society: Toward Democratic Consolidation'. *Journal of Democracy*, vol. 5, no. 3, pp. 4–17.

Doner, Richard F. (1991) 'Approaches to the Politics of Economic Growth in Southeast Asia'. *Journal of Asian Studies*, vol. 50, no. 4, pp. 818–849.

Economic Section (1998) '1998 Investment Climate Statement for Thailand'. Bangkok: Department of State, United States Embassy, http://usa.or.th/embassy/invcl98.htm.

Eldridge, Philip (1995) *Non-Governmental Organisations and Democratic Participation in Indonesia*. Kuala Lumpur: Oxford University Press.

Eley, Geoff (1992) 'Nations, Publics, and Political Cultures: Placing Habermas in the Nineteenth Century', in Craig Calhoun (ed.), *Habermas and the Public Sphere*, Cambridge, MA: The MIT Press, pp. 289–339.

Fairclough, Gordon (1996) 'Vox Populi'. *Far Eastern Economic Review*, 19 December.

—— (1997) 'Feeling Squeezed'. *Far Eastern Economic Review*, 9 January.

Fineman, Daniel (1997) *A Special Relationship: The United States and Military Government in Thailand, 1947–1958*. Honolulu: University of Hawaii Press.

Fishel, Thamora V. (1997) 'Mothers, Teachers and Hua Kanaen: Gender and the Culture of Local Politics in Thailand', in Virada Somswasdi and Sally Theobald (eds), *Women, Gender Relations and Development in Thai Society, Volume 2*. Chiang Mai: Women's Studies Center, Faculty of Social Sciences, Chiang Mai University, pp. 445–466.

Flaherty, Mark and Vesta Filipchuk (1994) 'Women in Local Governments in Northern Thailand'. *Canadian Journal of Development Studies*, vol. 15, no. 1, pp. 35–54.

Fowler, Alan (1991) 'The Role of NGOs in Changing State–Society Relations: Perspectives from Eastern and Southern Africa'. *Development Policy Review*, vol. 9, no. 1, pp. 53–84.

Fox, Jonathan (1994) 'The Difficult Transition from Clientelism to Citizenship: Lessons from Mexico'. *World Politics*, vol. 46, pp. 151–184.

Fox, Leslie (1995) *Civil Society: A Conceptual Framework*. Alexandria, VA: USAID Global Bureau/Center for Democracy.

Fraser, Nancy (1992) 'Rethinking the Public Sphere: A Contribution to the Critique of Actually Existing Democracy', in Craig Calhoun (ed.), *Habermas and the Public Sphere*, Cambridge, MA: MIT Press, pp. 109–142.

Frolic, B. Michael (1997) 'State-led Civil Society', in Timothy Brook and B. Michael Frolic (eds), *Civil Society in China*. New York: M. E. Sharpe, pp. 46–67.

Gawin Chutima (1994) 'Thai NGOs and Civil Society', in Isagani Serrano (ed.), *Civil Society in the Asia-Pacific Region*. Washington DC: CIVICUS, pp. 145–152.

Gellner, Ernest (1994) *Conditions of Liberty: Civil Society and Its Rivals*. Harmondsworth: Penguin.

Gender and Development Research Institute (GDRI) (1996) *6 Years GDRI*. Bangkok: GDRI.

Gill, Stephen (1995) 'Globalisation, Market Civilisation, and Disciplinary Neoliberalism'. *Millennium*, vol. 24, no. 3, pp. 399–423.

Girling, John L. S. (1981) *Thailand: Society and Politics*. Ithaca NY: Cornell University Press.

—— (1996) *Interpreting Development: Capitalism, Democracy and the Middle Class in Thailand*. Ithaca, NY: Cornell University Southeast Asian Studies Program.

Gramsci, Antonio (1971) *Selections from Prison Notebooks*. New York: International Publishers.

Grey, Dennis (ed.) (1988) *The King of Thailand in World Focus*. Bangkok: Foreign Correspondents' Club of Thailand.

Habermas, Jürgen (1989) *The Structural Transformation of the Public Sphere: An Inquiry into a Category of Bourgeois Society*. Trans. Thomas Burger with Frederick Lawrence. Cambridge, MA: MIT Press.

—— (1993) *L'espace public, avec une préface inédite de l'auteur.* Trans. Marc B. de Launay. Paris: Payot.

—— (1996) *The Structural Transformation of the Public Sphere.* Cambridge: Polity Press.

Hansen, Gary (1996) *Constituencies for Reform: Strategic Approaches for Donor-Supported Civic Advocacy Programs.* Arlington, VA: US Agency for International Development/Center for Development Information and Evaluation.

Hansen, Gary and Michael Calavan (1994) *The Development of Civil Society in Thailand: Donor Approaches and Issues.* Washington DC: US Agency for International Development.

Held, David (1987) *Models of Democracy.* Cambridge: Polity Press.

Hewison, Kevin (1989) *Bankers and Bureaucrats: Capital and the Role of the State in Thailand.* New Haven: Yale Center for International and Area Studies, Yale University Southeast Asian Monographs, no. 34.

—— (1993a) 'Nongovernmental Organizations and the Cultural Development Perspective: A Comment on Rigg (1991)'. *World Development,* vol. 21, no. 10, pp. 699–708.

—— (1993b) 'Of Regimes, State and Pluralities: Thai Politics Enters the 1990s', in Kevin Hewison, Richard Robison and Garry Rodan (eds) *Southeast Asia in the 1990s: Authoritarianism, Democracy and Capitalism.* Melbourne: Allen and Unwin, pp. 161–189.

—— (1993c) 'Thailand's Capitalism: Problems for an Economic Miracle'. *Development Bulletin,* no. 28, pp. 4–7.

—— (1996) 'Political Oppositions and Regime Change in Thailand', in Garry Rodan (ed.), *Political Oppositions in Industrialising Asia.* London: Routledge, pp. 72–94.

—— (1997a) 'The Monarchy and Democratisation', in Kevin Hewison (ed.), *Political Change in Thailand, Democracy and Participation.* London: Routledge, pp. 58–74.

—— (ed.) (1997b) *Political Change in Thailand: Democracy and Participation,* London: Routledge.

—— (1999a) *Localism in Thailand: A Study of Globalisation and Its Discontents.* Coventry: Centre for the Study of Globalisation and Regionalisation, University of Warwick, Working Paper no. 39/99, September.

—— (1999b) 'Thailand's Capitalism: The Impact of the Economic Crisis'. *UNEAC Asia Papers,* no. 1, pp. 21–49, http://www.une.edu.au/asiacenter/UNEAC_Asia_Papers.html.

—— (2000) 'Resisting Globalization: A Study of Localism in Thailand'. *The Pacific Review,* vol. 13, no. 2, pp. 279–296.

Hirsch, Philip (1994) 'The Thai Countryside in the 1990s'. *Southeast Asian Affairs 1994.* Singapore: ISEAS, pp. 320–334.

Holland, Stephen (1990) 'Development and Differentiation in Rural Thailand'. Unpublished D.Phil thesis, University of Oxford.

Humphery-Smythe, Veronica (1993) 'First Woman Governor Appointed: Sex Equality Still in Question'. *Thai Development Newsletter,* no. 22, pp. 11–12.

Hunsaker, Bryan (1996) 'The Political Economy of Thai Deforestation', in Bryan Hunsaker et al. *Loggers, Monks, Students, and Entrepreneurs: Four Essays on Thailand.* Dekalb, IL: Center for Southeast Asian Studies, Northern Illinois University, pp. 1–31.

Huntington, Samuel (1993) 'Modernization and Corruption', in Arnold J. Heidenheimer, Michael Johnston and Victor T. LeVine (eds) *Political Corruption: A Handbook.* Brunswick NJ: Transaction Publishers, pp. 377–388.

—— (1994) 'American Democracy in Relation to Asia', in Robert Bartley, Chan Heng Chee, Samuel P. Huntington and Shijuro Ogata (eds), *Democracy and Capitalism: Asian and American Perspectives*. Singapore: ISEAS, pp. 27–43.

ILO Regional Office for Asia and the Pacific, Bangkok (1998) 'The Social Impact of the Asian Financial Crisis'. Report for the ILO's High-Level Tripartite Meeting on Social Responses to the Financial Crisis in East and South-East Asian Countries. Bangkok, 22–24 April.

Jayasuriya, Kanishka (1999) 'Authoritarian Liberalism, Governance and the Emergence of the Regulatory State in Post Crisis East Asia', in Richard Robison, Mark Beeson, Kanishka Jayasuriya and Hyukrae Kim (eds), *Politics and Markets in the Wake of the Asian Crisis*. London: Routledge, pp. 315–330.

Jayasuriya, Laksari (1996) *The Sri Lankan Welfare State: Retrospect and Prospect*. Centre for Development Studies and Institute of Policy Studies Colombo, Sri Lanka, Monograph Series no. 1. Perth, WA: Edith Cowan University.

Ji Ungpakorn (1997) *The Struggle for Democracy and Social Justice in Thailand*. Bangkok: Arom Pongpangnan Foundation.

—— (1998) '"Thammarat" jak thatsana chonchan' [Good Governance from a Class Perspective] in Pitaya Wongkul (ed.), *Thammarat: jutplian prathet thai* [Good Governance: A Turning Point of Thailand?]. Bangkok: Vision Project, pp. 163–174.

—— (1999) *Thailand: Class Struggle in an Era of Economic Crisis*. Hong Kong: Asia Monitor Resource Centre.

Juree Vichit-Vadakan (1994) 'Women and the Family in Thailand'. *Law and Society Review*, vol. 28, no. 3, pp. 515–524.

—— (1997) 'Breaking down the Barriers: No Future for Women in Politics?' *Bangkok Post*, 25 March.

Kanin Boonsuwan (1998) *Khabuankanthamngan khong rabop ratthasapha tam ratthathammanon chabap mai* [How the Parliamentary System Works under the New Constitution]. Bangkok: Winyukorn Publishing.

Kasian Tejapira (1992) 'Commodifying Marxism: The Formation of Modern Thai Radical Culture, 1927–58'. Unpublished PhD thesis, Cornell University.

—— (1996) 'Globalizers vs. Communitarians: Post-May 1992 Debate among Thai Public Intellectuals'. Paper prepared for the Annual Meeting of the Association for Asian Studies, Honolulu.

—— (1998) 'Thammarat thammalae' [Good Governance]. *Nation Sudsapda*, June 18–24.

Keck, Margaret E. and Kathryn Sikkink (1998) *Activists beyond Borders: Advocacy Networks in International Politics*. Ithaca NY: Cornell University Press.

Kemp, Jeremy (1996) 'The Dialectics of Village and State in Modern Thailand', in Mason C. Hoadley and Christer Gunnarsson (eds), *The Village Concept in the Transformation of Rural Southeast Asia*. London: Curzon Press, pp. 44–63.

Keohane, Robert O. and Nye Jr., Joseph S. (1998) 'Power and Interdependence in the Information Age'. *Foreign Affairs*, September/October, pp. 81–94.

Keyes, Charles F. (1999) 'Buddhism Fragmented: Thai Buddhism and Political Order Since the 1970s,' Keynote Address presented at the Seventh International Conference on Thai Studies, Amsterdam, July 4–8.

Khanakammakan ronarong prachathippatai (1995) 'Phaenngan lae kitjakam kho ro po nai chuang 15 duan tulakhom 2537 – thanwakhom 2538'. [Campaign for Democracy 'CPD Plan and Activities between October 1994 and December 1995'] Mimeograph.

Khreuakhai phuying kap ratthathammanun (1997) 'Kho sanoe kaekhai phoemtoem rang ratthathammanun jak kanprachaphijan khong khreuakhai phuying kap ratthathammanun' [Women's Constitution Network, 'Proposal for Amending the Draft Constitution from Hearings of the Women's Constitution Network]. Mimeograph.

King, Daniel (1992) 'The Thai Parliamentary Election of 1992'. *Asian Survey*, vol. 32, no. 2, pp. 1109–23.

King, Daniel and Jim LoGerfo (1996) 'Thailand: Toward Democratic Stability'. *Journal of Democracy*, vol. 7, no. 1, pp. 102–117.

King, John K. (1954) 'Thailand's Bureaucracy and the Threat of Communist Subversion'. *Far Eastern Survey*, vol. 23, November, pp. 169–173.

Kitahara, Atsushi (1996) *The Thai Rural Community Reconsidered: Historical Community Formation and Contemporary Development Movements*. Bangkok: Political Economy Centre, Chulalongkorn University.

Kitching, Gavin (1982) *Development and Underdevelopment in Historical Perspective*. London: Methuen.

Klein, James R. (1998) *The Constitution of the Kingdom of Thailand, 1997: A Blueprint for Participatory Democracy*. Working Paper Series no. 8. Bangkok: The Asia Foundation, March.

Kobkua Suwannathat-Pian (1988) *Thai–Malay Relations: Traditional Intra-regional Relations from the Seventeenth to the Early Twentieth Centuries*. Singapore: Oxford University Press.

—— (1995) *Thailand's Durable Premier, Phibun through Three Decades, 1932–1957*. Kuala Lumpur: Oxford University Press.

Kolakowski, L. (1981) *Main Currents of Marxism: The Founders*. Oxford: Oxford University Press.

Korten, David C. (1990) *Getting to the 21st Century: Voluntary Action and the Global Agenda*. West Hartford, CON: Kumarian Press.

Levine, A. (1995) 'Democratic Corporatism and/versus Socialism', in Erik Olin Wright (ed.), *Association and Democracy*. London: Verso, pp. 157–166.

Likhit Dhiravegin (1985) *Thai Politics: Selected Aspects of Development and Change*. Bangkok: Tri-Sciences Publishing House.

—— (1992) *Demi Democracy: The Evolution of the Thai Political System*. Singapore: Times Academic Press.

Linz, Juan L. and Alfred Stepan (1996) *Problems of Democratic Transition and Consolidation*. Baltimore VA: Johns Hopkins University Press.

Local Administration Department (1996a) *Khomun saphatambon lae ongkan borihan suan tambon prajamphi 2539* [Data on Subdistrict Councils and Subdistrict Administrative Organisations, 1996]. Bangkok: Local Administration Department.

—— (1996b) *Khomun sathiti lae phonkanleuaktang samachik saphajangwat wan thi 24 thanwakhom 2538* [Statistical Data and Results of Provincial Councillor Elections, 24 December 1995]. Bangkok: Election Division, Local Administration Department.

Lockhart, Bruce M. (1990) 'Monarchy in Siam and Vietnam, 1925–1946'. Unpublished PhD dissertation, Cornell University.

Lummis, C. Douglas (1996) *Radical Democracy*. Ithaca NY: Cornell University Press.

MacEwan, Arthur (1999) *Neo-Liberalism or Democracy?* London: Zed Books.

McCargo, Duncan (1997) *Chamlong Srimuang and the New Thai Politics*. London: Hurst.

—— (1998) 'Alternative Meanings of Political Reform in Contemporary Thailand'. *The Copenhagen Journal of Asian Studies*, vol. 13, pp. 5–30.

—— (2000) *Politics and the Press in Thailand: Media Machinations*. London: Routledge.

—— (2001) 'Populism and Reformism in Contemporary Thailand'. *South East Asia Research*, vol. 9, no. 1, pp. 89–107.

McIntyre, Andrew (1999) 'Political Institutions and the Economic Crisis in Thailand and Indonesia', in T. J. Pempel (ed.), *Politics of the Asian Economic Crisis*. Ithaca NY: Cornell University Press.

Martinussen, John (1995) *Democracy, Competition and Choice: Emerging Local Government in Nepal*. Sage: New Delhi.

Medhi Krongkaew (1995a) 'The Political Economy of Decentralization in Thailand', in *Southeast Asian Affairs 1995*. Singapore: Institute of Southeast Asian Studies, pp. 343–361.

—— (1995b) 'Contributions of Agriculture to Industrialization', in Medhi Krongkaew (ed.), *Thailand's Industrialization and Its Consequences*. Basingstoke: Macmillan, pp. 33–65.

Mingsarn Kaosa-ard (1998) 'Economic Development and Institutional Failures in Thailand'. *TDRI Quarterly Review*, vol. 13 no. 1, pp. 3–11.

Ministry of Interior (1998) *Setthakit chumchon phung ton eng: naeo khwamkhit lae yutthasat* [The Self-Sufficient Economy: Thoughts and Strategies]. Bangkok: Ministry of Interior.

Missingham, Bruce (1996) 'Internal Colonialism and Environmental Conflict: The Case of Northeast Thailand'. Proceedings of the Sixth International Conference on Thai Studies, Chiang Mai, Thailand, vol. 2, pp. 187–203.

Mongkol Dhanthanin (1998) 'Setthakit chumchon choeng rabop: lakkan lae naeokan patibat' [The Community Economy System: Principles and Practices], in Ministry of Interior, *Setthakit chumchon phung ton eng: naeo khwamkhit lae yutthasat* [The Self Sufficient Economy: Thoughts and Strategies]. Bangkok: Ministry of Interior.

Morell, David and Chai-Anan Samudavanija (1981) *Political Conflict in Thailand: Reform, Reaction, Revolution*. Cambridge MA: Oelgeschlager, Gunn & Hain.

Muller, Jean-Daniel (1989) *Les ONG ambigües: Aide aux États, aides aux populations?* Paris: L'harmattan.

Munithi Arom Phongphangan (1990) *Prawattisat khabuankan raengngan Thai* [History of the Thai Labour Movement]. Bangkok: Phimtula.

Murashima, Eiji (1987) 'Local Elections and Leadership in Thailand: a Case Study of Nakhon Sawan Province'. *The Developing Economies*, vol. 25, pp. 363–385.

Muscat, Robert J. (1966) *Development Strategy in Thailand*. New York: Praeger.

Narongsak Datudom (1992) 'Raeng jungjai nai kansamak rap leuaktang pen samachik sapha jangwat nai jangwat phranakhon sri ayutthaya' [Motivation of Provincial Council Election Candidates: A Study of Ayutthaya Province]. MA thesis, Chulalongkorn University.

Naruemon Thabchumpon (1997) 'Economic Transition in Thailand: The Hidden Costs of Development', in Vinod Raina, Aditi Chowdhury and Sumit Chowdhury (eds), *The Dispossessed: Victims of Development in Asia*. Hong Kong: ARENA Press, pp. 420–457.

—— (1998) 'Grassroots NGOs and Political Reform in Thailand: Democracy behind Civil Society'. *The Copenhagen Journal of Asian Studies*, vol. 13, pp. 31–59.

—— (1999) 'Thailand: A Year of Diminishing Expectations', *Southeast Asian Affairs*. Singapore: ISEAS, pp. 311–335.

Naruemon Thabchumpon, Prapas Pintongtang and Somchai Prechasilapakul (1996) 'Khabuankan prachachon nai chonnabot kab khwamrunraeng khong rat' [Popular Movements in the Countryside and State Violence]. Unpublished manuscript.

National Archives (1985), File RA S.B. 15/5 'Miracles Happen, Gentlemen, But They Don't Come Cheap', *Leader Magazine.*
—— File RA S.B. 15/5 'Give More, Take Less, His Majesty King Bhumibol Adulyadej'.
National Economic and Social Development Board (NESDB) (1996) *The Eighth National Economic and Social Development Plan (1997–2001).* Bangkok: NESDB, Office of the Prime Minister.
National Human Rights Commission (NHRC) Act (1999) Bangkok: National Human Rights Commission
National Organizing Committee of the PP21 (1992) *Our Voice.* Bangkok: Union for Civil Liberty.
National Statistical Office (NSO) (1997) *Statistical Yearbook Thailand,* no. 44.
Neher, Clark D. (1972) 'The Politics of Change in Rural Thailand'. *Comparative Politics.* vol. 4, pp. 201–217.
—— (1979) *Modern Thai Politics: From Village to Nation.* Cambridge, MA: Schenkman Publishing Company.
—— (1995) 'Thailand's Politics As Usual'. *Current History,* vol. 94, no. 596, pp. 435–439.
Nelson, Michael (1994) 'Administration and Politics in Rural Thailand: Internal Differentiation and Expansion of the Political System'. Unpublished PhD thesis, University of Bielefeld.
—— (1998a) *Central Authority and Local Democratization in Thailand: A Case Study from Chachoengsao Province.* Bangkok: White Lotus.
—— (1998b) *Comparative Decentralization: Some Observations on Sub-national Governance in Thailand, France, Germany, and the United Kingdom.* Bangkok: Department of Government, Faculty of Political Science, Chulalongkorn University.
—— (2000) 'The Senate Elections of March 4, 2000 (etc., etc.)' *KPI Newsletter* vol. 1, no. 3, pp. 3–7.
—— (forthcoming) 'Thailand's House Elections of 6 Jan. 2001: Thaksin's Landslide Victory and Subsequent Narrow Escape', in Michael H. Nelson (ed.) *Thailand's New Politics: KPI Yearbook 2001.* Bangkok: White Lotus.
Nitirat Sapsomboon (1997) *Siang prachachon: warasan khong samatcha khonjon* [Voice of the People magazine], vol. 1, no.1. Bangkok: Forum of the Poor, pp. 58–64.
Ockey, James (1992) 'Business Leaders, Gangsters, and the Middle Class: Societal Groups and Civilian Rule in Thailand'. Unpublished PhD thesis, Cornell University.
—— (1997) 'Thailand: the Crafting of Democracy'. *Southeast Asian Affairs 1997.* Singapore: Institute of Southeast Asian Studies, pp. 301–316.
—— (1999) 'Creating the Thai Middle Class', in Michael Pinches (ed.), *Culture and Privilege in Capitalist Asia.* London: Routledge, pp. 230–250.
Office of the Civil Service Commission (OCSC) (1999) *Regulations of the Office of the Prime Minister on Good Governance. B.E. 2542.* Bangkok: Office of the Civil Service Commission.
Ongkan chaoban lae kreuakhai onkonphatthana ekkachon 11 khreuakhai khanakammakan prasanngan ongkon kanphatthana ekkachon ongkon prachathippatai prachakhompatirup kanmuang khreuakhai phuying ongkon raengngan haeng prathet Thai 28 ongkon thi prachum prachachon pheua ratthathammanun [People's Organizations and 11 NGO Networks, NGO-Cord, 29 Democracy Organizations, Forum for Political Reform, Women's Network, National Labour Organizations and The People's Assembly for

the Constitution] (1997) *Kho sanoe pheua ratthahthammanun* [Proposals for the Constitution]. Mimeograph.

Our Voice (1993) Bangkok: Asian Cultural Forum on Development (ACFOD).

Pasuk Phongpaichit (1999) 'Developing Social Alternatives: Walking Backwards into a Klong'. Paper presented to the Thailand Update Conference, Canberra, The Australian National University, 21 April.

Pasuk Phongpaichit and Chris Baker (1995) *Thailand: Economy and Politics*. Kuala Lumpur: Oxford University Press.

—— (1996) *Thailand's Boom!* Chiang Mai: Silkworm Books.

——(1997) 'Power in Transition: Thailand in the 1990s', in Kevin Hewison (ed.) *Political Change in Thailand: Democracy and Participation*. London: Routledge, pp. 21–41.

—— (2000) *Thailand's Crisis*. Chiang Mai/Copenhagen: Silkworm Books/NIAS.

Pasuk Phongpaichit, Sungsidh Piriyarangsan and Nualnoi Treevat (1995) 'Patterns and Processes of Social Exclusion in Thailand', in Gerry Rodgers, Charles Gore and Jose B. Figueiredo (eds), *Social Exclusion: Rhetoric, Reality, Responses*. Geneva: ILO, pp. 147–161.

—— (1996) *Challenging Social Exclusion: Rights and Livelihood in Thailand*. Geneva: International Institute for Labour Studies.

Petras, James (1999) 'NGOs: In the Service of Imperialism'. *Journal of Contemporary Asia*, vol. 29, no. 4, pp. 429–440.

Prajadhipok, King (1974) 'Problem of Siam', in Benjamin A. Batson (ed.), *Siam's Political Future: Documents from the End of the Absolute Monarchy*. Data Paper no. 96. Ithaca, NY: Southeast Asia Program. Department of Asian Studies, Cornell University, pp. 13–22.

Praphat Pintopaeng (1998) *Kanmuang bonthong thanon: 99 wan samatcha khonjon*. [Street Politics: 99 Days of the Forum of the Poor]. Bangkok: Krirk University Research Centre.

Prasan Maruekaphitak et al. (1998) *Anand Punyarachun chiwit, khwamkit lae kanngan khong adit nayok ratthamontri song samai* [Anand Punyarachun: The Life, Thought and Work of a Twice Former Prime Minister]. Bangkok: Amarin Publications.

Prawase Wasi (1991) 'So. No. Ph. Prawase Wasi, prathan munithi chumchon thongthin phatthana' [Prof. Dr Prawase Wasi, President of the Local Development Institute], in Phaisan Sanwoli (ed.) *Thotsawat ... ongkan phatthana ekkachon* [The Decade of NGOs]. Bangkok: Munithi asasamak pheua sangkhom, pp. 8–14.

—— (1996) *Kandoenthang haeng khwamkit: patirup kanmuang* [A Mind's Journey: Political Reform]. Bangkok: Mo Chao Ban.

—— (1998) 'Interview', in Chuchai Sohpawong and Uwadee Kadkarnkai (eds), *Prachasangkhom* [Civil Society]. Bangkok: Matichon, pp. 1–36.

—— (1999a) *Setthakit pho phiang lae prachasangkhom* [The Self-sufficient Economy and Civil Society]. Bangkok: Rural Doctors' Publishing.

—— (1999b) 'A Story of Sustainable Development'. *Bangkok Post*, 31 December.

—— (1999c) *Latthi thammakai kap bobat khong sangkhom thai* [The Thammakai Creed and the role of Thai Society] Bangkok: Samakhom sitkao Mahachulalongkon ratchawitthayalai .

Pridi Phanomyong's Concept of Democracy (1992) [Naeokhit prachathippatai khong Pridi Phanomyong]. Bangkok: The Pridi Phanomyong Foundation.

Prudhisan Jumbala (1998) 'Thailand: Constitutional Reform amidst Economic Crisis', *Southeast Asian Affairs*. Singapore: Institute of Southeast Asian Studies, pp. 265–291.

Prudhisan Jumbala and Maneerat Mitprasat (1997) 'Non-Governmental Organisations: Empowerment and Environment', in Kevin Hewison (ed.) (1997) *Political Change in Thailand: Democracy and Participation.* London: Routledge, pp. 195–216.

Quigley, Kevin F. (1996) 'Towards Consolidating Democracy: The Paradoxical Role of Democracy Groups in Thailand'. *Democratization,* vol. 3, no. 3, pp. 264–286.

Raignan khanakammathikan wisaman phijarana suksa naeothang kaekhai ratthathamanun haeng ratcha-anajak Thai 2 (1993) [Report of the Extraordinary House Committee Considering Approaches to Amend the Constitution of the Kingdom of Thailand]. Bangkok: Parliament of Thailand.

Ratana Tosakul Boonmathya (1999) 'Prachakhom – Civil Society in Thailand: the Case of Khon Kaen Civic Assembly (KKCA)'. Paper presented at the Seventh International Conference on Thai Studies, Amsterdam, 4–8 July.

Ratthathammanun thai: rang khosanoe pheua kan prachaphijan [Thai Constitution: Draft for Public Hearing] (1997) Bangkok: Civic Net.

Reinecke, Gerhard (1993) 'Social Security in Thailand: Political Decisions and Distributional Impact'. *Crossroads,* vol. 8, no. 1, pp. 78–115.

Rewadee Prasertcharoensuk (1996) 'Impacts of Trade Liberalisation on Thailand'. *Thai Development Newsletter,* no. 30, pp. 21–22.

Reynolds, Craig (1991) 'Introduction', in Craig Reynolds (ed.), *National Identity and Its Defenders: Thailand, 1939–1989.* Chiang Mai: Silkworm Books, pp. 1–39.

Rigg, Jonathan (1991) 'Grassroots Development in Rural Development: A Lost Cause?' *World Development,* vol. 19, no. 2/3, pp. 199–211.

Riggs, Fred W. (1962) 'Interest and Clientele Groups', in J. L. Sutton (ed.), *Problems of Politics and Administration in Thailand.* Bloomington: Indiana University Press, pp. 153–192.

——— (1963) *Census and Notes on Clientele Groups in Thai Politics and Administration.* Bloomington: Indiana University Department of Government, Institute of Training for Public Service.

Rodan, Garry (1997) 'Civil Society and Other Political Possibilities in Southeast Asia.' *Journal of Contemporary Asia,* vol. 27, pp. 156–178.

Rosenau, James N. and Mary Durfee (2000) *Thinking Theory Thoroughly: Coherent Approaches to an Incoherent World.* Boulder: CO: Westview Press.

Ruang Suksawasdi (1996) 'Alternative Agriculture: Act Now' *Thai Development Newsletter,* no. 30, pp. 24–26.

Rueschemeyer, Dietrich, Evelyne Huber Stevens and John D. Stephens (eds) (1992) *Capitalist Development and Democracy.* Cambridge: Polity Press.

Rüland, Jürgen and Bhansoon Ladavalya (1993) *Local Associations and Municipal Government in Thailand.* Germany: Freiburger Beitrage zu Entwicklung und Politik.

Saneh Chamarik (1998) 'Good governance kap thammarat' [Good Governance and Thammarat]. *Phujatkan Daily,* 21 May.

Sanitsuda Ekachai (1996) 'Woman and Democracy', *Bangkok Post,* 24 October.

——— (1997) 'Commentary', *Bangkok Post,* 30 January .

——— (1998) 'Why Did Things Go So Wrong?' *Bangkok Post,* 31 December.

Schaeffer, Robert (1993) 'Democratic Devolutions: East Asian Democratization in Comparative Perspective', in Ravi Arvind Palat (ed.), *Pacific-Asia and the Future of the World-System.* Westport, CON: Greenwood Press, pp. 169–180.

Schmidt, Johannes Dragsbaek (1993) 'Theory and Reality of Democracy and Thai Democratization'. *Kasarinlan: A Philippine Quarterly of Third World Studies,* vol. 8, no. 3, pp. 98–144.

—— (1996) 'Paternalism and Planning in Thailand: Facilitating Growth without Welfare', in Michael Parnwell (ed) *Uneven Development in Thailand*. Aldershot: Avebury, pp. 63–81.

—— (1997a) *Southeast Asia between Global Neoliberal Discipline and Local Quests for Welfare*. Working Paper no. 84, Murdoch: Asia Research Centre, Murdoch University.

—— (1997b) 'The Challenge from Southeast Asia: Between Equity and Growth', in Chris Dixon and David Drakakis-Smith (eds), *Uneven Development in Southeast Asia*. London: Ashgate Press, pp. 21–44.

—— (1997c) 'Globalization, Democracy and Social Welfare in Thailand'. Paper delivered to Workshop on Thailand: Social Issues in a Fast Developing Economy organized jointly between the European Institute for Asian Studies (EIAS, Brussels) and the Royal Thai Embassy, Brussels, 25 September.

Schmidt, Johannes Dragsbæk, Niels Fold and Jacques Hersh (eds) (1997) *Social Change in Southeast Asia*. Harlow: Longman.

Schmitter, Philippe C. and Terry Karl (1991) 'What Democracy Is ... and Is Not'. *Journal of Democracy*, vol. 2, no. 3, pp. 75–88.

Schumpeter, Joseph (1976) *Capitalism, Socialism and Democracy*. London: Allen and Unwin.

Scott, James C. and Benedict J. Kerkvliet (1977) 'How Traditional Rural Patrons Lose Legitimacy: A Theory with Special Reference to Southeast Asia', in Steffen W. Schmidt et al (eds), *Friends, Followers, and Factions: A Reader in Political Clientelism*. Berkeley CA: University of California Press, pp. 439–458.

Seri Phongphit (1989) *Development Paradigm. Strategy, Activities and Reflection*. Special issue of *RUDOC News*, vol. 4, no. 3/4.

Set Sayam [pseudony]) (1997) *Lathi boriphok niyom kap sangkhom* [Consumerism and Society]. Bangkok: Samaphan Publishers.

Siffin, William (1962) 'Economic Development', in Joseph L. Sutton (ed.), *Problems of Politics and Administration in Thailand*. Bloomington: Indiana University, pp. 125–151.

Sombat Chantornvong (1987) *Kanmuang ruang kanleuaktang: suksa chapho karani kanleuaktang thuapai pho so 2529* [Electoral Politics: A Case Study of the General Election 1986] Bangkok: Foundation for Democracy and Development Studies.

—— (1993) *Leuaktangwikrit: panha lae thang ok* [Thai Elections in Crisis: Problems and Solutions]. Bangkok: Kopfai.

—— (1998) 'The Political World of Sunthonphu', in Amara Pongsapich (ed.), *Traditional and Changing Thai World View*. Bangkok: Chulalongkorn University Press, pp. 63–96.

—— (2000) 'Local Godfathers in Thai Politics', in Ruth McVey (ed.), *Money and Power in Provincial Thailand*. Copenhagen: NIAS, pp. 53–73.

Sombat Raksakul (1994) 'A Grim Fight to Retain Traditional Influence.' *Bangkok Post Weekly*, 9 December.

Somchai Meesane (1997) 'Bureaucratic Reform.' *Bangkok Post*, 19 January.

Spindler, Kanjana (1993) 'May 1992: When the Tide Finally Turned'. *Thai Development Newsletter*, no. 22, pp. 53–54.

Srisuwan Kuankachorn (1996) 'Ongkon ekkachon kap kanphatthana prachathippatai nai prathet Thai' [NGOs and the Development of Democracy in Thailand], in Sungsidh Phiriyarangsan and Pasuk Phongpaichit (eds), *Jitsamnuk lae udomkan khong khabuankan prachathippatai ruamsamai* [Consciousness and Ideology of the Contemporary Democracy Movement]. Bangkok: Political Economy Centre, Chulalongkorn University, pp. 153–171.

—— (1998) 'The Roots of the Thai Crisis: A Failure of Development'. *Watershed*, vol. 3, no. 3, pp. 37–40.

Stewart, Robb (1999) 'Defending the Faith(s): Buddhism and Religious Freedom in Thailand,' paper presented at the Seventh International Conference on Thai Studies, Amsterdam, July 4–8.

Streckfuss, David (1995) 'Kings in the Age of Nations: the Paradox of *lèse-majesté* as Political Crime in Thailand,' *Comparative Studies in Society and History* vol. 37 no. 3, pp. 445–475.

—— (1998) 'The Poetics of Subversion: Civil Liberty and *lèse-majesté* in the Modern Thai State', unpublished Ph.D. dissertation, Department of History, University of Wisconsin-Madison.

Sungsidh Piriyarangsan (1998a) 'Setthakit chumchon phung ton eng: pratchaya thana lae anakhot' [The Self-reliant Economy: Philosophy, Status and Future], in Ministry of Interior *Setthakit chumchon phung ton eng: naeo khwamkhit lae yutthasat* [The Self-sufficient Economy: Thoughts and Strategies]. Bangkok: Ministry of Interior, pp. 31–46.

—— (1998b) 'Setthakit chumchon phung ton eng chabap mahatthai: prathet yakjon, prachachon mangkhang' [The Self-reliant Economy – Ministry of Interior document: Poor Country, Rich Population], in Ministry of Interior, *Setthakit chumchon phung ton eng: naeo khwamkhit lae yutthasat* [The Self-sufficient Economy: Thoughts and Strategies]. Bangkok: Ministry of Interior, pp. 47–58.

Sungsidh Piriyarangsan and Kanchada Poonpanich (1994) 'Labour Institutions in an Export-Oriented Country: A Case study of Thailand', in Gerry Rodgers (ed.), *Workers, Institutions and Economic Growth in Asia*. Geneva: ILO, pp. 211–253.

Surachart Bamrungsuk (1988) *United States Foreign Policy and Thai Military Rule 1947–1977*. Bangkok: Duang Kamol.

Surin Maisrikrod (1993) 'Emerging Patterns of Leadership in Thailand'. *Contemporary Southeast Asia*, vol. 15, no. 1, pp. 80–96.

Surin Maisrikrod and Duncan McCargo (1997) 'Electoral Politics: Commercialisation and Exclusion', in Kevin Hewison (ed.), *Political Change in Thailand: Democracy and Participation*. London: Routledge, pp. 132–148.

Suteera Thomson (1995) *Women in Decision-Making Positions: Politics and Administration*. Bangkok: GDRI.

Suteera Thomson and Maytinee Bhongsvej (1996) *Putting Women's Rights into the Constitution*. Bangkok: GDRI.

Suteera Thomson and Sheila Thomson (1994) *Women and Politics in Thailand: Options for the 1990s*. Bangkok: GDRI.

Suthy Prasertset (1995) 'The Rise of NGOs as [a] Critical Social Movement in Thailand', in Jaturong Boonyarattanasoontorn and Gawin Chuntima (eds), *Thai NGOs: The Continuing Struggle for Democracy*. Bangkok Thai NGO Support Project, pp. 97–134.

Tandon, Rajesh (1994) 'Civil Society, the State and the Role of NGOs', in Isagani Serrano (ed.) *Civil Society in the Asia-Pacific Region*. Washington DC: CIVICUS, pp. 117–136.

TDN (*Thai Development Newsletter*) (1991) no. 19, Bangkok: Thai Development Support Committee

—— (1993) no. 22, Bangkok: Thai Development Support Committee.
—— (1995) no. 29, Bangkok: Thai Development Support Committee.
—— (1997) no. 32, Bangkok: Thai Development Support Committee.
—— (1997) no. 34, Bangkok: Thai Development Support Committee.
—— (1998) no. 35, Bangkok: Thai Development Support Committee.

—— (1999) no. 39, Bangkok: Thai Development Support Committee.
Thai Red Cross (1999) http://www.redcross.or.th/backgnd/backgnd.html,
Thai Volunteer Service (1987) *Directory of Non-Government Development Organizations in Thailand*. Bangkok: Thai Volunteer Service.
Thailand Statistical Yearbook (n.d.) (Samut sathiti rai pi khong prathet thai v. 23 [1956–58]). Bangkok: National Statistical Office.
Thak Chaloemtiarana (1979) *Thailand: the Politics of Despotic Paternalism*. Bangkok: Social Science Association of Thailand.
Therborn, Goran (1988) *The Ideology of Power and the Power of Ideology*. London: Verso.
Thirayuth Boonmi (1998a) *Sangkhom khemkhaeng, thammarat haeng chat* [Strong/Civil Society: Good Governance]. Bangkok: Saithan Press.
—— (1998b) 'Thammarat: yutthasat thangrot khong phrathet thai' [Good Governance: The Strategy for Survival of Thailand]. *Matichon Sutsapda*, 27 January, pp. 12–13.
—— (1998c) *Thammarat kab kanpratirup sangkom* [Good Governance and Social Reform]. Bangkok: Amarin Printing.
Thitinan Pongsudhirak (1998) 'Thai People Feel the Squeeze'. *Bangkok Post*, 3 December.
Turton, Andrew (1987) *Production, Power and Participation in Rural Thailand: Experiences of the Poor Farmers' Groups*. Geneva: UNRISD.
—— (1989) 'Local Powers and Rural Differentiation', in Gillian Hart, Andrew Turton and Benjamin White (eds), *Agrarian Transformations: Local Processes and the State in Southeast Asia*. Berkeley CA: University of California Press, pp. 70–97.
Ubonrat Siriyuvasak (1991) 'The Environment and Popular Culture in Thailand.' *Southeast Asian Affairs*. Singapore: Institute of Southeast Asian Studies, pp. 298–310.
Ungpakorn, Giles (1999) 'Thai Workers in the 1990s'. Paper presented to the Seventh International Conference on Thai Studies, Amsterdam, 4–8 July.
UNDP (United Nations Development Program) (1998a) 'Gender Empowerment Measures', *Human Development Report*. New York: UNDP.
—— (1998b) 'Women's Participation in Economic and Political Life Index'. *Human Development Report*. New York: UNDP.
—— (1999) *Human Development Report of Thailand*. Bangkok: United Nations Development Program.
US Department of State (1956) *Background: Thailand*. Washington DC: Government Printing Office.
—— (1989) *Foreign Relations of theUnited States 1955–57*, vol. 22. Washington DC: Government Printing Office.
Vatikiotis, Michael (1996) 'Legal Relic'. *Far Eastern Economic Review*, 18 July, pp. 23–26.
Vatikiotis, Michael and Gordon Fairclough (1996a) 'Mission Impossible' *Far Eastern Economic Review* 28 November, pp. 16–18.
—— (1996b) 'Advice and Consent: Monarch's Moral Influence Prevails in Crises'. *Far Eastern Economic Review*, 13 June, p. 22.
Viboon Engakul (1985) 'Recognition of Human Rights under Thai Laws', in Harry Scoble and Lauries Wiseberg (eds), *Access to Justice: The Struggle for Human Rights in Southeast Asia*. London: Zed, pp. 97–100.
Vile, Maurice (1967) *Constitutionalism and the Separation of Powers*. Oxford: Clarendon Press.
Vitit Muntarbhorn (1998) 'Towards a Democratic Charter'. *Bangkok Post*, 10 June.

Vitit Muntarbhorn and Charles Taylor (1994) *Road to Democracy: Human Rights and Democratic Development in Thailand.* Montreal: International Center for Human Rights and Democratic Development.

Wade, Robert (1990) *Governing the Market: Economic Theory and the Role of Government in East Asian Industrialization,* New Jersey: Princeton University Press.

—— (1996) 'The Role of the State in East Asian Capitalism – Lessons for Eastern Europe', in Jacques Hersh and Johannes Dragsbaek Schmidt (eds), *The Aftermath of 'Real-Existing Socialism' in Eastern Europe: Between Western Europe and East Asia.* London: Macmillan, pp. 165–180.

Warren, Carol (1993) *Adat and Dinas: Balinese Communities in the Indonesian State,* Southeast Asia Social Science Monographs. Kuala Lumpur: Oxford Univ. Press.

Watershed: People's Forum on Ecology (1998) vol. 3, no. 2 (Nov 1997–Feb 1998).

WCN Newsletter (1997) *Jotmai khao khreukhai phuying kap ratthathammanun* [Women's Constitution Network Newsletter], no. 4, October–November.

Weber, Max (1970) 'Class, Status, Party', in H. H. Gerth and C. Wright Mills (eds), *From Max Weber.* London: Routledge & Kegan Paul, pp. 181–182.

Wedel, Paul (1988) 'A Royal Checkmate: 2 April 1981', in Dennis Grey (ed.), *The King of Thailand in World Focus.* Bangkok: Foreign Correspondents' Club of Thailand, pp. 94–95.

Wilson, Constance (1983) *Thailand: A Handbook of Historical Statistics.* Boston: D. K. Hall.

World Bank (1989) *Sub-Saharan Africa: From Crisis to Sustainable Growth.* Washington DC: The World Bank.

—— (1993) *The East Asian Miracle: Economic Growth and Public Policy.* New York: Oxford University Press.

—— (1997) *World Development Report.* New York: Oxford University Press.

Yeo, Eileen Janes (ed.) (1998) *Radical Femininity: Women's Self-Representation in the Public Sphere.* Manchester: Manchester University Press.

Yod Sukpattee (1998) 'Thammarat: pratchaya thang kanmuang khong Thirayuth Boonmi' [Good Governance: The Political Philosophy of Thirayuth Boonmi], in Pitaya Wongkul (ed.), *Thammarat: jutplian prathet thai?* [Good Governance: A Turning Point for Thailand?]. Bangkok: Vision Project, pp. 61–70.

Yupa Wanchai (1985) 'Thailand', in John Dixon and Hyung Shik Kim (eds), *Social Welfare in Asia.* London: Croom Helm, pp. 354–380.

NEWSPAPERS AND PERIODICALS (VARIOUS ISSUES)

Asiaweek
Bangkok Post
Far Eastern Economic Review
Friends of Women Newsletter
Jotmai Khao Kho Ro Po [CPD Newsletter].
Krungthep Thurakit
Matichon
The Nation
Nation Sutsapda
NESDB Newsletter
Phujatkan Daily
Thai Post
Thai Rath

INDEX

1932 revolution 21, 26. *See also* monarchy
1947 military coup 21, 26, 62. *See also* Plaek Phibunsongkhram
1951 military coup 62
1955–57 protests. *See* Hyde Park movement
1957 military coup 62. *See also* Sarit Thanarat
1973 popular uprising 1, 21, 26, 57
1974 constitution 58, 69–70n
1976 military coup 1, 21, 26
1981 (failed) military coup 66
1985 (failed) military coup 66
1991 constitution 59–60
1991 military coup 1, 21, 39. *See also* Assets Examination Committee, National Peace Keeping Council
1992 popular uprising 1, 21, 40–41, 143
1995 general election 12, 127, 172
1997 constitution 21–22, 73
  composition 10–12
  and CDA. *See* Constitutional Drafting Assembly
  and DDC. *See* Democratic Development Committee
  doubts about 206–207, 212, 218
  drafting 2, 13, 25, 221n. *See also* Constitutional Drafting Assembly
  effect on 2001 general election 203, 248
  and human rights 74–75, 78–90, 195, 197
  passage of 9, 44; reasons for ~ 52–53, 141–142
  a 'people's constitution' 9, 37
  position of monarch 59–66, 68–71
1997 economic crisis 1, 29, 91–92, 101–102, 146, 218–219
  causes 6, 14, 33, 92, 177
  ensures reforms passed 6, 13, 25, 52
  and localism 148. *See also* localism
  responses to 14, 15, 33, 143, 146–147, 189–193. *See also* 'good governance'; localism
2000 senate election 1, 17, 55, 197, 251, 256–257, 207–210. *See also* senators
2001 general election 1, 17, 55, 247–259 *passim*
  abuses 249–251. *See also* vote-buying
  assessment 220–221, 254–255
  dirtiest and most expensive Thai election 253

administration. *See* government
Administrative Courts established 1997 11
Anand Panyarachun, premier 5, 14, 22, 39, 46. *See also* 1992 popular uprising
Anna and the King, banned 79–81, 265. *See also* freedom of expression
anti-democratic behaviour 129–130. *See also* democracy and democratization
Assets Examination Committee 127–128. *See also* 1991 military coup; corruption

Bangkok
  as centre of power 8, 9, 93, 225–226
  growth of 119
  vs rural areas 5, 118, 133
  see also centralization; elite, urban; NGOs; urbanism
Banharn Silpa-archa 5
  approval of CDA 13, 42
  establishes PRC 13, 42
  support for reform 13, 24, 42
  see also Chart Thai Party
Bank of Thailand 196
  declining interest as career choice 8

reform needed 33
Bhumibol, King 157–158
  calls for greater self-sufficiency 6, 15–16, 148–149, 158, 161n. *See also* localism
  intervention in 1992 crisis 40, 65, 67
  as 'king-maker' 65
  role in the 1973 uprising 57–58
  see also monarchy
Bowornsak Uwanno 22, 41, 45
Buddhism
  Bramanism 168
  diversity of 77–78
  legitimizer of monarchy 64
  monks 76–78, 82, 116, 147, 166, 181n
  sangha, review of workings needed 2
  and self-reliance 150, 158
  see also freedom of religion; localism; Thammakai
bureaucracy 117
  accountability needed 43
  declining technocratic competence 8
  failings of as contributor to 1997 economic crisis 6
  importance in politics 8
  reform of 2, 33
  Thailand as a 'bureaucratic polity' 8
  traditional dominance of 225–226, 227. *See also* conservative forces; military
  see also Administrative Courts; centralization; conservative forces; Finance Ministry; Interior Ministry; local government
business sector 117
  government policy supports/reflects interests of 29, 95, 128, 190–191, 193
  immobility on constitutional reform 47
  MPs increasingly from 128, 133

capitalism. *See* development, mode of
CDA. *See* Constitutional Drafting Assembly
CDP. *See* cultural development perspective
centralization
  contributor to 1997 econ. crisis 6
  impediment to reform 8, 167, 225–226
  strength of 8, 167, 225–226
  top–down development. *See* neo-liberalism

see also Bangkok; bureaucracy; decentralization; local government
Chart Pattana Party 214, 247, 248, 253
Chart Thai Party 42, 214, 247, 248, 253, 256
Chatichai Choonavan
  overthrown by NPKC 39
  premier 1, 212
Chavalit Yongchaiyudh
  joins Thaksin government 255
  opposes draft 1997 constitution 44; ~ but allows passage 9, 44
  premier 4, 147, 193, 221, 229
  see also New Aspiration Party
Chuan Leekpai, premier 2, 22, 23, 40, 41, 147, 152, 193–194, 197, 210, 212, 226, 247, 256, 264
  see also Democrat Party
civil liberties. *See sub-entries under* freedom
  see also Constitutional Court; National Human Rights Commission
civil society 116, 119–121, 180n, 218, 259, 263
  characteristics 108, 126, 133–137, 139–141, 183–185
  elite- or state-led 102, 133–137, 263
  emergence crucial to political reform 18, 22, 138, 163, 261
  NGOs cannot replace State 14, 134
  promotes popular participation 139
  reform of 2, 224
  Thailand as a 263
community culture (school of thought)
  return to ideas of 6
  see also localism
conservative forces
  alliance with liberals and progressives to limit parliamentary power 4
  attack CDA 25
  participation in reform process 4
  resist substantive reform 2, 41
  see also bureaucracy; military
constitution
  16 Thai ~s since 1932 2
  constitutionalism as a political 'disease' 3
  limits on rights 129–130
  not all change reformist 3
  not the only area needing reform 2
  position of monarch 58–66, 68–71
  reform as instrument of day-to-day politics 2

INDEX

Thailand a 'constitutional polity' 3
  see also 1997 Constitution
Constitutional Court 60, 212, 222n
  acquittal of Thaksin 258
  arguments for 43
  credibility of 213, 258
  criticism of 85–86, 213, 258–259
  established 11, 85
  mandate 85–86
Constitutional Drafting Assembly 13, 42–44, 86
  elite-led 9, 37–39, 42–44
  established 13, 24–25
  immobilism of business sector 47
  NGO engagement 47–52
  opposition to 44, 52
  popular interest/involvement in 38, 142
  role of women's organizations 16, 49–50, 164, 173–178
consumerism 150. *See also* development, mode of
corruption
  as cause of leadership failure 6
  contributor to 1997 econ. crisis 6
  of government ministers 6–7, 220
  local-level 231–232, 244
  measures against 10–11, 182n
  reason for 1991 coup 39
  scale of 130
  see also Assets Examination Committee, National Counter-Corruption Commission; vote-buying
cultural development perspective 148, 152, 153, 156. *See also* community culture; localism

DDC. *See* Democratic Development Committee
decentralization 108, 195, 223
  democratic 17, 223–244 *passim*, 265
  problems with 224, 231–244 *passim*
  supported by king 6, 15–16
  see also local government; localism
democracy and democratization 93–94, 103, 126–127, 183–187, 196–199, 218
  from above 130–137, 184;
    ~ below 183, 184
  dependent on strength of middle class 131; ~ empowerment of subordinate classes 139, 141
  grassroots participation 14, 15, 183–187, 195–199, 218, 266

popular participation 139–140
  radical 138–141
  see also anti-democratic behaviour; development, mode of; liberalization; neo-liberalism; NGOs; political reform
Democrat Party 23, 115, 116, 194, 214, 216, 247–248, 252, 253, 255, 263. *See also* Chuan Leekpai
Democratic Development Committee 2, 25
  chairman Prawase Wasi 2, 22
  drafting of 1997 constitution 2
  established 1994 2, 41
  work of 23
demonstrations 52, 193, 194, 250
  see also 1973 popular uprising; 1992 popular uprising; (the) poor; popular unrest/conflict; social welfare; street politics
Department of Welfare 99–100
development, mode of
  and democracy 130–133
  opposition to 143, 149–150, 152–153, 159–160
  scepticism about 6. *See also* localism
Dhammachayo 75–77, 88n. *See also* Thammakai
district offices 226, 232. *See also* bureaucracy; local government

economic development
  approach to. *See* development, mode of; neo-liberalism
  destructiveness of 151–152
  success of 144–145
  uneven 128, 152, 187. *See also* (the) poor
  see also consumerism; industrialism; urbanism
education
  academic freedom 88n
  barriers to political office 10, 14, 51, 82–83, 122, 205, 212
  reform of ~ system 2
Election Commission 55, 206–210, 248
  established 1997 10, 204
  credibility of 17, 210, 250–251, 258
  membership 257
  powers and duties 204, 208, 210; controversy over ~ 17
elections
  campaigns increasingly violent and

285

competitive 214–217
control of. *See* Election Commission
fraud 6. *See also* corruption; vote-buying; vote-canvassing
free and fair 126. *See also* freedom
turnout 203, 208, 221n, 222n, 240;
~ as indicator of grassroots participation 197, 240. *See also* vote-buying
see date section for individual elections
see also electoral system; parliamentary politics; political parties
electoral system
for benefit of elites 7
exercise in benefit-sharing 7, 127, 255
reform 2; ~ ineffectiveness of 17
elite–grassroots conflict 12
'elite democracy' 15, 133–137
see also centralization; NGOs; popular power
elite, urban
centre of political power until 1980s 5, 94
constitution used to consolidate power 3, 265
see also development, mode of; middle class; NGOs
elites, provincial business
control of local government 230, 232–233, 237–239, 243. *See* local government
'dark influences' of 4–5, 246n. *See also* corruption
politicians. *See* rural politicians

Finance Ministry
declining interest as career choice 8
Forum of the Poor 15, 101, 121, 122, 188, 190, 193, 198. *See also* NGOs; (the) poor
freedom 126
academic 88n
of association 97
electoral 81–83, 89n, 126. *See also* political reform
of expression 14, 78–81, 88–89n
of information 11
of the press 39, 219–220
of religion 14, 74–78, 87–88n. *See also* Thammakai

general elections. *See* elections

see date section for individual elections
globalization 103, 144, 151, 153, 156–160. See also development, mode of; neo-liberalism
'good governance' 13, 29–35 *passim*, 45–46, 126, 134–135, 264, 265
conditions to establish 32–33
duties and responsibilities 34–35
involves social collaboration 30–31, 34
meaning 29–31, 35
as new source of legitimacy 31–32
reasons for 30, 134
World Bank promotion of 44, 163, 223
see also thammarat haengchat
government
of absolute monarch, abolished 1, 21, 26. *See also* monarchy
of Anand Panyarachun 5, 14, 22, 39, 46
Banharn. *See* Banharn Silpa-archa
centralism. *See* Bangkok; bureaucracy; centralization; decentralization
Chuan. *See* Chuan Leekpai; Democrat Party
of Chatichai Choonavan 1, 39, 212
of Chavalit Yongchaiyudh 4, 9, 44, 147, 193, 221, 229
civilian, rise of. *See* liberalization
of Kriangsak Chomanan 1
local. *See* local government
military. *See entries for* Sarit; Suchinda. *See also entries for* military coup *in date section. See also* military; National Peace Keeping Council
Phibun. *See* Plaek Phibunsongkhram
of Prem Tinsulanond 1, 66, 99
of Pridi Phanomyong 104n, 117
policy bias to business interests. *See* business sector
of Sanya Thammasak 65
Sarit. *See* Sarit Thanarat
of Suchinda Kraprayoon 27n, 39, 40
Thaksin. *See* Thaksin Shinawatra
of Thanom Kittikachorn 65, 67–68
transparent, etc. *See* 'good governance'
grassroots democracy. *See* democracy and democratization
grassroots organizations
partnership with the state 16;
~ seen as unworkable 15
see also NGOs

INDEX

health sector, reform of 2, 33
human rights 265
  1997 constitution 74–75, 78–90; ~
    seen as breakthrough 14
  consciousness as prerequisite of
    conditions 87
  as threat to national security 129–130
  see sub-entries under freedom
  see also National Human Rights
    Commission
Hyde Park movement 15, 108–124
  passim
  audience 115–119. *See also* (the) poor
  origins 108, 114. *See also* Phibun
  speakers 109, 110, 114–115
  support for Sarit 113–114
  venue for street politics 109–112. *See
    also* street politics
  see also democracy and democratization; grassroots participation

IMF. *See* International Monetary Fund
industrialism 150. *See also* development, mode of
Interior Ministry 251
  declining interest as career choice 8
  functions 226
  impedes substantive reform 2, 8, 53,
    231. *See also* conservative forces
  and localism 157
  perceived opportunism of 161n
  see also bureaucracy; local government
International Monetary Fund
  opposition to policies of 143, 147,
    158. *See also* localism; nationalism
  response to 1997 crisis 146–147

jao pho (godfathers) 38, 237, 238,
  251–252. *See also* rural politicians

kamnan. *See* sub-district heads
Kriangsak Chomanan, premier 1

labour 117–118
  control/repression of organized
    ~ 118, 119, 120, 128
  reverse migration in 1997 crisis 98,
    192
  union activity weak 96, 129, 183
  women 166
  see also social security
legal reform 33
liberal and progressive forces
  alliance with conservatives to limit
    parliamentary power 4
  emergence of 38
  importance of constitutional
    politics to 2
  see also NGOs
liberalization 1, 21, 144–145
  effected by military, bureaucratic
    and business elites 39
  see also democracy and democratization; political reform
local government
  corruption 7, 231–232
  reform 17, 231
  structure 226–227
  weakness of 8, 230–235
  workings of 17
  see also bureaucracy; centralization;
    decentralization; district offices;
    Interior Ministry; PAOs; provincial governors; SAOs; sub-district councils; subdistrict
    heads; village heads
'local powers' 224, 246n, 265. *See also
  jao pho*; PAOs; patron–client
  relations; rural politicians
localism 15–16
  criticism of 153–159
  origins 144–148
  populist nature 154–155
  principles of 6, 147–153
  supported by king 6, 15–16, 148–149
  see also Buddhism; community
    culture; cultural development
    perspective; decentralization;
    International Monetary Fund;
    nationalism; populism; self-reliance; self-sufficiency

media reform 33
members of parliament
  increased competition at
    elections 214–217
  increasingly from business
    sector 128
  list vs constituency 203–204, 211,
    214, 248–249
  poaching of MPs 10, 17, 205, 215
  qualification barriers 10, 82–83, 205
  see also corruption; parliamentary
    politics; political leadership;
    rural politicians
middle class
  beneficiaries of development 82, 187
  as bulwark of democracy 131

287

as centre of power/protest 26, 263
composition 117
focus of political studies 121
growth of 21, 131
NGOs. *See* NGOs
reaction to 1991 coup 39–40
voting behaviour 131, 133
see also bureaucracy; business sector; elite, urban; liberal and progressive forces
migration 150
to Bangkok 119
pattern of circular ~ 98
political impact of rural links 119
reverse ~ after 1997 crisis 98, 192
see also rural areas
military
authoritarian rule 1, 21
corruption 7
coups. *See date section for individual coups*
decline in power of 26
declining interest as career choice 8
growth of 117
reform of 2
see also bureaucracy; police
ministers, government
corruption and 6–7, 220
qualification barriers 10, 82–83, 204, 205, 214, 248
ministries. *See* Department of Welfare; Finance Ministry; Interior Ministry
modernization, modernity
vs community 155
and corruption 131–133
monarchy
absolute ~ ended in 1932 1
CDA draft as threat to 53, 54
centre of Thai socio-political life 58
leads modernizing reforms 1850–1932 26
lèse-majesté 80, 161n
powers of 14, 64, 264
role of 2, 14
succession 58, 59
wide popular support 14
see also Bhumibol, King
money politics 37, 253, 264
non-responsiveness of 52
reason for constitutional reform 52, 54
rural–urban divide pivotal to 37, 131
supposed decline 17
see also corruption, vote-buying

National Counter-Corruption Commission 60, 220, 258, 259
established 10–11
National Human Rights Commission
established 11, 84
mandate 84–85
scepticism about effectivess 13, 265
National Peace Keeping Council 39–40
criticizes 'parliamentary dictatorship' 39
see also 1991 military coup
national security 226. *See also* Interior Ministry
nationalism 148, 152, 157, 158, 247
cultural. *See* community culture; localism
see also Thai Rak Thai Party
NCC. *See* National Counter-Corruption Commission
New Aspiration Party 212–213, 248, 253, 255. *See also* Chavalit Yongchaiyudh
NGOs
alliances and links 3, 13, 16–17, 39, 49, 155, 189, 199, 220; ~ to middle class 187, 189, 195. *See also* liberal and progressive forces
cannot replace the State 14, 134
and central government 5, 15, 39, 136–137, 169–171
challenge the mainstream response to 1997 crisis 143
elite-urban. *See* ~ rural-popular *below*
emergence as significant political actors 143, 169, 183
foreign funding 48, 170, 176
grassroots 5, 15, 39, 136–137, 140, 173, 184–189, 194–199 *passim*, 218
and local government 234
political role 186–189; ~ in reform process 16, 169–171, 194–199. *See also* democracy and democratization: grassroots participation
reduced interest in directly political issues 50
rural-popular 190, 192, 194, 197, 199; ~ vs elite-urban 5, 16, 184, 187, 189, 194–195, 198, 224
see also Forum of the Poor; liberal and progressive forces; localism
NPKC. *See* National Peace Keeping Council

ombudsmen 11

INDEX

PAOs (Provincial Administrative Organizations) 226
  captured by local elite 237–239, 243
  failings of 235–244 *passim*
  origins 236
  vote-canvassing by councillors 239
  see also local government; SAOs
parliamentary politics
  'dictatorship' of 4, 39, 41
  factions and political clans 17. *See also* political parties
  failings of as contributor to 1997 economic crisis 6
  MPs. *See* members of parliament
  parties. *See* political parties
  popular interests not represented 7
  progressively institutionalized 1
  see also democracy and democratization; political reform
patron–client relations 131–132, 140, 141, 154, 265–266
  effect of decentralization 224
  see also corruption, vote-buying
Phao Siyanon 70n, 108–116 *passim*, 118, 122. *See also* 1947 military coup; Hyde Park movement
Phibun. *See* Plaek Phibunsongkhram
phuyaiban. *See* village heads
Plaek Phibunsongkhram, premier 15, 62, 70n, 107–118 *passim*, 122. *See also* 1947 military coup; Hyde Park movement
police
  corruption 7
  declining interest as career choice 8
  influence in elections 7
  growth of 117
  see also bureaucracy; military
political leadership
  failings of as contributor to 1997 economic crisis 6
  hard to attract capable and upstanding figures 6; ~ esp. with new constitution 214
  see also members of parliament: parliamentary politics; senators
political parties
  as collections of cliques 253, 255
  dilemmas of 209–215
  failings of 183
  importance to democracy 184
  reason for clique domination 37–38
  see also Democrat Party; Chart Pattana; Chart Thai ~ ; New Aspiration ~ ; Prachakorn Thai ~ ; Sammakhi Tham ~; Thai Rak Thai ~
political reform 125
  alternative meanings 4–6, 125, 133–135, 184
  building on legalism 4
  check power of provincial business elites 4–5
  democratic ideas 5, 183–184. *See also* NGOs
  desire for technocracy 5. *See also* neo-liberalism
  head off social disorder 4, 93
  limited progress 86, 248, 258–259
  role of 'Hyde Park' street politics 15, 108. *See also* Hyde Park movement
  role of NGOs 16, 169–171, 194–199
Political Reform Committee 13
politicians
  accountability needed 43
  see also political leadership; rural polticians
poor (peasantry, labourers, etc.)
  civil society and 102
  class consciousness of 141
  little benefit from development 152, 187
  NGOs and 122, 187. *See also* Forum of the Poor
  political representation/marginalization 93, 122, 187, 205
  problems ignored by government 193
  protest 15, 101, 109–112, 115–116, 121. *See also* street politics
  see also middle class; migration; rural areas
popular power
  behind democratic change 141–142
  vs elite power. *See* elite(s); neo-liberalism
  see also democracy and democratization: grassroots participation; demonstrations; popular unrest/conflict; street politics
popular unrest/conflict
  due to state policies 137; ~ uneven development 128–129
  as reason for political reform 4, 93
  repression of 129
  see also demonstrations; street politics
populism 154–155, 157, 158–160, 247

Prachakorn Thai Party 212, 214
Prawase Wasi 45, 134, 149, 150, 156, 158, 161n, 189–190
  advocates state–grassroots partnership 16, 133
  attacks 'parliamentary dictatorship' 4
  DDC chairman 2, 12, 22–23, 41
  strategy of 'social empowerment' 12, 190
PRC. *See* Political Reform Committee
Prem Tinsulanond, premier 1, 66, 99
Pridi Phanomyong, premier 104n, 117
provinces. *See* rural areas
provincial councils. *See* local government
provincial governors
  corruption 7
  influence in elections 7
  obstacles to reform 8
  role 226
  see also centralization; local government
public sphere/space 165–171 *passim*. *See also* political reform; women, Thai

reform. *See entries for* bureaucracy; civil society; constitutional reform; educational ~; electoral ~; health sector; media; military; universities; welfare
rural areas 119
  effect of migration. *See* migration
  most voters located here 5
  prime position in localism 152
  'rural machine politicians'. *See* rural politicians
  rural–urban divisions 5, 37, 101, 118, 128, 151, 155, 265
  voter behaviour 131. *See also* patron–client relations
  vs Bangkok 5, 118. *See also* Bangkok
  see also localism; NGOs; (the) poor; self-reliance; self-sufficiency;
rural politicians
  corruption 7, 131
  rise of 5, 39
  See also Banharn Silpa-archa, *jao pho*

SAOs (Subdistrict Administrative Organizations) 226, 228
  failings 230–235, 242–244
  formation 229

functions 230
membership 229, 232–233
operations 231–232
see also local government; subdistrict councils; subdistrict heads
Sammakhi Tham Party 40, 253
Sanoh Thienthong 5, 252
Sanya Thammasak, premier 65. *See also* 1973 popular uprising
Sarit Thanarat, Field Marshall 58, 59, 62, 65, 108, 113–114, 115, 120
  see also 1957 military coup; Hyde Park movement
self-reliance 149–150, 151, 157. *See also* Buddhism; localism
self-sufficiency 149, 151, 157
  supported by king 6, 15–16, 148–149
  see also localism
senators 197, 204
  selection 248
  see also 2000 senate election; parliamentary politics; political leadership
social collaboration. *See* good governance
social reform
  increased inequality 94, 128. *See also* economic development; (the) poor
  need for 2
  political agitation for. *See* NGOs
  see also democracy and democratization
social security
  expenditure 99
  ~ Act 97–98, 100, 110
  struggle for better protection 97, 110–111
  see also labour; welfare
state
  partnership with grassroots organizations 16; seen as unworkable 15. *See also* neo-liberalism; NGOs
  response to 1997 econ. crisis 14
  see also bureaucracy; centralization; government
State Audit Commission 11
street politics 15, 109–112, 121, 122, 194. *See also* demonstrations; Hyde Park movement; (the) poor
students 116
  lead 1973 uprising 21, 26
  reduced role in reform movement 26
subdistrict councils 226, 228–229. *See also* local government; SAOs

INDEX

subdistrict heads (*kamnan*)
  appointment 206, 227
  electoral activities 229–230, 240
  see also local government; SAOs
Suchinda Kraprayoon, premier 27n, 39, 40. *See also* 1991 military coup; 1992 popular uprising
Sulak Srivaraksa 153. *See also* Buddhism; localism

Thai Rak Thai Party 17, 215, 216, 220, 221, 247, 248, 252–255. *See also* Thaksin Shinawatra
Thaksin Shinawatra, premier 17, 220–221, 247, 248, 255–259. *See also* Thai Rak Thai Party
Thammakai (Buddhist group) 75–78
thammarat haengchat, meaning 35. *See also* 'good governance'
Thanom Kittikachorn, premier 65, 67–68

universities
  academic freedom. *See* freedom
  reform of 2, 33
urbanism 150. *See also* Bangkok; development, mode of; elite, urban

village heads (*phuyaiban*)
  appointment 206, 227
  electoral activities 229–230, 240
  see also local government; SAOs
vote-buying
  cause of clique domination 37–38
  exacerbated by reforms 7
  extent 127
  at local level 17, 227–228, 230, 233, 240–242, 265. *See also* PAOs; SAOs
  measures against 218, 246n; ~ in 1997 Constitution 10, 203–204
  persistence of 17, 207, 250
  results in illegal fund-raising 127
  turnout increased 240
  see also corruption; elections; rural areas; vote-canvassing

watthanatham chumchon. *See* cultural development perspective

welfare
  reform of 2, 104n
  theories often contradict democratization 103
  see also social security
Westernization
  forces of. *See* consumerism; development, mode of; globalization
  reaction to. *See* localism
women, Thai
  barriers to entry to public sphere 168–169
  constitutional equality 171
  and corruption 182n
  greater freedom of 166
  main actors in local economies 166
  under-represented in politics and bureaucracy 167, 178–179, 230, 234, 265
  see also public sphere/space; women's organizations
Women's Constitutional Network
  composition 49, 173
  involvement with CDA 49–50, 173–178. *See also* Constitutional Drafting Assembly
women's organizations
  Association for the Promotion of the Status of Women 170, 172
  emergence 16, 168, 169
  foreign links 170, 176
  Gender and Development Research Institute 170, 172–173, 178
  GenderWatch Group 170, 173
  political reform activities 169–173
  role in drafting 1997 Constitution 16, 49–50, 164, 173–178. *See also* Constitutional Drafting Assembly
  Women Lawyers' Association 171, 172, 175
  Women in Politics Institute 170, 176
  see also NGOs; Women's Constitutional Network
World Bank
  aid 192, 244
  policies criticized 153. *See also* development, mode of; IMF
  promotes 'good governance' 44, 163, 223. *See also* 'good governance'